HONDA CB/CL 450 1965-1974 K0 TO K7 WORKSHOP MANUAL

A Floyd Clymer Publication
This edition published in 2020 by
www.VelocePress.com

All rights reserved. This work may not be reproduced or transmitted in any form without the express written consent of the publisher.

INTRODUCTION

Welcome to the world of digital publishing ~ the book you now hold in your hand was printed using the latest state of the art digital technology. The advent of print-on-demand has forever changed the publishing process, never has information been so accessible and it is our hope that this book serves your informational needs for years to come. If this is your first exposure to digital publishing, we hope that you are pleased with the results. Many more titles of interest to the classic automobile and motorcycle enthusiast, collector and restorer are available via our website at www.VelocePress.com.

NOTE FROM THE PUBLISHER

The information presented is true and complete to the best of our knowledge. All recommendations are made without any guarantees on the part of the author or the publisher, who also disclaims any and all liability incurred with the use of the information contained in this manual.

TRADEMARKS

We recognize that some words, model names and designations, for example, mentioned herein are the property of the trademark holder. We use them for identification purposes only. This is not an official publication.

INFORMATION ON THE USE OF THIS PUBLICATION

This manual is an invaluable resource for those interested in performing their own maintenance. However, in today's information age we are constantly subject to changes in common practice, new technology, availability of improved materials and increased awareness of chemical toxicity. As such, it is advised that the user consult with an experienced professional prior to undertaking any procedure described herein. While every care has been taken to ensure correctness of information, it is obviously not possible to guarantee complete freedom from errors or omissions or to accept liability arising from such errors or omissions. Therefore, any individual that uses the information contained within, or elects to perform or participate in do-it-yourself repairs or modifications acknowledges that there is a risk factor involved and that the publisher or its associates cannot be held responsible for personal injury or property damage resulting from the use of the information or the outcome of such procedures.

MEASUREMENT & VALUES

The metric system is the primary measurement method used in both the manufacture of these motorcycles and this reproduction of the Factory Workshop Manual. As such, the reader is urged to verify that the conversion of those metric measurements to other forms of measurement is correct. All measurements and values are made without any guarantees on behalf of the publisher.

WARNING!

One final word of advice, this publication is intended to be used as a reference guide, and when in doubt the reader should consult with a qualified technician.

CONTENTS

SECTION ONE
COMPONENT CONSTRUCTION AND OPERATION..........................1

SECTION TWO
TUNE-UPS AND PERIODIC MAINTENANCE............................6

- Ignition timing
- Spark plugs
- Fuel system
- Oil filter
- Air cleaner
- Clutch
- Cam chain
- Drive chain
- Brakes
- Battery

SECTION THREE
ENGINE SERVICE...12

- Cylinder head
- Valves
- Camshaft assembly
- Cylinder
- Pistons
- Piston rings
- Crankcase
- Oil filter
- Clutch
- Crankshaft
- Transmission, 4-speed
- Transmission, 5-speed
- Shifting mechanism
- Kick starter
- Carburetor

SECTION FOUR
FRAME SERVICE..54

- Handlebar
- Hand controls
- Front fork
- Steering
- Fuel tank
- Kick stand
- Exhaust system
- Air cleaner
- Swinging arm
- Rear shock absorbers
- Front and rear wheels
- Brakes, drum and disc

SECTION FIVE
ELECTRICAL SERVICE..100

- Ignition system
- Generator
- Battery
- Electric starter
- Starting clutch
- Solenoid
- Horn
- Lighting
- Wire harness
- Continuity testing
- Condenser
- Coil

CONTENTS

SECTION SIX
WIRING DIAGRAMS 115

SECTION SEVEN
MECHANICAL AND VISUAL DIFFERENCES BY MODEL 123

SECTION EIGHT
GUIDE TO TROUBLESHOOTING 132
    Operating requirements   Piston seizure
    Starting difficulties   Vibration
    Poor idling   High oil consumption
    Misfiring   Clutch slippage
    Flat spots   Transmission problems
    Power loss   Poor handling
    Overheating   Brake malfunctions
    Backfiring   Lighting difficulties
    Engine noises

INDEX 136

SECTION ONE

COMPONENT CONSTRUCTION AND OPERATION

The 450 Honda engine is an air-cooled, four-stroke vertical twin. A pair of overhead camshafts distinguish the design. See **Figures 1 and 2** for details of engine construction.

Torsion bar valve springs cut down valve float or surging at high speeds, while an eccentric cam follower shaft does much to eliminate the need for frequent valve adjustment. Drive to the overhead camshafts is by a chain system using rollers to quiet the moving chain.

Engine lubrication is illustrated in **Figure 3.** Oil from the sump passes through a filter screen, the oil pump and into the lower crankcase. It then travels to the right crankcase cover through the oil filter into the upper crankcase. The crankshaft and transmission mainshaft are lubricated along with the intake and exhaust camshafts. Oil thrown from the camshaft lubricates the cam chain guide rollers and the torsion bar valve springs. The countershaft and kick starter pinion are lubricated by oil splashed from the oil pan.

Figure 4 shows the semi-hemispherical design of the combustion chambers. This arrangement promotes cooling and combustion efficiency. The head shape swirls and directs the gas-air mixture at the spark plug at the moment of firing, reducing the tendency of the engine to knock or ping with a lean mixture or poor grade of fuel.

Figure 5 shows clutch construction. The clutch provides a means of connecting and disconnecting the drive train at will. When the clutch is engaged (handle released) the clutch center hub is locked to the clutch pressure plate by friction between the clutch plates and friction discs through force exerted by the clutch springs. Power is transmitted from the crankshaft to the transmission by way of the primary drive gears.

When the clutch lever is operated to disengage the clutch, the clutch lifter thread rotates and moves inwards, pushing against the pressure plate and clutch springs through the steel ball, clutch lifter rod and clutch lifter joint piece. The friction discs and clutch plates separate to disengage power transmission.

Transmission operation is described here using the later model five-speed gearbox as an example. Four-speed gearbox assembly and disassembly are covered in the Engine Service section.

Refer to **Figures 6, 7, 8, 9, 10 and 11** for operation in neutral and the five gears. **Figure 6** shows the transmission in neutral. Mainshaft gears are prefaced with the initial "M" and

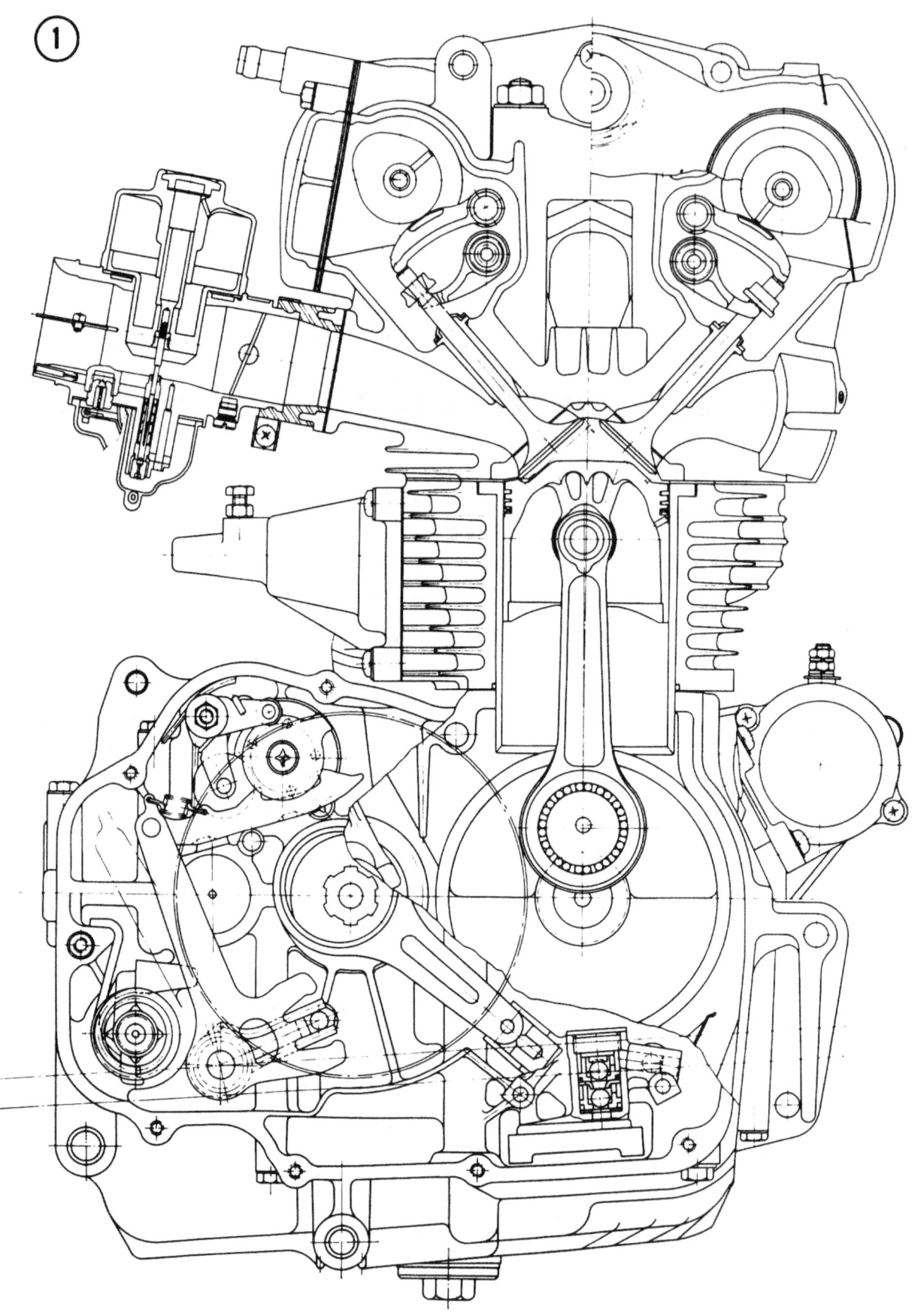

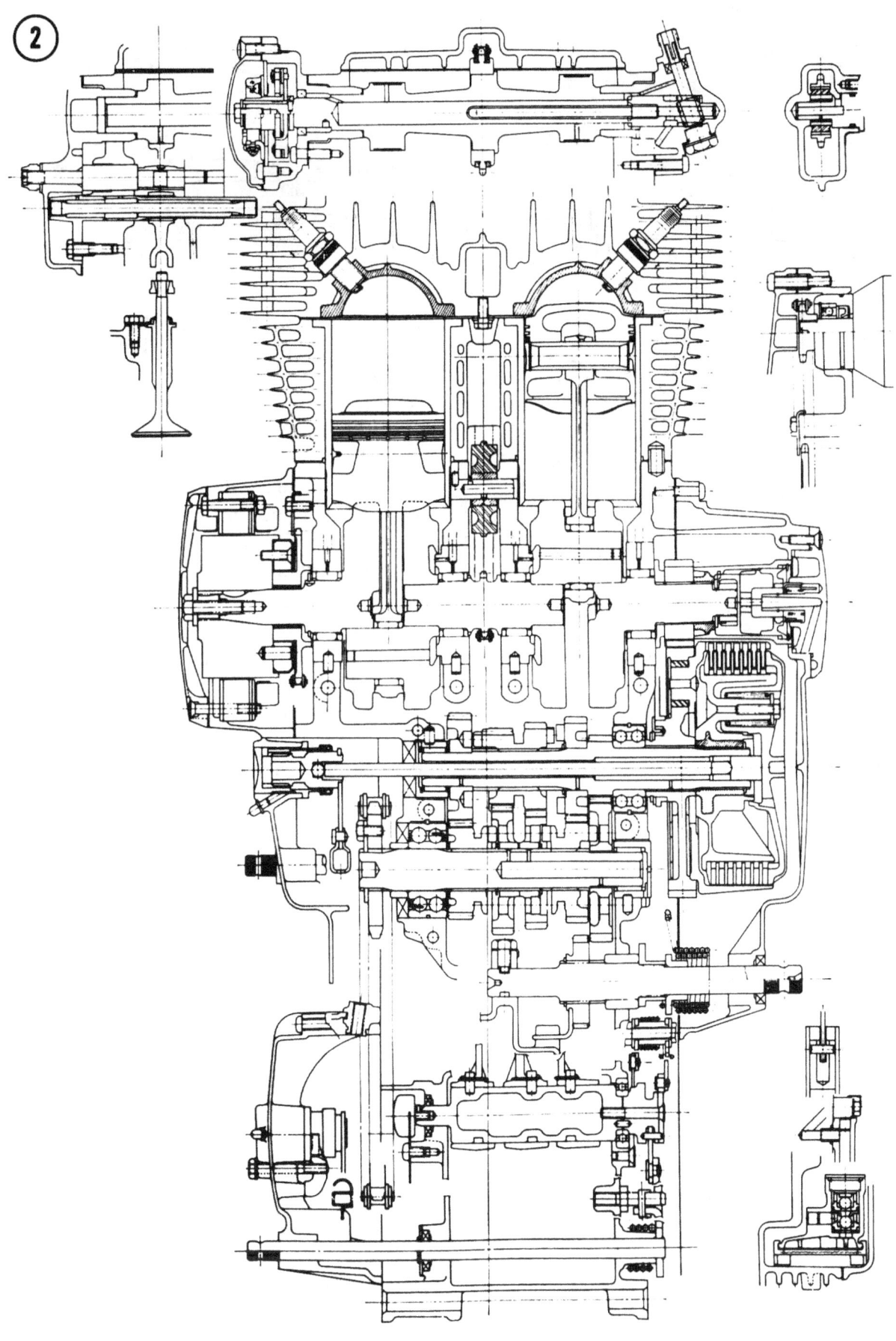

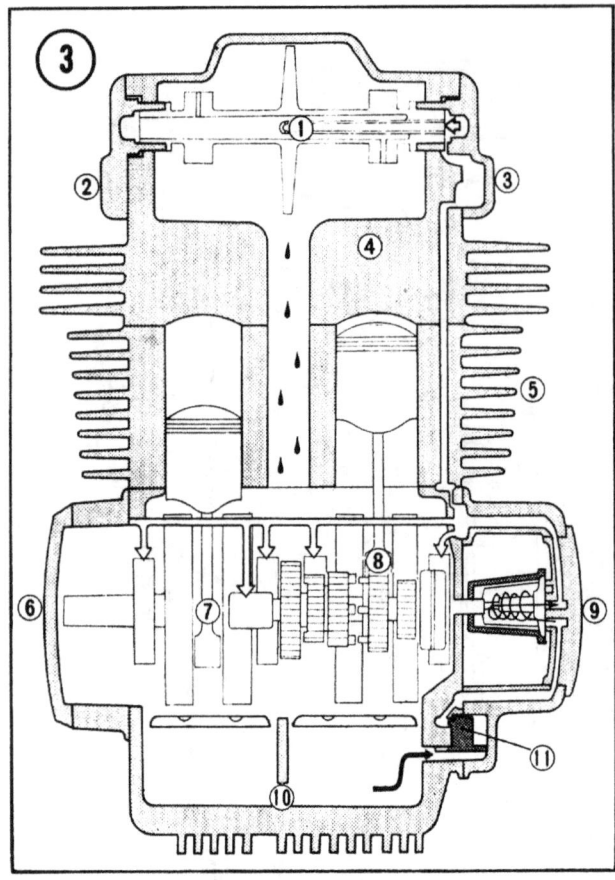
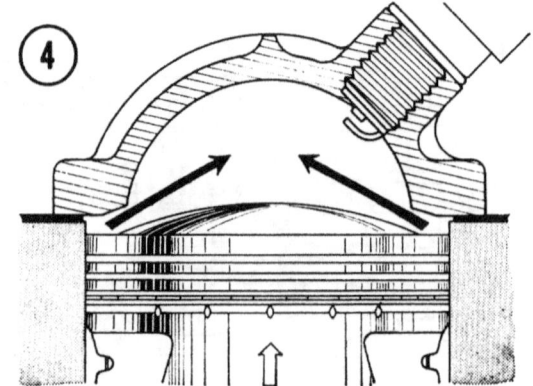

① To camshaft
② Left cover
③ Right cover
④ Cylinder head
⑤ Cylinder
⑥ Left crankcase cover
⑦ To mainshaft
⑧ To crankshaft
⑨ Right crankcase cover
⑩ Lower crankcase
⑪ Oil pump

countershaft gears are prefaced with a "C". Fixed mainshaft low gear (M1) is meshed with free-rotating countershaft low gear (C1), free-rotating mainshaft top gear (M5) is meshed with sliding countershaft top gear (C5), sliding mainshaft second and third gears (M2 and M3) are meshed with the free-rotating countershaft second and third gears (C2 and C3), and the free-rotating mainshaft fourth gear (M4) is meshed with the splined countershaft fourth gear (C4).

Figure 7 shows low gear power transmission. Power from the mainshaft low gear (M1) is transmitted to the free-rotating countershaft low gear (C1). Splined countershaft fourth gear (C4) is engaged to the countershaft low gear through a dog to drive the countershaft and the drive sprocket mounted on the countershaft end.

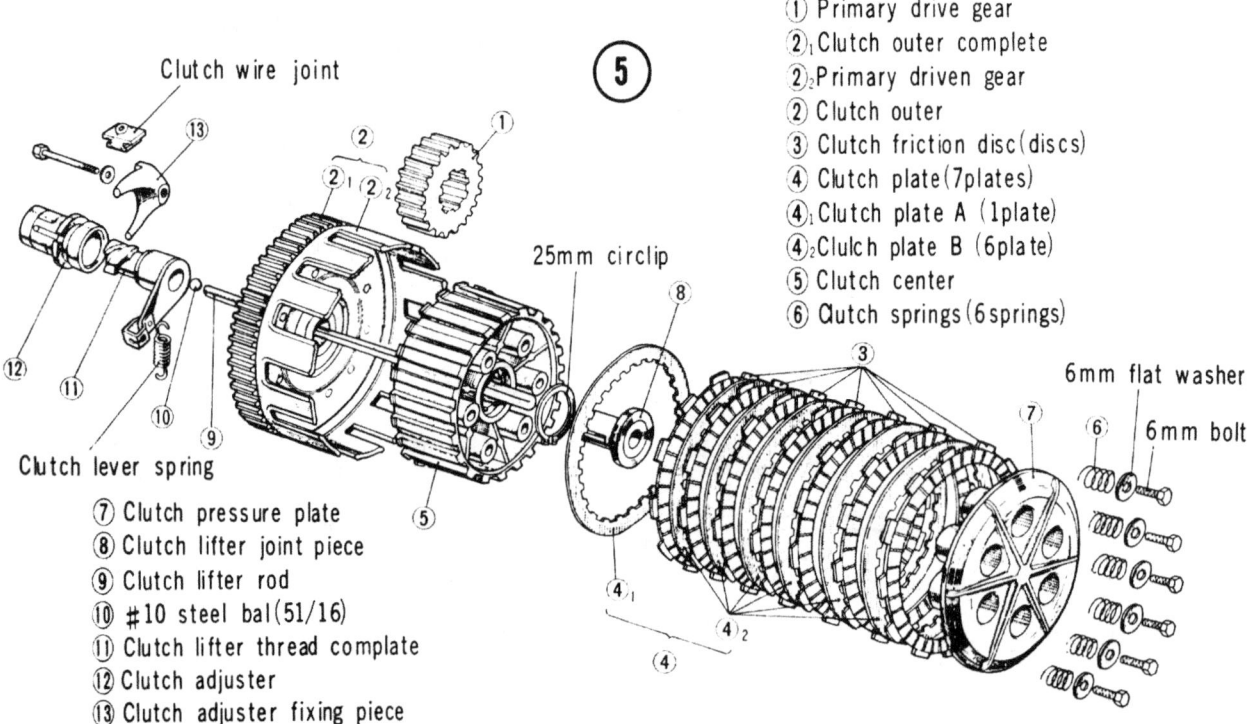

① Primary drive gear
②₁ Clutch outer complete
②₂ Primary driven gear
② Clutch outer
③ Clutch friction disc (discs)
④ Clutch plate (7 plates)
④₁ Clutch plate A (1 plate)
④₂ Clutch plate B (6 plate)
⑤ Clutch center
⑥ Clutch springs (6 springs)
⑦ Clutch pressure plate
⑧ Clutch lifter joint piece
⑨ Clutch lifter rod
⑩ #10 steel ball (51/16)
⑪ Clutch lifter thread complate
⑫ Clutch adjuster
⑬ Clutch adjuster fixing piece

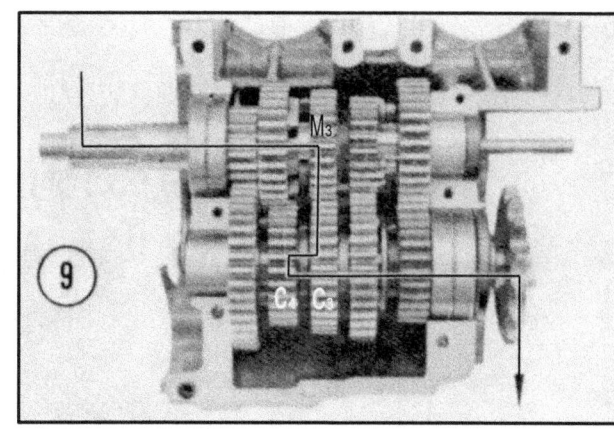

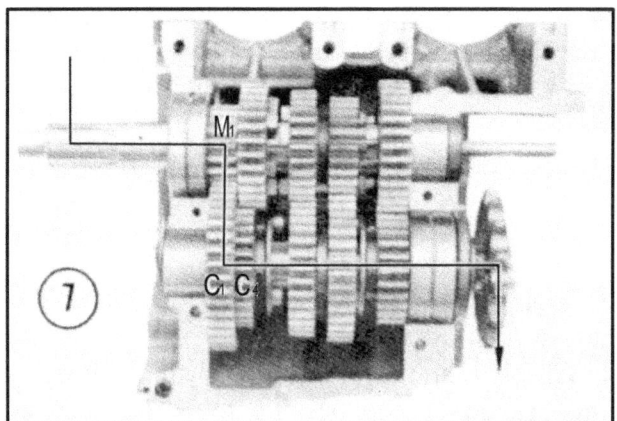

Figure 8 shows second gear operation. The mainshaft second gear (M2) transmits power to the free-rotating countershaft second gear (C2) which in turn transmits power to the countershaft top gear (C5) through a dog.

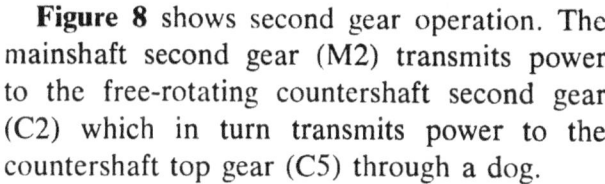

Figure 9 shows third gear operation. Power from the mainshaft third gear (M3) is transmitted to free-rotating countershaft third gear (C3). Splined countershaft fourth gear (C4) is engaged to the countershaft third gear through a dog and drives the countershaft.

Figure 10 shows fourth gear operation. Free-rotating mainshaft fourth gear (M4) is engaged to the mainshaft second and third gears (M2 and M3) by a dog. Power then flows from (M4) to the countershaft fourth gear (C4) and to the countershaft.

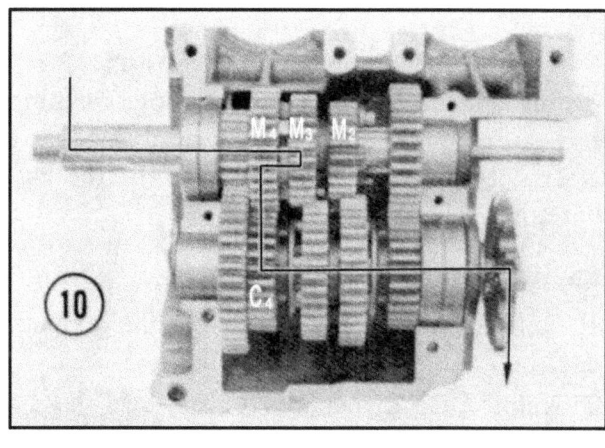

Figure 11 shows fifth or top gear operation. Free-rotating fifth gear on the mainshaft is engaged to the mainshaft second and third gears (M2 and M3) by a dog and transmits power to the countershaft fifth gear (C5) and to the countershaft.

SECTION TWO

TUNE-UPS AND PERIODIC MAINTENANCE

A normal tune-up usually consists of adjusting and checking ignition timing, cleaning and gapping the spark plugs, adjusting valve clearances and cleaning and adjusting the carburetors.

Ignition Timing and Point Gapping

1. Remove the point cover on the exhaust camshaft side of the left cylinder.

2. Remove the dynamo cover and turn the dynamo rotor until one set of points is opened to their fullest. Adjust the gap by loosening the breaker locking screw as shown in **Figure 1** to 0.3 to 0.4mm (0.012 to 0.016"). Adjust both sets of points to the same gap.

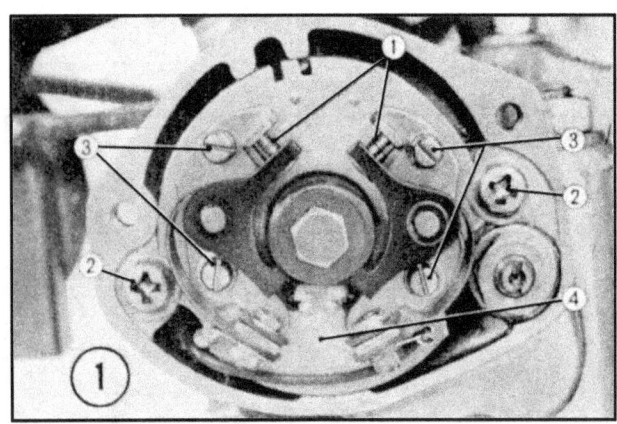

(1) Contact breaker point   (2) Screw a)
(3) Screw (b)   (4) Base plate

3. Tighten the locking screws and recheck the gap to make sure it remains correct.

4. Check that the points are clean, unburned and are contacting parallel to each other as shown in **Figure 2**.

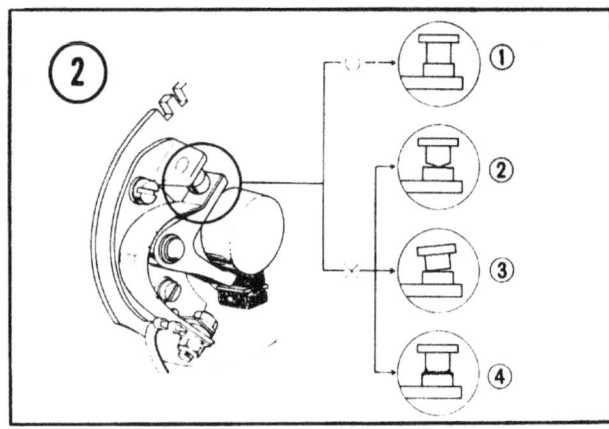

(1) Correct
(2) Contact is worn
(3) One side contact
(4) Contamination of the contact

5. To adjust ignition timing, make sure the left piston is on its compression stroke and then turn the dynamo rotor until the "LF" mark on the rotor lines up with the index mark as shown in **Figure 3**. The left set of points should be just opening when checked with a continuity tester. If adjustment is needed, loosen the

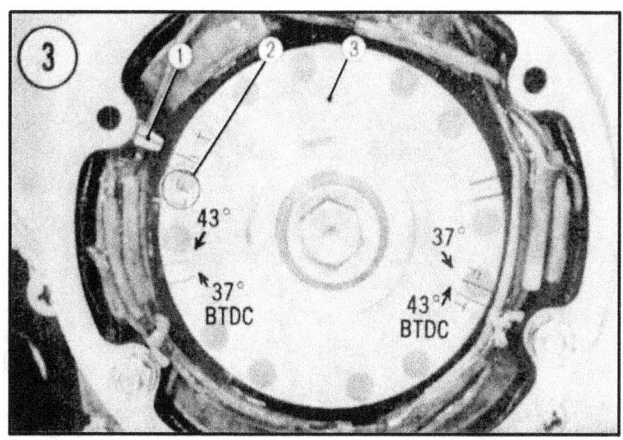

breaker base plate retaining screw (Phillips) as shown in **Figure 4** and adjust. Moving the base plate clockwise advances the timing and moving it counterclockwise retards the timing. Turn the rotor 180 degrees and match up the "F" to the index mark as before. Adjust the right set of points to just open by changing the point gap if necessary.

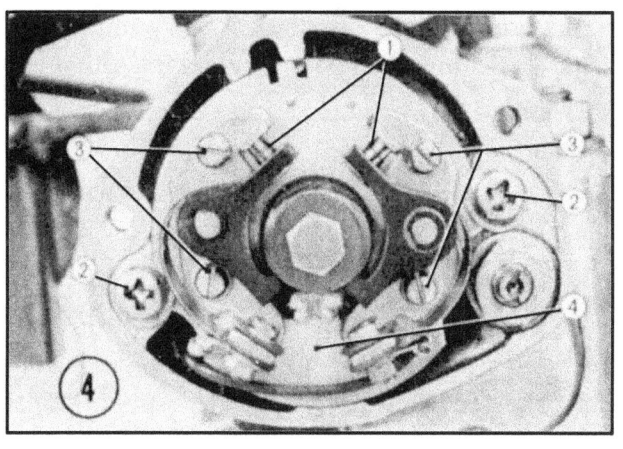

① Contact breaker point   ② Screw (a)
③ Screw (b)   ④ Base plate

6. Check the point gap by using a timing light if possible. The stator reference mark should appear between the two black marks which are 32 — 35 degrees (37° to 43° before TDC) before the "LF" and "L" marks.

Spark Plugs

1. Clean the spark plugs in a spark plug cleaner and gap them to 0.7 to 0.8mm (0.028 to 0.32").
2. Replace worn or burned plugs.

Adjusting Valve Clearances

1. Refer to the section in Section Three on adjusting tappet clearances.

Cleaning and Adjusting Carburetors

1. Remove the air cleaner boxes, air cleaners and carburetors. Refer to the section in Section Three on carburetor service for details of carburetor construction.

2. Disassemble and clean carburetor components in carburetor soaking solution. Blow air passages and jets clean and dry with compressed air, then reassemble the carburetors.

3. Set the idle adjustment as follows (5-speed carburetor shown; 4-speed has pilot screw underneath carburetor body): Adjust the idle stop screw shown in **Figure 5** so that both exhausts sound as nearly alike as possible, with the engine idle speed between 1.000 and 1.200 rpm. If engine idle speed doesn't decrease when the stop screws are unscrewed, adjust the throttle cable adjusters to give more slack in the cable.

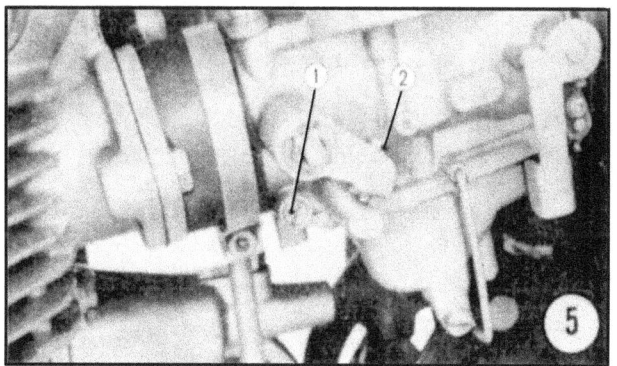

① Pilot screw   ② Stop screw

4. Starting with either carburetor, turn the pilot screw **Figure 5** in or out to obtain the highest idling speed possible. Do this with the other carburetor and then lower the idling speed with the stop screws and repeat the pilot screw adjustment until the engine is running smoothly and at the correct idling speed.

5. Synchronize the throttle valves so they open at the same time when the throttle is turned. Do this by placing your hand so both levers may be felt at the same time or watching that both begin to open simultaneously. Adjust the cable adjuster if necessary to correct. A Uni-Syn (air flow meter) will synchronize more accurately.

PERIODIC MAINTENANCE

Fuel System

1. Check the fuel system for free flow by disconnecting the fuel line at the petcock and turning it to the "on" position. Limited or no fuel flow could result from a dirty fuel cap vent, clogged lines, or a dirty strainer in the petcock. Disassemble and clean the faulty components. Refer to **Figures 6 and 7** for details of the petcock and gas filler cap. Cap shown is for 4-speed and early 5-speed models. Later models use a hinged cap with a latch designed to prevent accidental opening.

2. Inspect the petcock strainer and filter screen periodically.

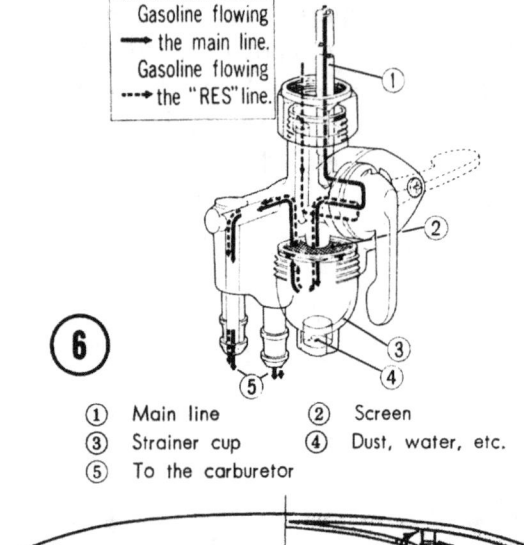

① Main line ② Screen
③ Strainer cup ④ Dust, water, etc.
⑤ To the carburetor

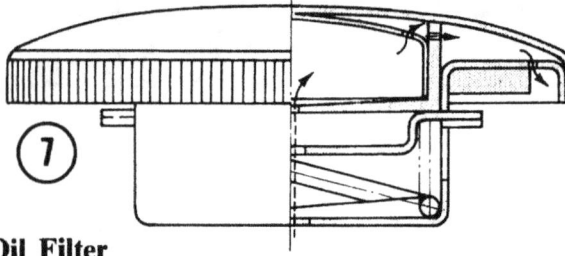

Oil Filter

1. Check the oil filter periodically and clean it thoroughly.

2. Remove the oil filter cover on the right crankcase cover. See **Figure 8**.

3. Remove the circlip, and pull the oil filter cap out of the oil filter rotor. Wash them in solvent or gasoline.

4. Reassemble, being sure to match the vane on the rotor cap to the groove on the inside wall of the rotor as shown.

5. Match the crankcase cover oil opening to the filter cover opening as shown in **Figure 9**.

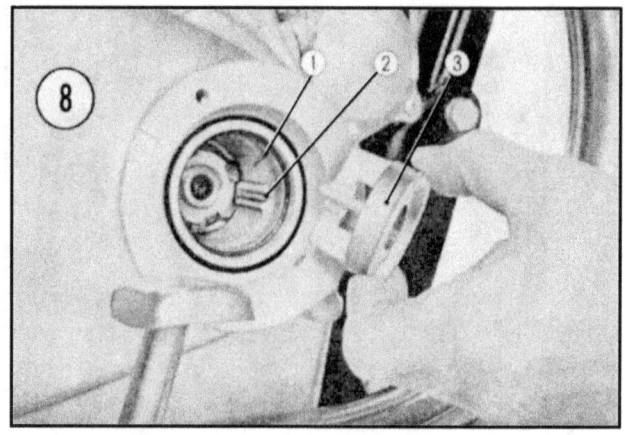

① Oil filter rotor ② Groove
③ Oil filter cap

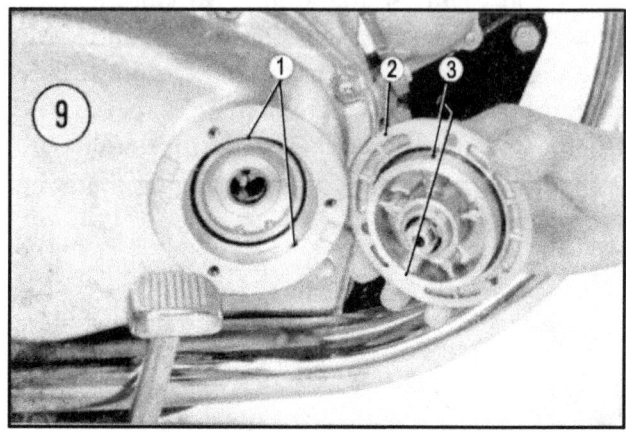

① Oil filter opening
② Oil filter cover
③ Oil guide (spring loaded)

Air Cleaner Service

1. Refer to **Figure 10** and remove the air cleaner case and covers and loosen the connecting tube set screw. Remove the elements and clean them by tapping or with compressed air.

① Air cleaner case
② Air cleaner cover
③ Air cleaner setting bolt
④ 6 × 10 hex bolt

2. Dry elements should be replaced if they become oil soaked.

3. When reassembling, be sure all joints, especially on the connecting tube, are airtight or unclean air may be sucked into the engine with resultant high wear.

4. Clean elements often if the motorcycle is driven under dusty conditions.

Clutch Adjustment

1. Clutch lever play is adjusted by loosening the locking nut at either end of the cable and turning the adjusting nut. Free play should be from 1.0 to 2.5 cm (0.4 to 1.0"). See **Figure 11.**

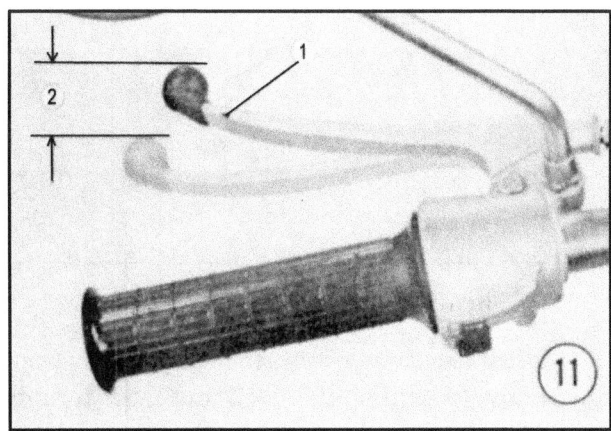

① Clutch lever   ② Free play

2. If the clutch still works improperly then it should be adjusted on the left crankcase cover as shown in **Figure 12**. Loosen the locking nut and turn the adjusting screw to the left to increase free play and to the right to decrease it. Do not turn more than 90° past index mark in either direction. Lubrication groove must align. Tighten the locking nut when the proper adjustment has been made.

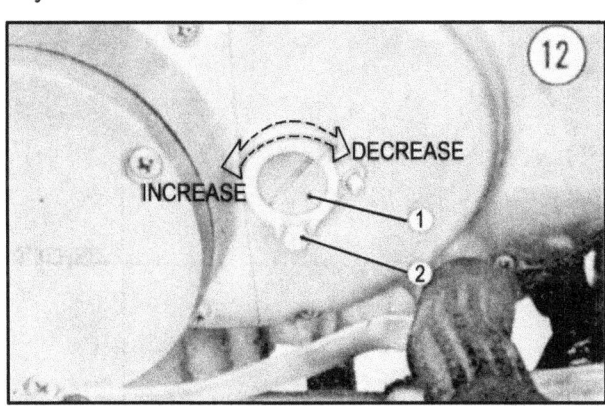

① Clutch adjuster   ② Locking bolt

Cam Chain Adjustment

1. The cam chain will wear and loosen up in time, requiring adjustment. Loosen the locking nut on the tensioner adjusting bolt and then the adjusting bolt itself. A spring operated mechanism automatically adjusts the tensioner. Retighten the bolt and locking nut. Do not push on the tensioner push rod as this will only result in shortening chain and roller life. See **Figure 13.**

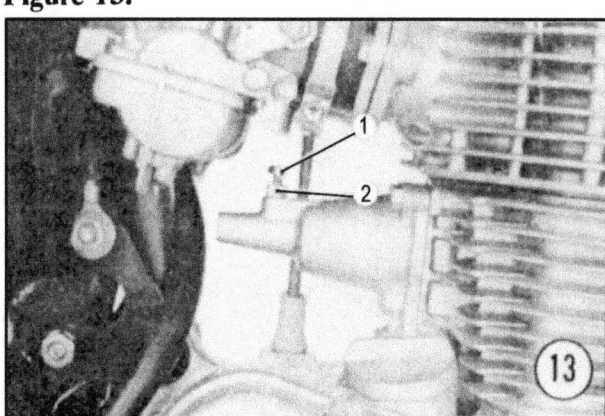

① Tensioner adjusting bolt   ② Locking nut

Lubrication

1. Engine oil should be changed after the first 300 miles and every 2,000 miles thereafter. Remove the drain plug on the bottom of the crankcase to drain the oil. See **Figure 14.**

2. Check oil level with the dipstick inserted in its opening but not screwed down, as shown in **Figure 15.**

3. Grease fittings should be lubricated with a multi-purpose grease type NLGI No. 2. See **Figures 16 and 17.**

4. Refer to the front fork section in Section Four for fork oil specifications and quantities.

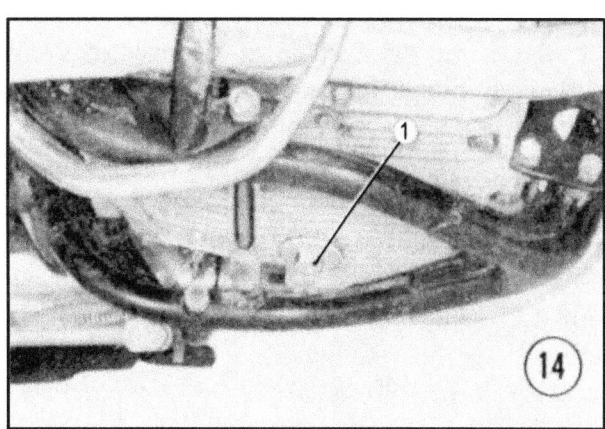

① Drain plug

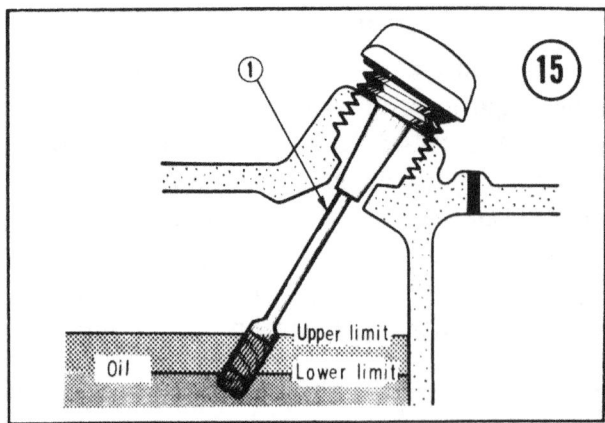

① Oil level gauge

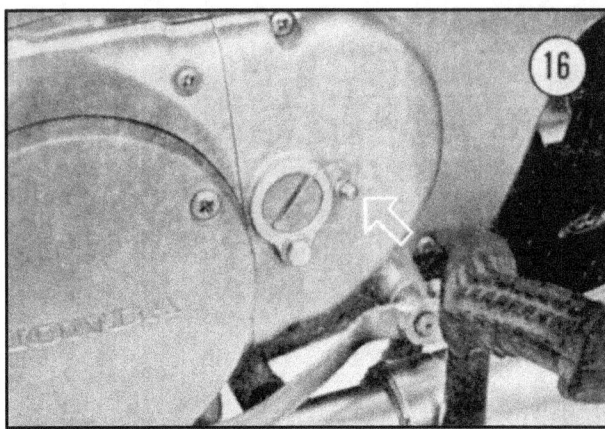

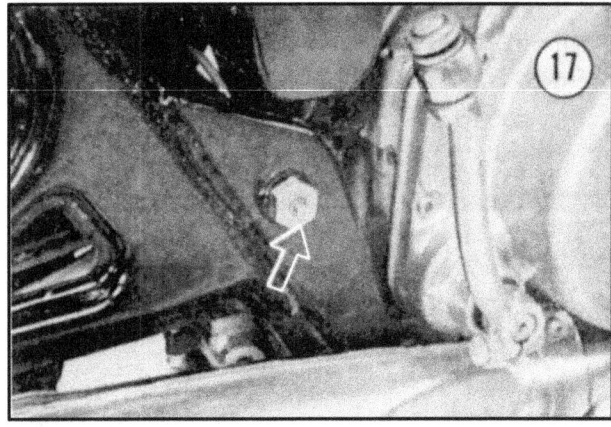

Drive Chain

1. Clean the drive chain at intervals of 6,000 miles, or more frequently if the motorcycle is ridden under severe conditions. Lubricate with a good quality chain lubricant whenever the chain appears dry.

2. Adjust chain play to 0.4 to 0.8" by loosening the axle nut and the adjuster lock nut and then screwing the adjuster in or out to obtain proper tension. Minimum play when bike is on wheels with rider on saddle is 0.4". Correct slack when on center stand is 0.8". Maximum play before readjustment is required is 1.5". Remember that adjusters on both sides of the rear wheel should be adjusted so the rear wheel remains in line with the front. Sight along the top run of the chain from the rear of the motorcycle to check.

3. Retighten the lock nut and axle nut firmly.

Brake Adjustment

1. With the drum type brakes, front brake lever free play should be 0.6 to 1.2". Adjustment is made by loosening the lock nut on the cable end, either at the wheel or at the lever. Normally the major adjustment is made at the wheel and the lever adjuster is used for fine adjustment. Refer to **Figure 18**.

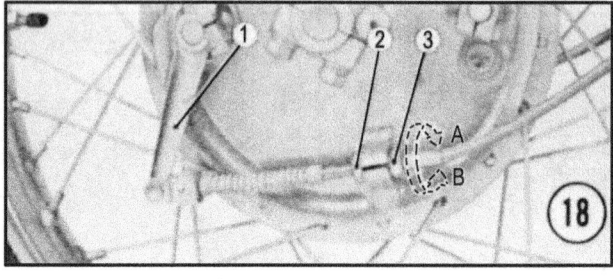

① Front brake arm ② Lock nut ③ Adjusting nut

2. Adjust lever play in the disc type front brake by loosening the lock nut and turning the adjusting screw to obtain the proper lever play. See **Figure 89**, Section Four.

3. Adjust the rear brake pedal free play to 0.8 to 1.2" by turning the adjusting nut on the brake rod. Turn it clockwise to decrease and counter-clockwise to increase free play. See **Figures 19 and 20**.

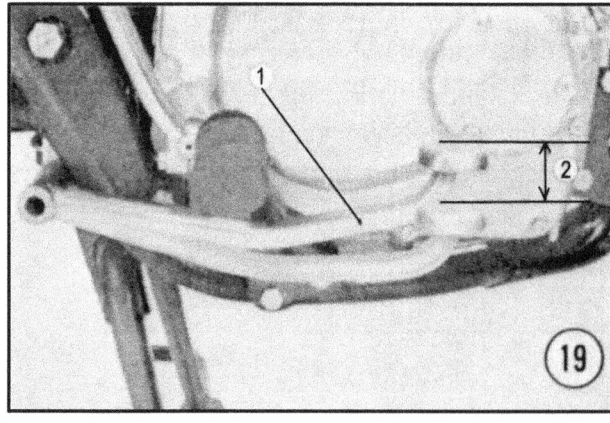

① Rear brake pedal ② Free play

Battery Service

1. Check the electrolyte level frequently and top up with distilled water if necessary.

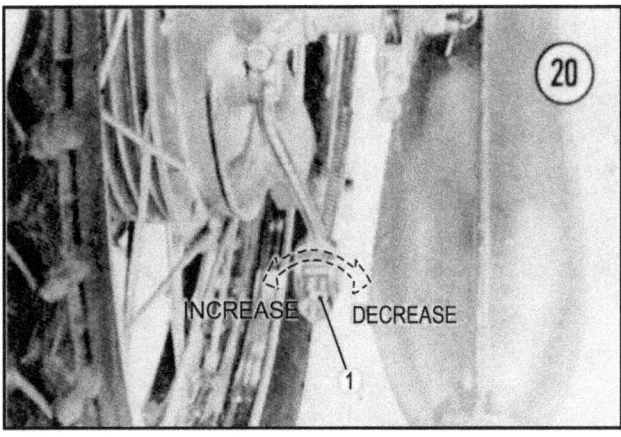

① Rear brake adjusting nut

2. Always disconnect the negative terminal first in removal and connect it last when installing the battery.

3. Apply grease to the terminals after connecting them to prevent corrosion.

Torque Specifications

1. Use the torque specification table **Figure 21** when servicing the machine to prevent parts from coming off or breaking.

2. Check spokes for tightness at least every 6,000 miles and tighten evenly to keep wheels aligned.

3. Check the following nuts and bolts frequently as they are prone to vibrate loose more frequently than the rest: handlebar mounting bolts, front fork cap bolts, steering stem nut, fork tube pinch bolts, front axle holder nuts, rear shock mounting nuts, rear wheel axle nut, front and rear brake stop arm nuts or bolts, and the wheel spokes.

Classification	No.	Location	Part tightened	Tightening torque	
Front fork	1	Front wheel axle	Front axle nut	750~850 kg cm	(54~61 lb ft)
	2	Front brake stopper arm	Front brake torque bolt	180~280 ″	(13~20 ″)
	3	Head light	Light case mounting bolt	400~500 ″	(29~58 ″)
	4	Fork top bridge	Front fork bolt	650~800 ″	(47~58 ″)
	5	Steering stem	Steering stem head nut	900~1200 ″	(65~87 ″)
	6	Fork top bridge	8×74 hex bolt	250~350 ″	(18~25 ″)
	7	Front fork bottom case	8 mm hex nut	180~280 ″	(13~20 ″)
	8	Steering case	Steering stem bottom bolt	400~500 ″	(29~58 ″)
	9	Front fender	6×16 hex bolt	80~120 ″	(6~ 9 ″)
Steering Handle	1	Handle pipe holder	8×32 hex bolt	250~350 ″	(18~25 ″)
	2	Handle lever	6 mm hex nut	80~120 ″	(6~ 9 ″)
	3	Handle pipe lower holder	8 mm hex nut	250~350 ″	(18~25 ″)
Frame	1	Engine monting	Engine hanger bolt (10 mm)	400~500 ″	(29~58 ″)
	2	Engine monting	Engine hanger bolt (8 mm)	180~280 ″	(13~20 ″)
	3	Main switch, Horn, 1G bracket	6×90 hex bolt	80~120 ″	(6~ 9 ″)
	4	Side stand	10 mm hex nut	400~500 ″	(29~58 ″)
	5	Rear cushion upper joint	10 cap nut	400~500 ″	(29~58 ″)
	6	Rear cushion lower	10 thin nut	400~500 ″	(29~58 ″)
	7	Rear cushion lower	Rear cushion lower bolt	400~500 ″	(29~58 ″)
	8	Rear fork pivot bolt	14 mm self-locking nut	700~900 ″	(51~65 ″)
	9	R. L. pillion step	10 mm hex nut	400~500 ″	(29~58 ″)
	10	Rear brake stopper arm	8 mm self-locking nut	200~280 ″	(15~20 ″)
	11	Rear whell axle	Rear axle nut	800~1200 ″	(58~87 ″)
	12	Handle lever pivot bolt	6 mm hex bolt	80~120 ″	(6~ 9 ″)
	13	Air cleaner	6 mm hex bolt	80~120 ″	(6~ 9 ″)
	14	Kick arm	8×32 hex bolt	180~280 ″	(13~20 ″)
	15	Exhaust pipe joint	Joint nut	80~120 ″	(6~ 9 ″)
	16	Final driven sprocket	10 mm thin nut	400~500 ″	(25~58 ″)
	17	Drive chain adjuster	Adjusting nut	150~190 ″	(11~14 ″)
	18	Drive chain case	6 mm hex bolt	80~120 ″	(6~ 9 ″)
	19	Fuel cock body	Joint nut	150~250 ″	(11~18 ″)

SECTION THREE

ENGINE SERVICE

Engine Removal

1. Shut off the fuel cock and remove the fuel lines and the fuel level tube. Lift up the seat and remove the gas tank.

2. Disconnect the throttle cables at the carburetors. Remove the air cleaner cases and loosen the carburetor insulating bands.

3. Remove the mufflers and exhaust pipes.

4. Disconnect the clutch cable.

5. Take off the gear shift lever and the left foot peg. Remove the front chain cover and the chain.

6. Unplug the generator cable connector and the contact point cable connector. **Figure 1.**

7. Remove the spark plug caps.

8. Disconnect the starter motor cable. **Figure 2.**

9. Disconnect the tachometer cable. **Figure 3.**

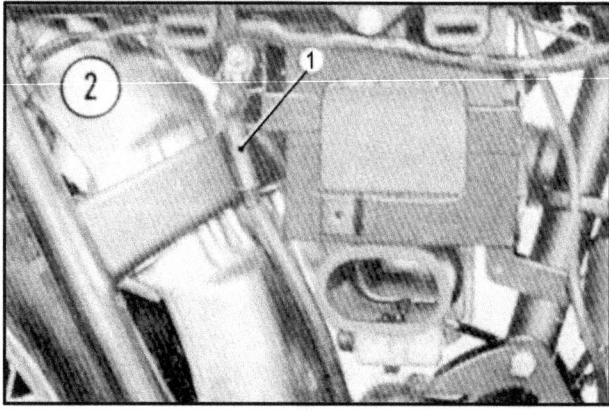

① Starting motor cable

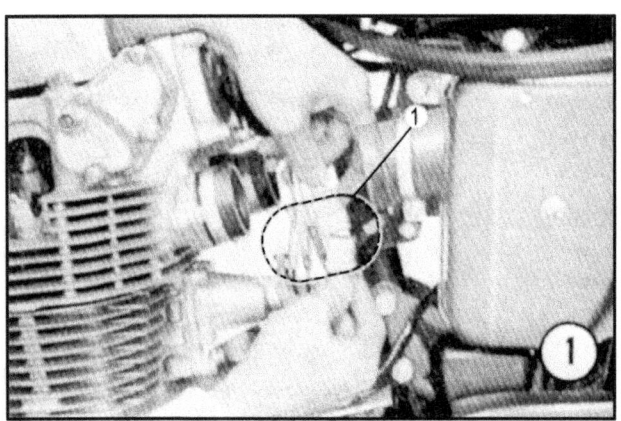

① Electrical leads

① Tachometer cable

10. Loosen and remove the 13 engine mounting bolts and lift out the engine from the left side. **Figure 4** shows the size bolts used, number 1 indicates 8mm bolts, and numbers 2, 3 and 4 indicate 10mm bolts.

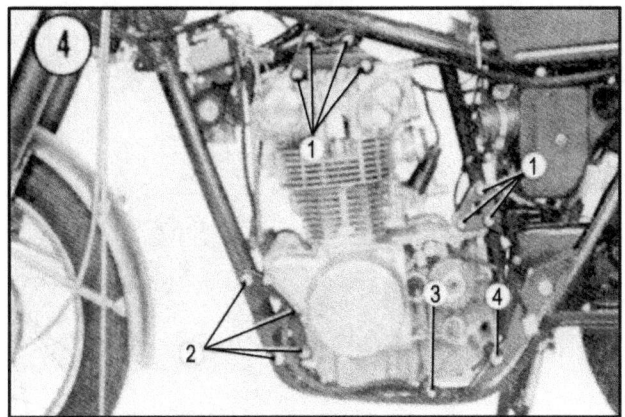

① 8mm bolt
② 10mm bolt
③ Engine hanger bolt
④ 10mm bolt

Replacement

1. Replace the engine in the reverse order of removal, following these additional guides: Install all engine mounting bolts from the right side of the frame putting the nuts on the left. All bolts should fit easily; if they have to be forced, check that everything is properly aligned.

2. Install the battery ground cable from the right side as shown in **Figure 5** and ensure the cable terminal, frame and bolt are free from rust, grease or paint.

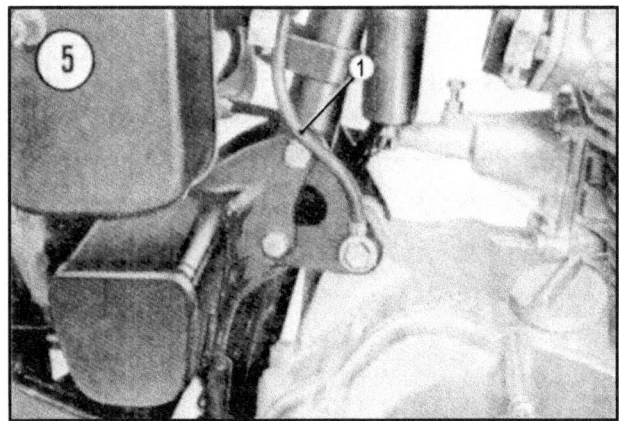

① Battery ground cable

3. When connecting the drive chain be sure the master link clip, number 3 in **Figure 6** is installed with its closed end pointing in the direction of normal chain movement.

4. Check that the steel ball has been installed

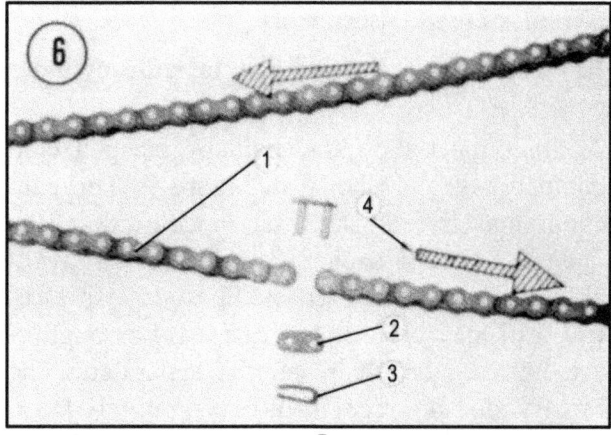

① Drive chain
② Drive chain joint
③ Drive chain joint clip
④ Rotation of direction

in the clutch lifter rod before the drive chain cover is installed. **Figure 7**.

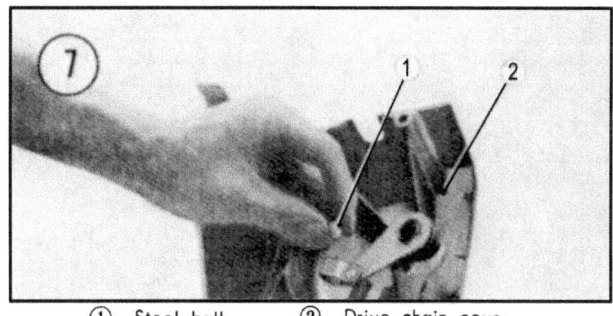

① Steel ball
② Drive chain cover

Cylinder Head

Note: The oil breather on models prior to engine serial numbers CB 450E-3000542, CL 450E-100-2569, is installed on the intake cylinder head cover. For a period the breather was located on the exhaust cover as shown in **Figure 8**. Current models have the breather in its original position on the intake cover.

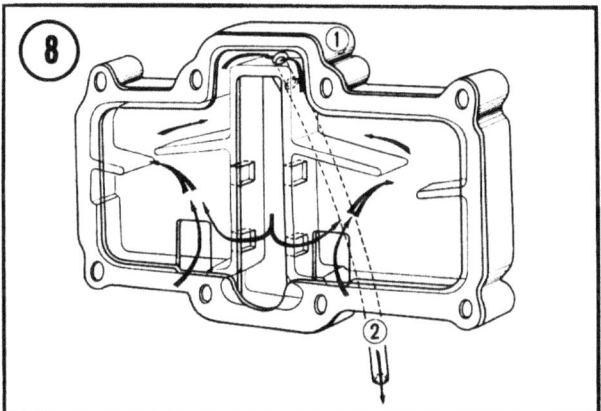

① Cylinder head cover A assembly
② Breather pipe

Cylinder Head Disassembly

1. Take off the intake and exhaust cylinder covers.

2. Disconnect the cam chain by using a cam chain breaker as shown in **Figure 9**. The cam chain master link is lighter in color than the normal links. If a chain breaker is not available, a small grinder wheel chucked in an electric drill may be used to grind away enough of the link so the chain can be separated. The factory doesn't recommend this but no harm will result if extreme care is used. Removing the spark plugs will permit the engine to be turned over easily so the master link may be found.

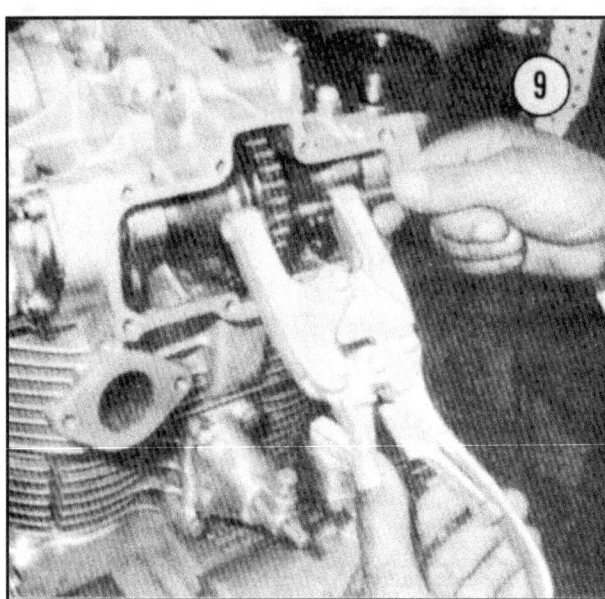

3. Hook wires in the ends of the cam chain so the chain doesn't drop into the crankcase as shown in **Figure 10**.

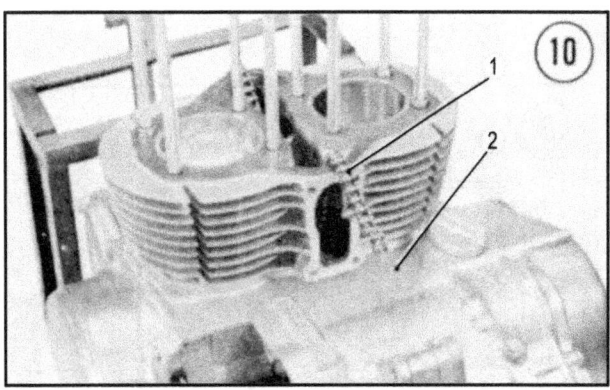

① Cam chain ② Wire

4. Remove the six hex head and two cap nuts securing the head. Loosen them in the reverse of the tightening sequence shown in **Figure 13**.

Cylinder Head Inspection and Cleaning

1. Inspect gasket, head and cylinder surfaces for evidences of blow-by or warping. **Figure 11.**

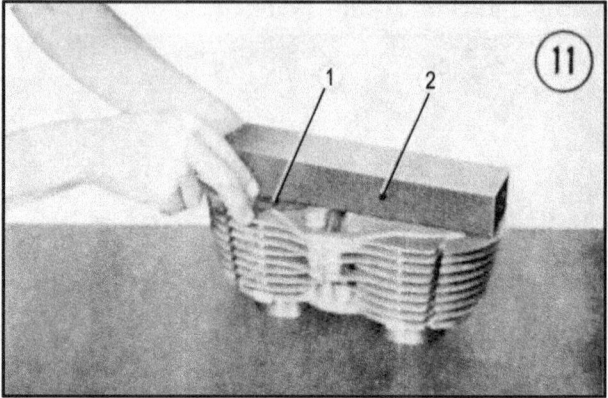

① Thickness gauge
② Square scale

2. Surfaces warped more than 0.05mm (0.002") will have to be lapped flat.

3. Clean the head, removing carbon with a carbon scraper and washing the head in solvent. Screwdrivers or chisels should not be used as scratches in the combustion chamber may form hot spots, causing pre-ignition.

Cylinder Head Reassembly

1. Replace the cylinder head gasket. Check that the three 12mm guide pins, and the two stud gaskets shown in **Figure 12** are in place. Number 1 shows the head gasket, number 2 shows the guide pins and number 3 shows the stud gaskets.

2. Lower the head into place making sure the guide pins enter the head and the cam chain is properly routed.

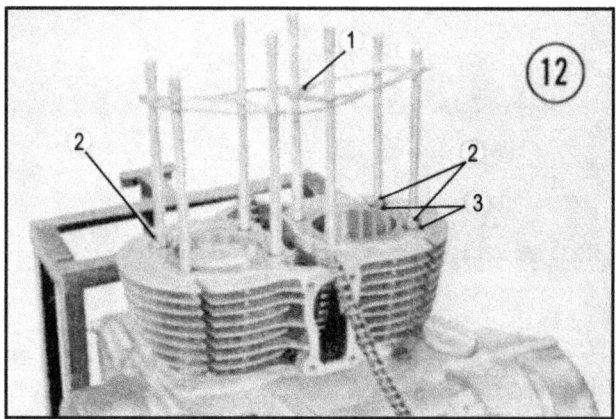

① Cylinder head gasket
② 12mm guide pins
③ Cylinder stud gaskets

3. Install the copper sealing washers and cap nuts on the two right-hand studs. The flat washers and hex nuts go on the other six studs. Torque the nuts in the sequence shown in **Figure 13** to 21.7 ft-lbs.

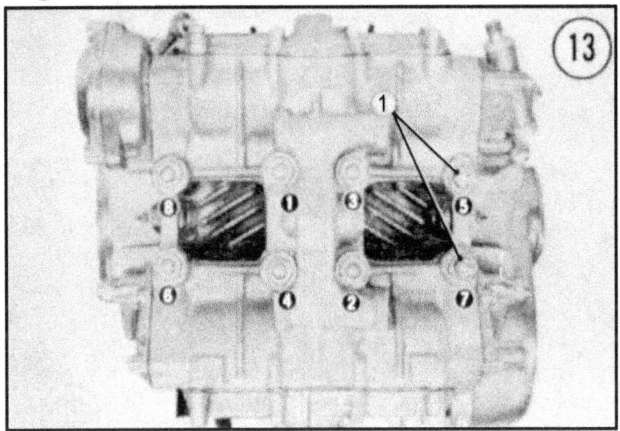

① Cap nuts

Valve Timing

1. Align the timing mark on each camshaft with its corresponding mark on the right-hand bearing as shown in **Figure 14**.

① Matching mark   ② Bearing
③ Cam shaft

2. Align the LT mark on the generator rotor with the index mark on the stator to bring the left piston to top dead center. Refer to **Figure 15**.

3. Connect the cam chain using the special tool as shown in **Figure 16**, noting that the tool will not work if the new link is positioned on a sprocket. Alignment of the valve timing marks should now be rechecked.

Cam Chain Tensioner Installation

1. If the tensioner has been dismantled, push the tensioner roller assembly toward the inside of the tensioner and secure it with the ad-

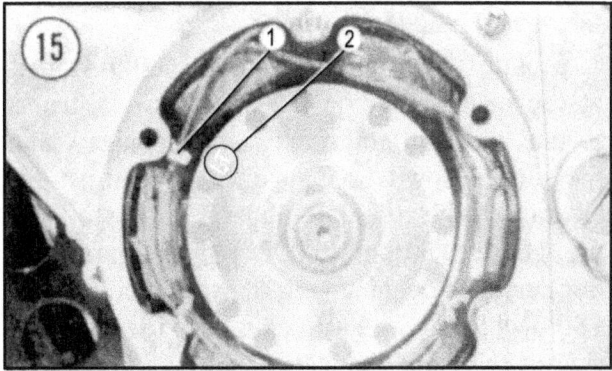

① Index mark   ② "LT" mark

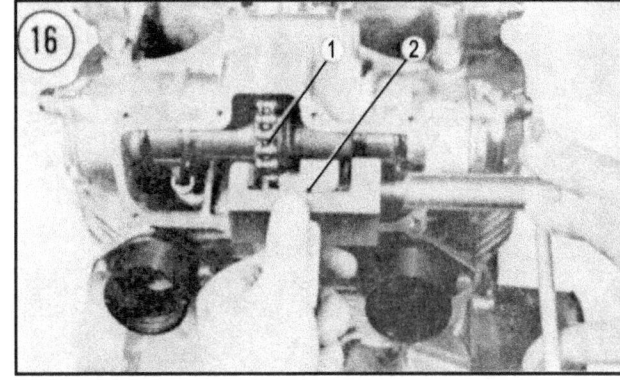

① Cam chain   ② Cam chain pincher

justing bolt and lock nut. Bolt it to the cylinder with the four 6mm hex nuts. Cam chain tension must then be adjusted per the following section.

Cam Chain Tensioner Adjustment

1. Loosen the lock nut and the adjustment bolt to free the push bar. Tighten the push bar after rotating the crankshaft to ensure the roller and cam chain are properly intermeshed. Lock the adjustment bolt with the lock nut, without putting pressure on the push bar. The spring will provide the proper tension. Refer to **Figure 17**.

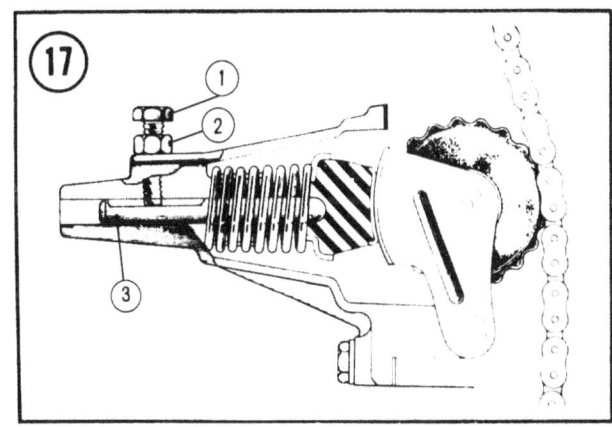

① Tensioner adjusting bolt   ② Lock nut   ③ Push bar

Adjusting Tappet Clearance

1. Rotate the crankshaft so the left piston is at top dead center on the compression stroke. Rotate the cam follower shaft keeping within the range shown in **Figure 19** and adjust the clearance with a feeler gauge as shown in **Figure 18** to 0.03mm (0.002"). This should be done with the engine cold. Turn the crankshaft 180 degrees and adjust clearances for the other side in the same manner.

2. Replace both cylinder head covers.

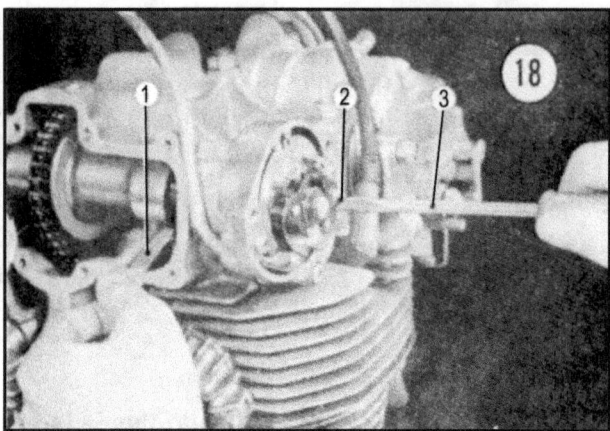

① Thickness gauge   ② Cam follower shaft
③ Screw driver

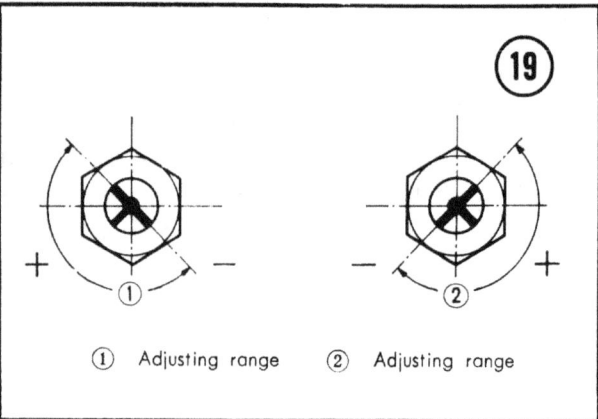

① Adjusting range   ② Adjusting range

Camshaft and Cam Follower Disassembly
(Refer to **Figures 20 and 21**).

1. Remove the cylinder head.
2. To remove the inlet camshaft, remove the cam follower shaft lock nuts from both sides.
3. Remove the cylinder head side covers and the inlet camshaft.
4. To remove the exhaust camshaft, loosen the lock nut from the right side and take off the tachometer gear box.
5. Remove the contact point cover.

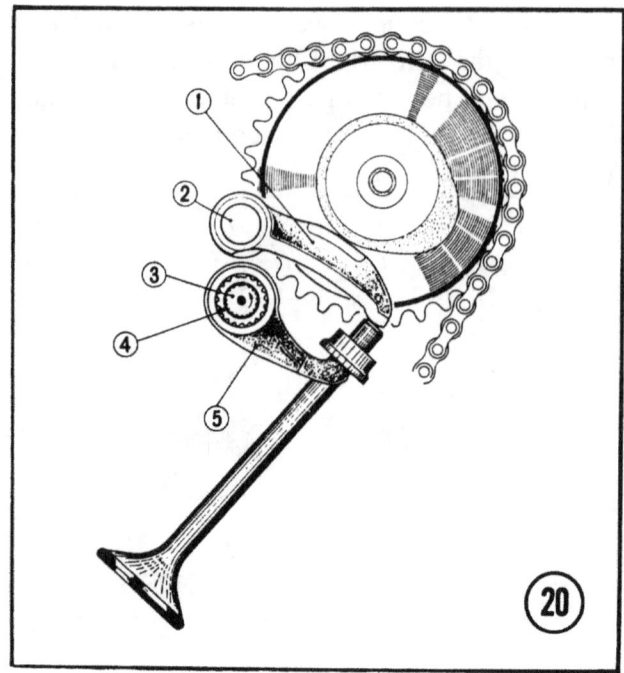

① Cam follower   ② Cam follower shaft
③ Torsion bar valve spring   ④ Outer torsion bar
⑤ Outer arm

6. Loosen the lock nut and remove the contact point assembly.
7. Remove the spark advance mechanism and the contact point base.
8. The exhaust camshaft can now be removed.

Camshaft and Cam Follower Inspection

1. Inspect the camshaft and cam follower shaft and arm to ensure that all dimensions in the accompanying table fall within the serviceable limits. Refer to **Figures 22, 23, 24 and 25**.
2. Check the cam sprocket for damage or worn teeth and replace if necessary. The damper ring must not be broken.

Camshaft and Cam Follower Reassembly

1. Starting with the inlet side, assemble the cam follower and the cam follower shaft. Refer to **Figure 21** to ensure correct placement.

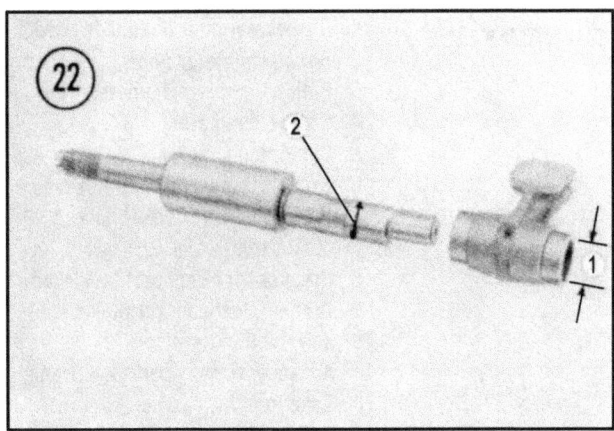

① Cam follower bearing diameter
② Cam follower shaft journal

	Item	Standard value	Serviceable limit
1	Cam follower bearing diamter ①	10.20~10.218 mm (0.4016~0.4023 in)	Replace if over 10.28 mm (0.4047 in)
2	Cam follower shaft journal ②	10.166~10.184 mm (0.3992~0.4009 in)	Replace if under 10.10 mm (0.3976 in)
3	Camshaft journals, inlet and exhaust	21.967~21.980 mm (0.8648~0.8654 in)	Replace if under 21.92 mm (0.8622 in)
4	Cam lift, inlet and exhaust	4.688~4.728 mm (0.1846~0.1853 in)	Replace if under 4.65 mm (0.1830 in)
5	Breaker point shaft runout	0.01 mm max (0.0004 in)	Replace if over 0.05 mm (0.002 in)

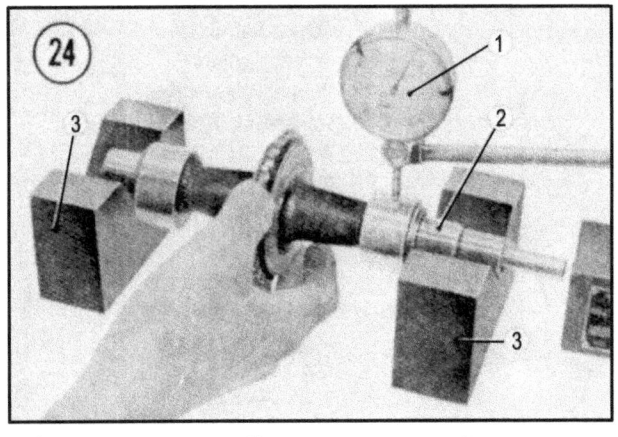

① Dial gauge ② Cam shaft ③ V block

2. Insert the inlet camshaft in place in the cylinder head with the oil pipe fitting on the right side.

3. Install both cylinder head side covers and check that the camshaft is free to rotate without binding.

4. Tighten the lock nut temporarily.

5. On the exhaust side, insert the cam follower and cam follower shaft into the cylinder head, then insert the exhaust camshaft.

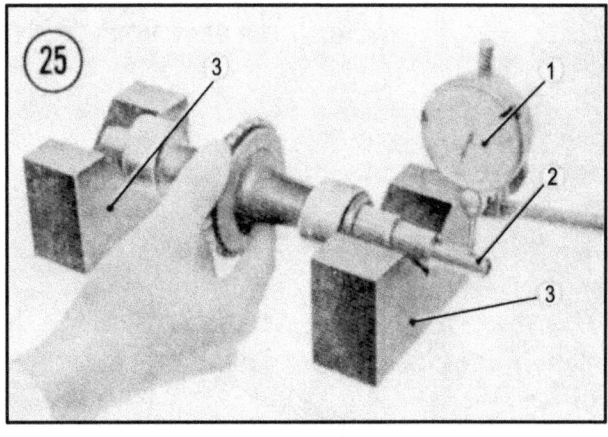

① Dial gauge ② Cam shaft ③ V block

6. Assemble the drive pinion and the tachometer gear box as shown in **Figures 26, 27**. Don't forget the washer shown by number 2 in the photo.

① Pinion
② Washer
③ Gear box

7. Slip the gearbox assembly in place and secure it. Be sure it is properly meshed with the camshaft.

8. Attach the breaker point base and check that the camshaft is free to rotate.

9. Install the spark advance assembly and the contact point assembly. Tighten the lock nut temporarily.

10. Camshaft end play should be checked to ensure it is within 0.05 to 0.35mm (0.002 to 0.014"). Shims are available for adjusting this clearance in 0.1 and 0.2mm (0.004 and 0.008").

11. Valve clearance will now have to be adjusted as outlined previously.

TACHOMETER GEAR BOX — POINT BASE — BREAKER

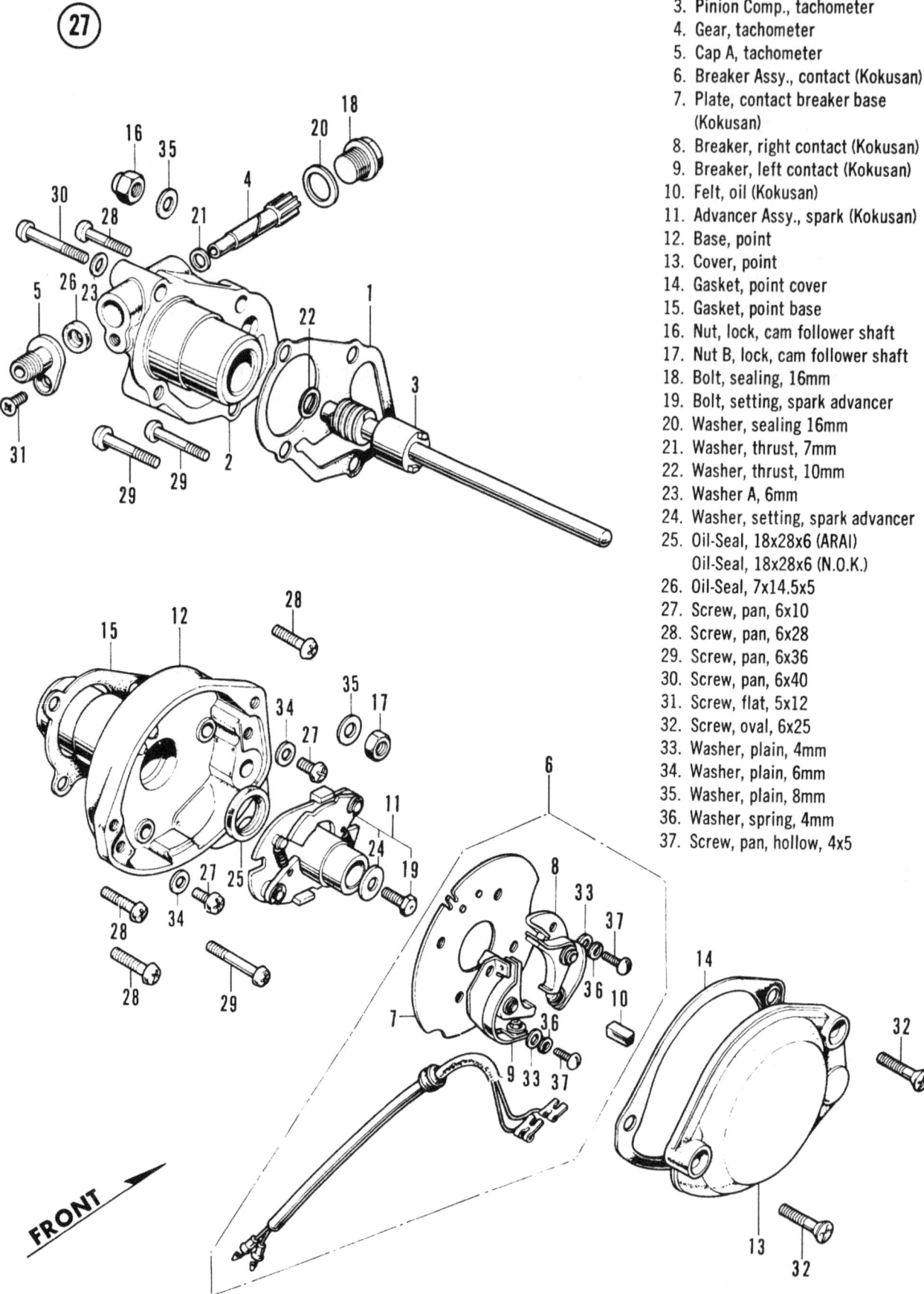

1. Gasket, cylinder head side cover
2. Box, tachometer gear
3. Pinion Comp., tachometer
4. Gear, tachometer
5. Cap A, tachometer
6. Breaker Assy., contact (Kokusan)
7. Plate, contact breaker base (Kokusan)
8. Breaker, right contact (Kokusan)
9. Breaker, left contact (Kokusan)
10. Felt, oil (Kokusan)
11. Advancer Assy., spark (Kokusan)
12. Base, point
13. Cover, point
14. Gasket, point cover
15. Gasket, point base
16. Nut, lock, cam follower shaft
17. Nut B, lock, cam follower shaft
18. Bolt, sealing, 16mm
19. Bolt, setting, spark advancer
20. Washer, sealing 16mm
21. Washer, thrust, 7mm
22. Washer, thrust, 10mm
23. Washer A, 6mm
24. Washer, setting, spark advancer
25. Oil-Seal, 18x28x6 (ARAI)
    Oil-Seal, 18x28x6 (N.O.K.)
26. Oil-Seal, 7x14.5x5
27. Screw, pan, 6x10
28. Screw, pan, 6x28
29. Screw, pan, 6x36
30. Screw, pan, 6x40
31. Screw, flat, 5x12
32. Screw, oval, 6x25
33. Washer, plain, 4mm
34. Washer, plain, 6mm
35. Washer, plain, 8mm
36. Washer, spring, 4mm
37. Screw, pan, hollow, 4x5

Valve and Torsion Bar Spring Disassembly

1. Refer to **Figures 28, 29, 30,** for details of valve and torsion bar disassembly, assembly and construction.

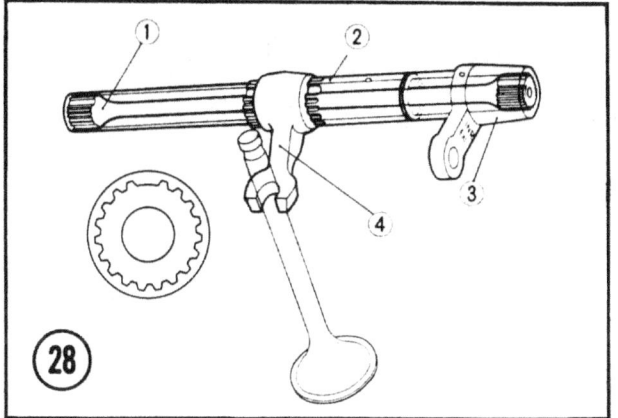

① Torsion bar (Valve spring)
② Torsion bar outer
③ Torsion bar holder
④ Torsion bar outer arm

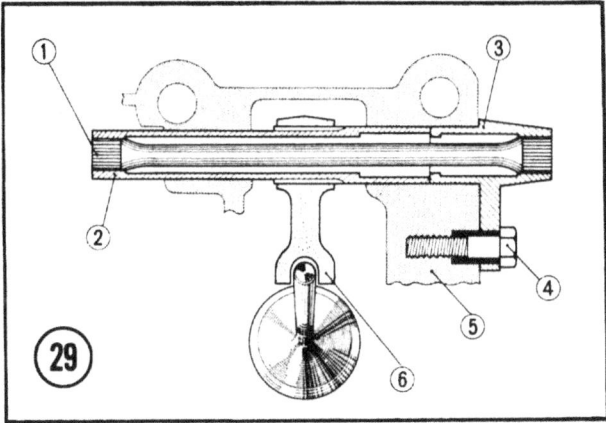

① Torsion bar ② Torsion bar outer
③ Torsion bar holder ④ Setting bolt
⑤ Cylinder head ⑥ Torsion bar outer arm

2. Dismantle the cam follower and camshaft as described above.

3. Unscrew the torsion bar holder bolt, putting tension on the torsion bar arm in the direction of the arrow marked on the end of the torsion bar (valve spring) to relieve tension on the bolt. Pull out the torsion bar assembly and repeat the procedure for all valves. Keep respective torsion bar and valve assemblies separated so they may be reinstalled correctly. Use extreme care when handling torsion bars as even small nicks or scratches may cause failure.

4. Remove the valve retainer and cotter.

5. Remove the 6mm valve guide stop bolt and then the stop. Remove the valve guide seal cap. Refer to **Figure 31**. The valve can now be removed through the combustion chamber.

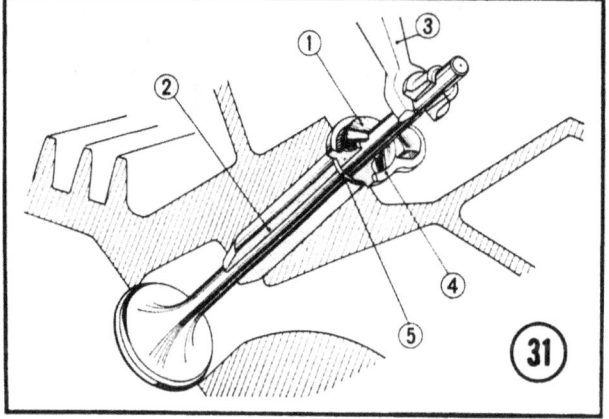

① Valve guide seal cap
② Valve guide
③ Torsion bar outer arm
④ Valve guide stop
⑤ O ring

Valve Inspection and Service

1. Inspect the valve and valve guide to ensure that their critical dimensions fall within the limits given in the accompanying table. **Figure 32**. Also check the valve face for evidences of blow-by, burning or wear and repair or replace as necessary. The valve head thickness shouldn't be less than 0.5mm (0.020") after refacing.

2. If a valve is being replaced because of a worn stem, the valve guide will also be worn, necessitating its replacement. Valve guides should be slightly undersize and reamed to fit. Always use new O rings under the flange of the valve guide.

3. Check valve seat width by smearing the valve face with a coat of bluing or red lead and inserting the valve in its guide. Hold it tightly in place and rotate the valve through a complete revolution. The width and condition of the valve seat will be clearly indicated. Width should fall between 1.0 and 1.3mm (0.0394 and 0.0512"). The seat should be remachined as in the following step if it is over 2.0mm (0.0787").

4. Valve seat recutting should be done by only the most experienced mechanics and with the necessary seat cutters.

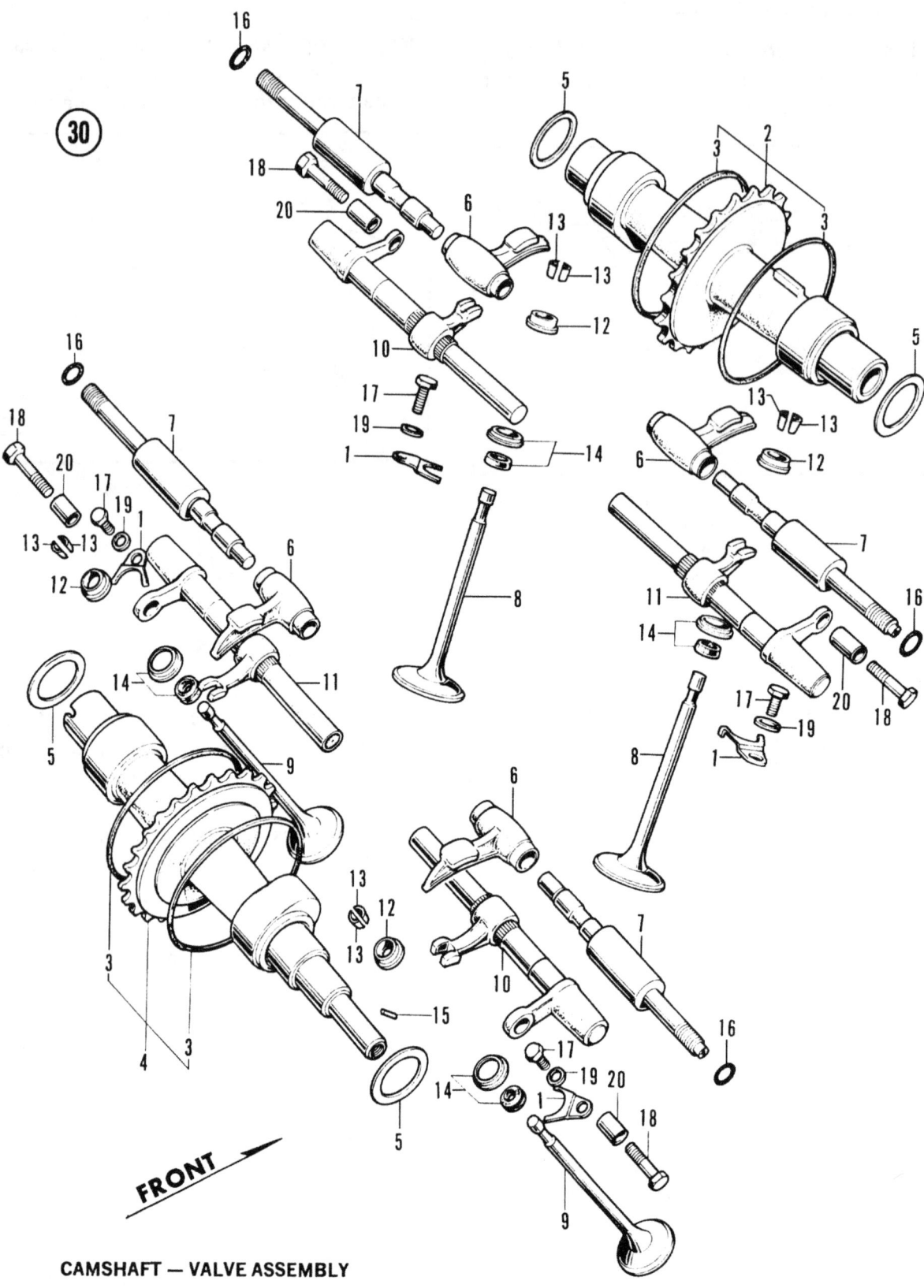

CAMSHAFT — VALVE ASSEMBLY

1. Stopper, valve guide
2. Camshaft Comp., inlet
3. Ring, cam chain damper
4. Camshaft Comp., exhaust
5. Spacer, camshaft (0.1mm)
   Spacer, camshaft (0.2mm)
6. Follower, cam
7. Shaft, cam follower
8. Valve, inlet
9. Valve, exhaust
10. Spring A Assy., torsion bar valve
11. Spring B Assy., torsion bar valve
12. Retainer, valve spring
13. Cotter, valve
14. Cap, valve guide seal
15. Pin, knock, 3x6.8
16. O-Ring, 7.8x2.2
17. Bolt, hex., 6x12
18. Bolt, hex., 6x28
19. Washer, spring, 6mm
20. Pin, knock, 8x12A

	Item	Standard value	Serviceable limit
1	Valve stem diameter, inlet	6.974~6.988 mm (0.2746~0.2751 in)	Replace if under 6.96 mm (0.2740 in)
2	Valve stem diameter, exhaust	6.968~6.982 mm (0.2743~0.2749 in)	Replace if under 6.95 mm (0.2736 in)
3	Straightness of valve stem	Within 0.02 mm (0.0008 in)	Replace if over 0.02 mm (0.0008 in)
4	Concentricity of valve face	0.03 mm TIR (0.0012 in)	Replace if over 0.03 mm (0.0012 in)
5	Valve guide diameter, inlet & exhaust	7.0~7.01 mm (0.2756~0.2760 in)	Replace if over 7.05 mm (0.2776 in)

5. Valves should be lapped in if any wear is noted in the seats. Use a valve lapping compound, following instructions on the container and using a suction cup lapping tool. Wash all traces of lapping compound away when the job is finished and check the seat with bluing as in the valve seat width test.

Valve and Torsion Bar Valve Spring Reassembly

1. Inspect the torsion bar for cracks or rust before assembling.

2. Refer to **Figure 33** to ensure that torsion bars are not interchanged.

3. Assemble the outer arm and the torsion bar into the cylinder head, fitting the outer arm onto the shaft of the bar as it is passed into the cylinder head, as shown in **Figure 34**.

4. Assemble valve into head and secure, ensuring the guide seal cap is not loose and the

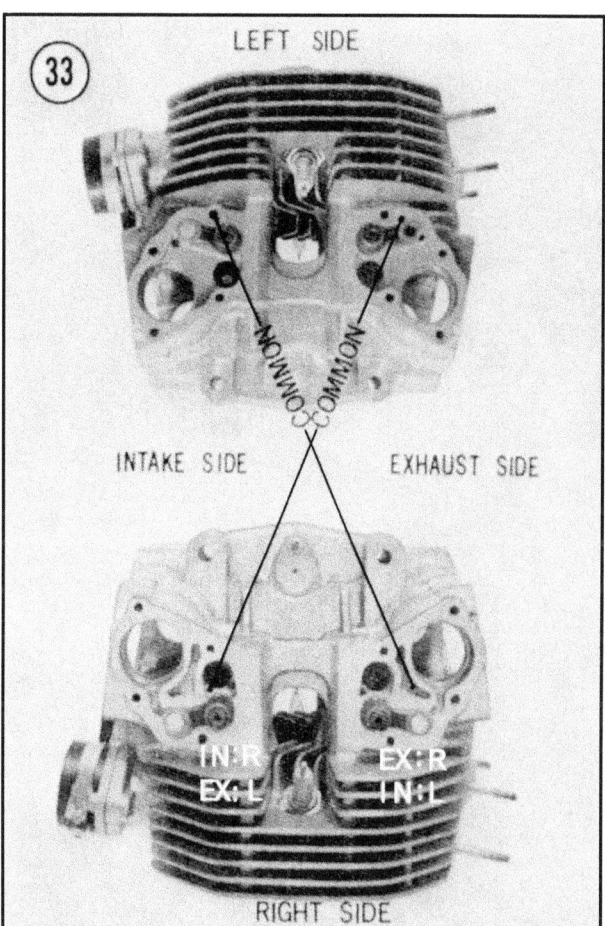

valve stem and fork of the outer arms is not binding.

5. Insert the dowel pin to hold the torsion bar holder in place and tighten the bolt to 3.7 to 4.63 ft-lbs.

Cam Chain Guide Roller Disassembly

1. Refer to **Figures 35, 36,** to identify the various rollers for disassembly and service.

2. To remove the guide roller "T", remove either the inlet or exhaust camshaft and then take out the guide roller pin.

3. To remove the guide rollers "A" and "R" remove the bracket bolts and then the rollers.

4. To remove guide roller "B", remove the cylinder and then the guide roller pin and the roller.

Cam Chain Guide Roller Reassembly

1. Oil all moveable parts before assembling the rollers as they will not receive oil for some time after the engine is started.

2. Assemble the rollers in the following order: A, C and R, followed by the others. Check

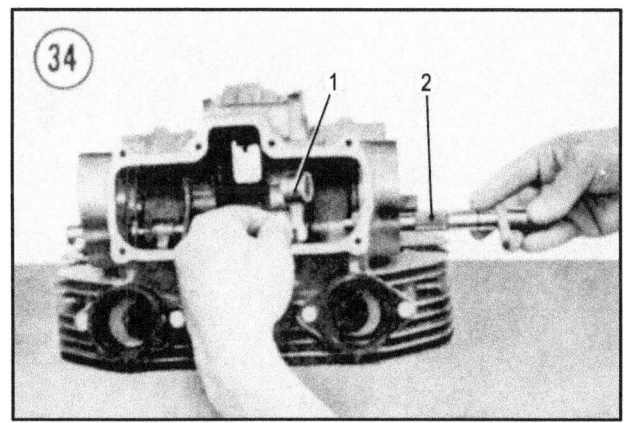

① Torsion bar outer arm   ② Torsion bar valve spring

CAM CHAIN — TENSIONER — GUIDE ROLLER

1. Chain, cam (DK219-64L)
2. Joint, cam chain (DK219)
3. Tensioner Comp., cam chain
4. Spring, tensioner
5. Bar Comp., push
6. Gasket, cam chain tensioner
7. Roller Comp., front cam chain guide
8. Roller B, cam chain guide
9. Pin B, cam chain guide roller
10. Roller, cam chain guide
11. Pin A, cam chain guide roller
12. Roller Comp., rear cam chain guide
13. Pin, knock, roller stay
14. Bolt, tensioner adjusting
15. O-Ring, 16.4 x 2.4
16. Bolt, hex., 6x16
17. Bolt, hex., 6x25
18. Screw, pan, 6x10
19. Nut, hex., 6mm
20. Washer, plain, 6mm
21. Washer, spring, 6mm
22. Pin, knock, 4x8B

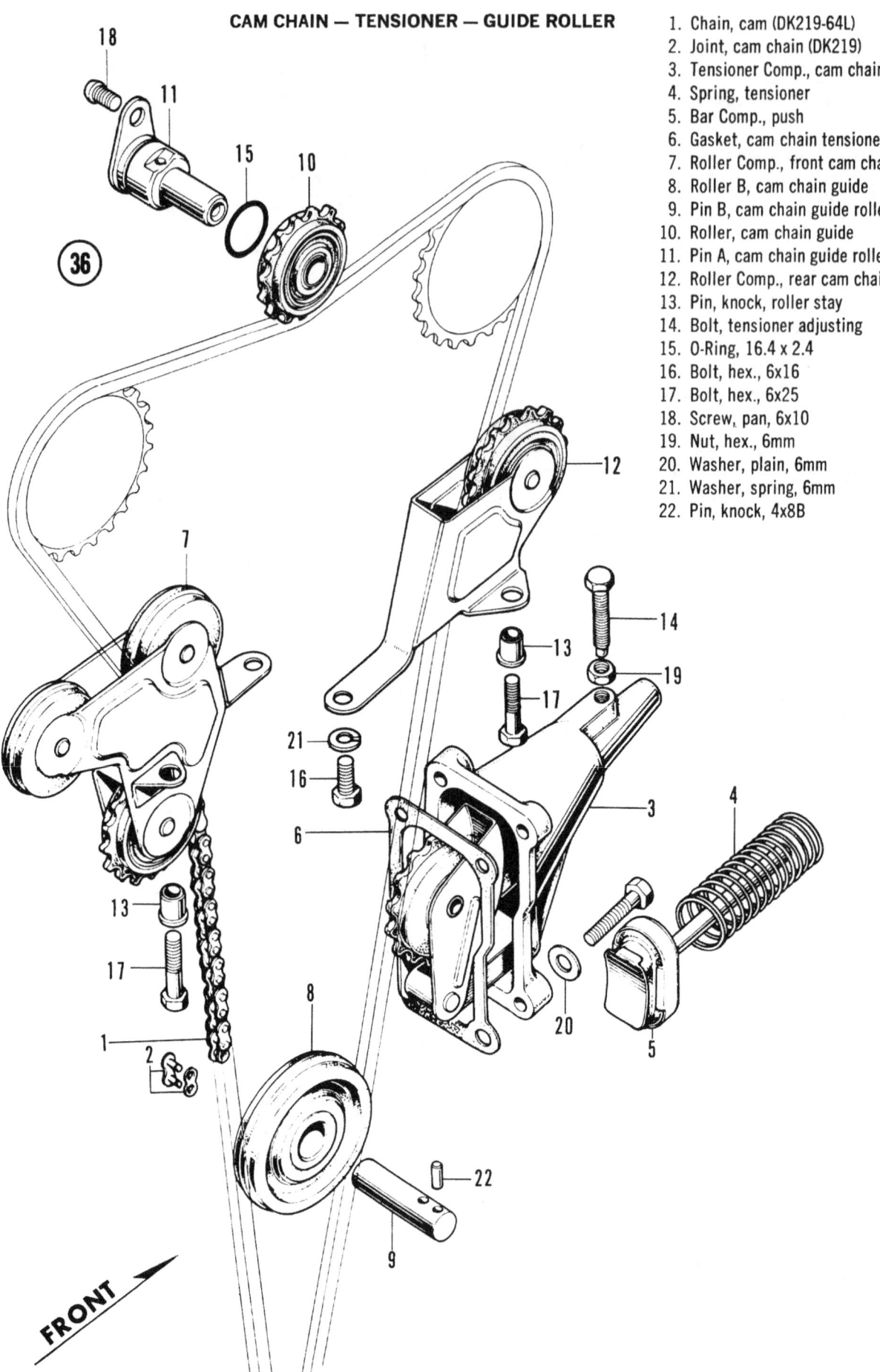

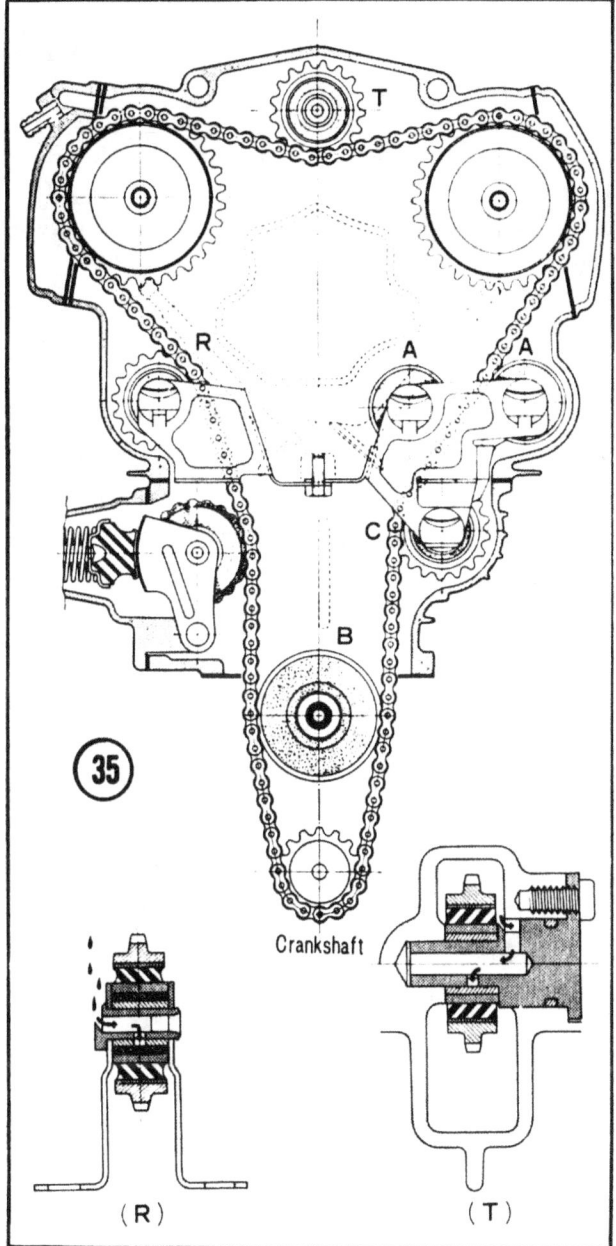

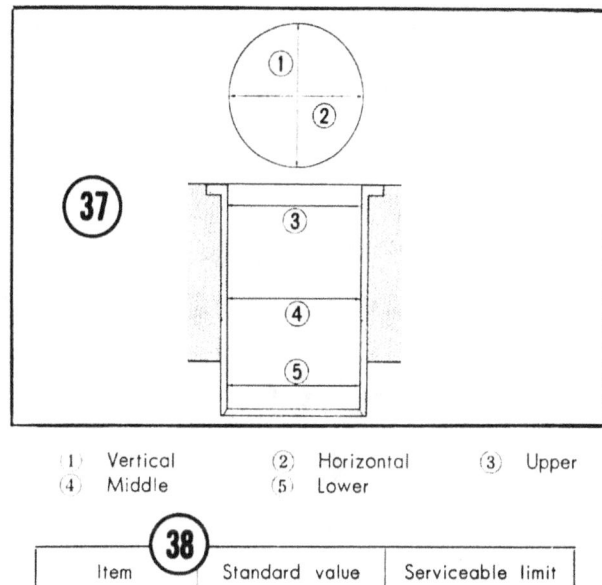

(1) Vertical   (2) Horizontal   (3) Upper
(4) Middle   (5) Lower

Item	Standard value	Serviceable limit
Cylinder barrel	70.0~70.01 mm (2.756~2.7564 in)	Boring necessary when over 70.11 mm (2.76 in)
Cylinder out-of-round	Less than 0.005 mm (0.0002 in)	Boring necessary when over 0.05 mm (0.002 in)
Cylinder taper	Less than 0.005 mm (0.0002 in)	Boring necessary when over 0.05 mm (0.002 in)

Sleeves and liners are not available separately and purchase of the entire block is required.

3. If the piston only is replaced without boring the cylinder, a ridge reamer should be used to remove the ridge which forms at the top of the cylinder. Refer to **Figure 39**.

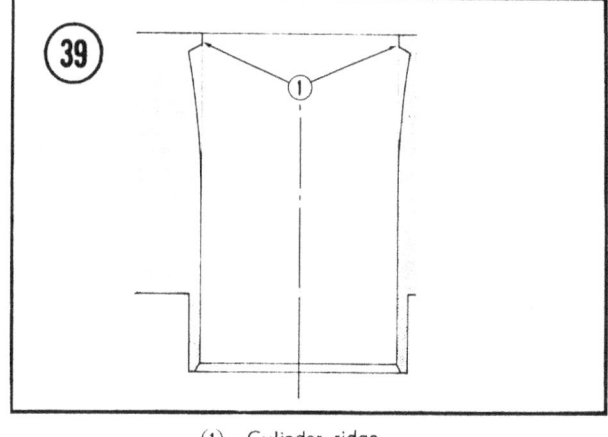

(1) Cylinder ridge

that all are operating freely before proceeding with further reassembly.

Cylinder Disassembly

1. Remove the cylinder head and then the cylinder, as discussed earlier in this section.

Cylinder Inspection

1. Measure the cylinder with an inside micrometer or cylinder gauge, taking measurements as shown in **Figure 37**. Compare the figures to those shown in the accompanying table to determine if boring or liner replacement will be necessary. **Figure 38**.

2. If the cylinder needs reboring more than 1.0mm (0.040") the sleeves should be replaced.

Cylinder Reassembly

1. Install the base gasket and two locating pins on the crankcase and ensure an O ring is installed on the cylinder skirt.

2. Space the piston ring gaps around the piston, approximately 120 degrees apart to avoid

blow-by. Secure the rings in their grooves with ring compressors as shown in **Figure 40** and carefully lower the cylinder into place.

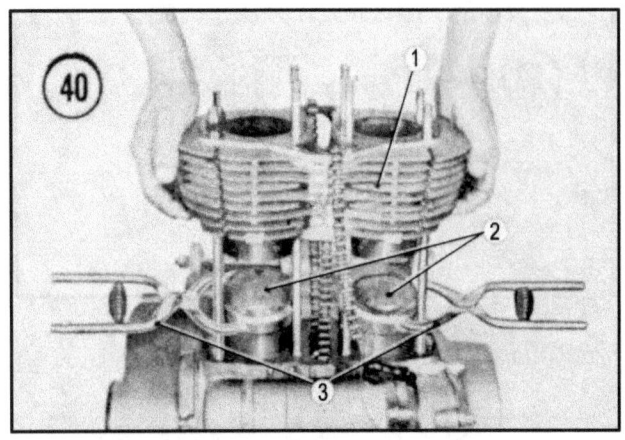

① Cylinder ② Piston
③ Piston ring compressor

Piston and Piston Ring Disassembly

1. Wrap a clean rag around the connecting rod as shown in **Figure 41** to prevent a dropped circlip from falling in the crankcase. Remove the circlip and push out the piston pin.

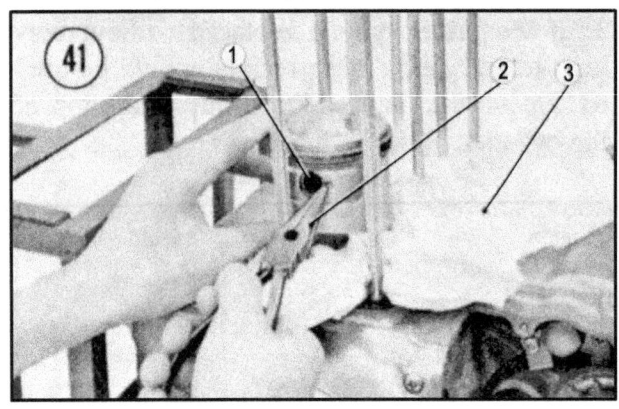

1 Piston pin clip 2 Long nose pliers ③ Rags

2. Lift the piston free of the connecting rod.

3. Remove the rings from the piston, preferably with a ring remover. They can be removed by hand if care is used to avoid twisting them.

Piston and Piston Ring Inspection

1. Clean carbon from the piston head and ring grooves using a carbon scraper and groove cleaner. Emery paper should not be used.

2. Measure piston diameter in two axes as shown in **Figure 42**. Measurement "D" should

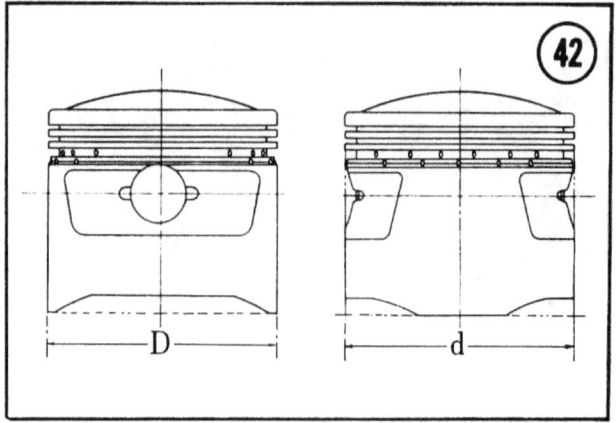

be 69.95 to 69.97mm (2.754 to 2.755") and measurement "d" should be "D" minus 0.24 mm (0.0095") to 0.26mm (0.0102").

3. Oversize pistons come in four sizes from D=70.22mm (2.765") in increments of 0.25-mm (0.01").

4. Measure ring groove clearances as shown in **Figure 43** and use the accompanying table to determine replacement needs. **Figure 44.**

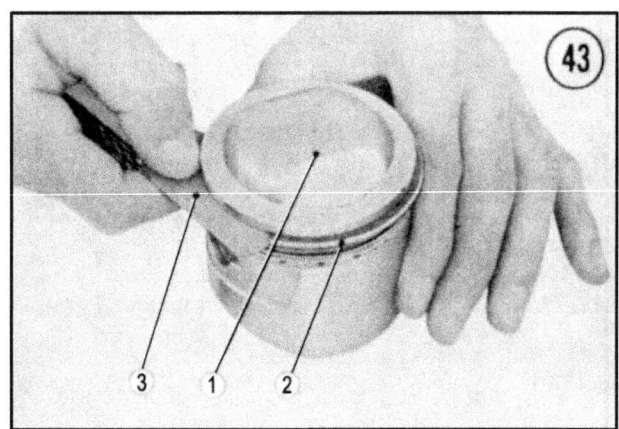

① Piston ② Piston ring ③ Thickness gauge

Item	Standard value	Serviceable limit
Top ring	0.040~0.070 mm (0.0016~0.0028 in)	Replace if over 0.15 mm (0.006 in)
2nd ring	0.020~0.045 mm (0.0008~0.0018 in)	Replace if over 0.15 mm (0.006 in)
Oil ring	0.010~0.040 mm (0.0004~0.0016 in)	Replace if over 0.1 mm (0.004 in)

5. Measure piston pin diameter and use the table to determine serviceable limits. **Figure 45.**

6. Insert the rings one at a time into the cylinder bore as shown in **Figure 46** and measure their end gap with a feeler gauge. The table gives serviceable limits. **Figure 47.**

Item	Standard value	Serviceable limit
Piston pin dia.	16.994~17.00 mm (0.6690~0.6693 in)	Replace if under 16.95 mm (0.6673 in)
Piston pin bore	17.002~17.008 mm (0.6693~0.6696 in)	Replace if over 17.1 mm (0.6732 in)

Figure 45

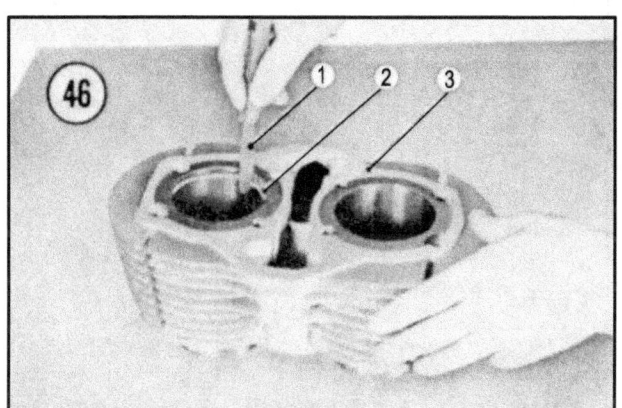

① Thickness gauge ② Piston ring ③ Cylinder

Figure 46

Item	Standard value	Serviceable limit
Top, Second ring	0.3~0.5 mm (0.012~0.03 in)	Replace if over 0.8 mm (0.031 in)
Oil ring	0.2~0.4 mm (0.008~0.016 in)	Replace if over 0.8 mm (0.031 in)

Figure 47

7. Ring tension must be measured with a tension measuring instrument as shown in **Figure 48**. See the table for limits. **Figure 49**.

8. Measure rings with a micrometer to check serviceable limits (as shown in the table) for proper width and thickness. **Figure 50**.

Piston and Piston Ring Reassembly

1. Cover the crankcase opening with a clean rag and install the piston on the connecting rod. Be sure the "E" mark on the piston head is pointed toward the front (exhaust) side of the engine.

2. The piston pin should be an easy push fit and is secured with new piston pin clips. Slide the clips around after installation so that their cut ends are away from the cut portion of the clip groove as shown in **Figure 51**.

3. Install the rings on the piston, starting with the bottom ring and working up. Roll the rings

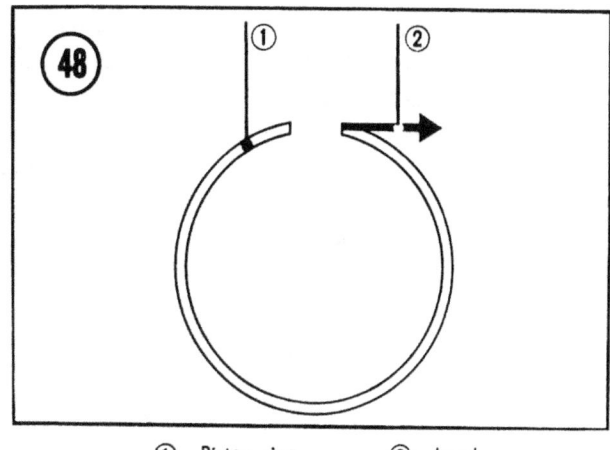

① Piston ring ② Load

Figure 48

Item	Standard value	Serviceable limit
Top, ring	0.92~1.37 kg (2.0~3.0 lb)	Replace if under 0.6 kg (1.3 lb)
Second ring	0.75~1.15 kg (1.65~2.5 lb)	Replace if under 0.5 kg (1.1 lb)
Oil ring	1.47~2.14 kg (3.2~4.7 lb)	Replace if under 1.2 kg (2.6 lb)

Figure 49

Item		Standard value	Serviceable limit
Width	All rings	3.1~3.3 mm (0.122~0.130 in)	Replace if under 2.9 mm (0.1141 in)
Thickness	Top	1.45~1.465 mm (0.057~0.058 in)	Replace if under 1.4 mm (0.0551 in)
	2nd	1.475~1.485 mm (0.0580~0.0584 in)	Replace if under 1.43 mm (0.566 in)
	Oil	2.48~2.495 mm (0.0976~0.0982 in)	Replace if under 2.4 mm (0.0944 in)

Figure 50

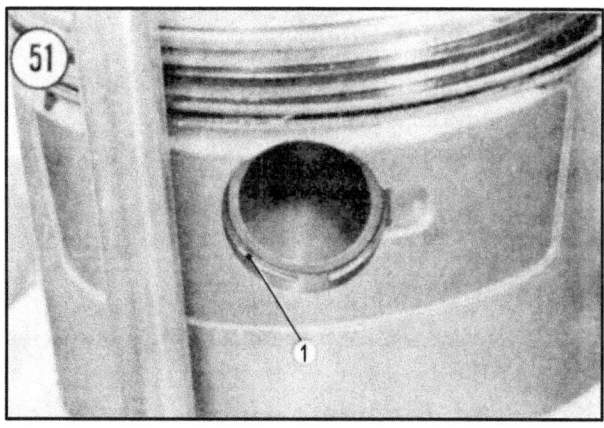

① Piston pin clip

Figure 51

around in their grooves as shown in **Figure 52** to ensure they are free to operate properly and that the grooves are clean.

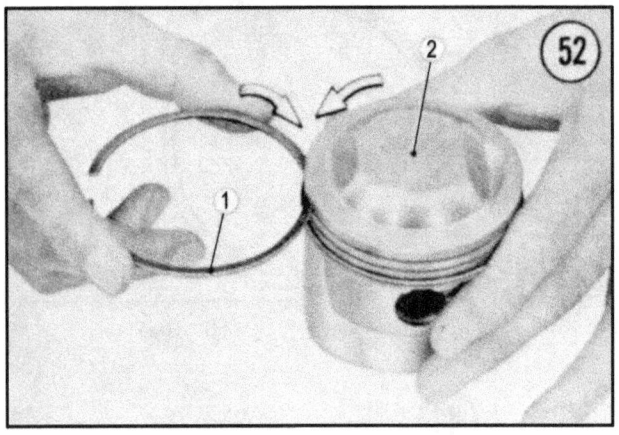

① Piston ring   ② Piston

4. The rings must be installed with the manufacturers mark UP as shown in **Figure 53**. Use a ring installing tool if at all possible.

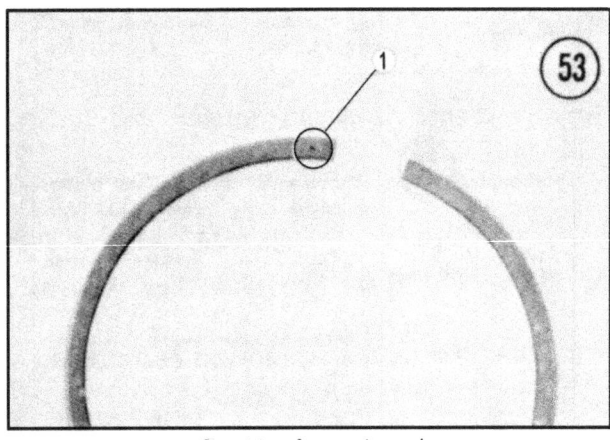

(1) Manufacturer's mark

5. Stagger the ring gaps 120 degrees apart to prevent blow-by and use a ring compressor on each piston when lowering the cylinder in place. Install the cam chain and cam chain guide roller at this time.

6. Check that the cam chamber gasket is properly seated and install the cylinder head as previously instructed.

Right Crankcase Cover Disassembly

1. Refer to **Figure 54** for details of the crankcase cover and oil filter construction.
2. Drain the engine oil and remove the kick starter from its shaft.
3. Remove the mounting screws and take off the cover.

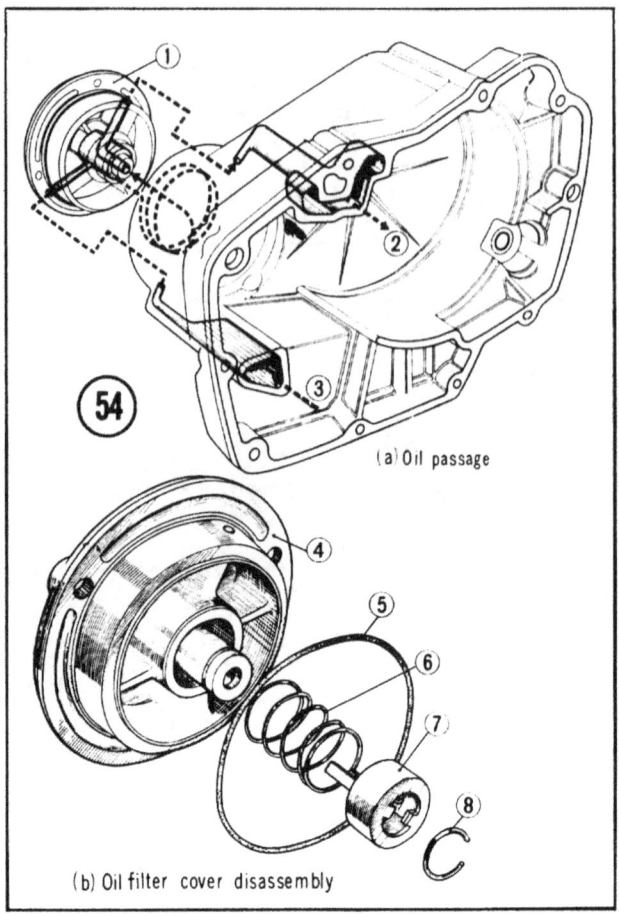

(a) Oil passage

(b) Oil filter cover disassembly

① Oil filter cover
② To upper crank case
③ From lower crankcase
④ Oil filter cover
⑤ 57.8 × 6.2 O-ring
⑥ Oil guide metal spring
⑦ Oil guide metal
⑧ Oil guide metal stop ring

Right Crankcase Cover Reassembly

1. Inspect the crankcase and oil filter covers for cracks and damage to the mating surfaces. Repair or replace as necessary.
2. Inspect the O ring and gasket and replace if necessary.
3. Match up the punch marks on the kick starter arm and shaft when installing.
4. Tighten all case screws uniformly.

Oil Filter Disassembly

1. Remove the right crankcase cover and then the circlip and oil filter cap as shown in **Figure 55**.
2. Straighten the pawls of the spring washer so the lock nut may be removed with a 16mm T-handle wrench as shown in **Figure 56**. The filter rotor can then be removed.

① 8mm bolt   ② Spanner

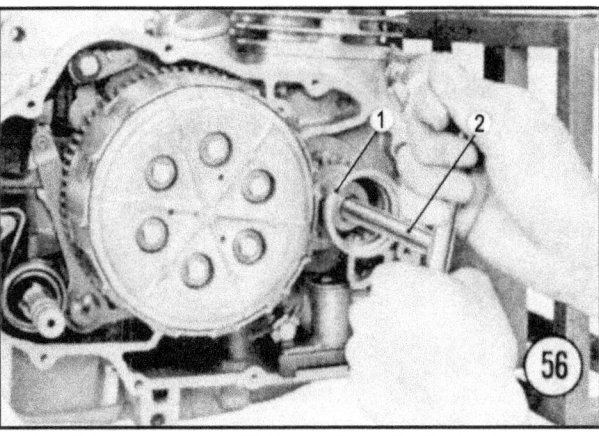

① Oil filter rotor   ② 16mm T-handle lock nut wrench

Oil Filter Reassembly

1. Clean the inside of the oil filter rotor and reassemble. Follow the reverse order of assembly.

2. Be sure the mounting nut is tight and locked in place with the tongued washer as shown in **Figure 57.** Note that the oil filter cap is aligned to fit in a groove within the rotor wall as shown is **Figure 58.** Secure the filter cap with the circlip.

① 16 mm lock nut   ② Oil filter rotor
③ Tongued washer

① Oil filter rotor
② Oil filter cap

Clutch Disassembly

1. Remove the right crankcase cover.

2. Remove the oil filter.

3. Refer to **Figure 59** for details of clutch construction.

4. Remove the six 6mm bolts on the clutch pressure plate. Remove the pressure plate, friction discs and clutch plates as shown in **Figure 60.**

5. Remove the circlip and pull off the clutch center hub as shown in **Figure 61.**

① Friction disc and clutch plates

① Clutch center   ② 25mm circlip   ③ Plier

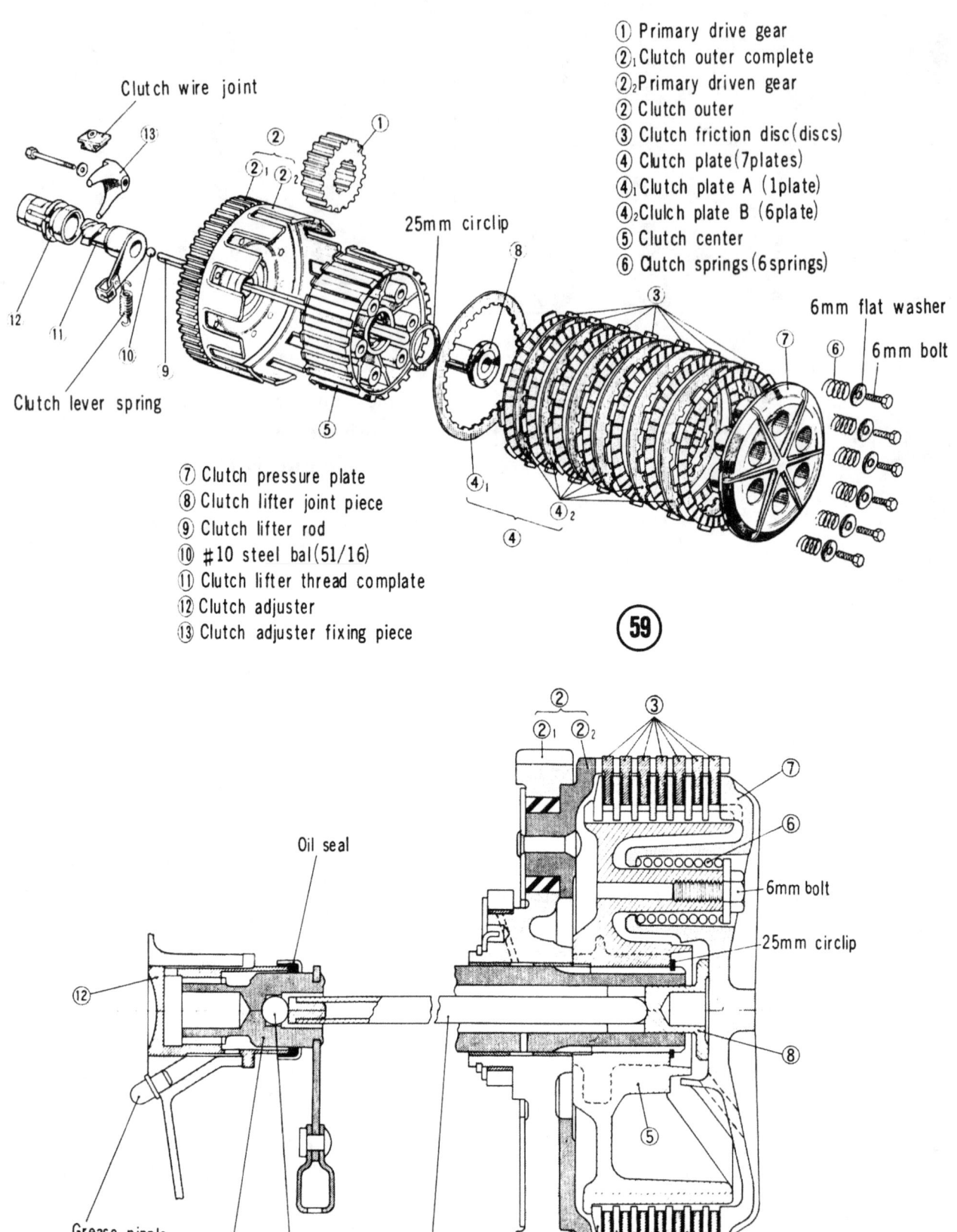

6. Straighten the lock washers on the oil pump bolts and remove them. The clutch outer hub and oil pump are then removed as a unit. Refer to **Figure 62**.

7. Refer to **Figures 63, 64, 65** for details of oil pump construction.

① Clutch outer
② Oil pump

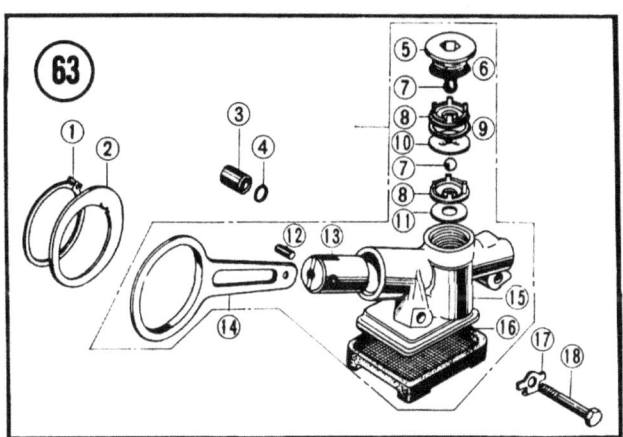

① 32 mm circlip
③ 8×12 Knock pin
⑤ Oil pump ball stopper bolt
⑦ #10 Steel ball
⑨ Rubber ring
⑪ Rubber seat
⑬ Pump plunger
⑮ Oil pump body
⑰ 6 mm lock washer

② Pump rod side washer
④ 8×1.5 O ring
⑥ 17×2.5 O ring
⑧ Oil pump ball seat
⑩ Oil pump ball stopper
⑫ Oil pump plunger pin
⑭ Pump rod
⑯ Filter screen
⑱ 6×28 hex bolt

Clutch Inspection

1. Inspect clutch components and repair or replace them if dimensions fall outside limits given in the accompanying tables. **(Figure 66)**.

Clutch Reassembly

1. Reassemble the clutch is the reverse order, referring to **Figure 59** again for details.

1. Friction disc

Item	Standard value	Serviceable limit
Friction disc thickness	3.42~3.58 mm (0.135~0.141 in)	Replace if under 3.1 mm (0.122 in)

2. Backlash

Item	Standard value	Serviceable limit
Friction disc and clutch outer	0.3 mm max. (0.012 in)	Replace if over 0.8 mm (0.032 in)

3. Clutch plate distortion.

Item	Standard value	Serviceable limit
Clutch plate A and B	0.15 mm max. (0.006 in)	Repair or replace if over 0.35 mm (0.014 in)

4. Clutch spring

Item	Standard value	Serviceable limit
Free length	40.1 mm (1.575 in)	Replace if under 3.94 mm (1.55 in)
With load	31.6~34.1 kg/56.6 mm (81.585~77.175 lbs/1.047 in)	—

5. Clutch center

Item	Standard value	Serviceable limit
Radial clearance between clutch center and main shaft	0.020~0.062 mm (0.0008~0.0024 in)	Replace if over 0.12 mm (0.0047 in)

2. Install the oil pump rod with care as reversing it will render the pump inoperable. Replace the oil pump lock washer each time the pump is removed and check that the 8x15 O ring installed around the pump pin is in place and undamaged.

Left Crankcase Cover Disassembly

1. Remove the neutral switch. Refer to **Figure 67**.

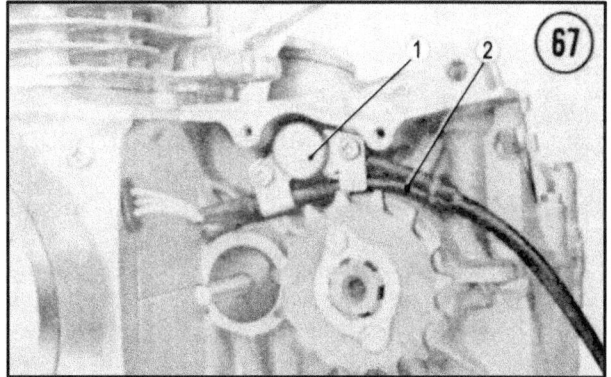

① Neutral switch
② Generator cord

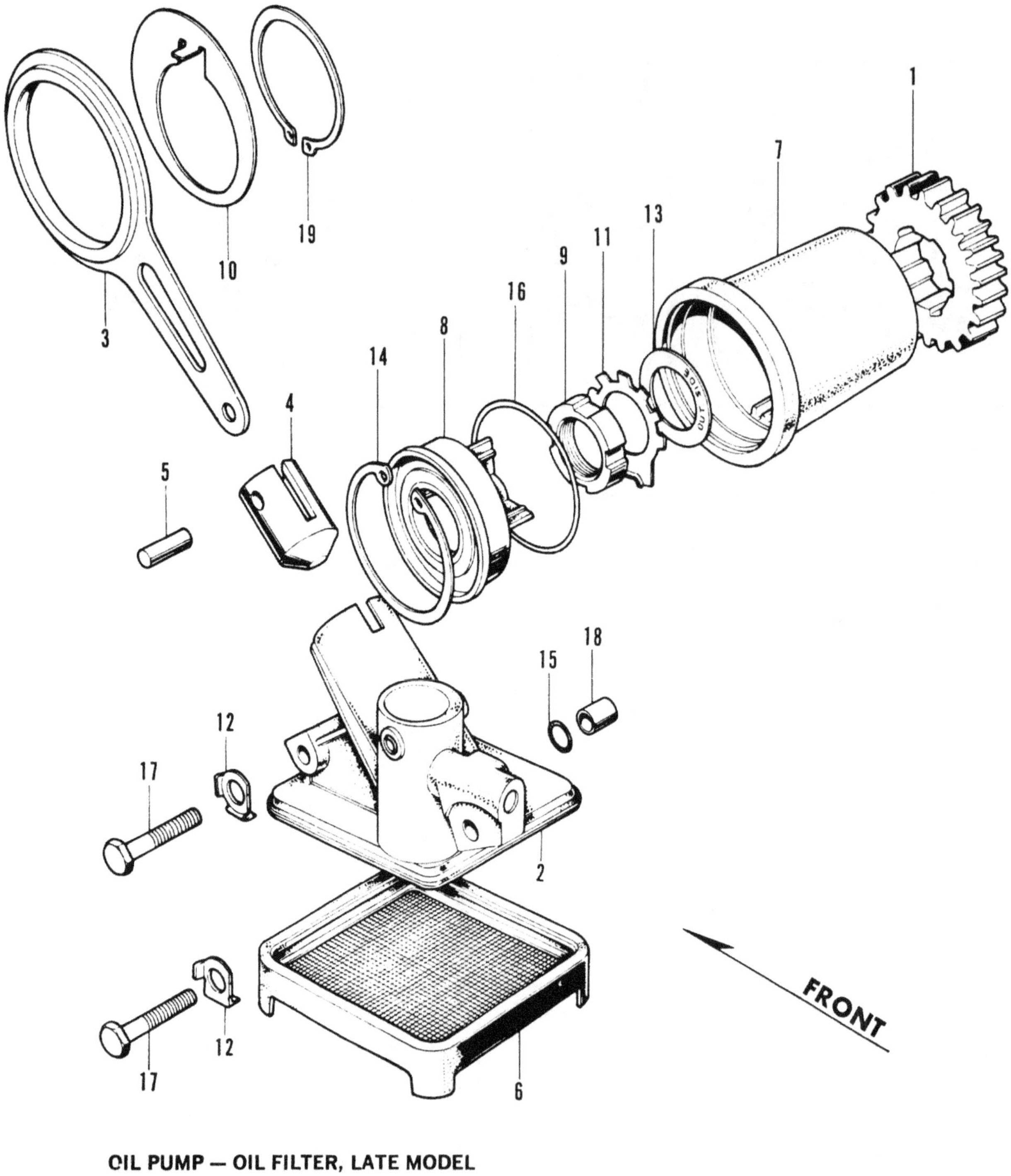

OIL PUMP — OIL FILTER, LATE MODEL

1. Gear, primary drive (23T)
2. Pump Assy., oil
3. Rod, pump
4. Plunger, pump
5. Pin, oil pump plunger
6. Screen, filter
7. Rotor, oil filter
8. Cap, oil filter
9. Nut, lock, 16mm
10. Washer, pump rod side
11. Washer, lock, 16mm
12. Washer, lock, 6mm
13. Washer, lock, oil filter rotor
14. Circlip, internal, 45mm
15. O-Ring, 8x15
16. O-Ring, 41x2
17. Bolt, hex., 6x28
18. Pin, knock, 8x12A
19. Circlip, external, 32mm

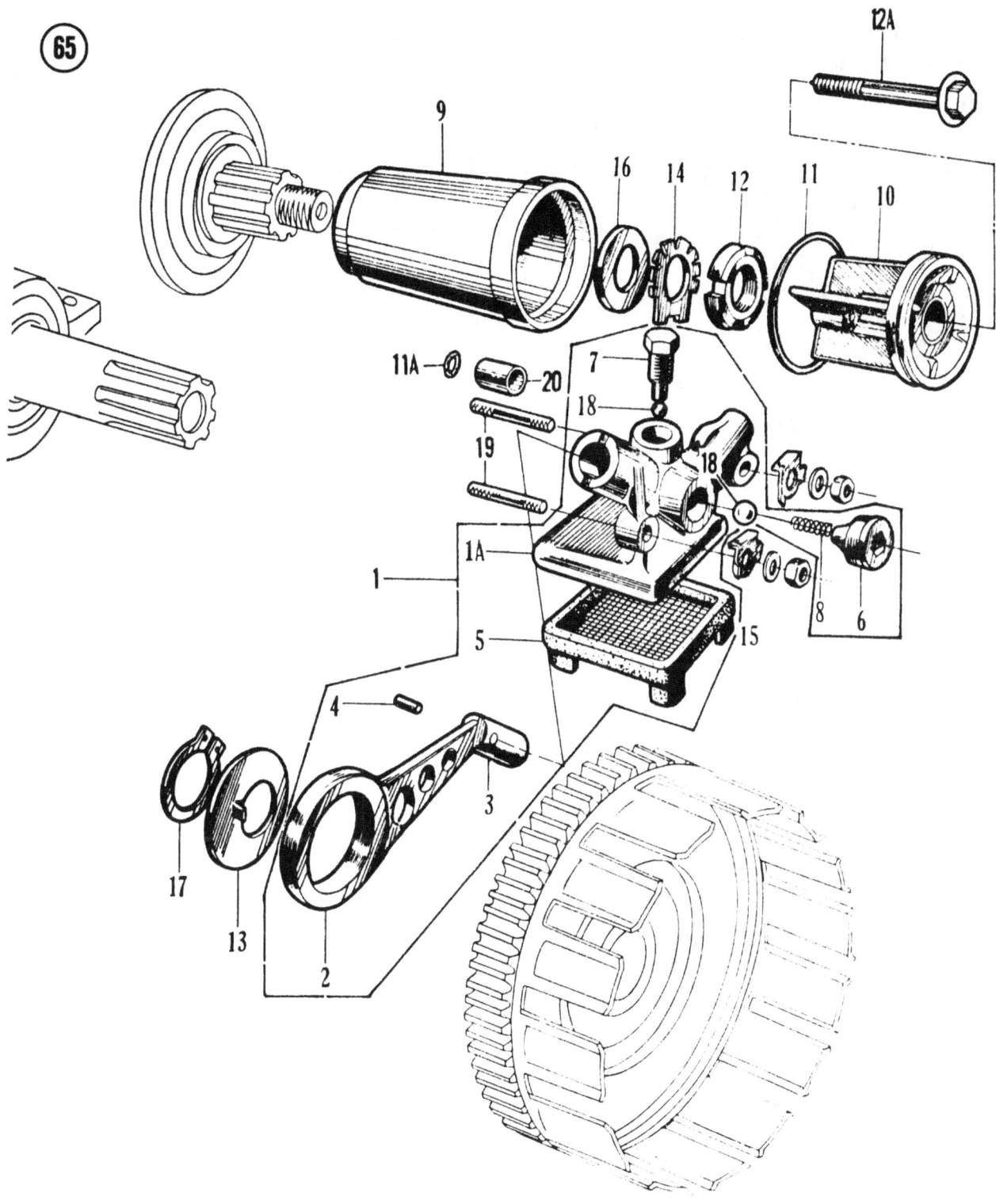

OIL PUMP, EARLY MODEL

1. Pump Assy., oil
1A. Body, pump
2. Rod, pump
3. Plunger, pump
4. Pin, pump plunger
5. Screen, filter
6. Guide, pump outlet valve
7. Bolt, pump suction valve
8. Spring, pump suction valve
9. Rotor, oil filter
10. Cap, oil filter
11. O-Ring, 42.3x2
11A. O-Ring, 8x1.5
12. Nut, lock, 16mm
12A. Bolt, oil filter cap
13. Washer, pump rod side
14. Washer, lock, 16mm
15. Washer, lock, 6mm
16. Washer, 16mm
17. Circlip, 34mm
18. Ball, steel, #10
19. Stud bolt, 6x34
20. Pin, knock, 8x10

2. Remove the left crankcase cover. Loosen the mounting nut to remove the generator stator from the crankcase cover.

3. Use a generator rotor puller as shown in **Figure 68** to remove the generator rotor.

① Generator rotor   ② T-handle gererator rotor puller

4. Loosen the bolt and remove the starting sprocket set plate. Take out the starting motor and driven sprocket at the same time. Refer to **Figure 69**.

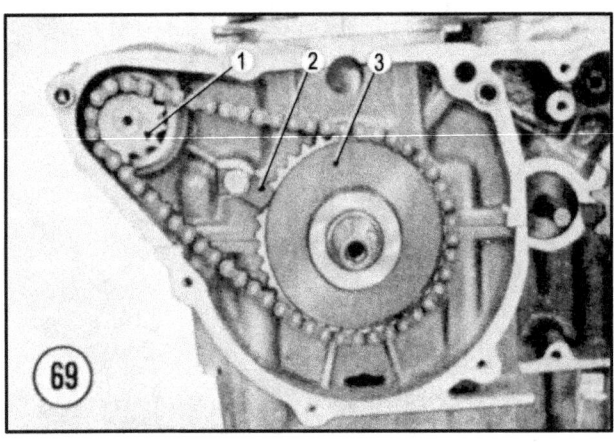

① Starting motor sprocket
② Starting sprocket set plate
③ Starting sprocket

Left Crankcase Cover Reassembly

1. Fit the chain to both sprockets and install them both at the same time.

2. Install the starting sprocket set plate and secure.

3. Insert the key in its slot and install the generator rotor.

4. Replace the cover gasket if it is damaged and replace the cover.

5. Install the neutral switch.

Upper and Lower Crankcase Disassembly (See Figures 70, 71 and 72)

1. Refer to **Figures 73, 74, and 75** for details of oil flow in the cases and location of the oil separator.

2. Remove the left crankcase cover, the generator and the starting clutch as previously outlined.

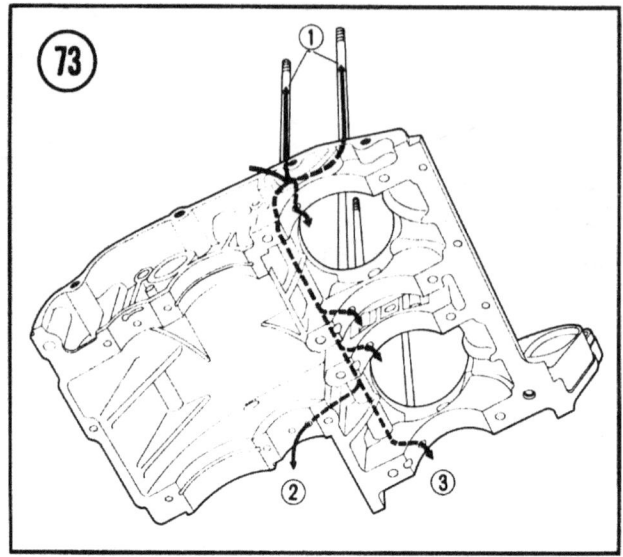

① To camshaft   ② To mainshaft
③ To crankshaft

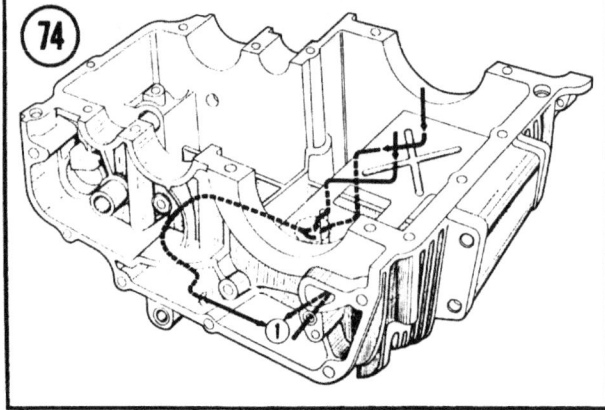

① Oil pump

① Oil separator

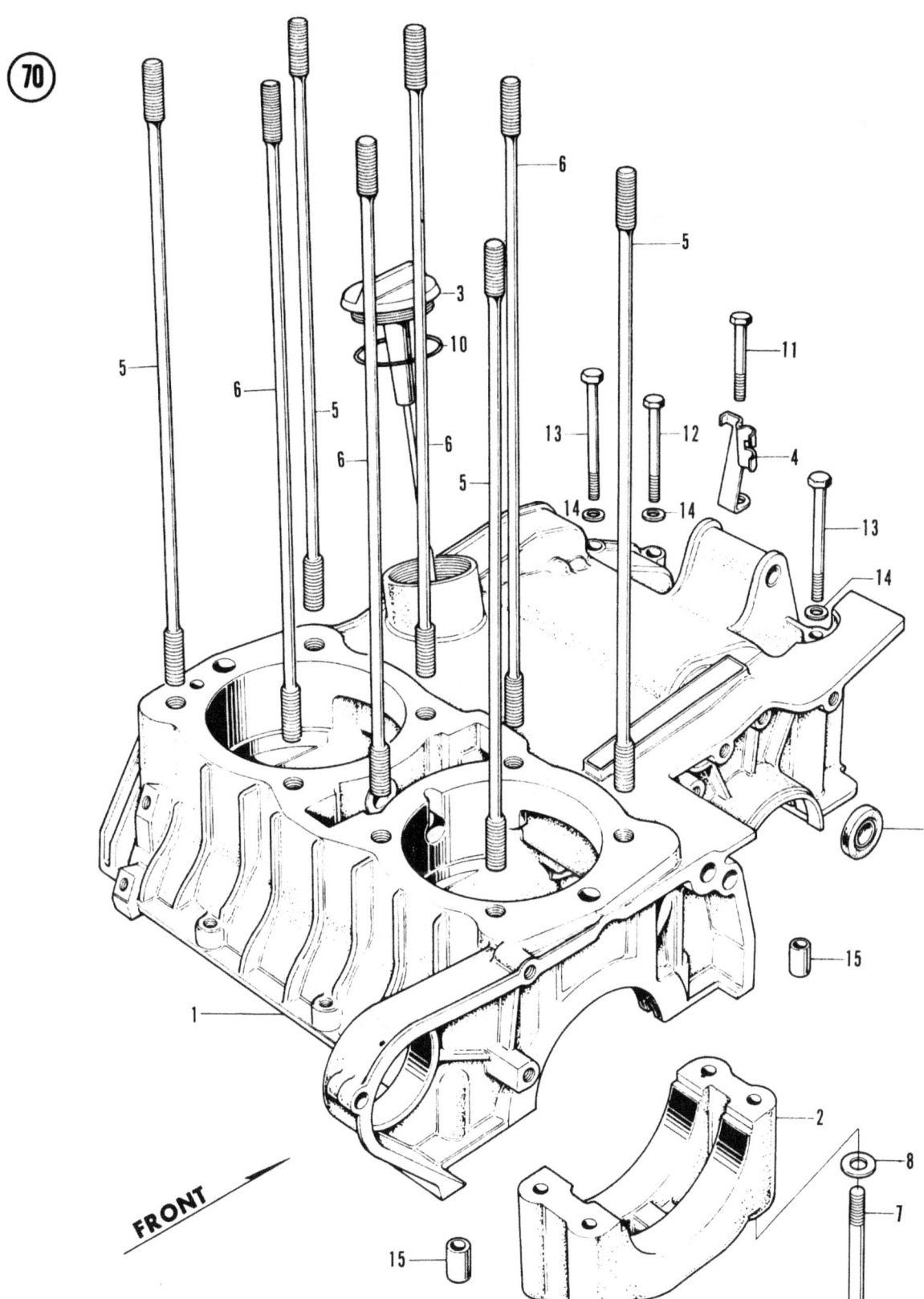

UPPER CRANKCASE, 5-SPEED

1. Crankcase Comp., upper
2. Cap, center bearing
3. Gauge, oil level
4. Clamper, dynamo cord
5. Bolt A, cylinder stud
6. Bolt B, cylinder stud
7. Bolt hex., 8x71
8. Washer, head, 8mm
9. Oil-Seal, 12x25x4.5 (ARAI)
10. O-Ring, 37.2 x 2.3
11. Bolt, hex., 6x40
12. Bolt, hex., 6x63
13. Bolt, hex., 6x80
14. Washer, plain, 6mm
15. Pin, knock, 10x14A

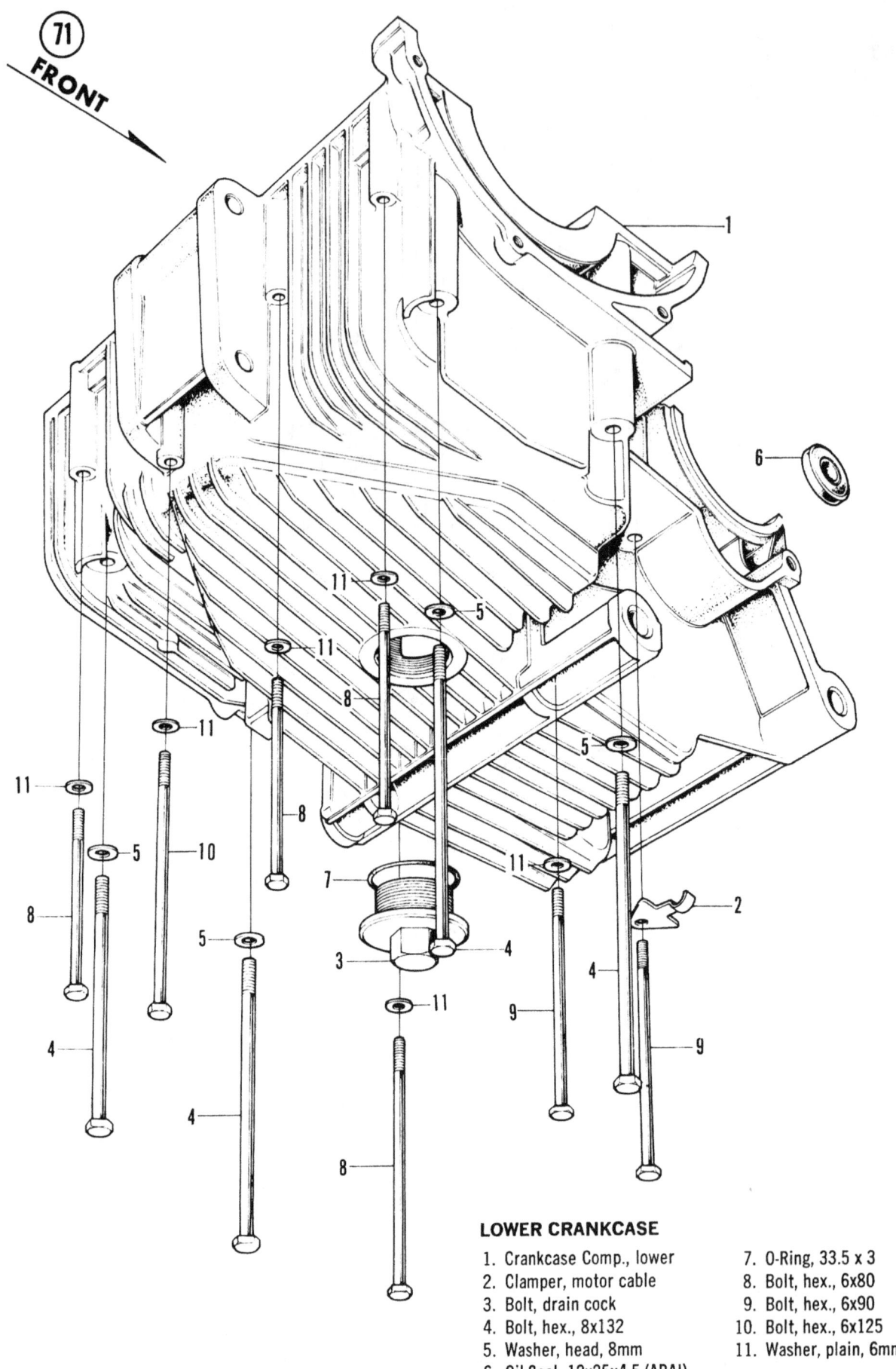

LOWER CRANKCASE

1. Crankcase Comp., lower
2. Clamper, motor cable
3. Bolt, drain cock
4. Bolt, hex., 8x132
5. Washer, head, 8mm
6. Oil-Seal, 12x25x4.5 (ARAI)
7. O-Ring, 33.5 x 3
8. Bolt, hex., 6x80
9. Bolt, hex., 6x90
10. Bolt, hex., 6x125
11. Washer, plain, 6mm

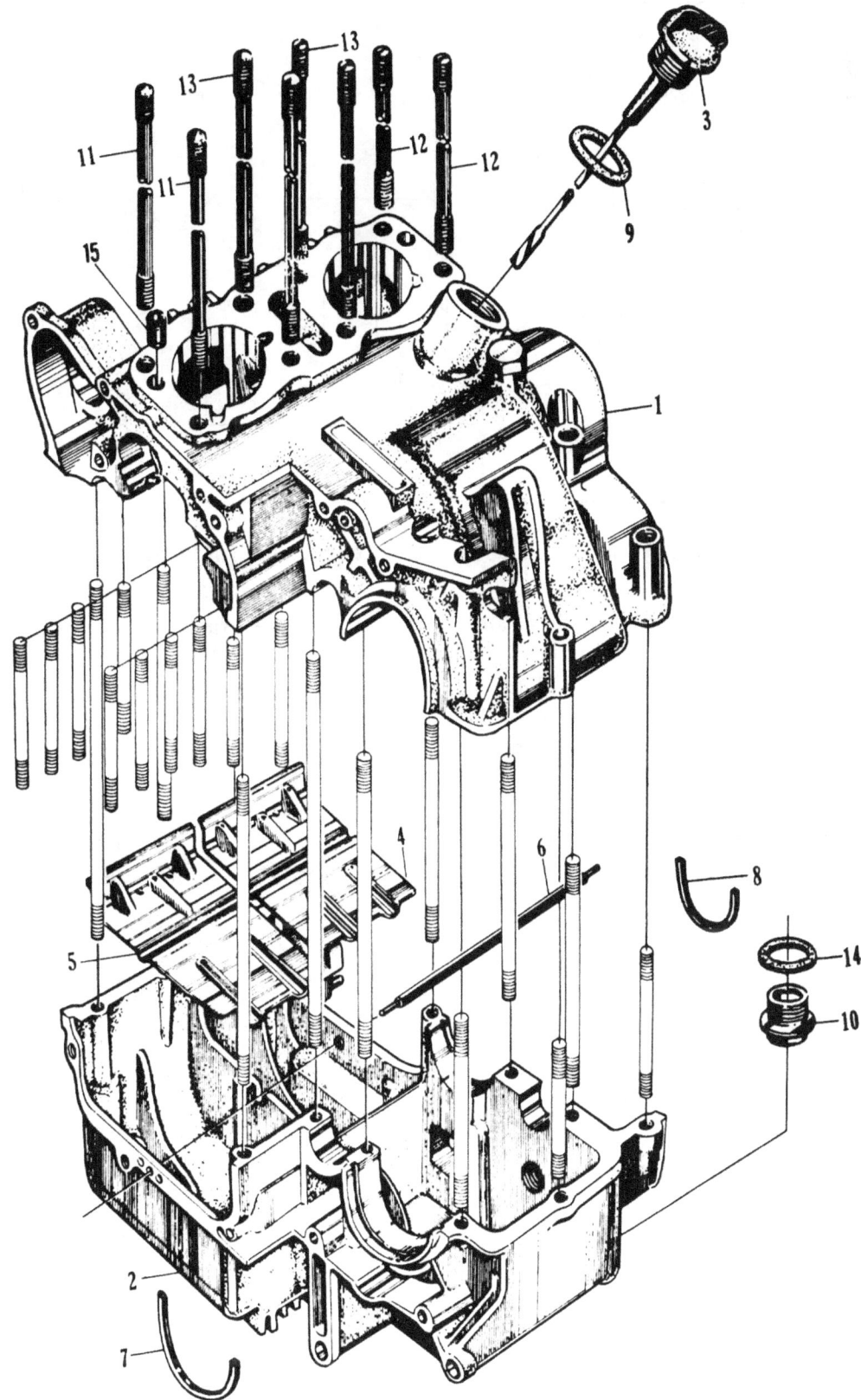

UPPER & LOWER CRANKCASE, 4-SPEED

1. Crankcase, upper
2. Crankcase, under
3. Gauge, oil level
4. Separator, right, oil
5. Separator, left, oil
6. Bar, oil separator setting
7. Ring, bearing setting, 57mm
8. Ring, bearing setting, 52mm
9. O-Ring, 37.2 x 2.3
10. Bolt, drain cock
11. Stud A, cylinder
12. Stud B, cylinder
13. Stud C, cylinder
14. O-Ring, 33.5x3
15. Pin, knock, 10x16

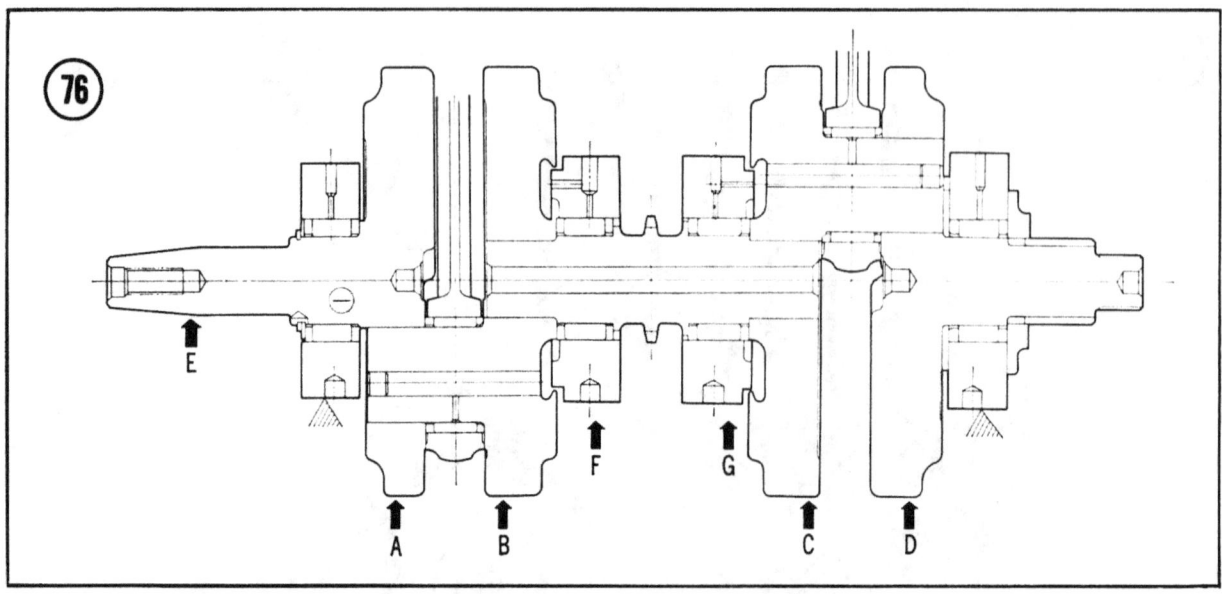

3. Remove the oil filter and clutch as previously outlined.

4. To remove the gear shift spindle, remove its left circlip and pull out the spindle. Be careful not to damage the drum stop cam plate.

5. Take out the four 6mm bolts on the upper side, the four 8mm bolts and seven 6mm bolts on the lower side, and remove the lower case.

Upper and Lower Crankcase Inspection

1. Check the crankcase mating surfaces for evidence of oil leaks or damaged faces. Small nicks and scratches may be repaired with an oil stone. Use extreme care.

Upper and Lower Crankcase Assembly

1. Before assembling the cases, be sure all traces of old gasket cement, oil, etc. are removed from the mating surfaces. Coat the lower case with gasket cement on the mating surfaces only. Keep excess cement off dowel pin holes.

2. Ensure that the kick starter is properly installed in the lower case, route the cam chain and assemble the cases.

3. Handle the starting motor and generator wiring with care.

Crankshaft Disassembly

1. Remove cylinder head, cylinder, pistons and split the cases as discussed earlier.

2. Remove the center bearing bolts and remove the crankshaft.

Crankshaft Inspection

1. Refer to **Figures 76, 77, 78, 79 and 80** to determine crankshaft serviceable limits. Five-speed crankshaft illustrated; 4-speed is measured in the same manner.

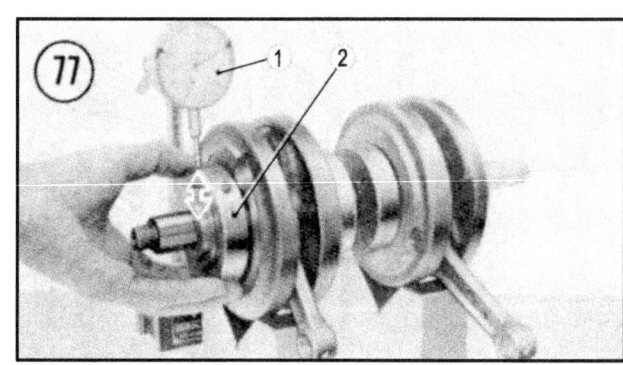

① Dial gauge ② Outer race

78	Item		Standard value	Serviceable limit
1	Crankshaft run-out	A, B, C and D	0.05mm max. (0.002 in)	Replace if over 0.2 mm (0.008 in)
		E, F and G	0.02mm max. (0.001 in)	Replace if over 0.1 mm (0.004 in)
2	Main bearing radial clearance		0.006~0.014mm (0.0002~0.0005 in)	Replace if over 0.03 mm (0.001 in)
3	Connecting rod small end		17.016~17.034 mm (0.6699~0.6706 in)	Replace if over 17.07 mm (0.6721 in)
4	Connecting rod large end radial clearance		0~0.008 mm (0~0.0003 in)	Replace if over 0.05 mm (0.0020 in)
5	Connecting rod large end side clearance		0.07~0.33 mm (0.0028~0.0130 in)	Replace if over 0.5 mm (0.0197 in)
6	Connecting rod large end tilt		0.2~1.0 mm (0.008~0.04 in)	Replace if over 3.0 mm (0.1181 in)

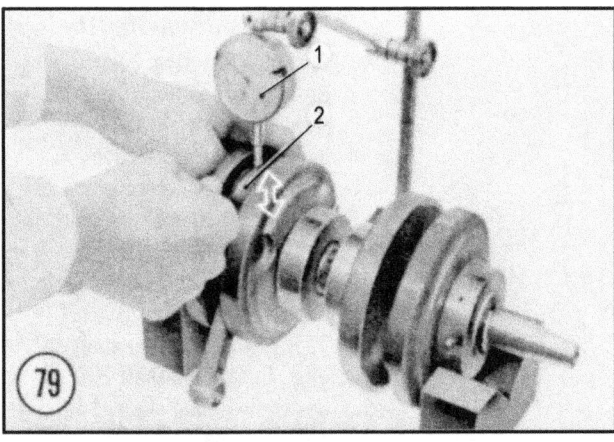

① Dial gauge
② Connecting rod

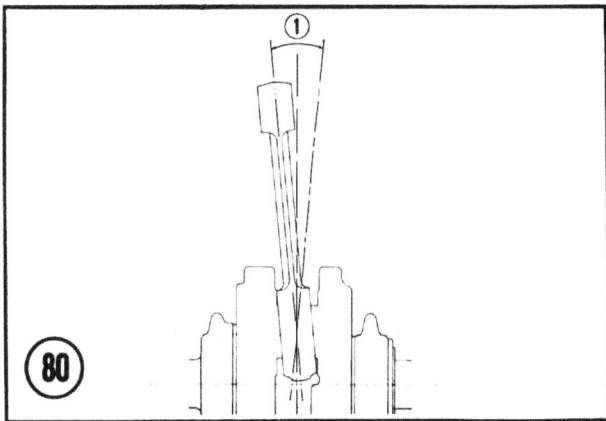

① Maximum swinging

Crankshaft Reassembly

1. Install the bearing caps noting in **Figure 81** that those with dowel pins can only be installed in one way. Torque the caps down to 11.6 to 15.2 ft-lbs.

① Dowel pin

Transmission Disassembly

NOTE: Early models of the CB 450 were equipped with a four-speed transmission. Service procedures and specifications vary between the four and five-speed models. **Determine which transmission you have and use the appropriate section of this book.** See **Figures 82 and 83**.

Four-Speed Transmission Disassembly

1. Refer to **Figures 83 and 84,** for details, and disassemble the transmission after splitting the cases.

Four-Speed Transmission Inspection

1. Measure the countershaft and mainshaft bushings outer diameter as shown in **Figure 85.** Standard size is 20mm -0.020 for M and -0.041 for C. Replace if the measurement is less than 19.94mm.

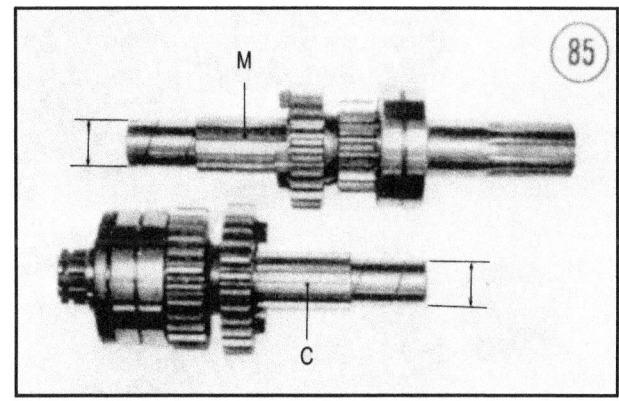

2. Measure the backlash of gears M and M^3 and C and C^3 using a dial gauge and V-blocks as shown in **Figure 86.** The standard is 0.030 to 0.096mm and more than 0.12mm indicates replacement is necessary.

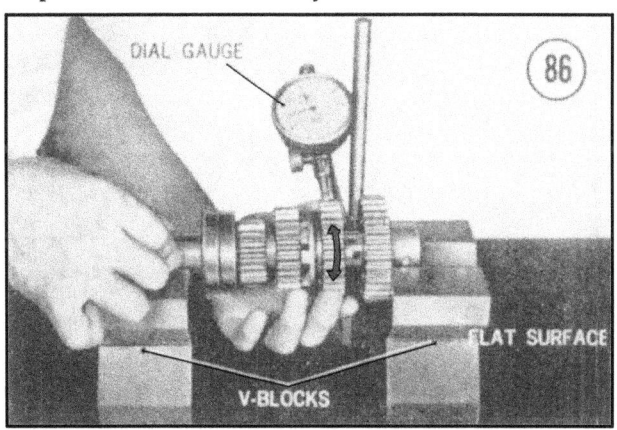

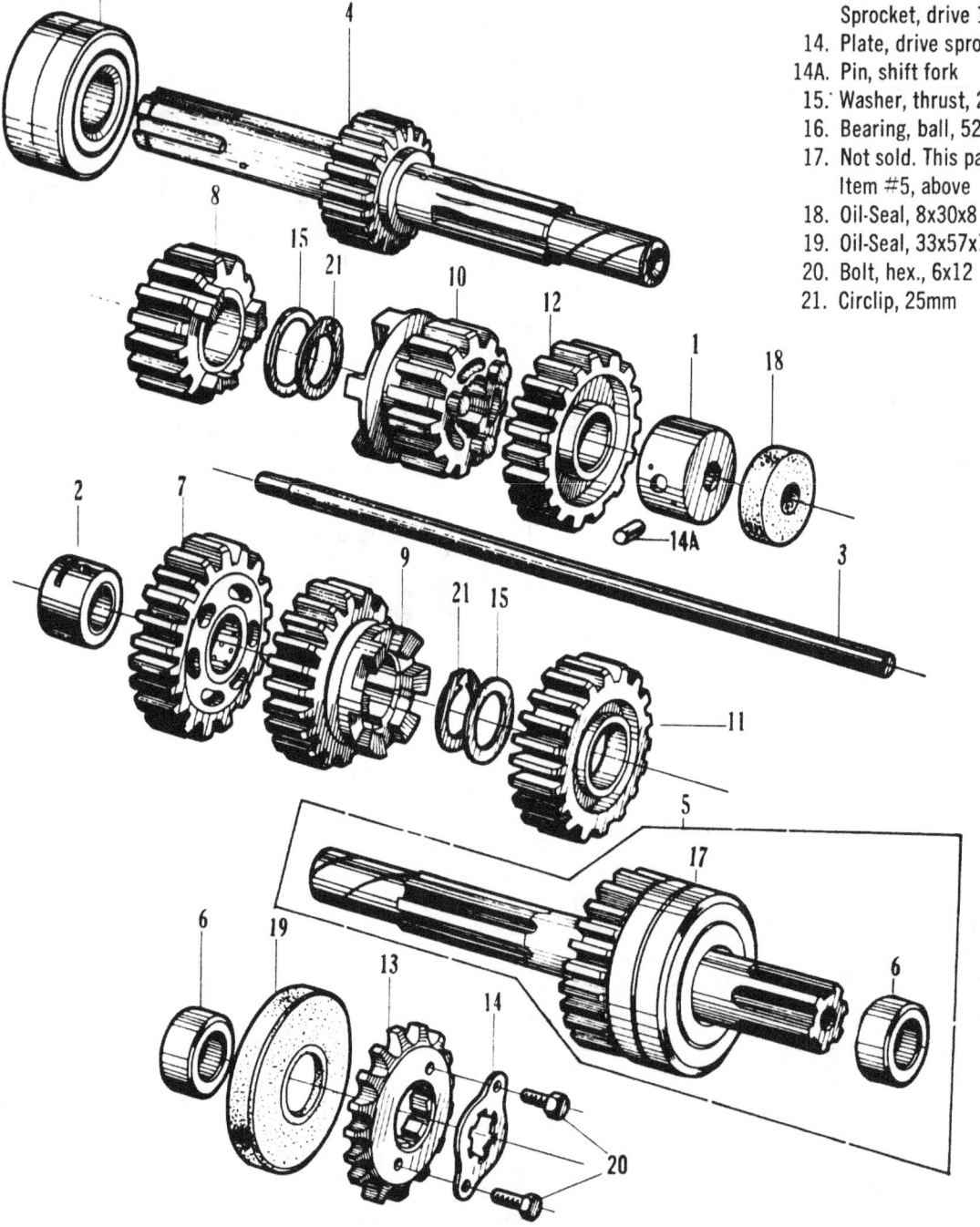

4-SPEED TRANSMISSION

1. Bushing A, bearing, 20mm
2. Bushing B, bearing, 20mm
3. Rod, clutch lifter
4. Shaft, main, transmission 17T
5. Shaft, counter, transmission 28T
6. Not sold. This part is included in Item #5, above
7. Gear, low, counter shaft 41T
8. Gear, second, main shaft 25T
9. Gear, second, counter shaft 35T
10. Gear, third, main shaft 29T
11. Gear, third, counter shaft 30T
12. Gear, top, main shaft 31T
13. Sprocket, drive 15T
    Sprocket, drive 16T
14. Plate, drive sprocket fixing
14A. Pin, shift fork
15. Washer, thrust, 25mm
16. Bearing, ball, 5205HS
17. Not sold. This part is included in Item #5, above
18. Oil-Seal, 8x30x8
19. Oil-Seal, 33x57x7
20. Bolt, hex., 6x12
21. Circlip, 25mm

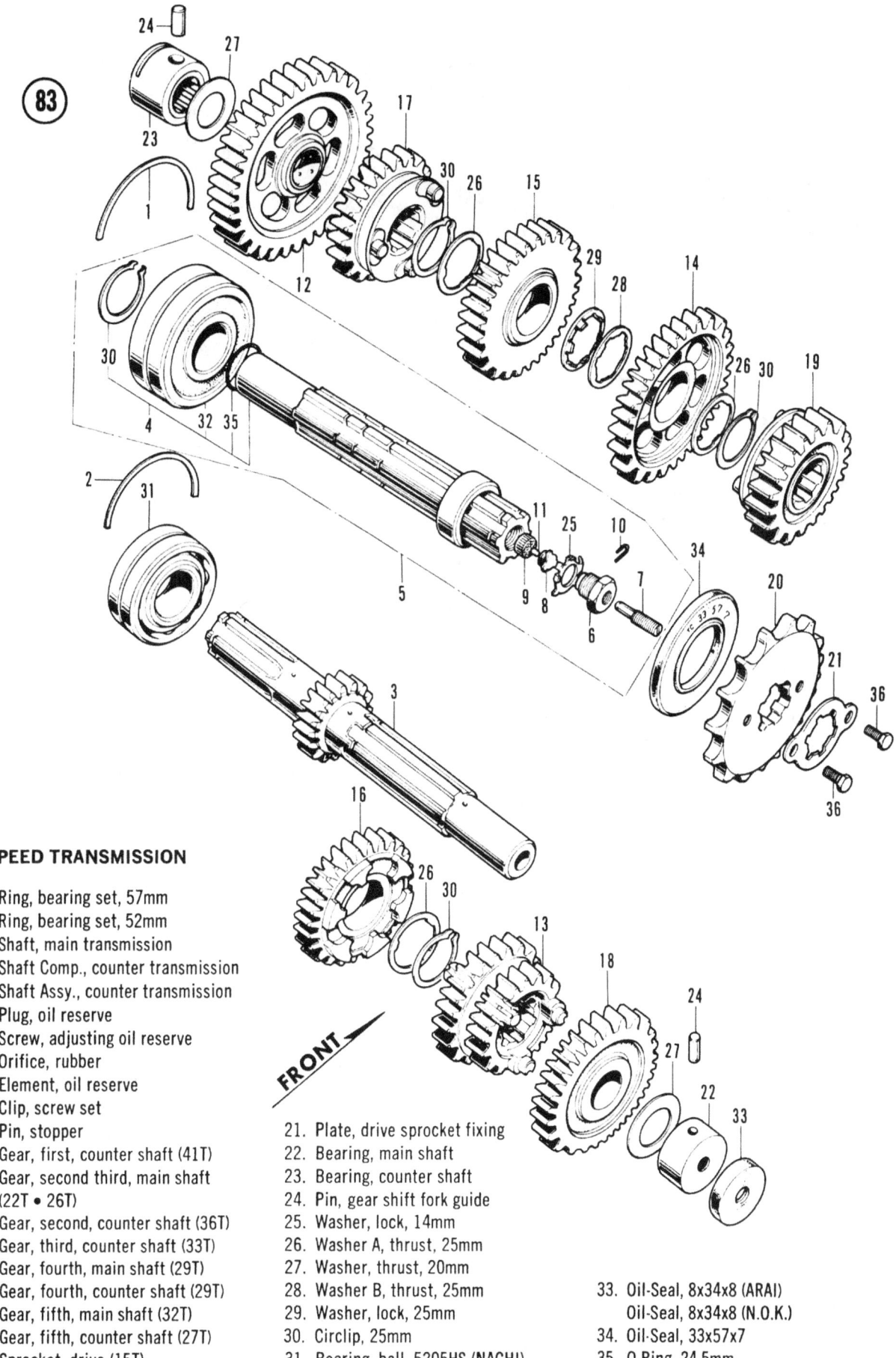

5-SPEED TRANSMISSION

1. Ring, bearing set, 57mm
2. Ring, bearing set, 52mm
3. Shaft, main transmission
4. Shaft Comp., counter transmission
5. Shaft Assy., counter transmission
6. Plug, oil reserve
7. Screw, adjusting oil reserve
8. Orifice, rubber
9. Element, oil reserve
10. Clip, screw set
11. Pin, stopper
12. Gear, first, counter shaft (41T)
13. Gear, second third, main shaft (22T • 26T)
14. Gear, second, counter shaft (36T)
15. Gear, third, counter shaft (33T)
16. Gear, fourth, main shaft (29T)
17. Gear, fourth, counter shaft (29T)
18. Gear, fifth, main shaft (32T)
19. Gear, fifth, counter shaft (27T)
20. Sprocket, drive (15T)
    Sprocket, drive (Optional part 16T)
21. Plate, drive sprocket fixing
22. Bearing, main shaft
23. Bearing, counter shaft
24. Pin, gear shift fork guide
25. Washer, lock, 14mm
26. Washer A, thrust, 25mm
27. Washer, thrust, 20mm
28. Washer B, thrust, 25mm
29. Washer, lock, 25mm
30. Circlip, 25mm
31. Bearing, ball, 5205HS (NACHI)
32. Bearing, special ball, 5205 (NACHI)
33. Oil-Seal, 8x34x8 (ARAI)
    Oil-Seal, 8x34x8 (N.O.K.)
34. Oil-Seal, 33x57x7
35. O-Ring, 24.5mm
36. Bolt, hex., 6x12

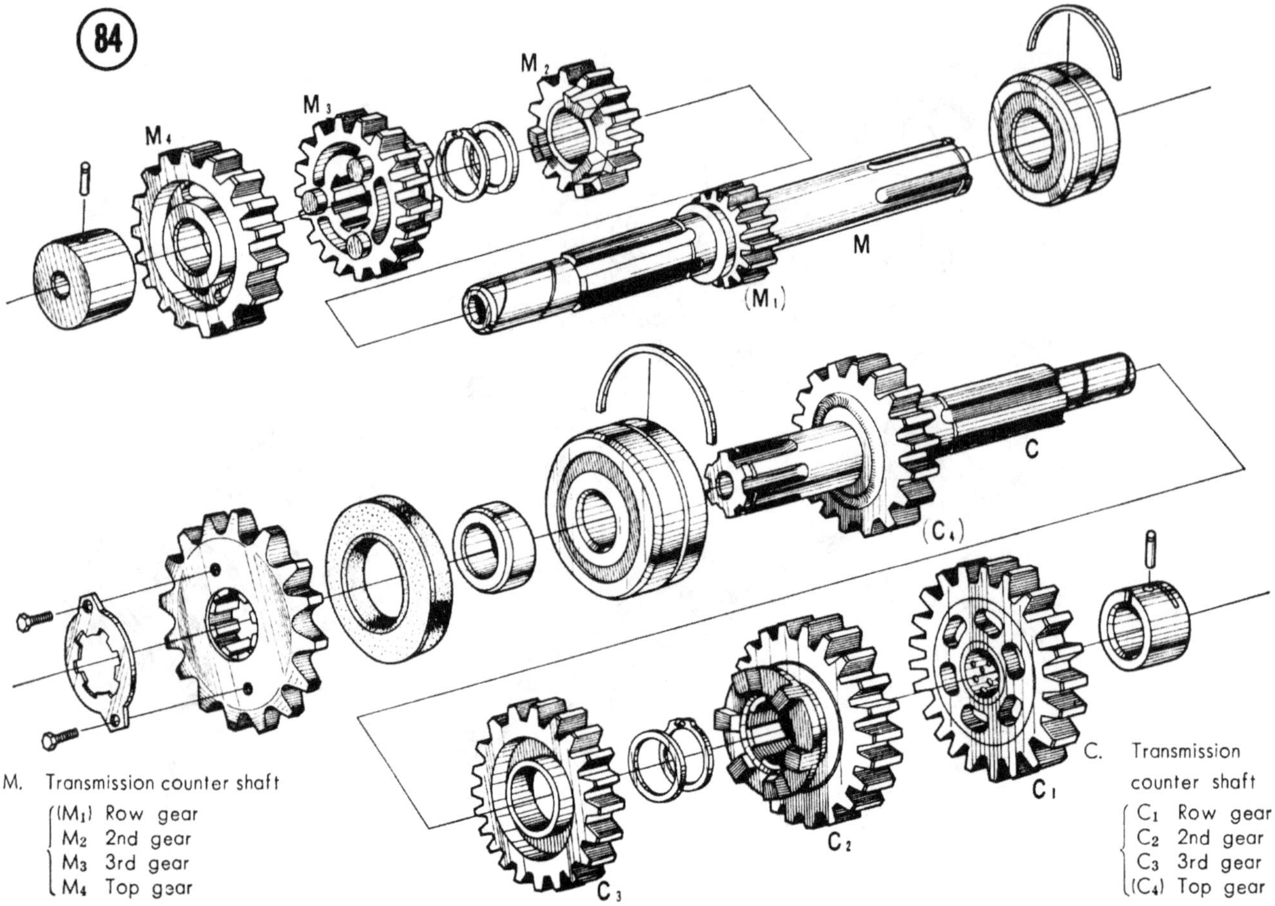

(84)

M. Transmission counter shaft
- (M_1) Row gear
- M_2 2nd gear
- M_3 3rd gear
- M_4 Top gear

C. Transmission counter shaft
- C_1 Row gear
- C_2 2nd gear
- C_3 3rd gear
- (C_4) Top gear

3. Check the backlash of transmission gears as shown in **Figure 87**. The standard is 0.094 to 0.188. For low gear the standard is 0.032 to 0.096mm. Replace if either is in excess of 0.21mm.

4. Measure the bearing bushing inside diameter of both M and C. The standard is 20mm +0.028 for M and +0.007 for C. Replace if either is more than 20.06mm.

5. Measure the inside diameter of C^1. The standard is 20 to 20.021mm. Replace if more than 20.08mm.

6. Measure the double row ball bearing radius direction clearance as shown in **Figure 88**. Standard is 0.010 to 0.025 and replacement is indicated if the measurement exceeds 0.05mm.

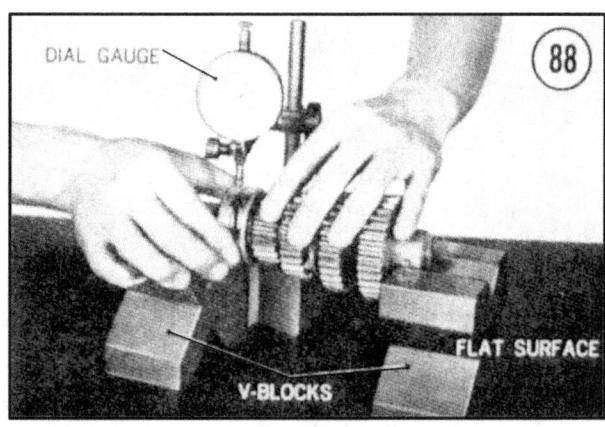

Four-Speed Transmission Reassembly

1. Refer to **Figure 84** and reassemble in the reverse order of disassembly.

2. Note the position of the thrust washers and circlips installed next to M^2 and C^3 gears.

3. Note that the bearing with the oil groove is installed on the countershaft and the bearing

without a groove goes on the mainshaft.

4. Check that the bearing set rings and locating pins are aligned and fit in the upper rankcase.

5. Fit the right side shift fork in gear C^2 and the left side shift fork in gear M^3, fit the mainshaft and countershaft together.

Four-Speed Transmission
Gear Shift Disassembly

1. Remove the gear shift spindle, separate the upper and lower crankcase halves and remove the transmission gears. Refer to **Figure 89**.

2. Refer to **Figure 90** and remove the shift drum stop.

3. Remove the shift fork guide pin clip and remove the guide pin. Refer to **Figure 91**.

4. Remove the shift drum guide screw and pull out the shift drum.

Four-Speed Transmission
Gear Shift Inspection

1. Refer to the table for correction limits for the gear shift forks. All dimensions are in millimeters. (**Figure 92**).

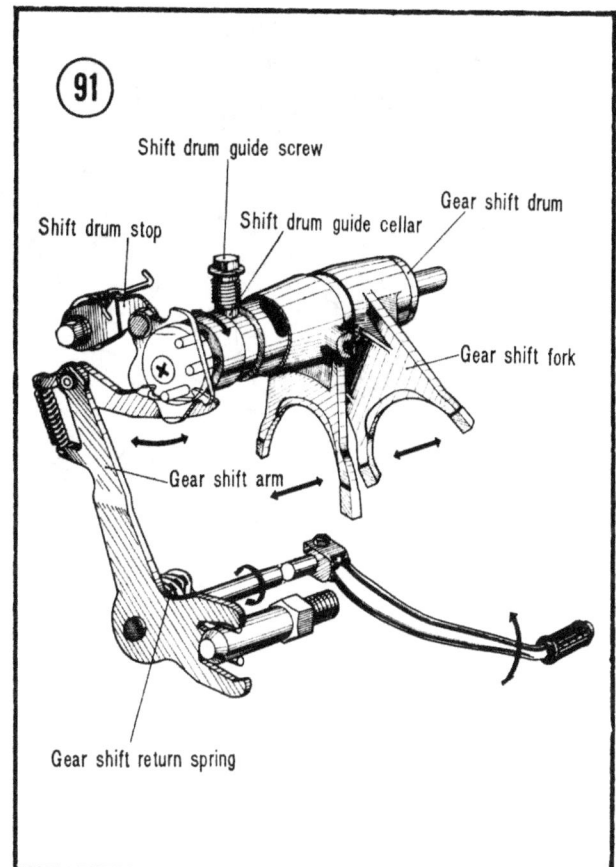

92	Standard	Limit for correction
Inside diameter	$34\phi \begin{array}{c}+0.025\\-0\end{array}$	Replace if more than 34.1ϕ
End thickness	$5\phi \begin{array}{c}+0\\-0.1\end{array}$	Replace if less than 4.6
Fork end bending to left or right	Within 0.1	Replace if more then 0.8

2. Measure the gear shift drum and case clearance with a feeler gauge as shown in **Figure 93**. The standard is 0.05 to 0.125mm and replacement is indicated if the clearance is more than 0.2mm.

3. The gear shift drum outside diameter must not be less than 11.9mm.

4. The standard gear shift drum groove width is 6.1 plus 0.1 or minus 0mm. Replace if it exceeds 6.5mm.

5. Measure the clearance between the gear shift spindle and the lower case. Standard is 0.032 to 0.086mm and replacement is indicated if the measurement exceeds 0.13mm.

Four-Speed Transmission
Gear Shift Reassembly

1. Insert the shift drum and shift forks.

2. Insert the shift drum guide screw along with its collar and tighten it.

3. Refer to **Figure 94** and insert the guide pin in the drum groove and set the clip, ensuring its direction matches that in the diagram.

4. Refer to **Figure 95** for details of the shift drum stop and install.

5. Assemble the transmission gears, join the

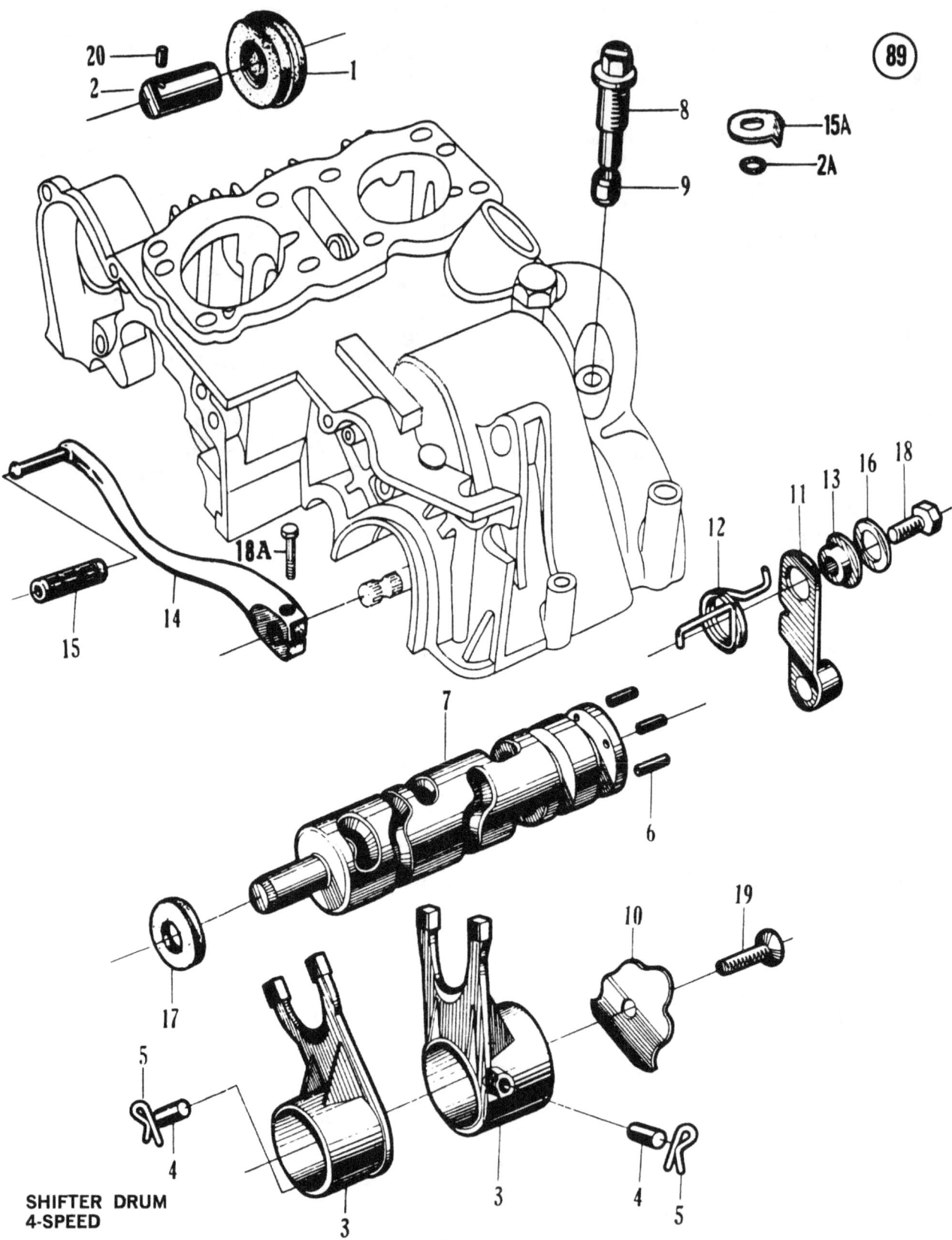

SHIFTER DRUM 4-SPEED

1. Roller B, cam chain guide
2. Pin B, cam chain guide roller
2A. O-Ring, 11x1.8
3. Fork, gear shift
4. Pin, gear shift fork guide
5. Clip, gear shift guide pin
6. Pin, gear shift drum
7. Drum, gear shift
8. Screw, shift drum guide
9. Collar, shift drum guide
10. Plate, drum stopper cam
11. Stopper, shift drum
12. Spring, shift drum stopper
13. Collar, shift drum stopper
14. Pedal, gear change
15. Rubber, change pedal
15A. Washer, lock, 12mm
16. Washer, 6mm
17. Oil-Seal, 12x25x4.5
18. Bolt, hex., 6x18
18A. Bolt, hex., 6x18
19. Screw, cross, 6x16
20. Pin, knock, 4x8

Gear shift drum and case clearance measurement

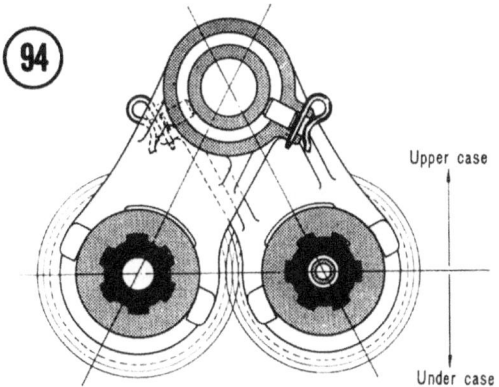

Gear shift fork guide pin clip installing direction

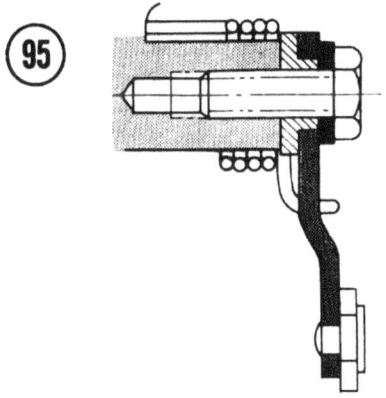

Shift dium stop installation diagram

outside diameter as shown in **Figures 97 and 98.** Refer to the table for serviceable limits. **(Figure 99)**

2. Refer to **Figure 96** for identification of gears and then measure spline clearances as shows in **Figure 100.** Refer to the table for serviceable limits. **(Figure 101)**

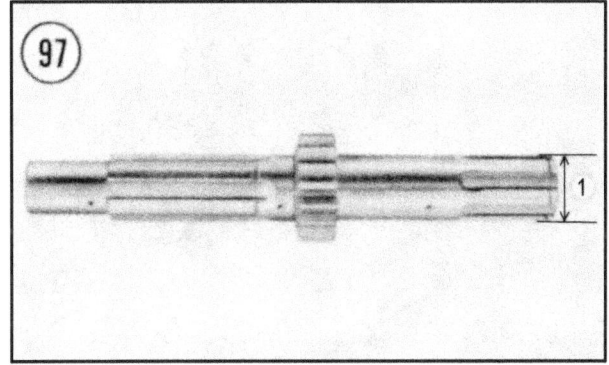

① Main shaft outside diameter

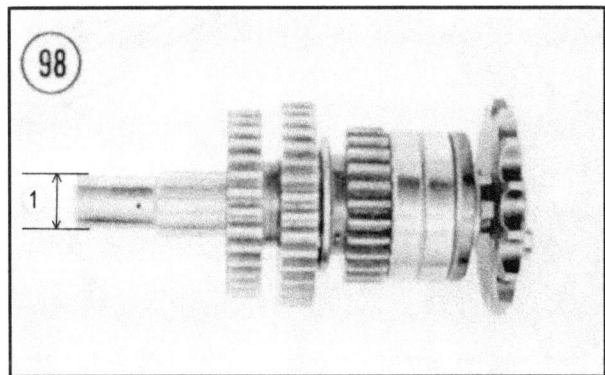

① Counter shaft outside diameter

Item	Standard value	Serviceable limit
Shaft O.D.	19.959~19.98 mm (0.7858~0.7866 in)	Replace if under 19.94 mm (0.785 in)

Item	Standard value	Serviceable limit
Spline clearance	0.03~0.096 mm (0.0012~0.0038 in)	Replace if over 0.15 mm (0.0059 in)

crankcase halves and insert the gear shift spindle including the washer and circlip on the left side. Check for proper operation.

Five-Speed Transmission Disassembly

1. Refer to **Figures 96 and 82** for details of the five-speed transmission.
2. Split the engine cases for access to the transmission and disassemble.

Five-Speed Transmission Inspection

1. Measure the mainshaft and countershaft

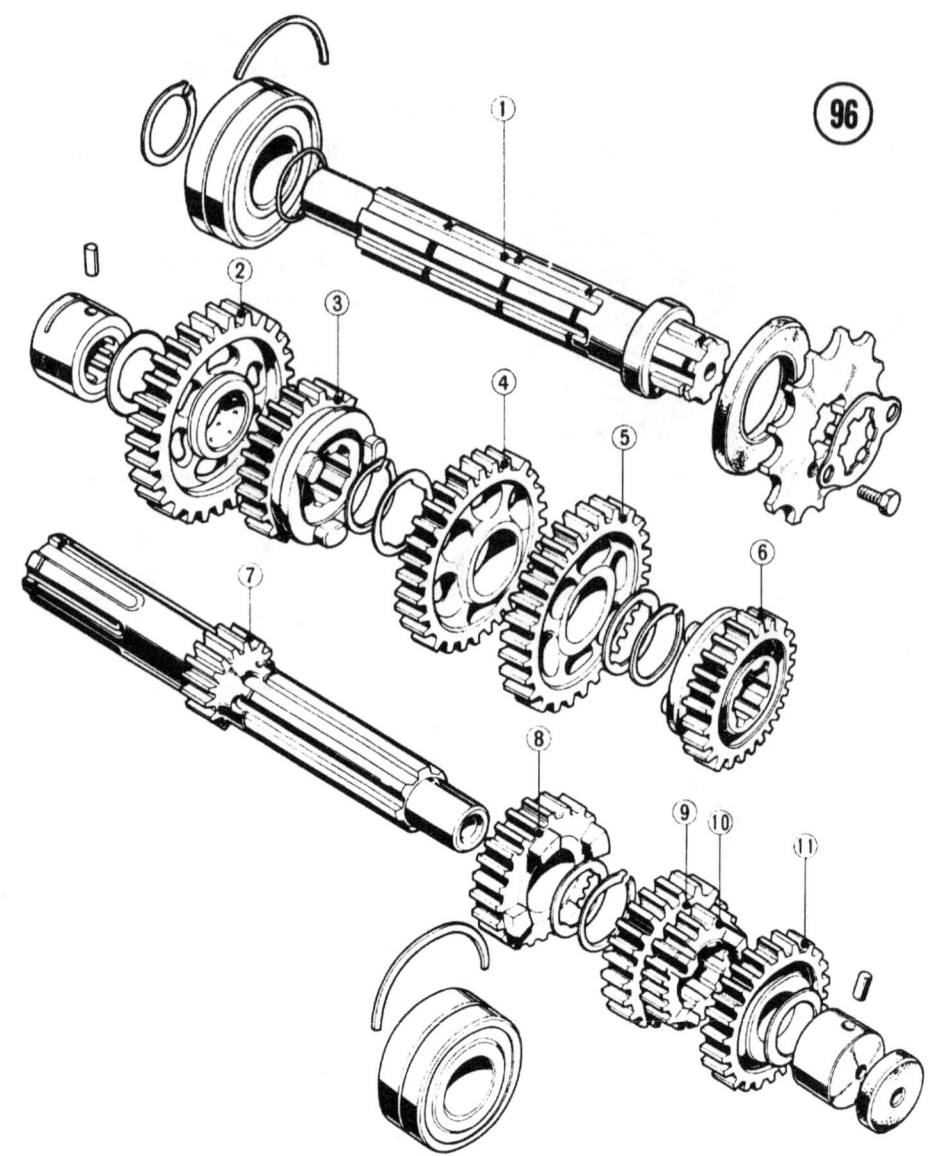

① Counter shaft ② Counter shaft low gear ③ Counter shaft fourth gear ④ Counter shaft third gear
⑤ Counter shaft second gear ⑥ Counter shaft top gear ⑦ Main shaft ⑧ Main shaft fourth gear
⑨ ⑩ Main shaft second-third gear ⑪ Main shaft top gear

3. Measure backlash as shown in **Figure 102**. The table gives serviceable limits. (**Figure 103**)

Item		Standard value	Serviceable limit
Backlash	Low	0.032~0.096 mm (0.0013~0.0038 in)	Replace if over 0.15 mm (0.006 in)
	2nd	0.089~0.179 mm (0.0035~0.0071 in)	Replace if over 0.2 mm (0.08 in)
	3rd, 4th, Top	0.094~0.188 mm (0.0037~0.0074 in)	Replace if over 0.21 mm (0.0082 in)

4. Measure the mainshaft and countershaft bearing inside diameter and refer to the table. (**Figure 104**)

Item	Standard value	Serviceable limit
Bearing I.D.	20.02~20.033 mm (0.7882~0.7887 in)	Replace if over 20.06 mm (0.789 in)

5. Measure the bore of gear C1 and refer to the table. (Figure 105)

Item (105)	Standard value	Serviceable limit
Bore Dia.	20.0~20.021 mm (0.7874~0.7882 in)	Replace if over 20.05 mm (0.789 in)

6. Measure the double row ball bearing clearance as shown in **Figure 106** and refer to the table. (Figure 107)

Item (107)	Standard value	Serviceable limit
Diametrical Clearance	0.01~0.025 mm (0.0004~0.001 in)	Replace if over 0.05 mm (0.002 in)

Five-Speed Transmission Assembly

1. Refer to **Figure 96** for details and assemble in reverse order of disassembly.

2. Note the thrust washers and circlips on gears M4, C2 and C3.

4. The bearing with the oil groove is installed on the countershaft and the plain bearing goes on the mainshaft.

5. Don't forget the bearing set ring and the dowel pin.

6. Fit the left shift fork on gear C4, the right shift fork on gear C5 and the center shift fork between gears M2 and M3.

7. Fit the mainshaft and the countershaft together and install them in place.

Five-Speed Transmission Gear Shift Disassembly

1. Refer to **Figures 108, 109, and 110** for details of the gear shift.

2. Remove the gear shift spindle, separate the

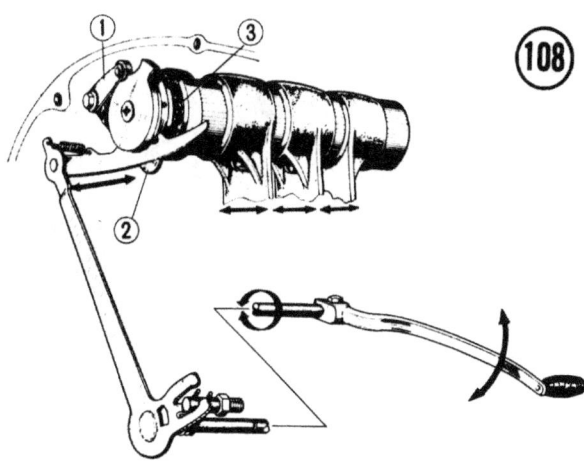

① Neutral stopper ② Shift drum stopper ③ Ball bearing

crankcase halves and disassemble the transmission gears.

3. Take out the 6mm bolt and remove the neutral stopper and shift drum stopper.

4. Unscrew the Phillips head screw and remove the bearing set plate as shown in **Figure 111.**

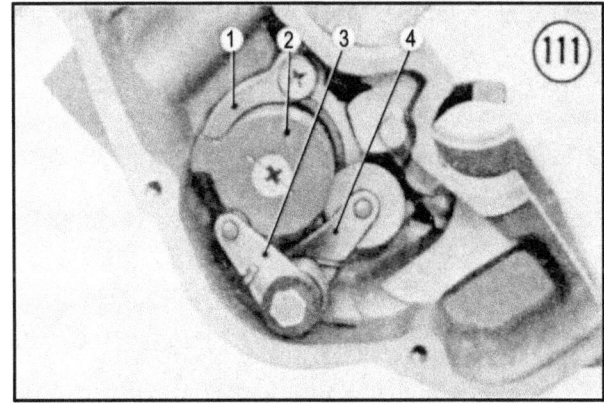

① Bearing set plate
② Gear shift drum
③ Shift drum neutral stopper
④ Shift drum stopper

5. Take out the shift fork guide pin clip and pull out the guide pin.

6. The gear shift drum can now be removed by gently tapping the case on the side of the neutral switch mount.

Five-Speed Transmission Gear Shift Inspection

1. Refer to the accompanying table, (**Figure 112**) make the necessary measurements to determine serviceable limits for the gear shift fork and drum guide grooves. **Figure 113** shows method for measuring fork end bending.

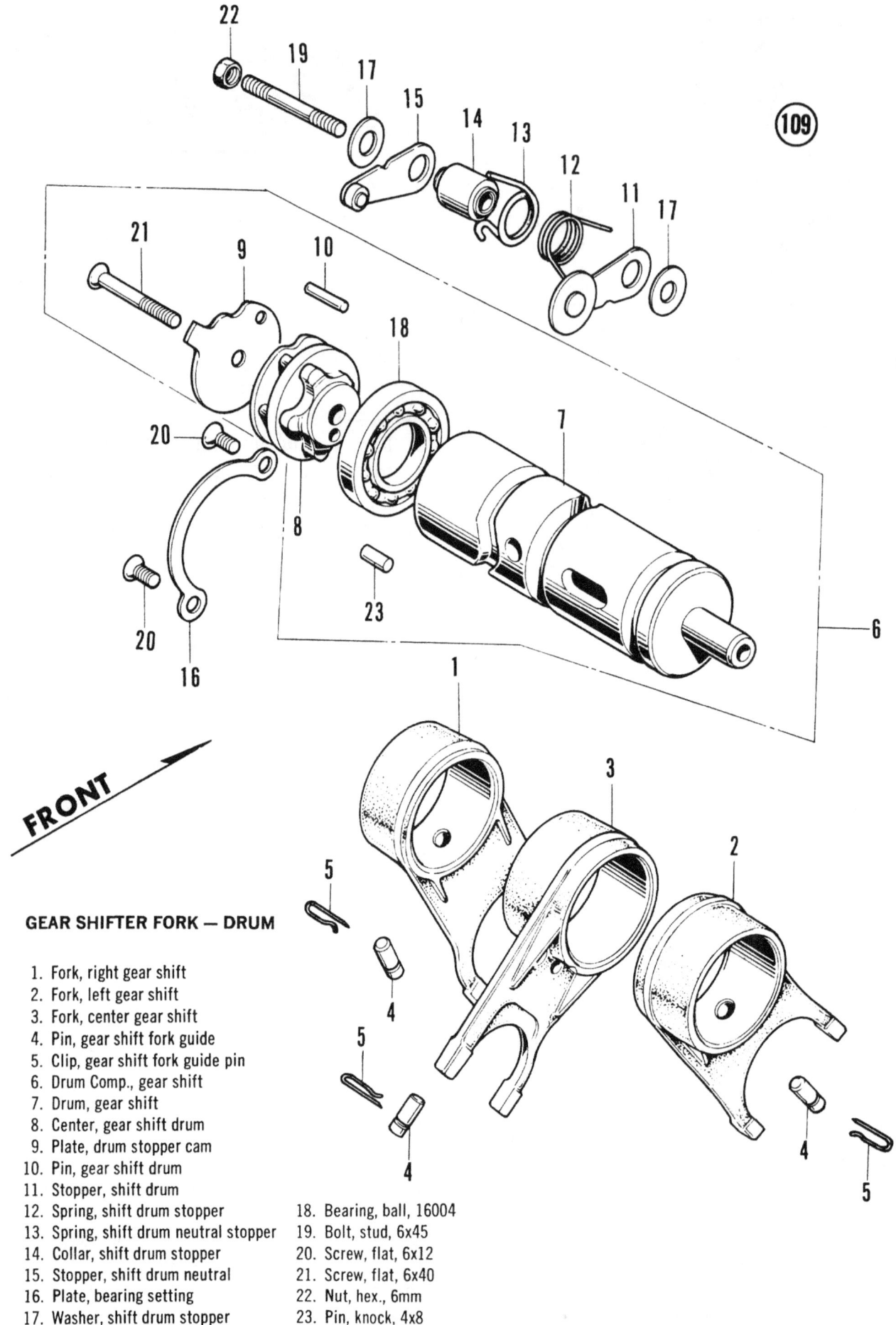

GEAR SHIFTER FORK — DRUM

1. Fork, right gear shift
2. Fork, left gear shift
3. Fork, center gear shift
4. Pin, gear shift fork guide
5. Clip, gear shift fork guide pin
6. Drum Comp., gear shift
7. Drum, gear shift
8. Center, gear shift drum
9. Plate, drum stopper cam
10. Pin, gear shift drum
11. Stopper, shift drum
12. Spring, shift drum stopper
13. Spring, shift drum neutral stopper
14. Collar, shift drum stopper
15. Stopper, shift drum neutral
16. Plate, bearing setting
17. Washer, shift drum stopper
18. Bearing, ball, 16004
19. Bolt, stud, 6x45
20. Screw, flat, 6x12
21. Screw, flat, 6x40
22. Nut, hex., 6mm
23. Pin, knock, 4x8

GEAR SHIFT SPINDLE — CHANGE PEDAL

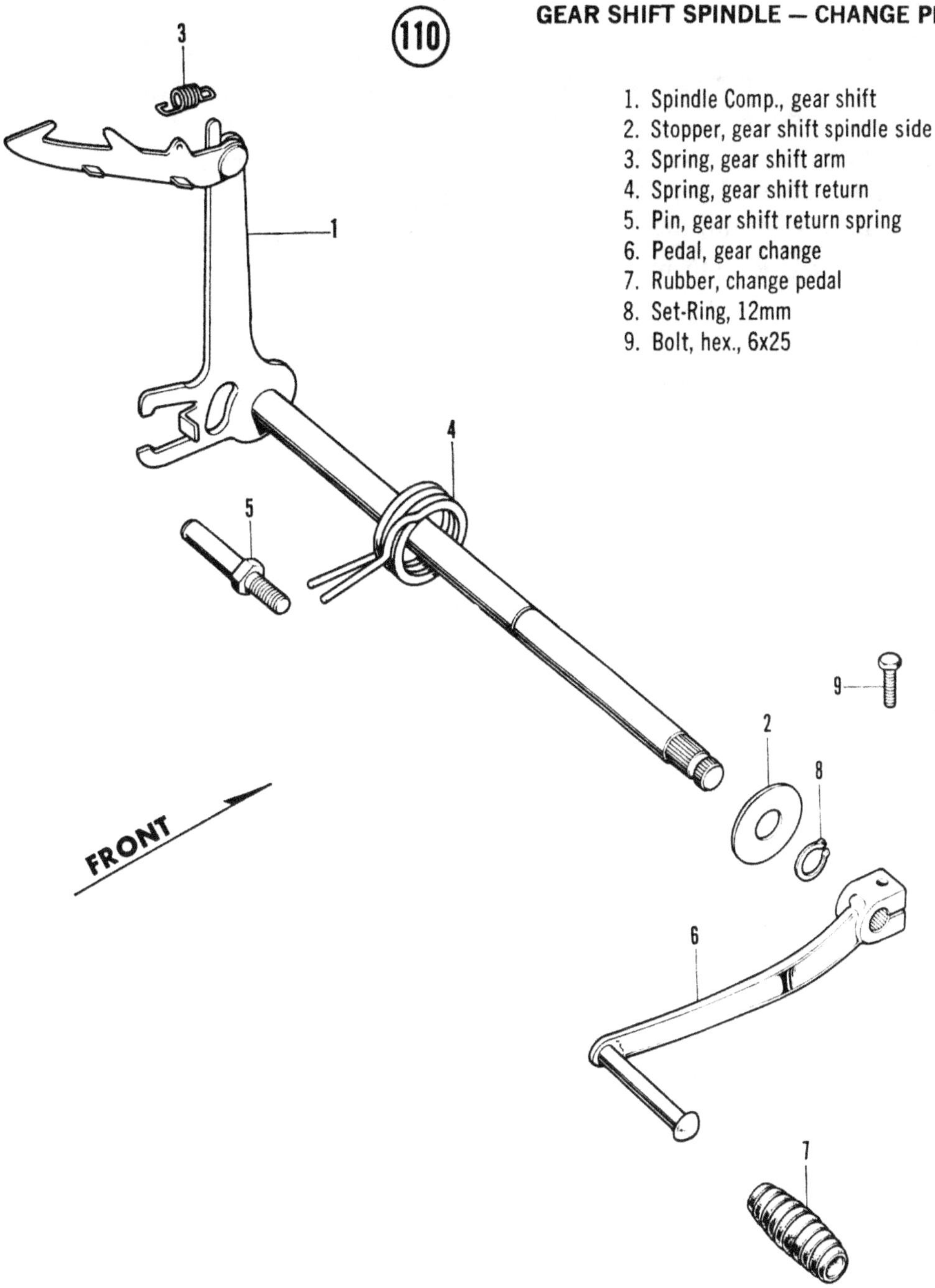

1. Spindle Comp., gear shift
2. Stopper, gear shift spindle side
3. Spring, gear shift arm
4. Spring, gear shift return
5. Pin, gear shift return spring
6. Pedal, gear change
7. Rubber, change pedal
8. Set-Ring, 12mm
9. Bolt, hex., 6x25

Item		Standard value	Serviceable limit
Inside Dia.		34.0~34.025 mm (1.3385~1.339 in)	Replace if over 34.1 mm (1.3425 in)
End thickness	Left Right	4.93~5.0 mm (0.1941~0.1968 in)	Replace if under 4.6 mm (0.181 in)
	Center	5.93~6.0 mm (0.2334~0.236 in)	Replace if under 5.6 mm (0.2205 in)
Bend in fork end (left, right)		Within 0.1mm (0.004 in)	Replace if over 0.8 mm (0.031 in)

Gear shift drum guide grooves

Item	Standard value	Serviceable limit
Groove width	6.05~6.15 mm (0.238~0.242 in)	Replace if over 6.5 mm (0.256 in)

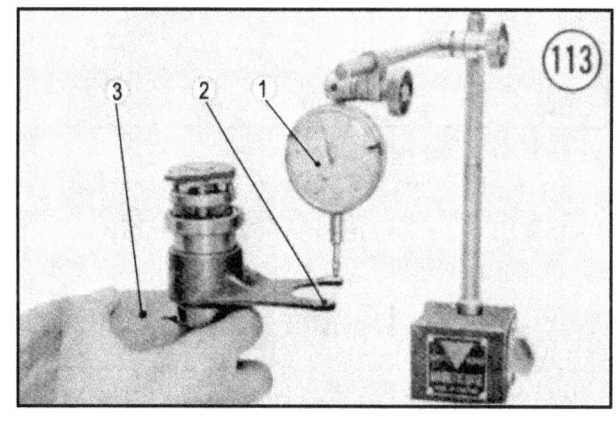

① Dial gauge ② Gear shift fork ③ V-block

Five-Speed Transmission
Gear Shift Reassembly

1. Fit the gear shift drum into the upper case. Check that the shift forks are in their proper locations. Right and left forks are stamped "R" and "L" for identification. Use care not to damage the oil seal pressed into the crankcase.
2. Insert the shift fork guide pin into the shift fork and lock with a clip. Refer to **Figures 114 and 115**. Install the bearing set plate, the neutral stopper and shift drum stopper.

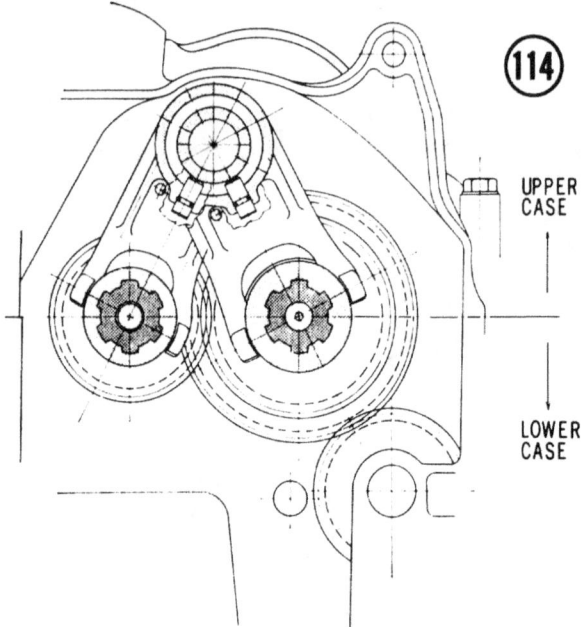

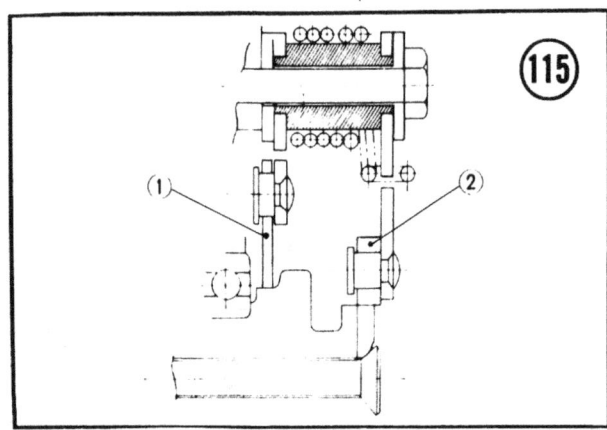

(1) Shift drum stopper
(2) Shift drum neutral stopper

3. Install the transmission gear assembly.
4. Assemble the crankcase halves.
5. Fit the gear shift spindle, installing a washer on the left side and securing it with the circlip.
6. Check the shift fork action for smoothness and continue assembly of the remaining parts.

Kick Starter Disassembly

1. Split the crankcase halves.
2. Remove the kickstarter spring, the 25mm circlip, unscrew the 8mm lock bolt and remove the washer. Refer to **Figures 116 and 117** for details.
3. Remove the starter spindle.

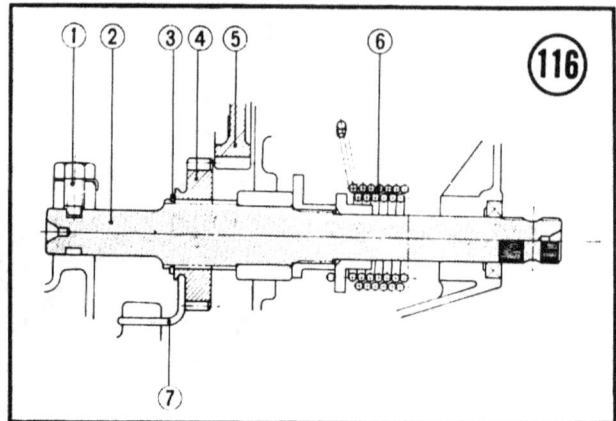

(1) 8mm set bolt
(2) Kick starter spindle
(3) 25mm cir-clip
(4) Kick starter pinion
(5) Counter shaft low gear
(6) Kick starter spring
(7) Friction spring

Kick Starter Inspection

1. Check the pinion and spindle for excessive wear or damage and replace if necessary.

Kick Starter Assembly

1. Refer to **Figure 116** for details and reassemble in reverse order of disassembly. Always use a new 8mm lock washer.

Carburetor Construction

1. Carburetor changes have been made on various models of the 450. However, all carburetors used are similar in construction and operation. Refer to the drawing and photos for details. Minor details may not be the same as on your model, but the figures may be used for reference. See **Figures 118, 119, and 120**.

Carburetor Adjustment

1. Refer to **Figure 121** for details of the carburetor circuit involved in the four phases of operation. "a" shows idling operation. Fuel mixture comes from the pilot outlet and is controlled by the pilot screw. "b" shows low and cruising speed operation. Fuel mixture comes

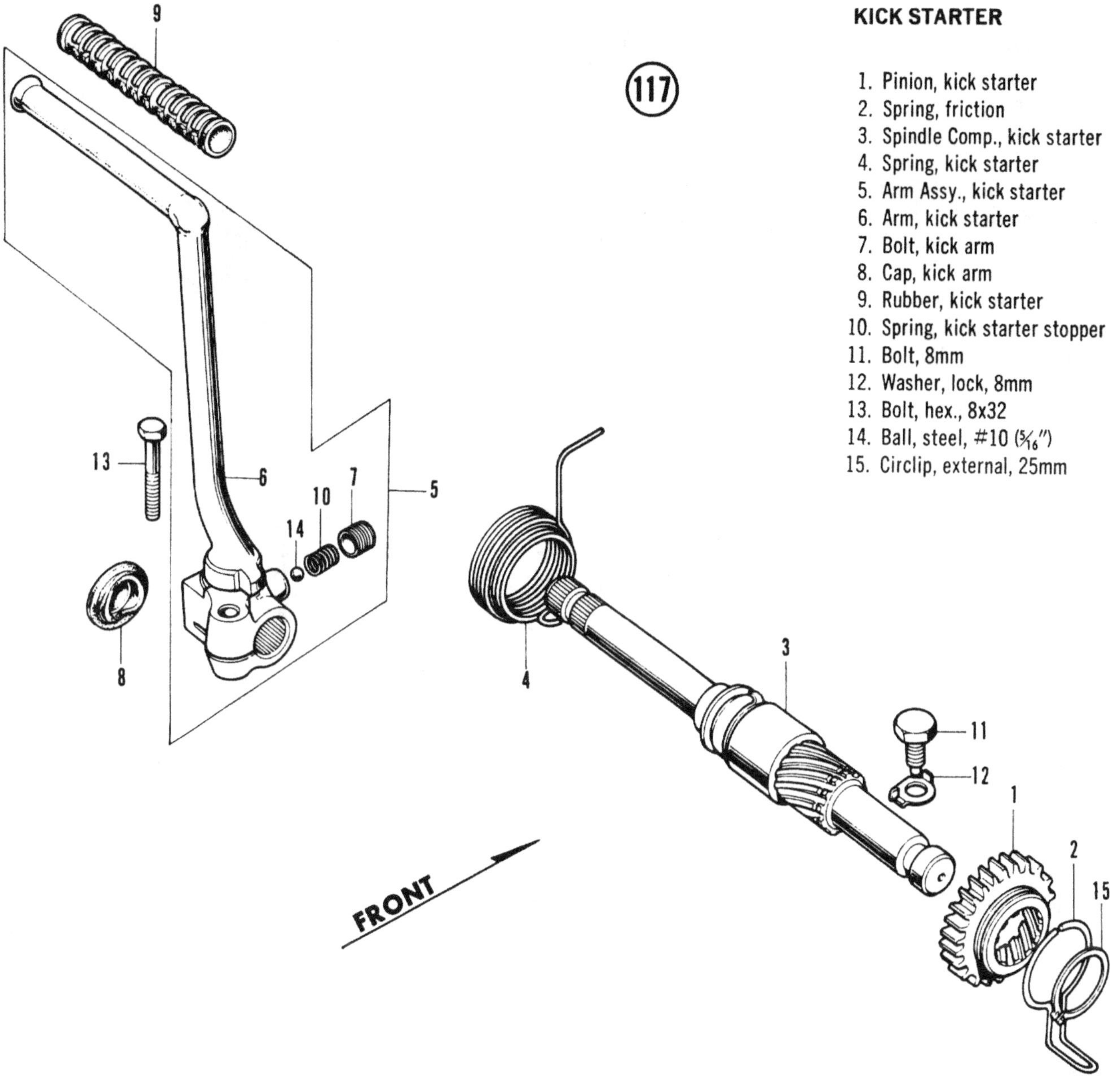

KICK STARTER

1. Pinion, kick starter
2. Spring, friction
3. Spindle Comp., kick starter
4. Spring, kick starter
5. Arm Assy., kick starter
6. Arm, kick starter
7. Bolt, kick arm
8. Cap, kick arm
9. Rubber, kick starter
10. Spring, kick starter stopper
11. Bolt, 8mm
12. Washer, lock, 8mm
13. Bolt, hex., 8x32
14. Ball, steel, #10 (5/16")
15. Circlip, external, 25mm

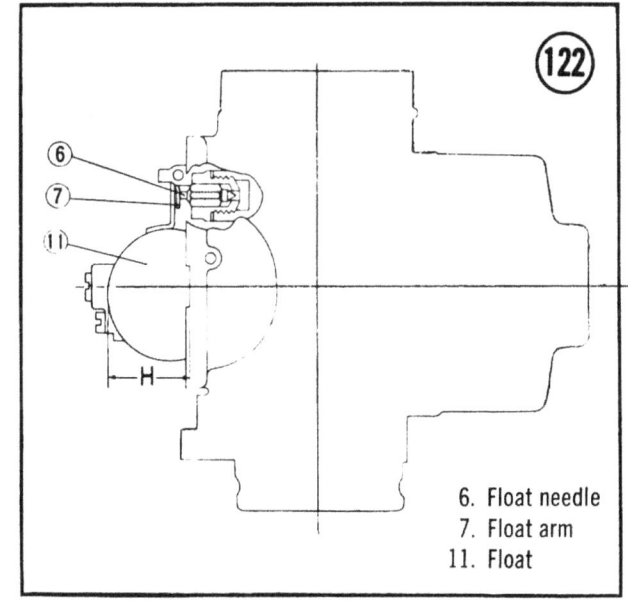

6. Float needle
7. Float arm
11. Float

mainly from the pilot bypass and is adjusted by changing inside diameter of the slow jet. "c" shows medium speed operation. The vacuum piston has started rising and fuel mixture is obtained from the needle jet. The quantity is regulated by the position of the jet needle. "d" shows high speed, full-throttle operation. Fuel mixture now is regulated by the size of the main jet.

2. Refer to the section on tuning for idle adjustment and throttle valve settings.

3. Refer to **Figures 122 and 123** for details of

RIGHT CARBURETOR, 5-SPEED, KEIHIN 14H

1. Carburetor Assy., right
2. Piston Comp., vacuum
3. Cylinder Comp., vacuum
4. Float
5. Valve-Set, float
6. Pin, float arm
7. Washer, float chamber
8. Jet, needle
9. Holder, needle jet
10. Holder, jet needle
11. Lever, throttle, right
12. Plate, stay, right
13. Nut, hex., 7mm
14. Needle, jet
15. Screw, pilot
16. Screw, throttle stop
17. Screw, drain
18. Screw, needle setting
19. Screw, plug, 8⌀
20. Bolt, hex., 5x18
21. Stopper, vacuum piston
22. O-Ring, 2.8⌀
23. Spring, torsion coil, right
24. Spring, throttle stop
25. Clip, float chamber setting
26. Washer, fiber, 9⌀
27. Spring, pilot screw
28. Washer, fiber, 6⌀
29. Joint, connector
30. Washer, tongued, 5mm
31. Washer, serrated lock, 7⌀
32. Washer, lock, 7⌀
33. Washer, fiber, 8⌀
34. Jet, main (#110)
    Jet, main (#115)
    Jet, main (#120)
    Jet, main (#125)
    Jet, main (#130)
    Jet, main (#135)
    Jet, main (#140)
    Jet, main (#145)
    Jet, main (#150)
35. Jet, slow (#38)
    Jet, slow (#40)
    Jet, slow (#42)
    Jet, slow (#45)
36. Jet, pilot (#35)
    Jet, pilot (#38)
    Jet, pilot (#40)
    Jet, pilot (#42)
    Jet, pilot (#45)
37. Screw, pan, 5x10
38. Screw, pan, 5x16
39. Nut, hex., 5mm
40. Washer, spring, 5mm

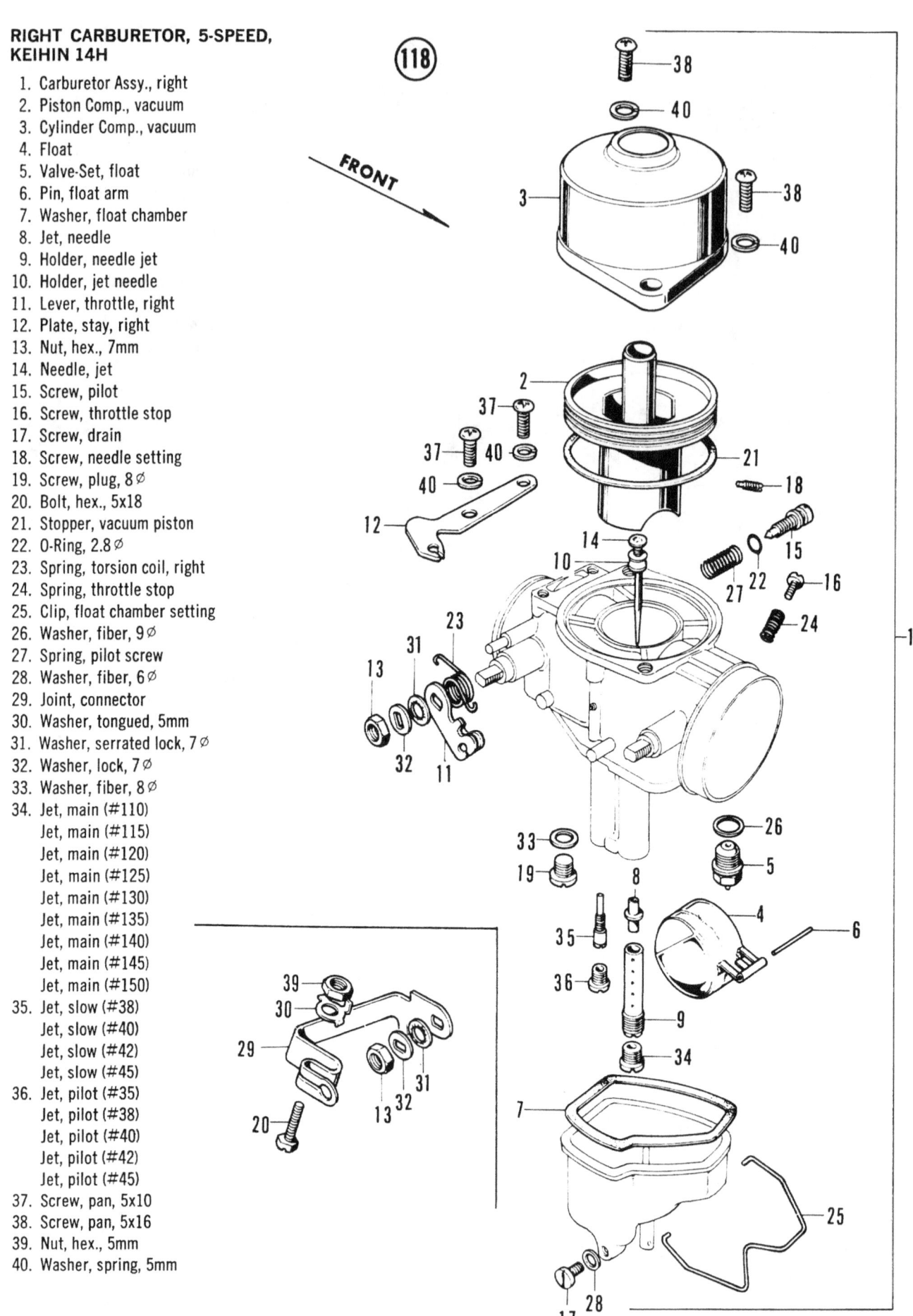

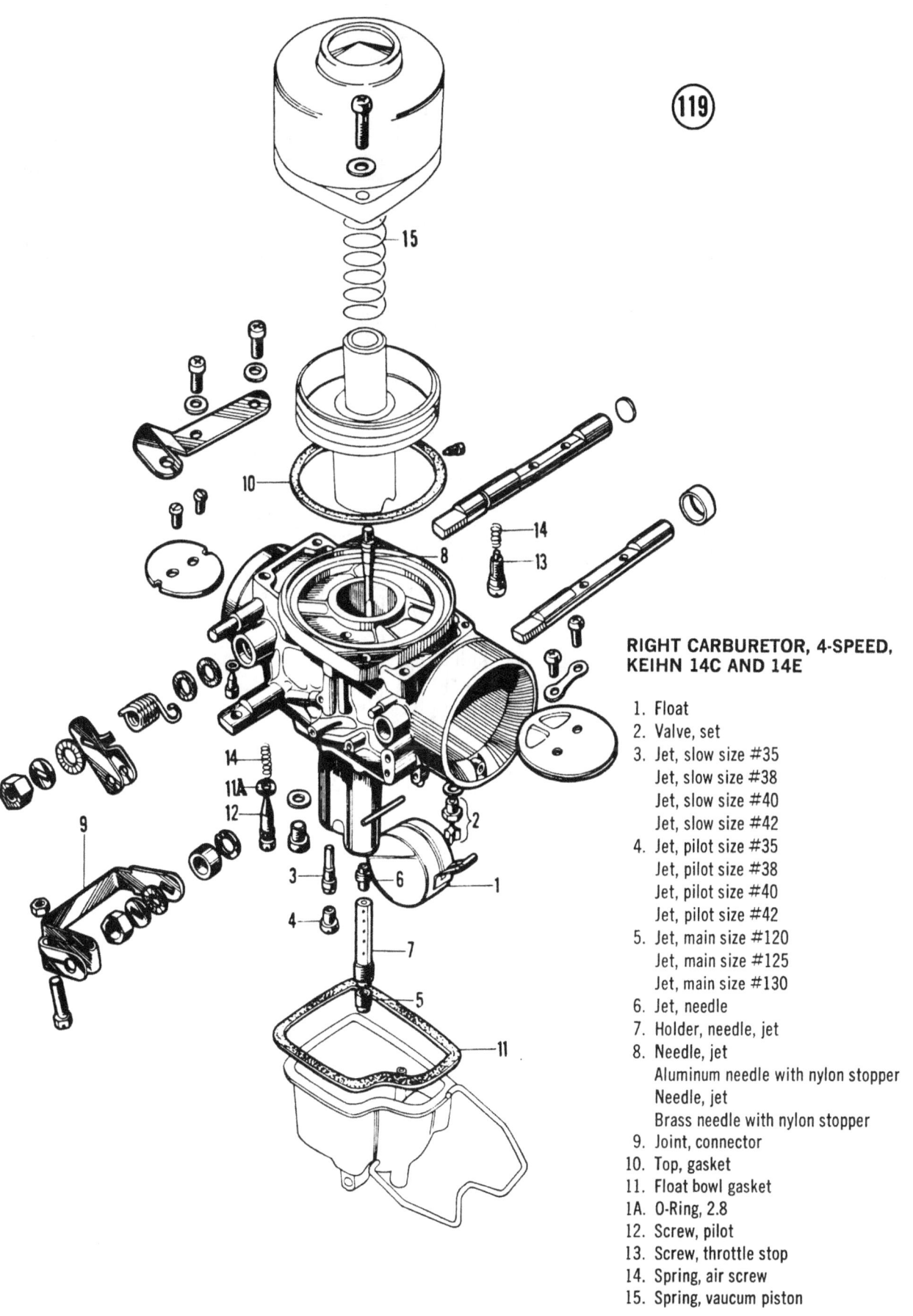

RIGHT CARBURETOR, 4-SPEED, KEIHN 14C AND 14E

1. Float
2. Valve, set
3. Jet, slow size #35
   Jet, slow size #38
   Jet, slow size #40
   Jet, slow size #42
4. Jet, pilot size #35
   Jet, pilot size #38
   Jet, pilot size #40
   Jet, pilot size #42
5. Jet, main size #120
   Jet, main size #125
   Jet, main size #130
6. Jet, needle
7. Holder, needle, jet
8. Needle, jet
   Aluminum needle with nylon stopper
   Needle, jet
   Brass needle with nylon stopper
9. Joint, connector
10. Top, gasket
11. Float bowl gasket
1A. O-Ring, 2.8
12. Screw, pilot
13. Screw, throttle stop
14. Spring, air screw
15. Spring, vaucum piston

(120)

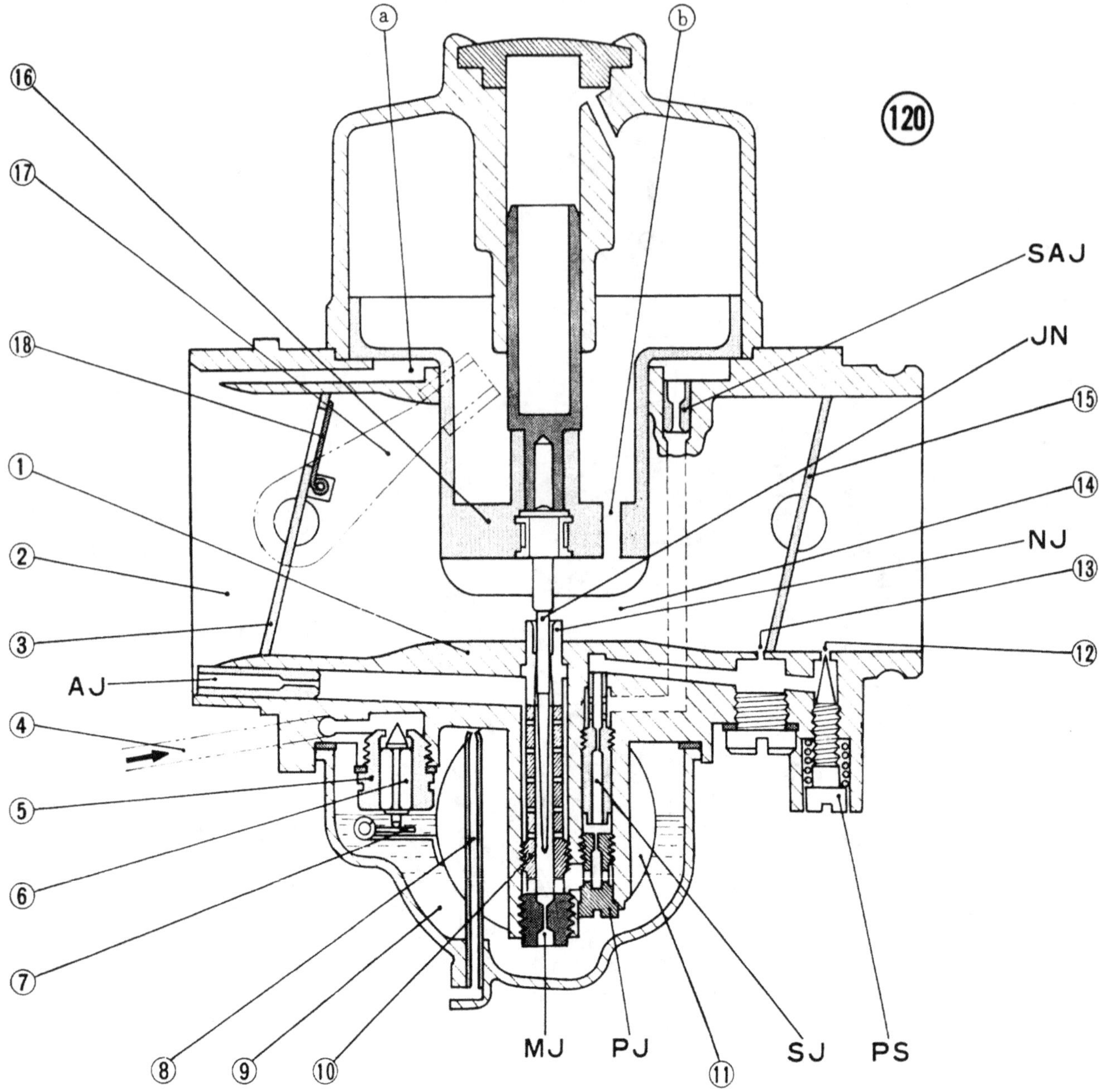

1. Venturi	6. Float needle	11. Float	16. Vacuum piston	MJ Main jet
2. Air intake	7. Float arm	12. Pilot outlet	17. Choke lever	NJ Needle jet
3. Choke valve	8. Overflow tube	13. Pilot bypass	18. Relief valve	PS Pilot screw
4. Fuel inlet	9. Float chamber	14. Venturi	AJ Air jet	SAJ Slow air jet
5. Needle seat	10. Jet body	15. Throttle valve	JN Jet needle	SJ Slow jet

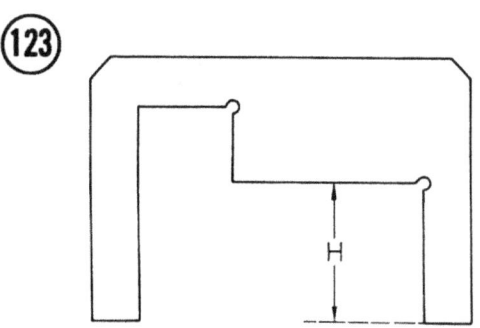

(123)

float level adjustment. Distance "H" on the gauge is 20mm. Turn the carburetor vertically as shown and move the float back and forth so the float valve head and the float arm just contact each other. "H" is then checked with the gauge. Bend the float arm carefully to obtain the correct setting if necessary.

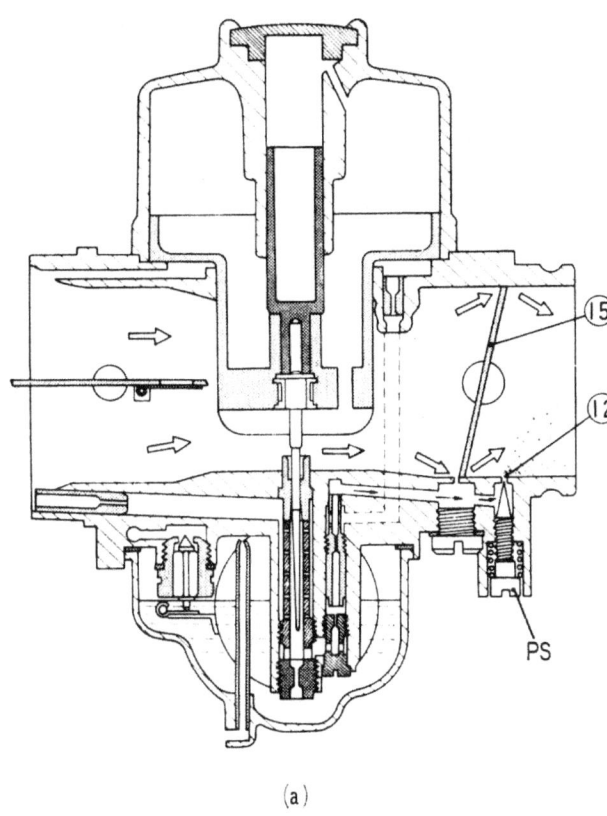

(a)

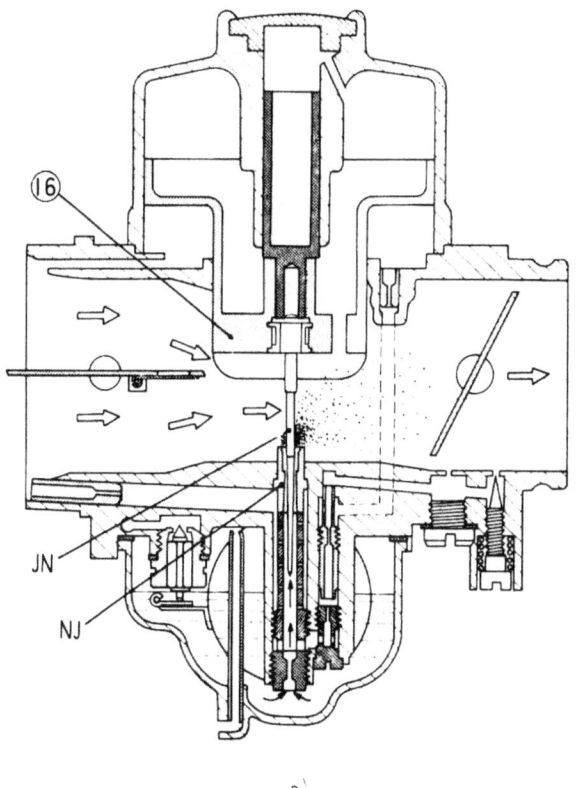

(c)

⑫⑴

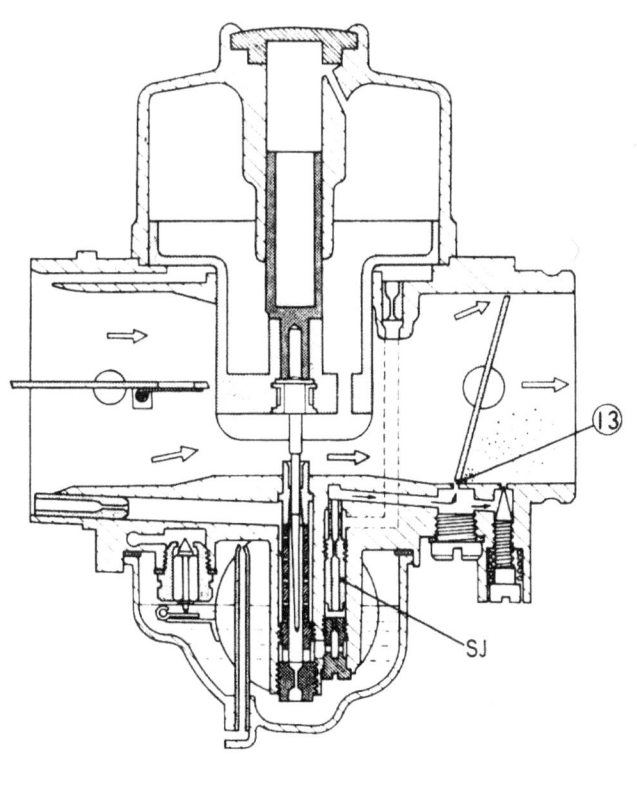

(b)

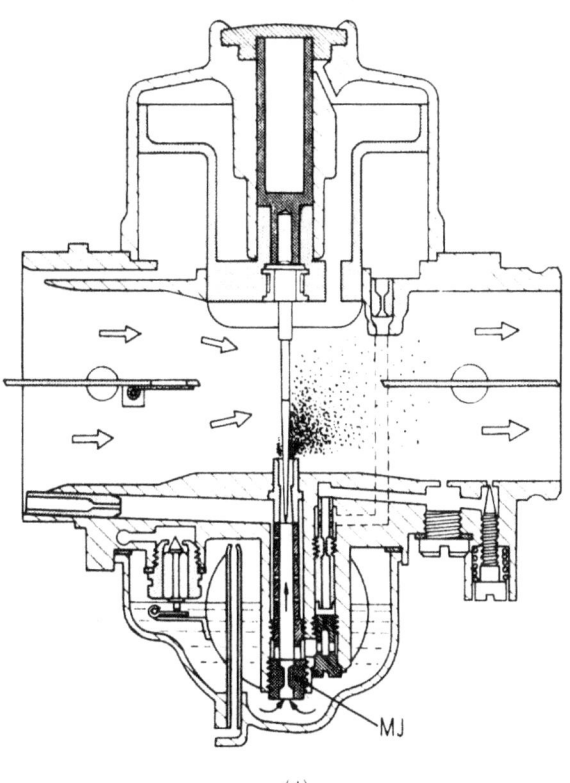

(d)

SECTION FOUR

FRAME SERVICE

Handlebar and Hand Control Disassembly

1. To remove the handlebars disconnect the front brake cable at the wheel end by loosening the locking nut and then the adjusting nut. Push the brake arm to obtain slack, remove the cotter pin and disconnect the cable end as shown in **Figures 1 and 2**. For details of handlebar disassembly, refer to **Figures 3, 4, 5, 6 and 7**.

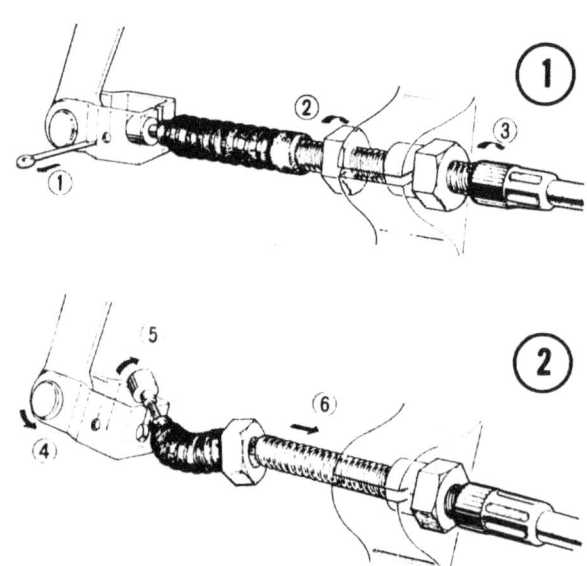

2. Remove both brake and clutch cables at the handlebar end by lining up the slots on the adjuster and holder so the cable may be slipped through as shown. Line the cable up with the slot in the lever and remove. Refer to **Figure 8**.

3. To disconnect the clutch cable at the engine, remove the gear shift lever, the drive chain cover, and then slip the cable out of the clutch lifter.

4. To remove the throttle cable from the hand throttle, unscrew the starter switch assembly and separate the two halves of the switch. This will expose the throttle cable so that it can be removed.

5. To remove the throttle cable at the carburetor, loosen the lock nut and then the adjusting nut as shown in **Figure 9**.

6. If necessary, the electrical leads for the horn, starter motor, and light dimmer switch (and turn signals if the machine is so equipped) may be disconnected in the wiring harness located in the headlight case.

7. Finally, remove the handlebars by unscrewing the four bolts from the handlebar clamps.

Handlebar and Hand Control Inspection

1. Inspect all cables for bends, kinks and evidences of fraying. Replace if necessary. Oil them before reassembly.

2. The throttle assembly must work freely and smoothly throughout its entire range. Re-

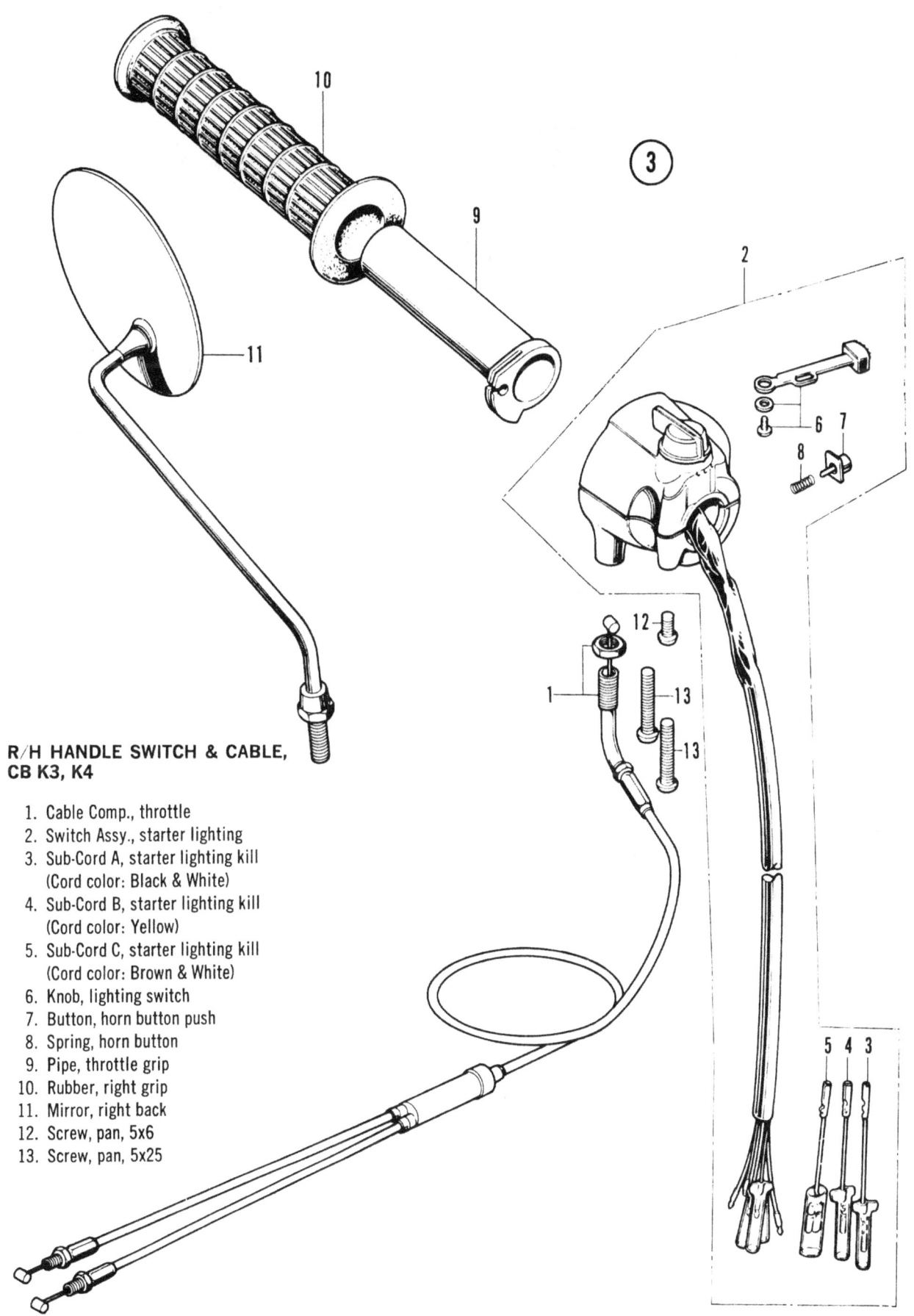

R/H HANDLE SWITCH & CABLE, CB K3, K4

1. Cable Comp., throttle
2. Switch Assy., starter lighting
3. Sub-Cord A, starter lighting kill (Cord color: Black & White)
4. Sub-Cord B, starter lighting kill (Cord color: Yellow)
5. Sub-Cord C, starter lighting kill (Cord color: Brown & White)
6. Knob, lighting switch
7. Button, horn button push
8. Spring, horn button
9. Pipe, throttle grip
10. Rubber, right grip
11. Mirror, right back
12. Screw, pan, 5x6
13. Screw, pan, 5x25

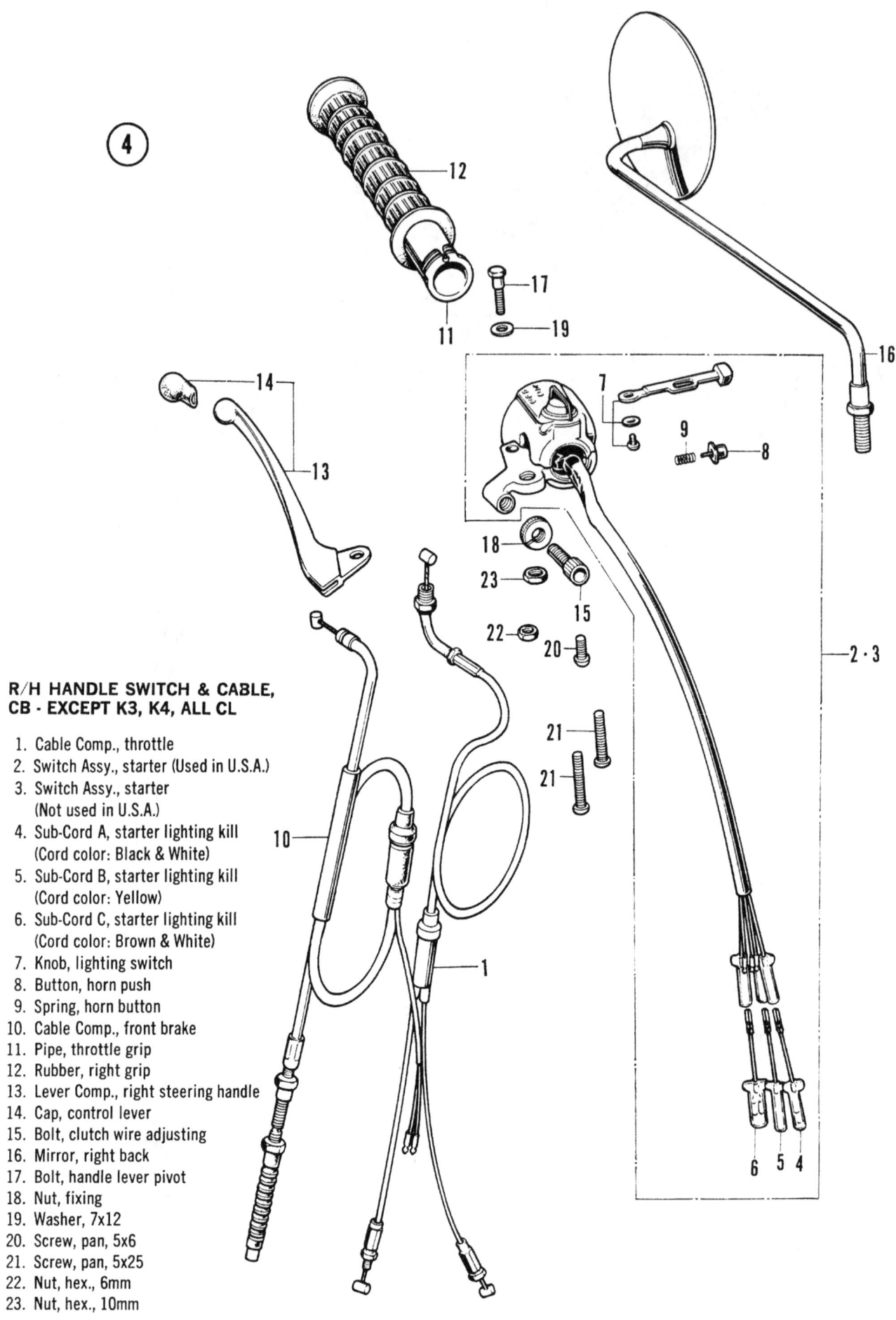

R/H HANDLE SWITCH & CABLE, CB - EXCEPT K3, K4, ALL CL

1. Cable Comp., throttle
2. Switch Assy., starter (Used in U.S.A.)
3. Switch Assy., starter (Not used in U.S.A.)
4. Sub-Cord A, starter lighting kill (Cord color: Black & White)
5. Sub-Cord B, starter lighting kill (Cord color: Yellow)
6. Sub-Cord C, starter lighting kill (Cord color: Brown & White)
7. Knob, lighting switch
8. Button, horn push
9. Spring, horn button
10. Cable Comp., front brake
11. Pipe, throttle grip
12. Rubber, right grip
13. Lever Comp., right steering handle
14. Cap, control lever
15. Bolt, clutch wire adjusting
16. Mirror, right back
17. Bolt, handle lever pivot
18. Nut, fixing
19. Washer, 7x12
20. Screw, pan, 5x6
21. Screw, pan, 5x25
22. Nut, hex., 6mm
23. Nut, hex., 10mm

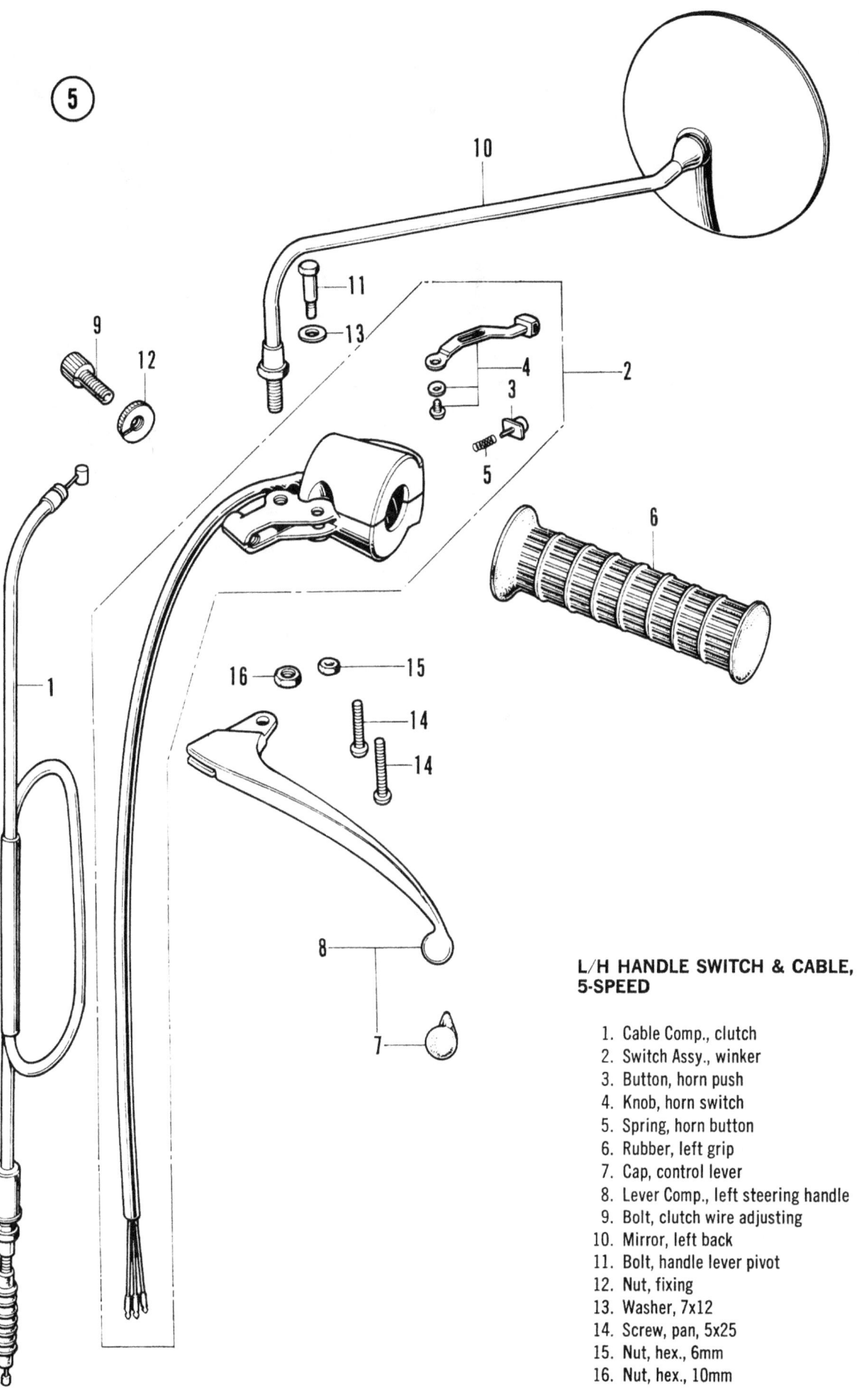

L/H HANDLE SWITCH & CABLE, 5-SPEED

1. Cable Comp., clutch
2. Switch Assy., winker
3. Button, horn push
4. Knob, horn switch
5. Spring, horn button
6. Rubber, left grip
7. Cap, control lever
8. Lever Comp., left steering handle
9. Bolt, clutch wire adjusting
10. Mirror, left back
11. Bolt, handle lever pivot
12. Nut, fixing
13. Washer, 7x12
14. Screw, pan, 5x25
15. Nut, hex., 6mm
16. Nut, hex., 10mm

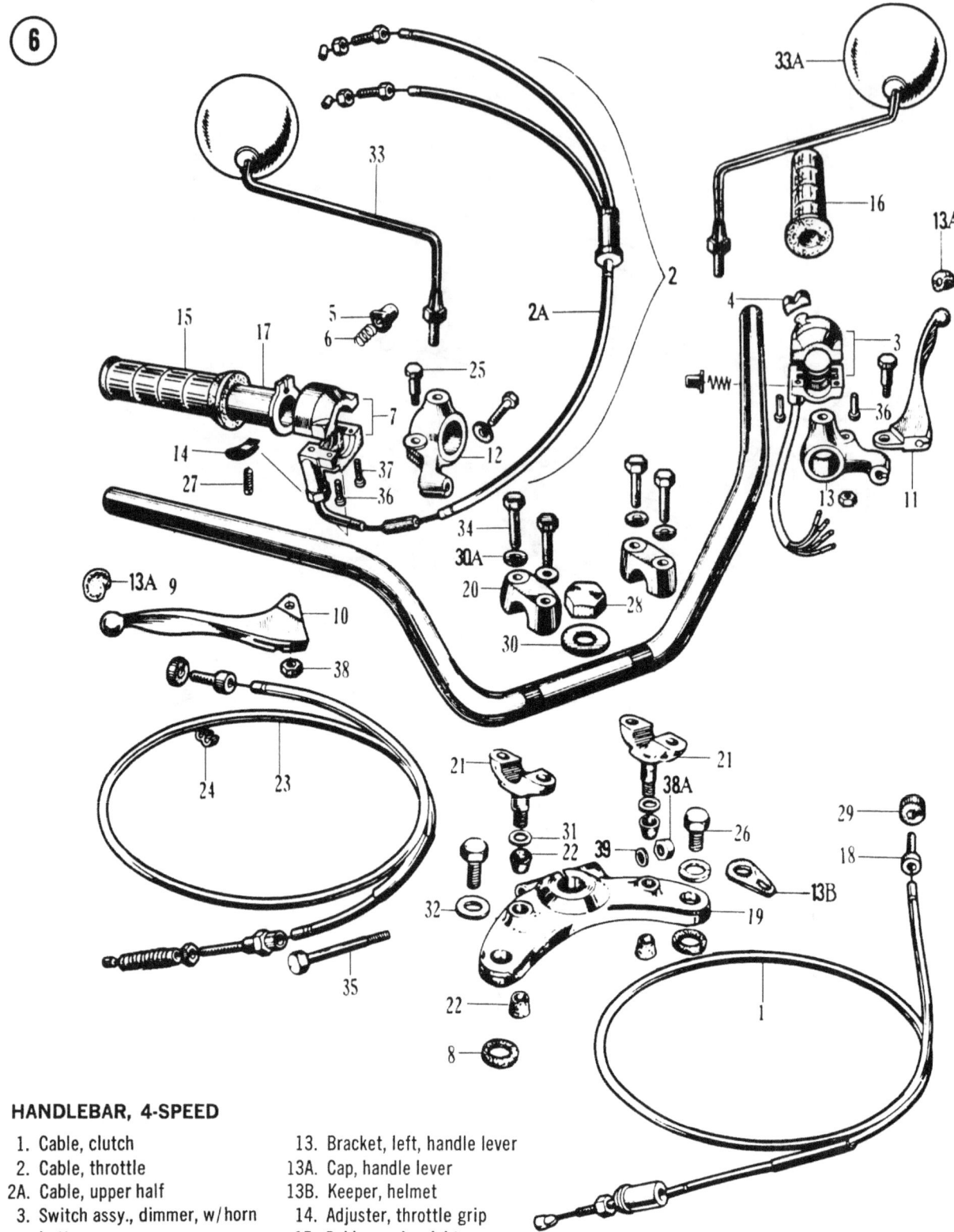

HANDLEBAR, 4-SPEED

1. Cable, clutch
2. Cable, throttle
2A. Cable, upper half
3. Switch assy., dimmer, w/horn button
4. Knob, horn button switch
5. Button, horn button switch push
6. Spring, push button
7. Switch assy., starter
8. Cushion, front fork cover
9. Pipe, steering handle
10. Lever, right steering handle
11. Lever, left steering handle
12. Bracket, right, handle lever
13. Bracket, left, handle lever
13A. Cap, handle lever
13B. Keeper, helmet
14. Adjuster, throttle grip
15. Rubber, grip, right
16. Rubber, grip, left
17. Pipe, throttle grip
18. Bolt, clutch cable adjusting
19. Bridge, fork top
20. Holder, handle pipe
21. Holder, lower, handle pipe
22. Rubber, handle cushion
23. Cable, front brake
24. Clip, front brake cable
25. Bolt, handle lever pivot
26. Bolt, front fork
27. Screw, throttle grip adjuster
28. Nut, steering stem
29. Nut, fixing
30. Washer, steering stem
30A. Washer, special, 8mm
31. Washer, handle cushion
32. Washer, front fork
33. Mirror, back, right
33A. Mirror, back, left
34. Bolt, hex., 8x32
35. Bolt, hex., 8x74
36. Screw, cross, 5x14
37. Screw, Cross, 5x22
38. Nut, hex., 6mm
38A. Nut, hex., 8mm
39. Washer, flat, 8mm

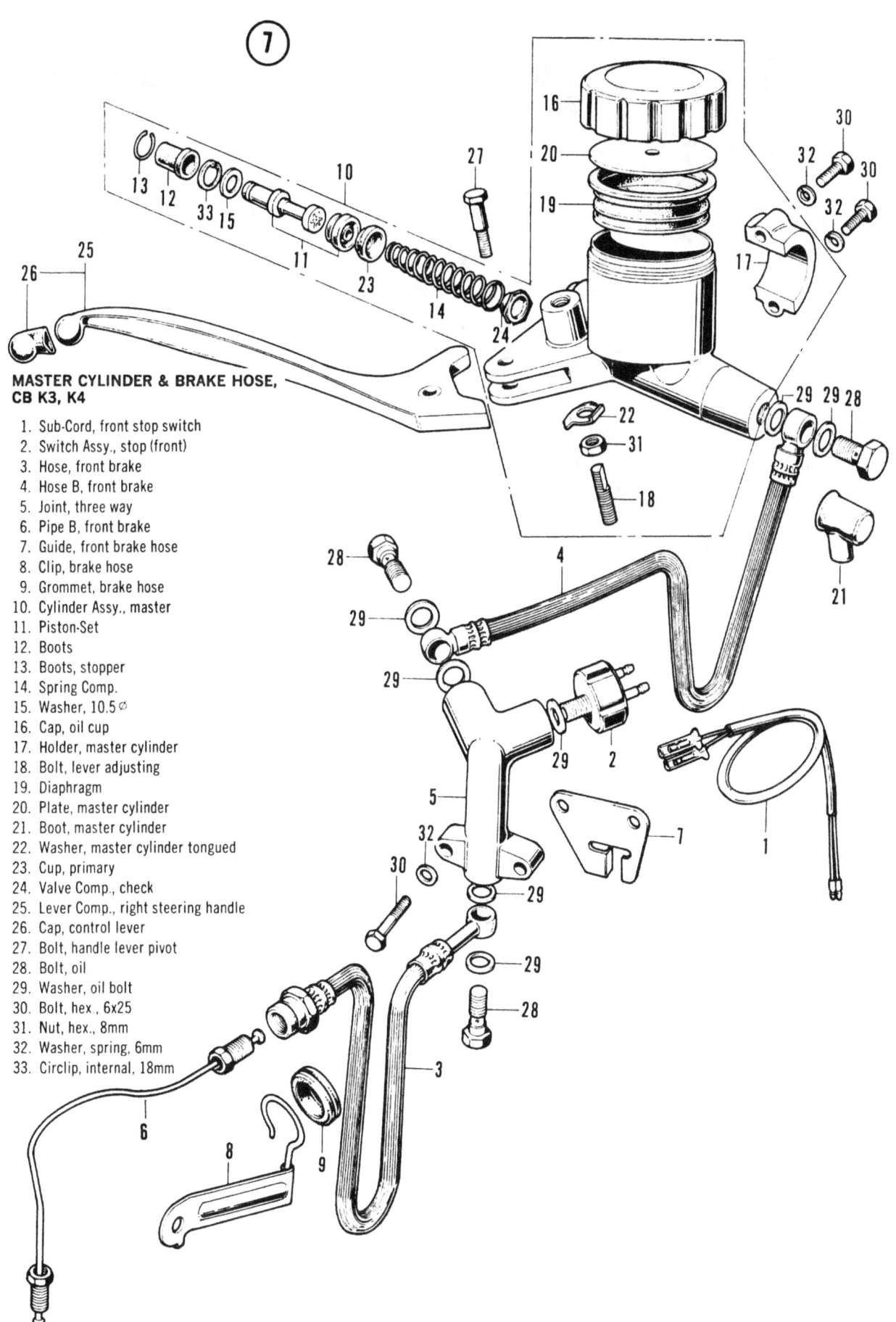

MASTER CYLINDER & BRAKE HOSE, CB K3, K4

1. Sub-Cord, front stop switch
2. Switch Assy., stop (front)
3. Hose, front brake
4. Hose B, front brake
5. Joint, three way
6. Pipe B, front brake
7. Guide, front brake hose
8. Clip, brake hose
9. Grommet, brake hose
10. Cylinder Assy., master
11. Piston-Set
12. Boots
13. Boots, stopper
14. Spring Comp.
15. Washer, 10.5 ⌀
16. Cap, oil cup
17. Holder, master cylinder
18. Bolt, lever adjusting
19. Diaphragm
20. Plate, master cylinder
21. Boot, master cylinder
22. Washer, master cylinder tongued
23. Cup, primary
24. Valve Comp., check
25. Lever Comp., right steering handle
26. Cap, control lever
27. Bolt, handle lever pivot
28. Bolt, oil
29. Washer, oil bolt
30. Bolt, hex., 6x25
31. Nut, hex., 8mm
32. Washer, spring, 6mm
33. Circlip, internal, 18mm

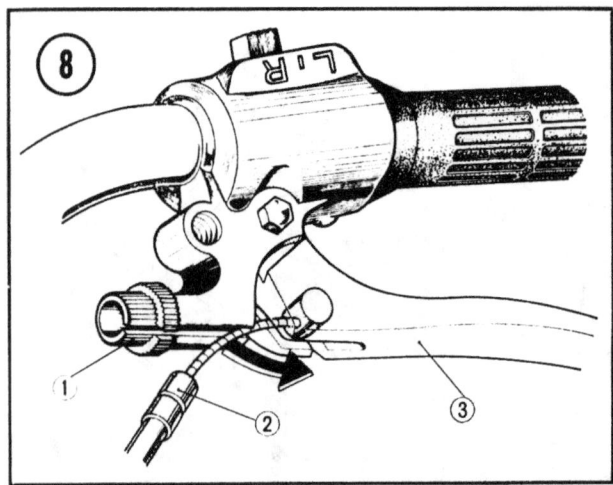

① Adjusting bolt ② Clutch cable ③ Clutch lever

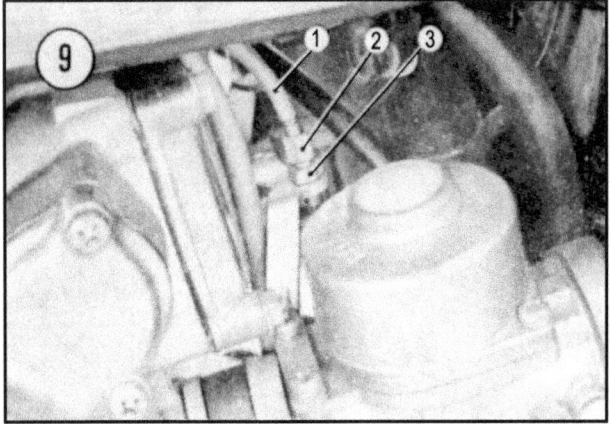

① Throttle cable
② Throttle cable adjuster
③ Lock nut

pair or replace as necessary. Grease the hand levers lightly at friction points.

3. Check wiring and switches for proper operation.

4. Check the handlebars for bends or other damage.

Handlebar and Hand Control Reassembly

1. Route the necessary electrical leads through the center hole in the top fork crown and mount the handlebars in place.

2. Connect the throttle cable and adjust play as outlined in the first section. Refer to **Figure 10**.

3. Connect the clutch cable and front brake cable to left and right hand levers, respectively. Adjust both cables at their lower ends for proper operation. The adjusters on the handlebars are for fine adjustment and should only be used after the lower adjustments have been made.

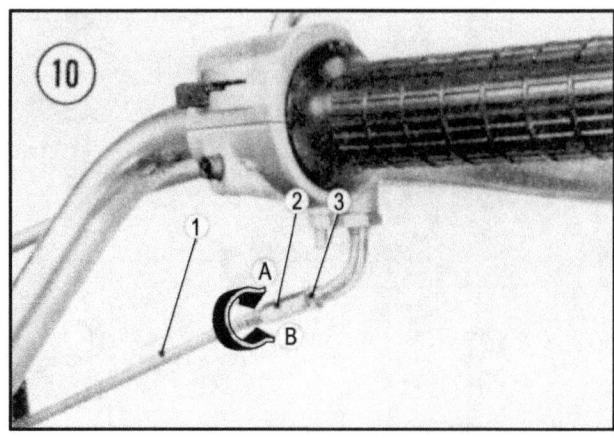

① Throttle cable
② Throttle cable adjuster
③ Lock nut

4. Connect the electrical connections inside the headlight case and replace the headlight and rim. See **Figure 11**.

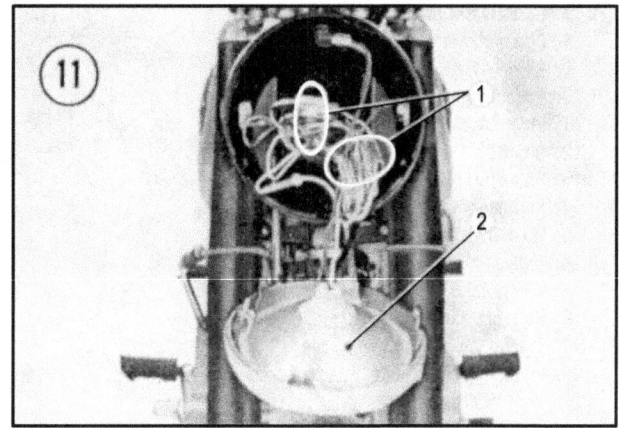

① Leads conectors
② Head light

Fork Crown Disassembly

1. Refer to **Figures 12, 13 and 14** for details of fork crown (triple clamp) disassembly. Remove the handlebars and extract the lock pin so the steering damper may be pulled out.

2. Disconnect the speedometer and tachometer cables and then the instruments themselves.

3. Unscrew the fork cap bolts, remove the steering stem nut and then loosen the fork clamp bolt.

4. Temporarily replace the handlebars in their holders and secure them lightly. Remove the handlebar lower holder bolts. The washers, cushion rubbers and lower holders may now be removed.

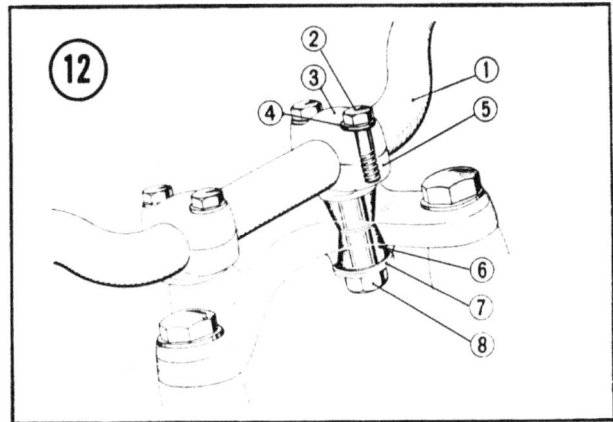

① Handle bar
② 8 mm bolt
③ Handle bar pipe upper holder
④ 8 mm flat washer
⑤ Handle bar pipe under holder
⑥ Handle cushion rubber
⑦ Washer
⑧ 10 mm nut

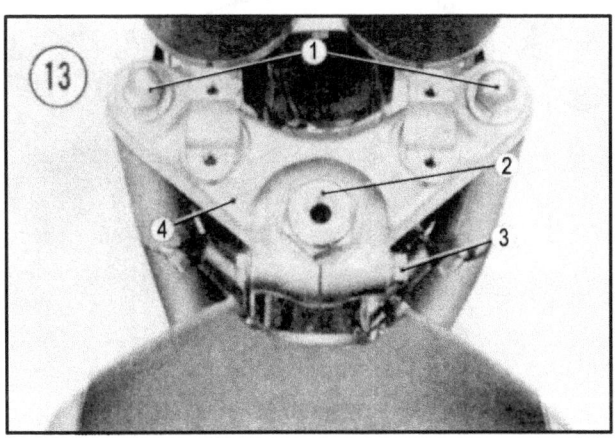

① Front fork bolt
② Steering stem nut
③ 8 mm bolt
④ Fork top bridge

Fork Crown Inspection

1. Check the crown carefully for cracks or damage and inspect the rubber cushions for wear or deterioration and replace if necessary.

Fork Crown Reassembly

1. Assemble the fork crown in reverse order of disassembly and fit the handlebars. Check headlights, horn and turn signals for proper operation.

Front Fork Disassembly

1. Note the various types of front forks used on the CB and CL 450's. The earlier models shared the same type of fork using two-piece fork springs. Later models used an interior fork spring on the CB 450 and an exterior fork spring covered by a rubber boot on the CL 450. If your bike has the front disc brake, refer to the last type of fork. If any doubt exists as to the type forks used on your bike, compare the type with the diagrams given. All the forks are basically similar but for the most clarity we have treated them in three separate sections and identified them under the headings of: Two-piece spring (early type), One-piece spring, and Disc brake.

**Front Fork Disassembly
(Two-piece spring) See Figure 15 for details.**

1. Remove the front wheel, front fender, and front brake stop bolt.

2. Loosen the pinch bolt on the bottom triple clamp as shown in **Figure 16** (CB K1 illustrated; others similar). Remove the front fork bolt (cap) and pull the entire fork tube assembly downwards and out of the triple clamp. The bottom clamp may be spread with a screwdriver or wedge to facilitate fork tube removal.

3. Drain oil from the bottom tube by removing the drain bolt or turning the assembly upside down.

4. Unscrew the fork seal housing, using the special tool as shown in **Figure 17,** and remove the fork pipe assembly. The two fork springs, along with their joint piece, may then be removed from the bottom case.

5. Continue disassembly, removing parts in the following order and referring to **Figure 18** for details: Fork piston snap ring, front fork piston, front damper valve, fork valve stop ring, fork pipe stop ring, front fork pipe guide and seal housing. Note that the seal housing

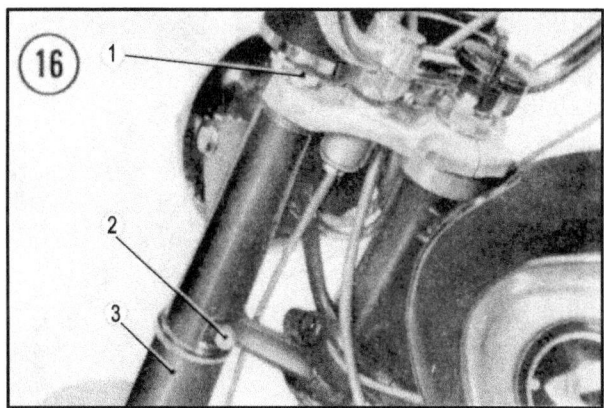

① Front fork bolt
② 10 mm bolt
③ Front cushion assembly

(14) STEERING STEM & FENDER, 5-SPEED (CB)

1. Clip, tachometer cable
2. Grommet, wire
3. Clip, speedometer cable
4. Race, steering top ball
5. Race, steering bottom ball
6. Dust-Seal, steering head
7. Stem Comp., steering (black)
8. Race, steering top cone
9. Race, steering bottom cone
10. Cover Comp., handle lock case
11. Washer, steering head dust-seal
12. Thread Comp., steering head top
13. Lock Comp., handle
14. Spring, handle lock
15. Fender Comp., front (chrome)
16. Piece, fender setting
17. Stay A, front fender
18. Stay B, front fender
19. Nut, steering stem
20. Washer, steering stem
21. Bolt, hex., 6x12
22. Bolt, hex., 6x25
23. Bolt, hex., 8x25
24. Bolt, hex., 10x40
25. Screw, pan, 3x8
26. Screw, oval, 5x25
27. Nut, hex., 5mm
28. Washer, plain, 3mm
29. Washer, plain, 5mm
30. Washer, plain, 6mm
31. Washer, plain, 8mm
32. Washer, plain, 10mm
33. Washer, spring, 5mm
34. Washer, spring, 8mm
35. Ball, steel, RB8 (¼")

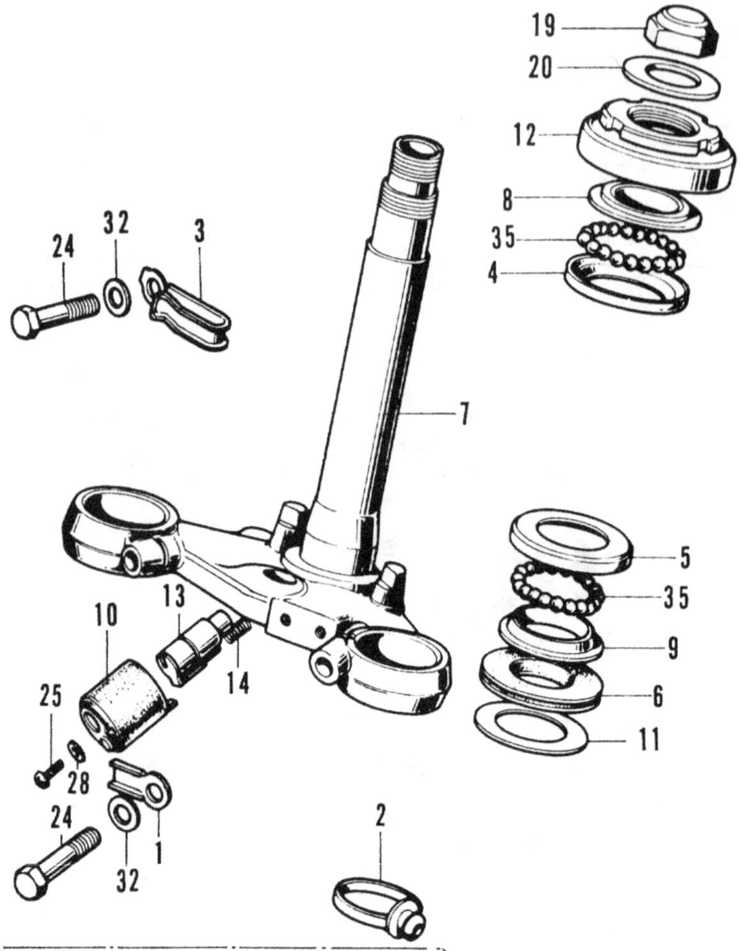

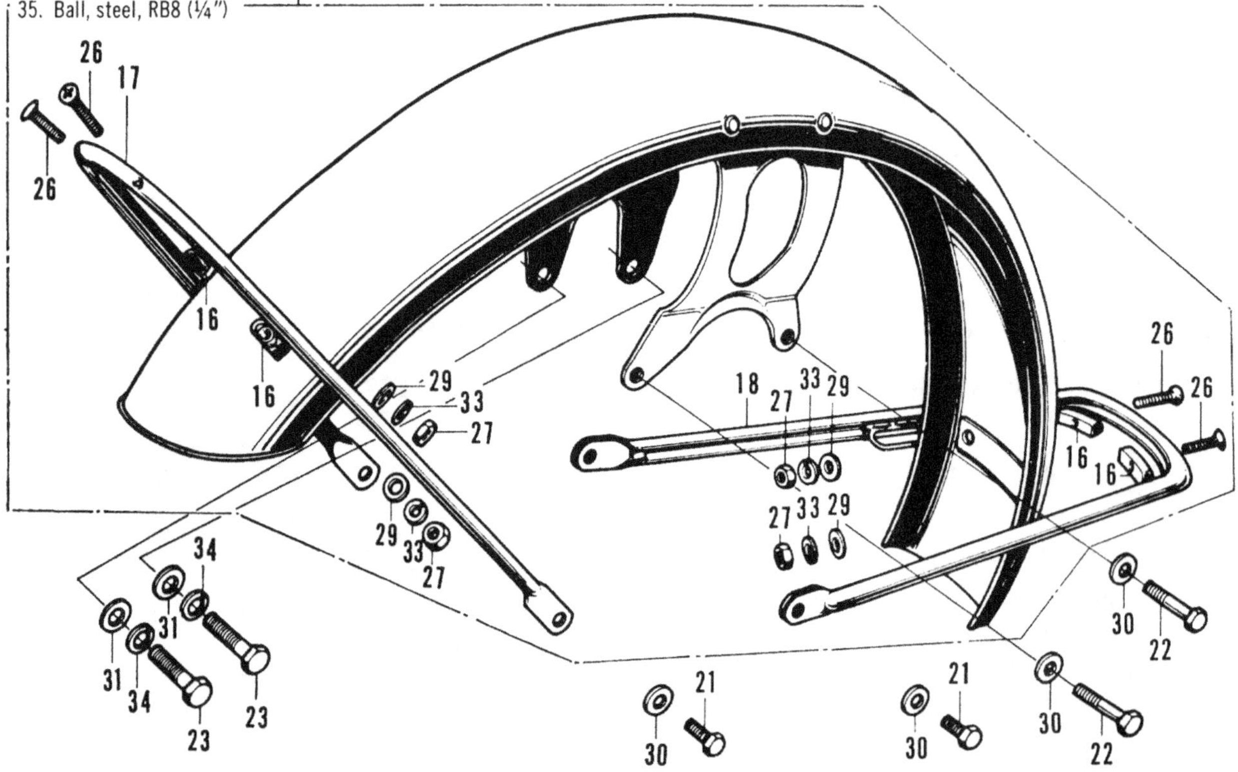

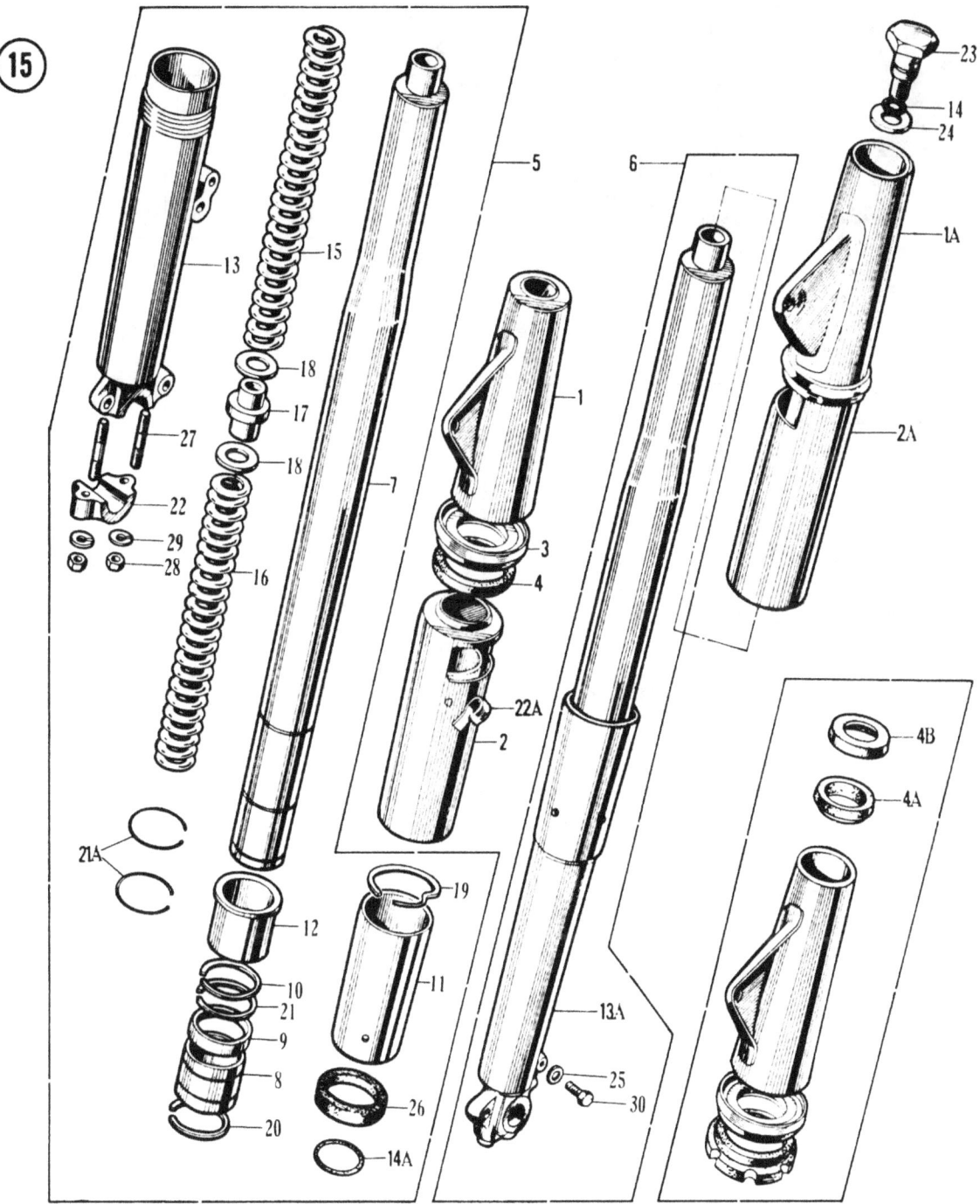

FRONT FORK

1. Cover, upper, right front fork
   Cover, right front fork
1A. Cover, upper, left front fork
    Cover, left front fork
2. Cover, under, right front fork
2A. Not available, use item #2
3. Rib, front fork
4. Cushion, front fork cover
4A. Cushion, front fork upper cover
4B. Cap, front fork upper cover
5. Cushion assy., right front
6. Cushion assy., left front
7. Pipe, front fork
8. Piston, front fork
9. Valve, front damper
10. Ring, fork pipe stopper
11. Housing, front fork seal
12. Guide, front fork pipe
13. Case, bottom, right front fork
13A. Case, bottom, left front fork
14. O-Ring, 9.4x2.4
14A. O-Ring, 40.5x3
15. Spring A, front cushion
16. Spring B, front cushion
17. Piece, front cushion spring joint
18. Washer, front cushion spring
19. Retainer, front fork oil seal
20. Ring, fork piston snap
21. Ring, fork valve stopper
21A. Ring, piston stopper
22. Holder, front axle
22A. Clip, speedometer cable
23. Bolt, front fork
24. Washer, front fork
25. Packing, drain cock
26. Oil-Seal, 334610
27. Stud, 8x49
28. Nut, hex., 8mm
29. Washer, spring, 8mm
30. Bolt, hex., 6x8

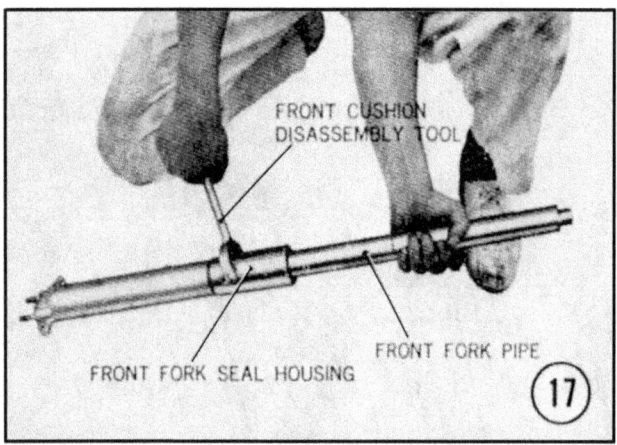

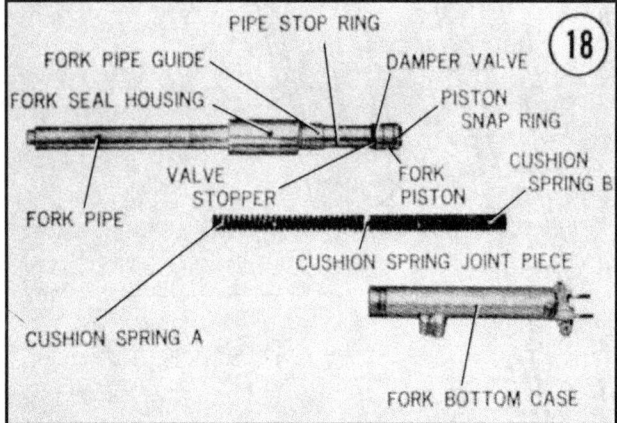

should be removed from the front fork pipe only when oil seals need replacing.

6. To replace the oil seal, remove the retainer as shown in **Figure 19** and then the seal.

7. Use care to avoid damaging the fork tubes and piston.

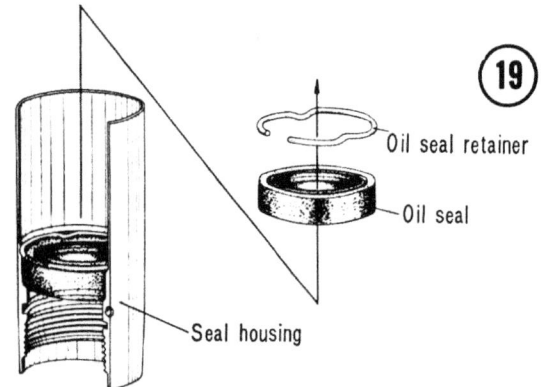

Front Fork (Two-piece spring) Inspection

1. Refer to the accompanying tables to determine condition of front fork parts and repair or replace as necessary. **(Figure 20)**

Front Fork (Two-piece spring) Reassembly

1. Clean all parts thoroughly.

1. Measurment of front cushion springs (A) and (B).

Spring A	Standard	Service Limit
Weight	30 ± 1.8 kg Length (176.2)	
	60 ± 3.6 kg (155.4)	
Unloaded Length	197 mm	Replace when less than 191 mm
Right Angle to End Surface	Within $\pm 1°$	

Spring B	Standard	Service Limit
Weight	50 ± 3.0 kg Length (184.4)	
	$100 + 6.0$ kg (153)	
Unloaded Length	215 mm	Replace when less than 209 mm
Right Angle to End Surface	Within $\pm 1°$	

2. Measurement of front fork piston.

	Standard Value	Service Limit
Outside diameter	$37.5 \phi \begin{array}{c} -0.025 \\ -0.050 \end{array}$	Replace when less than 37.5ϕ
Inside diameter	Within 0.008	Replace when more than 0.015
Taper	Within 0.015	Replace when more than 0.03

3. Measurement of front fork pipe (outside diameter and straightness).

	Standard Value	Service Limit
Outside diameter	$33 \phi + 7 \begin{array}{c} -0.025 \\ -0.050 \end{array}$	
Elliptic wear	0.015	Replace when more than 0.03
Deflection	Within 0.04	Replace when more than 0.1

4. Measurement of front fork pipe guide.

	Standard Value	Service Limit
Full length	36	
Inside diameter	$33 \phi \begin{array}{c} +0.039 \\ -0 \end{array}$	
Outside diameter	$37.5 \phi \begin{array}{c} -0.009 \\ -0.034 \end{array}$	

Measurement of front fork bottom case.

20	Standard Value	Service Limit
Inside diameter	37.5 +0.039 −0	
Elliptic wear		
Taper		

2. Reassemble the front fork pipe components in reverse order of disassembly. Install the seal housing from the mounting side of the fork piston in such a way that the oil seal lip is not damaged. Check the action of the front damper valve on the fork pipe after installation as shown in **Figure 21**.

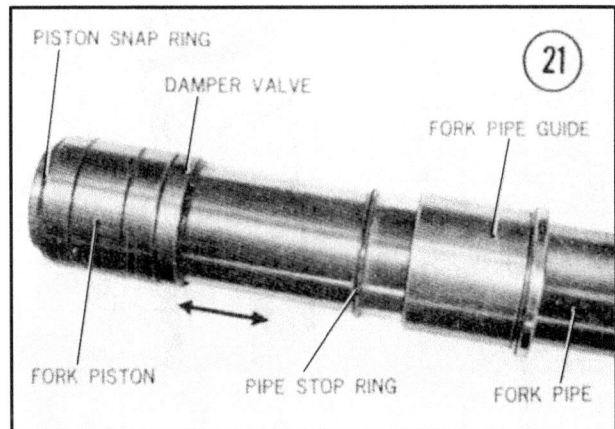

3. Install the fork pipe into the bottom case, fitting the springs in place at the same time. Use the special tool to tighten the seal housing.

4. Insert the fork tubes in place in the triple clamps. On the CB model, add 7.3 ounces (230cc) of 10W-30 motor oil; on the CL, add 9.6-10.0 ounces (285-295cc). Replace the fork bolts (caps) and tighten the 10mm pinch bolts.

5. Replace front fender, wheel, and brake stop bolt and check the forks for smooth action by locking the front brake and pushing down on the handlebars.

Front Fork Disassembly (One-piece spring)

1. Remove the front wheel, front fender and front brake stop arm bolt.
2. Remove the headlight assembly.
3. Remove the pinch bolt on the lower triple crown and the front fork bolt (cap). Detach the fork tube assembly by pulling it down and out.

The bottom clamp may be spread with a screwdriver or wedge to facilitate fork tube removal.

4. Drain oil from the tube by removing the drain plug or by turning the assembly upside down.

5. On the CL 450 remove the rubber boot and on the CB 450 remove the front fork under cover. Remove the front cushion spring and the 47mm internal circlip as shown in **Figure 22**.

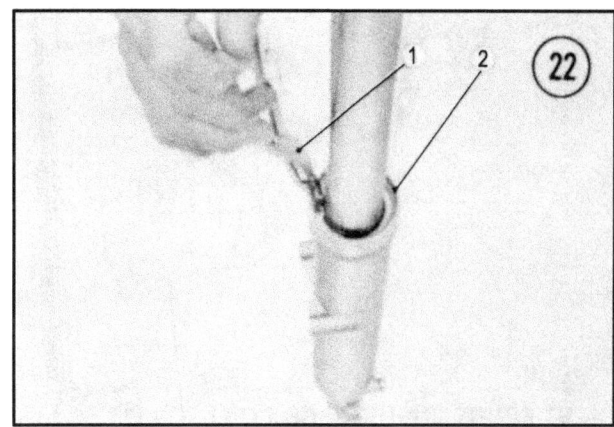

① Pliers (close)
② 47 mm intenal circlip

6. Pull out the bottom pipe and disassemble the front fork pipe assembly in this order, referring to **Figure 23**: Fork piston snap ring, fork piston, piston stopper ring, front damper valve, front valve stopper ring, fork pipe stopper ring and front fork pipe guide. See **Figures 24 and 25** for additional details.

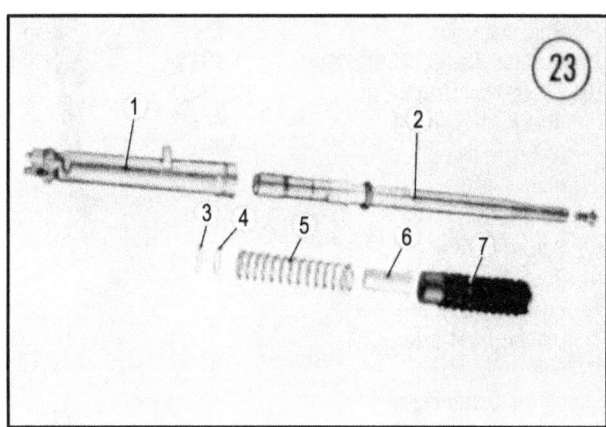

① Fork bottom case
② Fork pipe
③ 47 mm internal circlip
④ Spring seat
⑤ Front cushion spring
⑥ Spring guide
⑦ Front fork boot

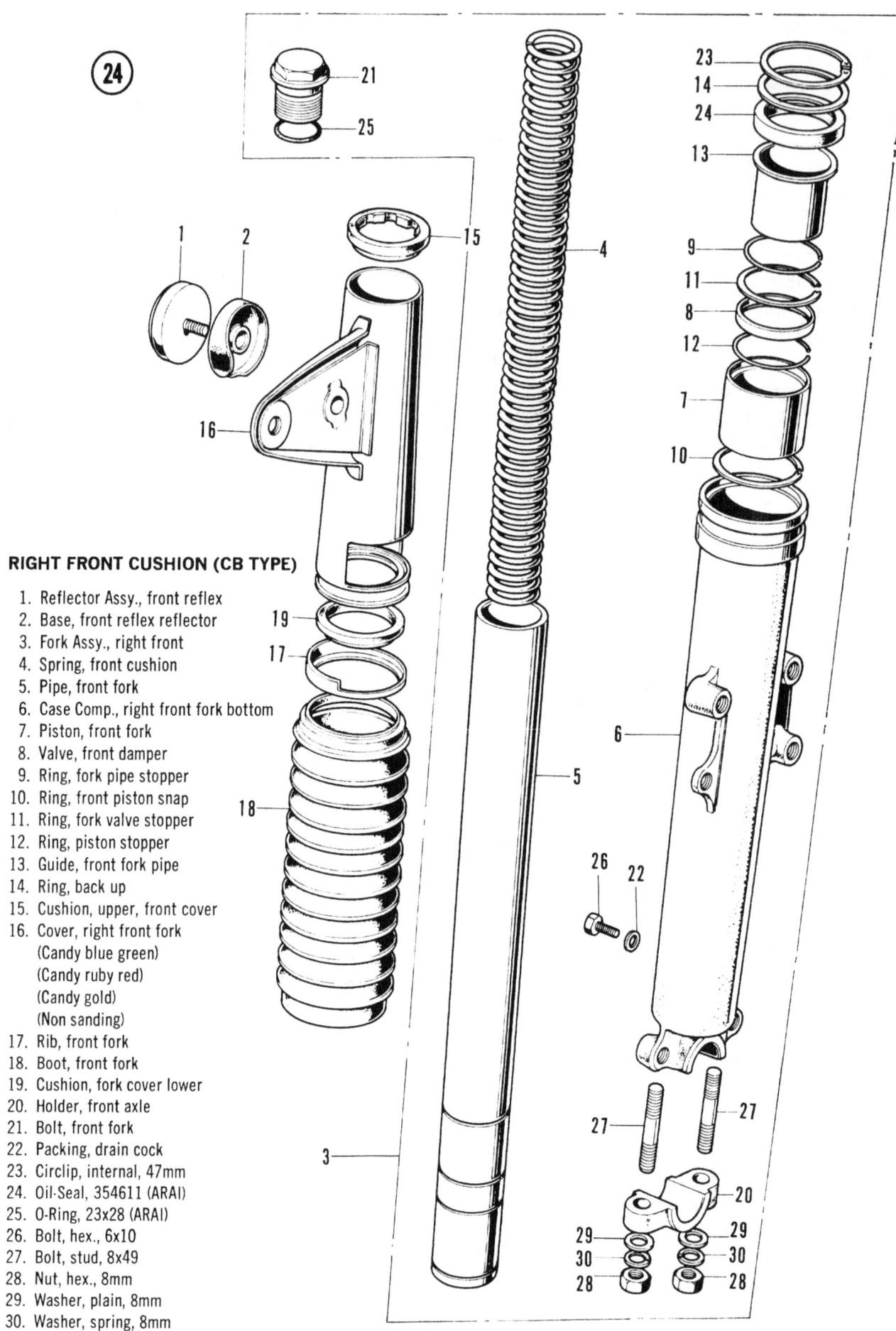

RIGHT FRONT CUSHION (CB TYPE)

1. Reflector Assy., front reflex
2. Base, front reflex reflector
3. Fork Assy., right front
4. Spring, front cushion
5. Pipe, front fork
6. Case Comp., right front fork bottom
7. Piston, front fork
8. Valve, front damper
9. Ring, fork pipe stopper
10. Ring, front piston snap
11. Ring, fork valve stopper
12. Ring, piston stopper
13. Guide, front fork pipe
14. Ring, back up
15. Cushion, upper, front cover
16. Cover, right front fork
    (Candy blue green)
    (Candy ruby red)
    (Candy gold)
    (Non sanding)
17. Rib, front fork
18. Boot, front fork
19. Cushion, fork cover lower
20. Holder, front axle
21. Bolt, front fork
22. Packing, drain cock
23. Circlip, internal, 47mm
24. Oil-Seal, 354611 (ARAI)
25. O-Ring, 23x28 (ARAI)
26. Bolt, hex., 6x10
27. Bolt, stud, 8x49
28. Nut, hex., 8mm
29. Washer, plain, 8mm
30. Washer, spring, 8mm

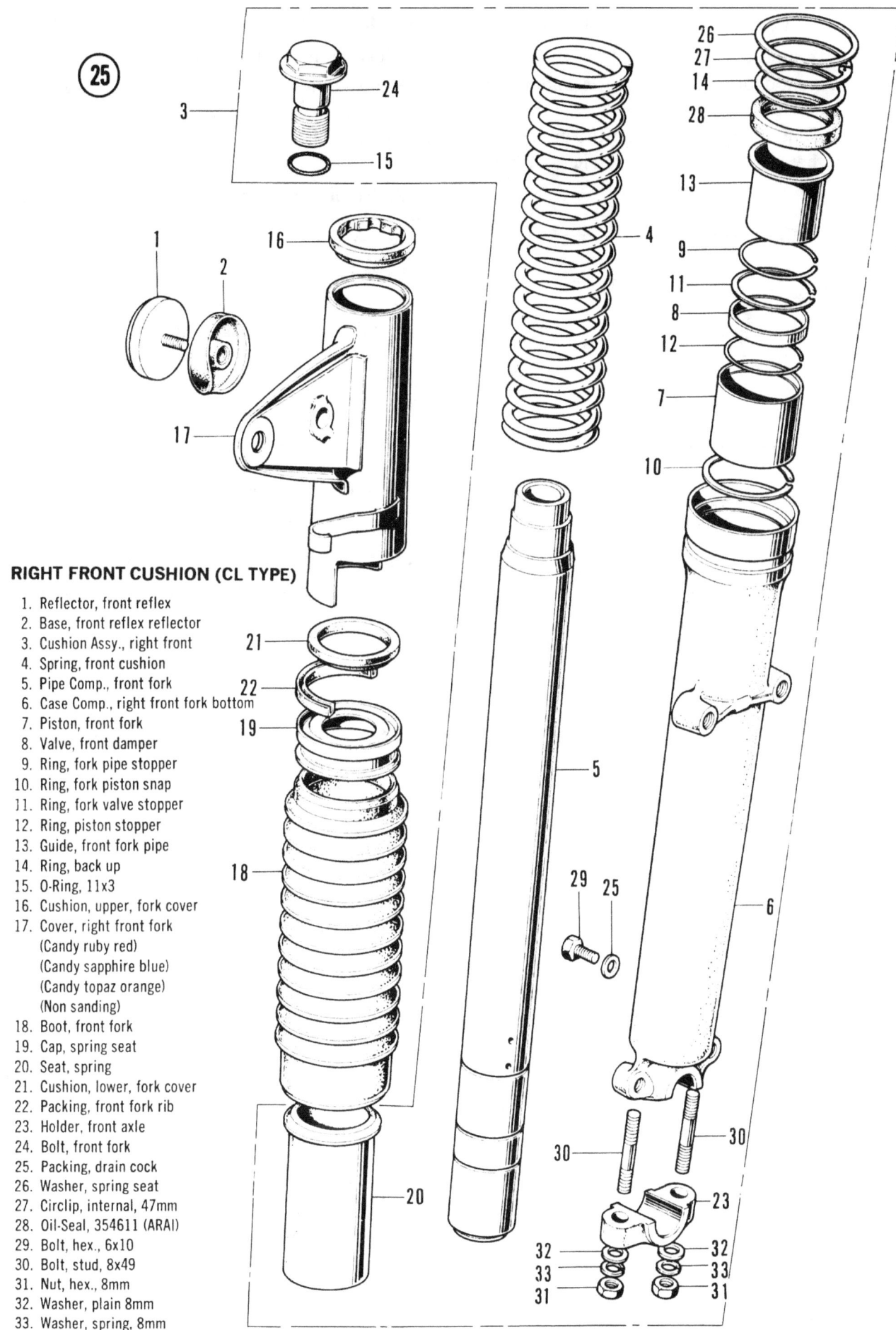

RIGHT FRONT CUSHION (CL TYPE)

1. Reflector, front reflex
2. Base, front reflex reflector
3. Cushion Assy., right front
4. Spring, front cushion
5. Pipe Comp., front fork
6. Case Comp., right front fork bottom
7. Piston, front fork
8. Valve, front damper
9. Ring, fork pipe stopper
10. Ring, fork piston snap
11. Ring, fork valve stopper
12. Ring, piston stopper
13. Guide, front fork pipe
14. Ring, back up
15. O-Ring, 11x3
16. Cushion, upper, fork cover
17. Cover, right front fork
    (Candy ruby red)
    (Candy sapphire blue)
    (Candy topaz orange)
    (Non sanding)
18. Boot, front fork
19. Cap, spring seat
20. Seat, spring
21. Cushion, lower, fork cover
22. Packing, front fork rib
23. Holder, front axle
24. Bolt, front fork
25. Packing, drain cock
26. Washer, spring seat
27. Circlip, internal, 47mm
28. Oil-Seal, 354611 (ARAI)
29. Bolt, hex., 6x10
30. Bolt, stud, 8x49
31. Nut, hex., 8mm
32. Washer, plain 8mm
33. Washer, spring, 8mm

Front Fork (One-piece spring) Inspection

1. Refer to the accompanying tables to determine condition of front fork parts and repair or replace as necessary. Inspect the bottom surface of the damper valve and the upper surface of the piston for any scratches. (**Figure 26**)

Figure 26

Item	Standard value	Serviceable limit
Spring load	178.5 mm/26.1~28.9 kg (7.03 in/57.5~63.7 lb)	—
Free length	211.9 mm (8.35 in)	Replace if under 205 mm (8.06 in)
Tilt	Within 1.5°	—

Front fork piston

Item	Standard value	Serviceable limit
Outside diameter	39.425~39.45 mm (1.552~1.553 in)	Replace when less than 39.4 mm (1.551 in)
Inside diameter	Within 0.008 mm (0.0003 in)	Replace when more than 0.015 mm (0.0006 in)
Taper	Within 0.015 mm (0.0059 in)	Replace when more than 0.03 mm (0.0012 in)

Front fork pipe

Item	Standard value	Serviceable limit
Outside diameter	34.90~34.915 mm (1.551~1.552 in)	
Elliptic wear	0.015 mm (0.00059 in)	Replace when more than 0.03 mm (0.0012 in)
Deflection	Within 0.04 mm (0.0016 in)	Replace when more than 0.1 mm (0.0039 in)

Front fork pipe guide

Item	Standard value	Serviceable limit
Full length	35.0 mm (1.378 in)	
Inside diameter	35.0~35.039 mm (1.378~1.380 in)	
Outside diameter	39.466~39.539 mm (1.551~1.556 in)	

Front fork bottom case

Item	Standard value	Serviceable limit
Inside diameter	39.5~39.539 mm (1.555~1.557 in)	

Front Fork (One-piece spring) Reassembly

1. Clean all parts thoroughly.

2. Reassemble the front fork pipe components in reverse order of disassembly, referring to **Figure 23**. Check the damper valve for smooth action.

3. Assemble the bottom pipe and the fork pipe using special tools Nos. 07054-29201 and 07057-29201 (oil seal driving guide and oil seal driving weight) to avoid damaging the oil seal.

4. Install the fork tubes into the triple clamps and tighten the pinch bolts on the bottom clamp. Fill the tubes with 285-295cc of 10W-30 motor oil and replace the fork bolts (caps).

5. Replace the front fender, wheel, headlight assembly and brake stop bolt. Check the forks for smooth action by locking the front brake and pushing down on the handlebars.

Front Fork (Disc Brake) Disassembly

1. Refer to **Figure 27** for details of front fork design and construction.

2. Remove the front wheel as outlined in the section on servicing front wheel and disc brake.

3. Remove the caliper setting bolts along with the adjuster nut shown in **Figure 28** and remove the caliper.

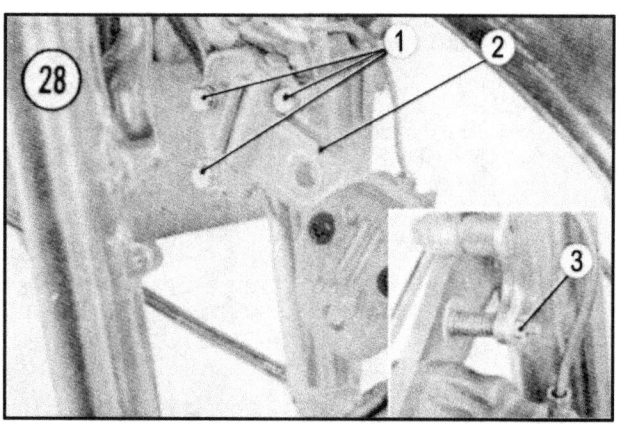

① Caliper setting bolts
② Caliper assembly　③ Adjuster nut

4. Loosen the fork tube mounting bolts on both the triple clamps and pull the fork tubes out in a downward direction.

5. Separate the front fork pipe from the bottom case by removing the circlip shown in **Figure 29**.

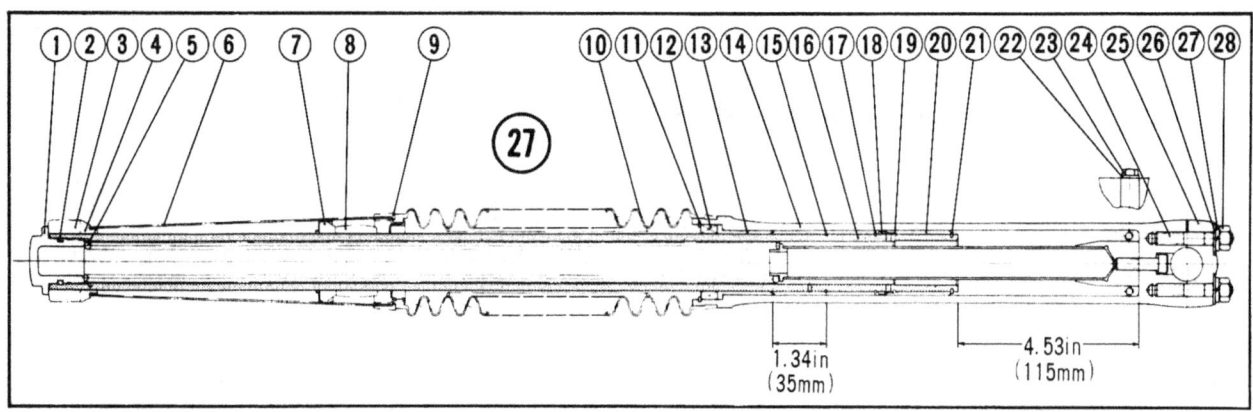

① Front fork bolt
② 23×2.8 "O" ring
③ Fork top bridge
④ Fork cover upper cushion
⑤ Front cushion spring
⑥ Front fork cover
⑦ Fork cover lower cushion
⑧ Steering stem
⑨ Front fork rib
⑩ Front fork boot
⑪ 47 mm circlip
⑫ 354611 oil seal
⑬ Front fork pipe guide
⑭ Front fork bottom case
⑮ Fork pipe stopper ring
⑯ Front fork pipe
⑰ Fork valve stopper ring
⑱ Front damper valve
⑲ Piston stopper ring
⑳ Front fork piston
㉑ Fork piston snap ring
㉒ Drain cock packing
㉓ 6 mm hex bolt
㉔ 8 mm stud bolt
㉕ Front axle holder
㉖ 8 mm flat washer
㉗ 8 mm spring washer
㉘ 8 mm hex nut

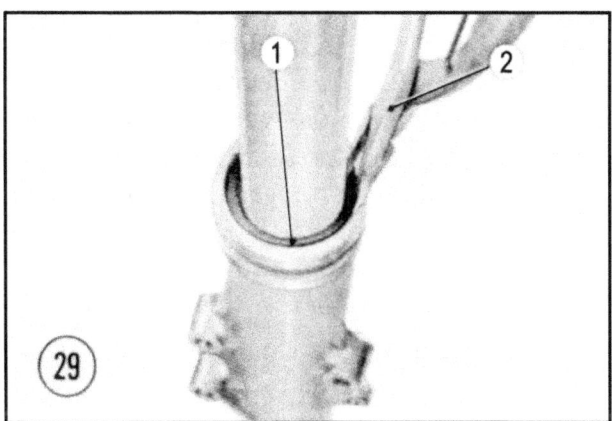

① Internal circlip ② Pliers

6. Refer to **Figure 30** and remove the fork piston snap ring, the front fork piston and the front fork damper valve from the front fork pipe.

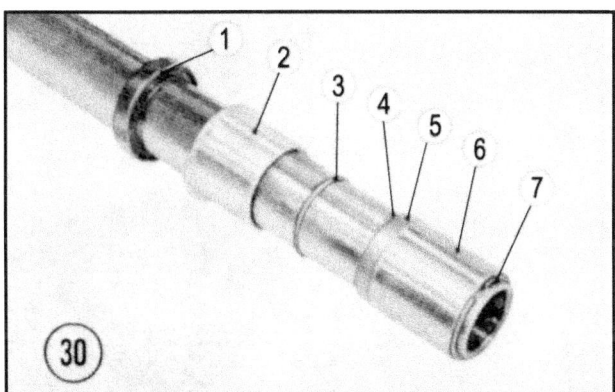

① 354611 oil seal   ⑤ Front damper valve
② Front fork pipe guide ⑥ Front fork piston
③ Fork pipe stopper ring ⑦ Fork piston snap ring
④ Fork valve stopper ring

Front Fork (Disc Brake) Inspection

1. Use a micrometer as shown in **Figure 31** to measure the front fork piston diameter. If it is less than 1.551" (39.40mm), it should be replaced.

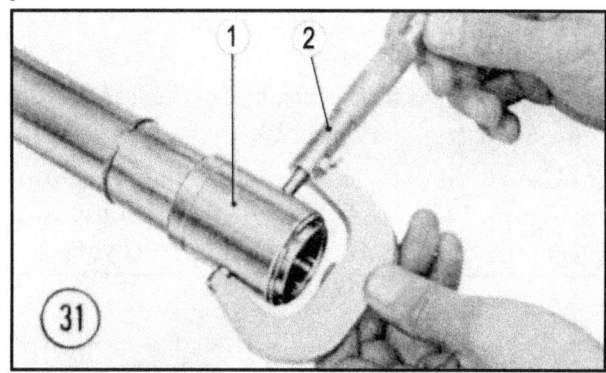

① Front fork piston
② Micrometer

2. Use a cylinder gauge or inside micrometer as shown in **Figure 32** to measure the fork bottom case inner diameter. If it is more than 1.562" (39.68mm) it should be replaced.

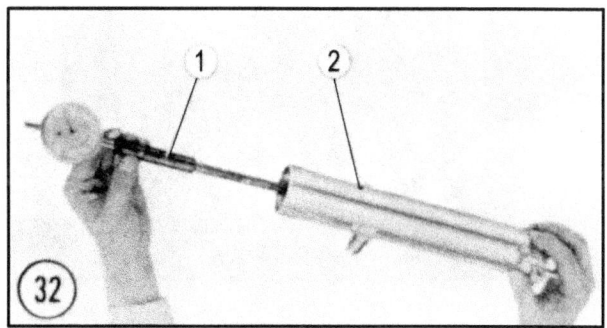

① Cylinder gauge ② Bottom case

Front Fork (Disc Brake) Reassembly

1. Clean all parts thoroughly.

2. Assemble the pipe guide, stopper rings, damper valve, piston and snap ring on the front fork pipe. Refer to **Figure 30.**

3. Assemble the front fork pipe and bottom case and install the oil seal using special tools Nos. 07054-30001 and 07057-29201 (oil seal driving guide and oil seal driving weight). Avoid damaging the oil seal during installation. See **Figure 33.**

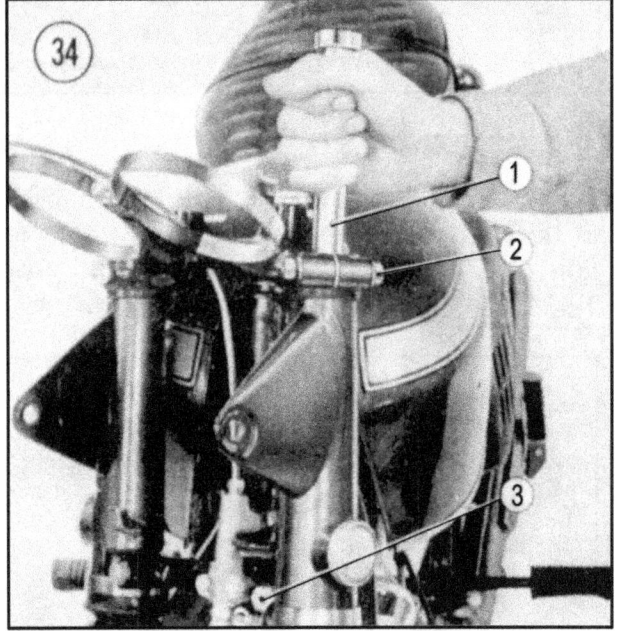

① Oil seal driving weight
② Oil seal driving guide
③ Oil seal

4. Install the internal circlip at the top of the bottom case. See **Figure 29.**

5. Use a front fork assembling bar as shown in **Figure 34** if possible to fit the fork tubes in place. Install the fork tube upper covers between the upper and lower cushion rubbers and push the fork tubes in place. Temporarily tighten the lower pinch bolts.

6. Fill the fork tubes with 7.0-7.3 oz. (220-230cc) of good quality 10W-30 motor oil and replace the fork bolts (caps).

7. Tighten the fork tube pinch bolts shown in **Figure 34.**

8. Refer to the section on the front disc brake to adjust the front brake caliper.

Steering Stem Disassembly

1. Remove the handlebars, front wheel, front fork tubes, the top triple clamp, and the fork tube covers.

2. On models with the disc brake, remove the master cylinder body and disconnect the clutch cable from the clutch lever. Remove the switch assembly from the right handlebar and disconnect the throttle cable. Detach the headlight case and disconnect the wiring. Remove the handlebars. Remove the speedometer and tachometer from the top bridge. Loosen the stem nut, the fork top bolts (caps), the three pinch bolts and remove the top bridge.

3. Remove the steering stem top thread as shown in **Figure 35** and pull the stem out of the head pipe taking care not to lose any of the 37 steel ball bearings.

Steering Stem Inspection

1. Inspect the ball bearings, cone and ball races, steering head dust seal and top end of the steering stem for wear or damage.

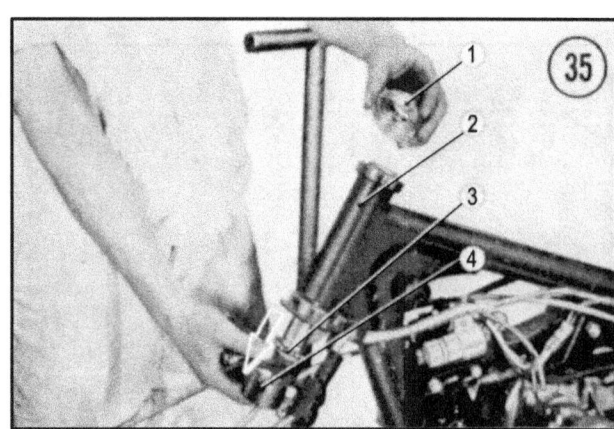

① Front fork assembling bar
② Front fork pipe setting bolt (8 mm)
③ Front fork pipe setting bolt (10 mm)

① Steering head top thread
② Head pipe
③ # 8 Steel balls
④ Steering stem

Steering Stem Reassembly

1. Replace the steering lock on the steering stem.

2. Use grease to keep the ball bearings in place in their races (18 in the upper and 19 in the lower) and insert the steering stem into the head pipe.

3. Replace the steering head top thread and adjust very carefully so that while there is no horizontal or vertical play, the steering assembly will still turn to the locks under its own weight after an initial assist. See **Figures 36 and 37.**

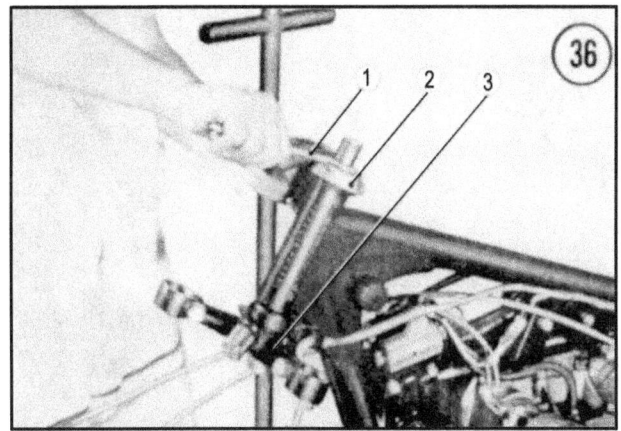

① 48mm pin spanner
② Steering head top thread
③ Steering stem

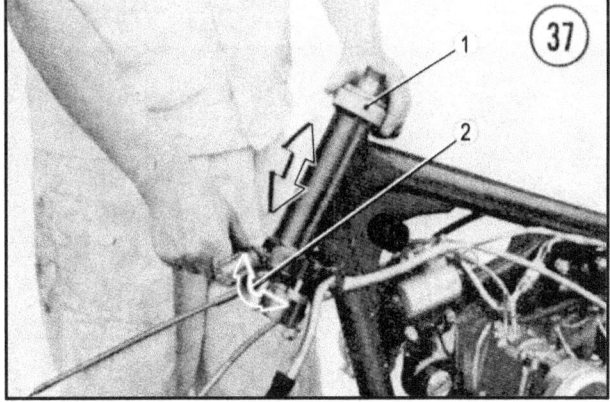

① Steering head top thread
② Steering stem

4. Replace components previously removed.

5. On models with the disc brake, route cables, wire harness and brake hose as shown in **Figure 38**. The throttle cable **must not** be routed through brake and clutch cable guide between handlebar mounting bolts, otherwise it may be pulled when the motorcycle is steered to one side, preventing carburetor throttle valves from closing.

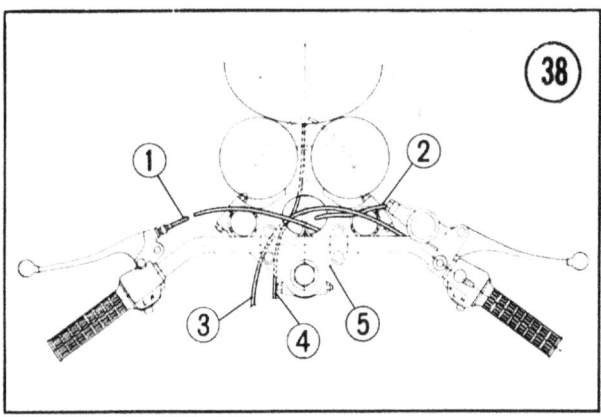

① Clutch cable   ④ Wire harness
② Front brake hose   ⑤ Fork top bridge
③ Throttle cable

Fuel Tank Removal

1. Unlatch the seat and swing up out of the way. Shut off the gasoline petcock and remove the fuel line.

2. If a fuel level tube is fitted, detach it and plug up any openings to prevent gas from draining. Detach the tank at its rear fitting and pull it to the rear and up to remove. The tank side cover can be removed by removing the emblem and the side cover mounting bolt and sliding the cover toward the front.

3. Remove the fuel petcocks by loosening the joint nut shown in **Figure 39**.

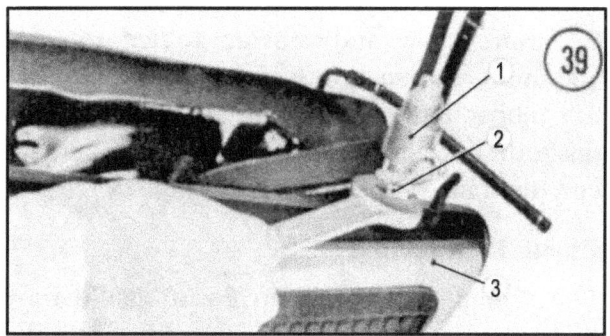

① Fuel cock assembly
② Joint nut
③ Fuel tank

Fuel Tank Inspection

1. Inspect the fuel tank for damage or leaks. An underwater pressure test may be used if low pressure only is applied.

2. Inspect the filler cap vent for clogging, the rubber cushions for wear or deterioration, the valve cock O ring and filler cap gasket for damage and repair or replace as necessary.

3. Inspect the fuel line for kinks or aging.

Fuel Tank Reassembly

1. Refer to **Figure 40** for details of fuel cock reassembly and replace in the tank.

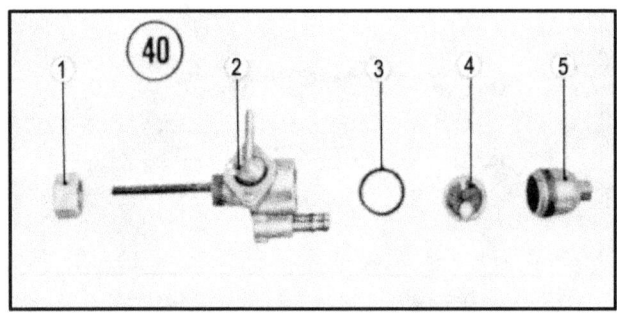

① Joint nut
② Fuel cock body
③ Cock packing
④ Screen
⑤ Fuel strainer cup

2. Install the side covers making sure a proper length bolt is used as shown in **Figure 41.** Too long a bolt will puncture the tank.

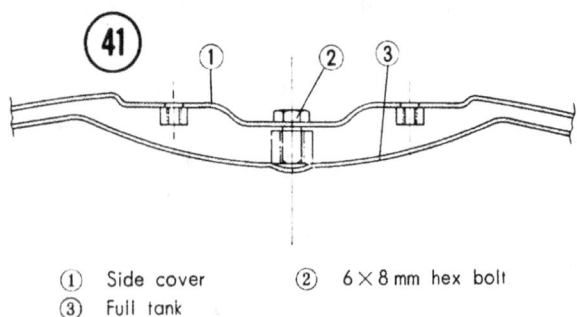

① Side cover
② 6 × 8 mm hex bolt
③ Full tank

3. Ensure cables and leads are routed properly and are in no danger of being pinched. Replace the rubber cushions and install the tank. Replace the fuel lines and fuel level tube and secure the tank and seat.

Frame Disassembly

1. A complete frame strip down should only be necessary if alignment is incorrect as a result of collision damage, or if painting is contemplated. Refer to **Figures 42 and 43** for details of earlier and later model frames. **Figure 44** shows the frame with attaching nuts and bolts.

Frame Inspection

1. Inspect all joints for cracks.
2. Inspect the steering head pipe for damage or misalignment.
3. Check the two steering head ball races for wear or scratches.
4. Ball races are an easy driving fit in the steering head pipe should they need replacement.

Frame Reassembly

1. Refer to individual component sections in this manual for proper reassembly and adjustment.

Kick Stand Service

1. Refer to **Figure 45** for details of kick stand construction. Note that the brake pedal is mounted on the kick stand pivot pipe.
2. Inspect the main stand pivot pipe, the brake

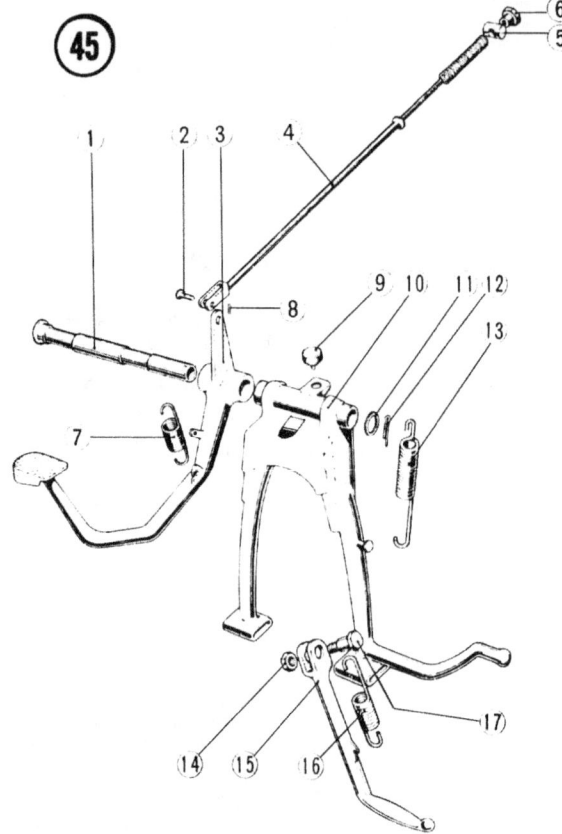

① Main stand pivot pipe
② Brake rod joint pin
③ Brake pedal
④ Rear brake rod
⑤ Rear brake arm joint
⑥ Rear brake adjusting nut
⑦ Rear brake spring
⑧ 1.6 mm split pin
⑨ Main stand stopper rubber (For CL 450)
⑩ Main stand
⑪ 19 mm washer
⑫ 2.5 mm split pin
⑬ Main stand spring
⑭ 10 mm hex nut
⑮ Side stand bar
⑯ Side stand spring
⑰ Side stand pivot screw

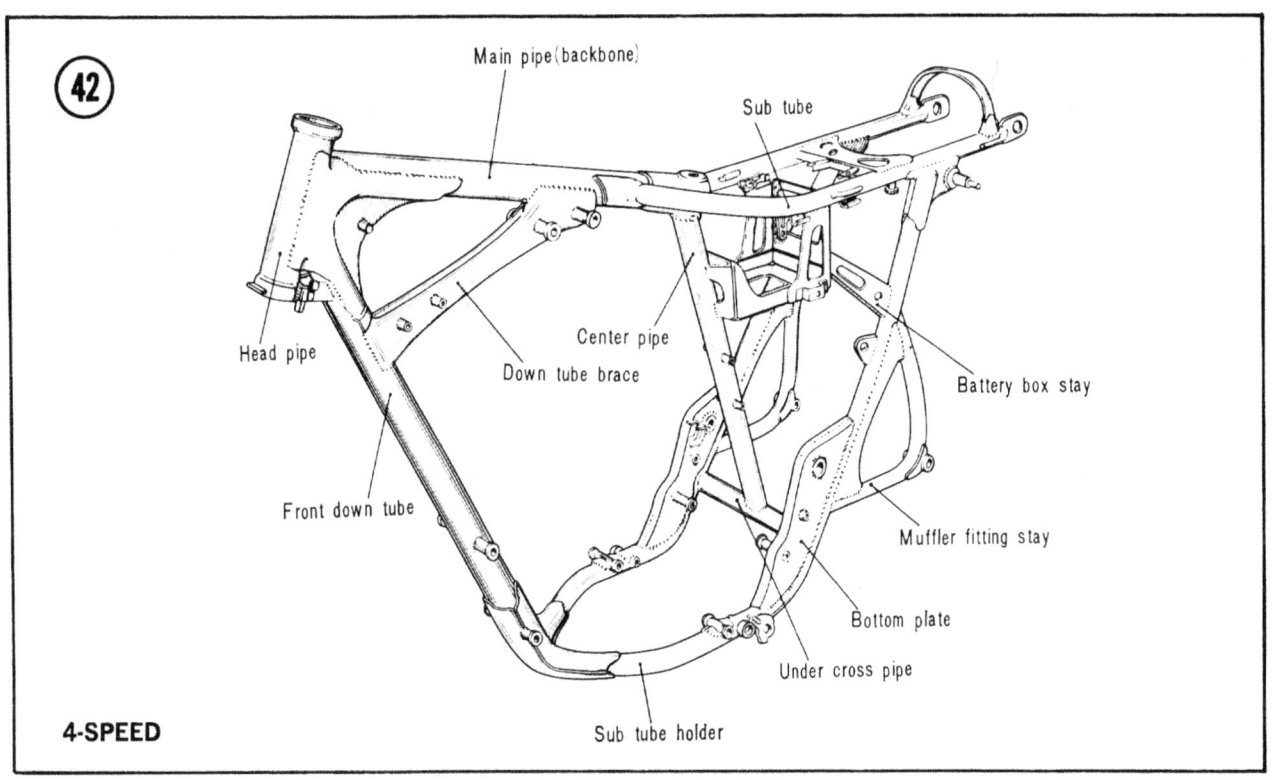

4-SPEED

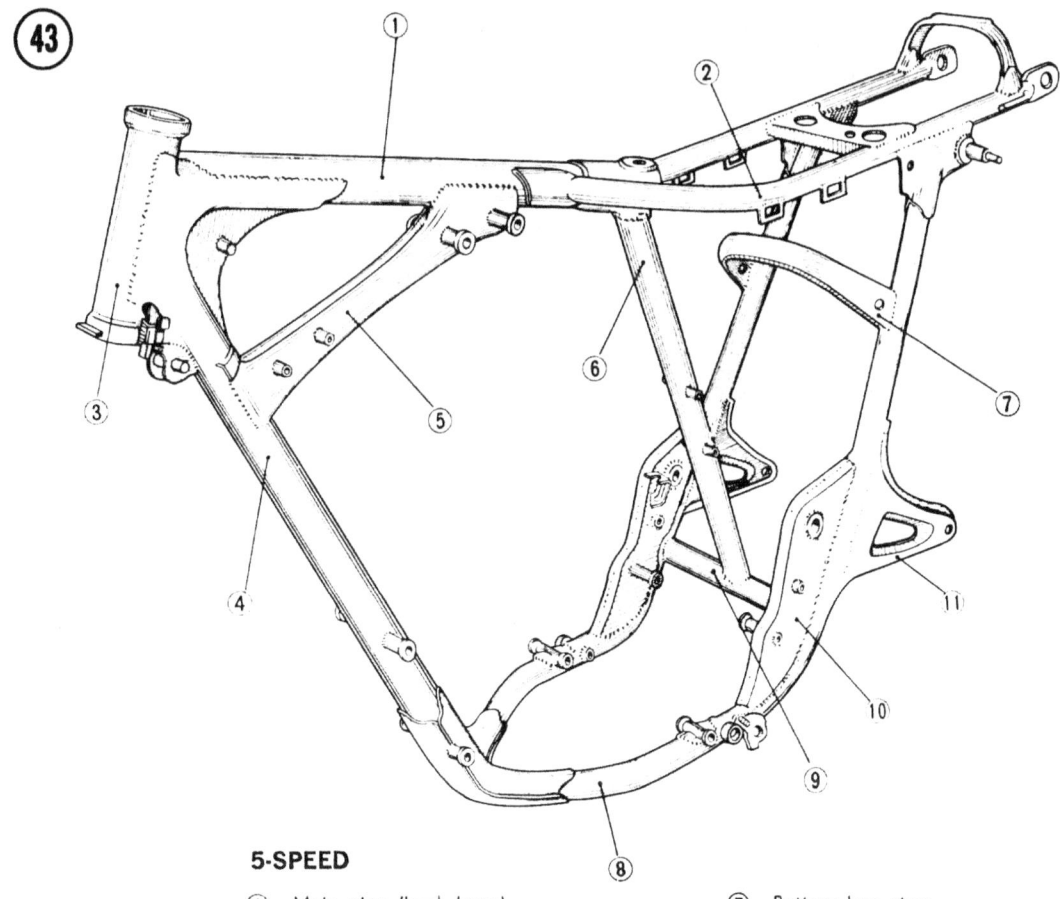

5-SPEED

① Main pipe (back bone)
② Sub tube
③ Head pipe
④ Front down tube
⑤ Down tube brace
⑥ Center pipe
⑦ Battery box stay
⑧ Sub tube holder
⑨ Under cross pipe
⑩ Bottom plate
⑪ Muffler fitting stay

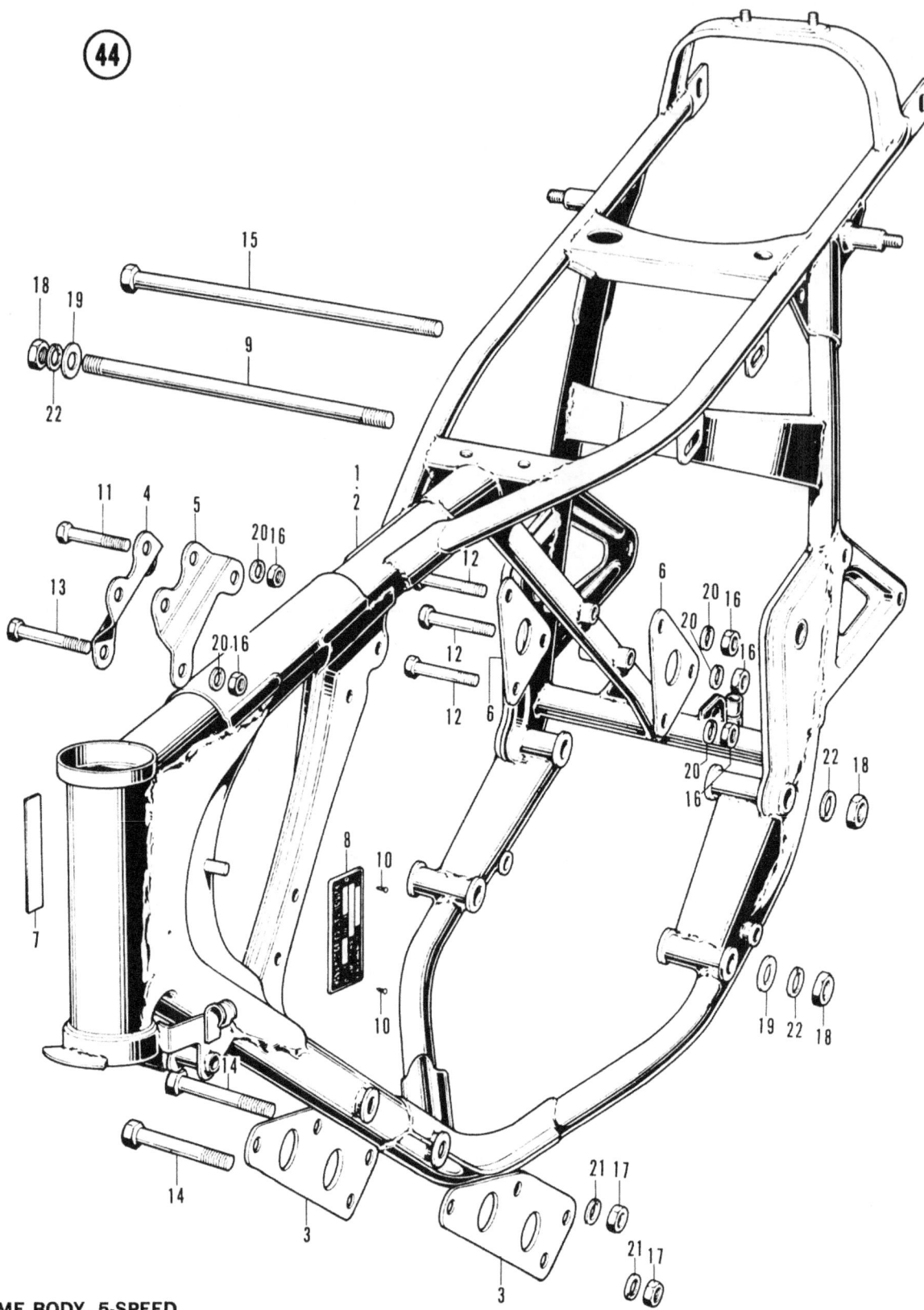

FRAME BODY, 5-SPEED

1. Body Comp., frame (Black) (Not used in Germany)
2. Body Comp., frame (Black) (Used in Germany)
3. Plate, front engine hanger (Black)
4. Plate, right upper engine hanger (Black)
5. Plate, left upper engine hanger (Black)
6. Plate, rear engine hanger (Black)
7. Plate, name (Not used in U.S.A.)
8. Plate, registered number (Used in Germany)
9. Bolt, engine hanger (12mm)
10. Screw, rivet, 1.5x5 (Used in Germany)
11. Bolt, hex., 8x57
12. Bolt, hex., 8x70
13. Bolt, hex., 8x87
14. Bolt, hex., 10x90
15. Bolt, hex., 12x275
16. Nut, hex., 8mm
17. Nut, hex., 10mm
18. Nut hex., 12mm
19. Washer, plain, 12mm
20. Washer, spring, 8mm
21. Washer, spring, 10mm
22. Washer, spring, 12mm

pedal pivot hole and the main stand mounting hole for wear. Use the accompanying tables to determine serviceable limits.

3. When reassembling, use a new cotter pin at the brake rod joint and be careful to avoid overtorqueing the bolt shown in **Figure 46.** Fill the inside of the pivot pipe with grease.

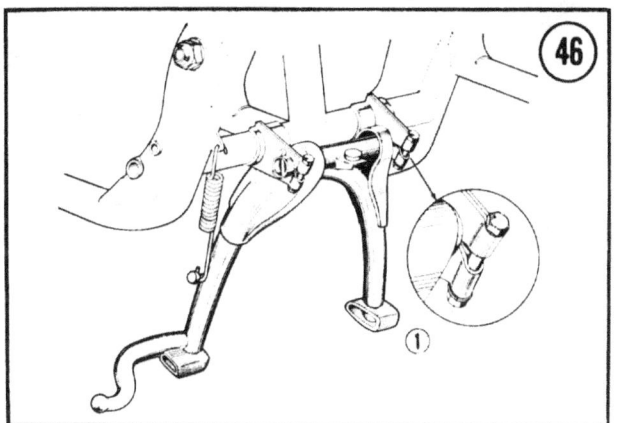

4. Adjust the stop light switch and rear brake for proper operation.

Muffler and Exhaust Pipe Service

(See **Figure 47**)

1. Removal of these items is straightforward. Reassembly will be facilitated if the exhaust pipe is fitted in place and the bolts shown in **Figure 48** are tightened loosely until the mufflers have been installed. When the mufflers are in place the exhaust pipe joint nuts should be tightened fully.

① Exhaust pipe joint nut
② Exhaust pipe

Air Cleaner Service

1. Air cleaner construction is similar on all models. Refer to **Figures 49 and 50,** for details.

2. To remove the filters, detach the air cleaner case, the air cleaner cover mounting bolt and the air cleaner cover. Remove the air

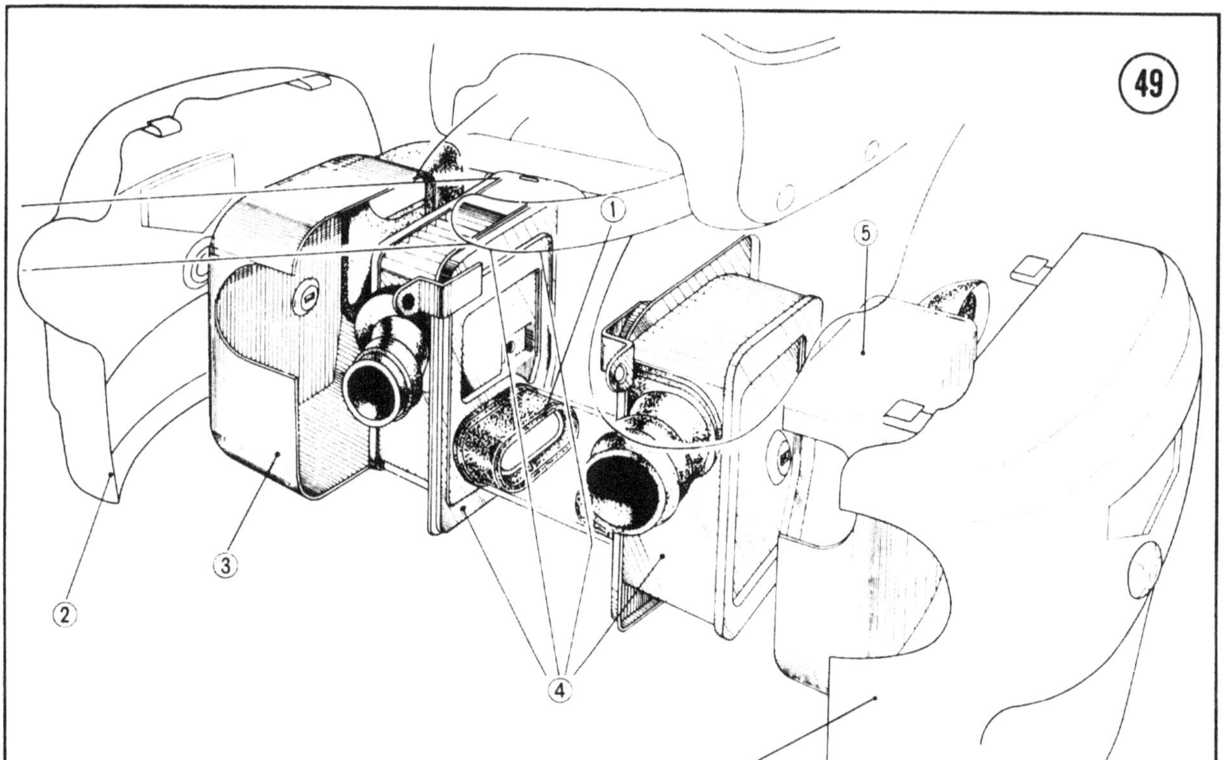

① Air cleaner joint tube
② Air cleaner case
③ R. air cleaner cover
④ Air cleaner element
⑤ L. air cleaner cover
⑥ L. air cleaner case

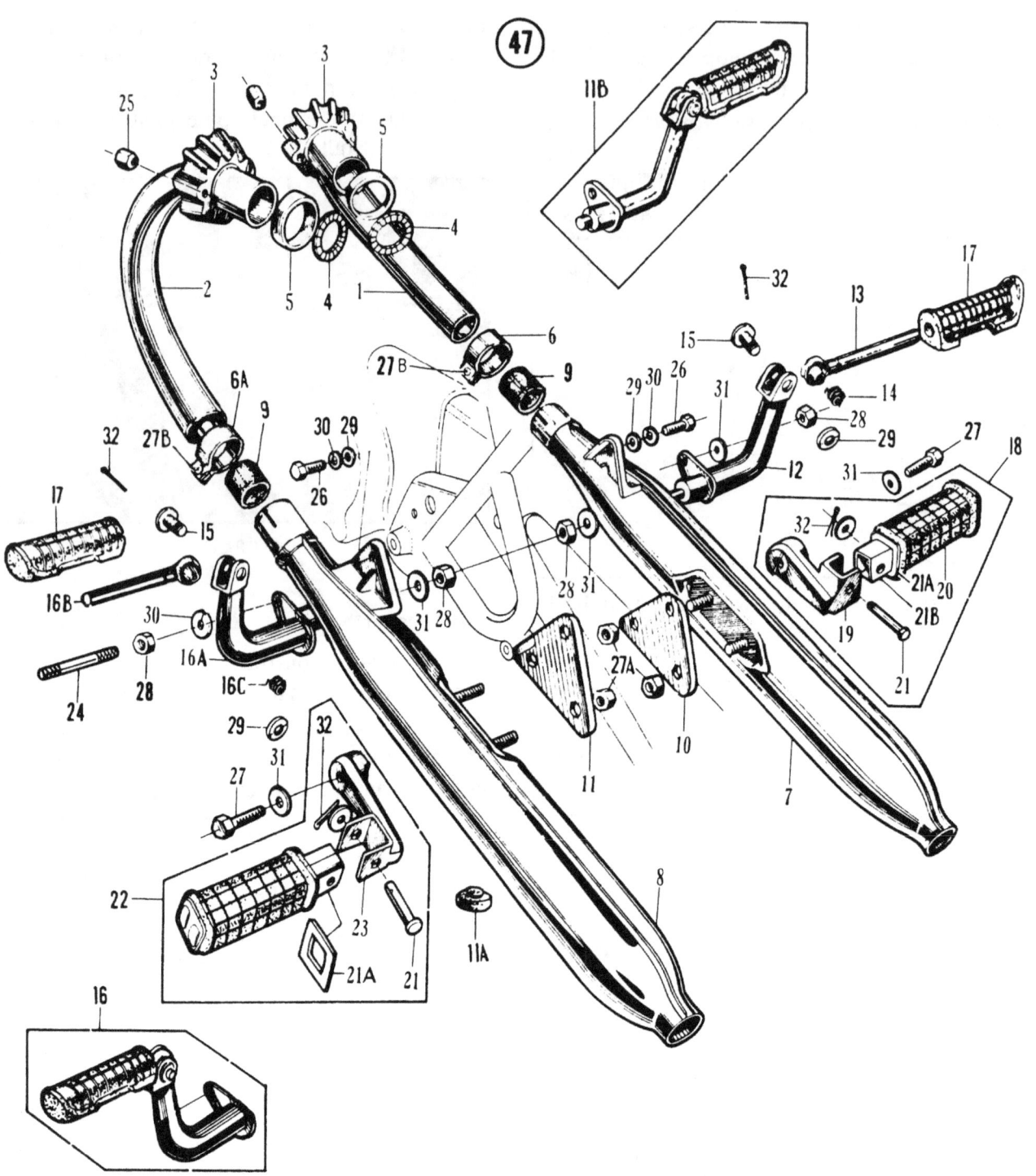

MUFFLER & STEP BAR, 4-SPEED

1. Pipe, exhaust, right
2. Pipe, exhaust, left
3. Joint, exhaust pipe
4. Gasket, exhaust pipe
5. Collar, exhaust pipe joint
6. Band, right muffler
6A. Band, left muffler
7. Muffler, right
8. Muffler, left
9. Packing, muffler
10. Bracket, right muffler
11. Bracket, left muffler
11A. Rubber, side stand stopper
11B. Bar assy., right step
12. Bar, right step
13. Arm, right step
14. Spring, right step return
15. Pin, step bar joint
16. Bar assy., left step
16A. Bar, left step
16B. Arm, left step
16C. Spring, left step return
17. Rubber, step
18. Step assy., right pillion
19. Arm, right pillion step
20. Rubber, pillion step
21. Pin, pillion step
21A. Washer, pillion step
21B. Bar, pillion step
22. Step assy., left pillion
23. Arm, left pillion step
    Arm, left pillion step
24. Bolt, stud, 10x310
25. Nut, exhaust pipe joint
26. Bolt, hex., 8x18mm
27. Bolt, hex., 10x60
27A. Nut, hex., 8mm
27B. Screw, cross, 6x14
28. Nut, hex., 10mm
29. Washer, flat, 8mm
30. Washer, spring, 8mm
31. Washer, spring, 10mm
32. Pin, cotter, 1.6x15

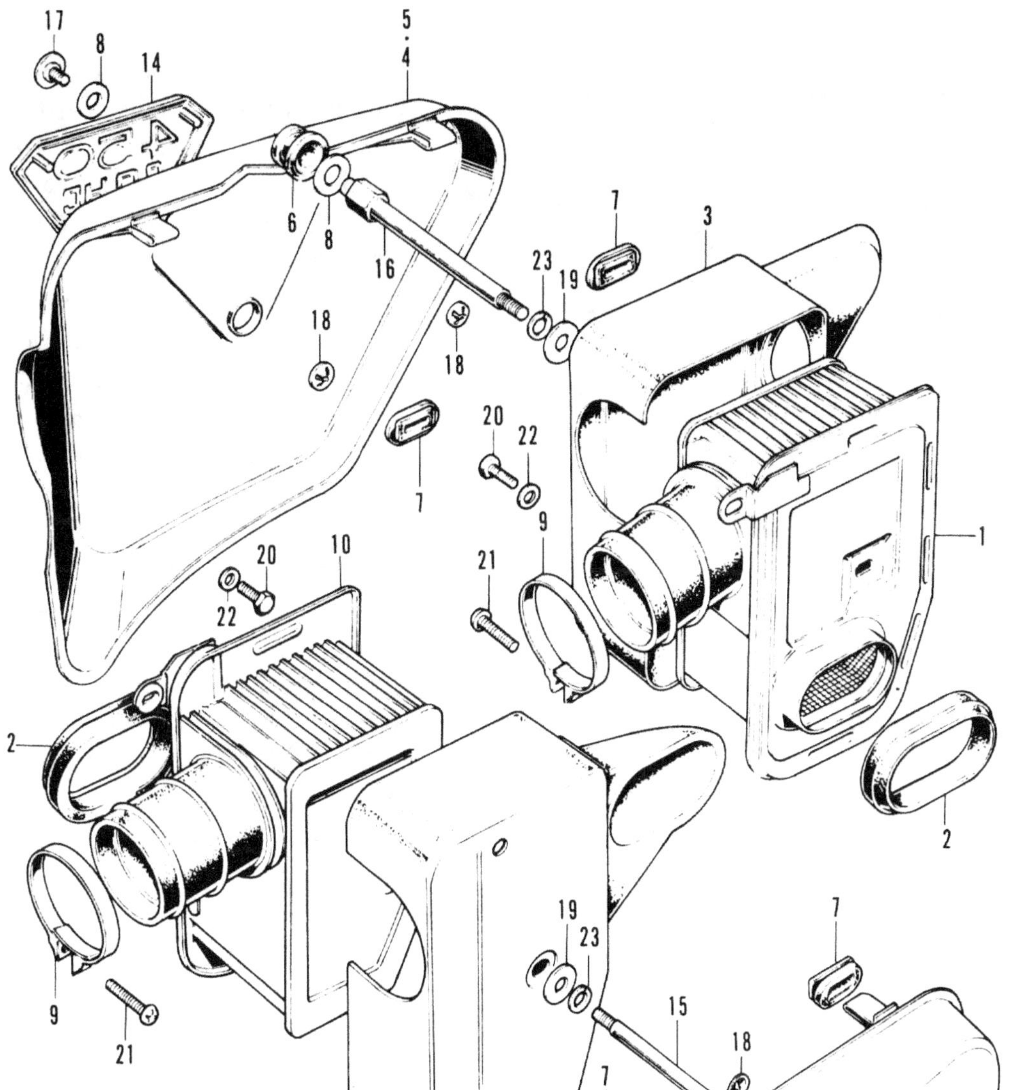

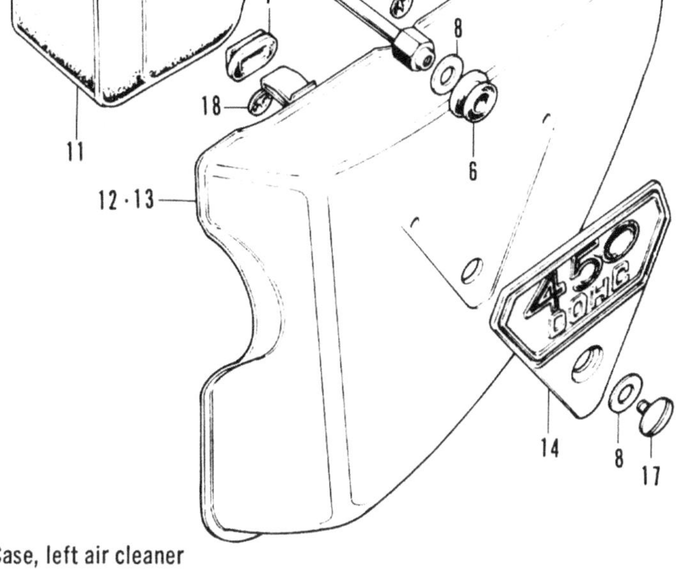

AIR CLEANER & CASE, 5-SPEED

1. Element, right air cleaner
2. Tube, air cleaner joint
3. Cover, right air cleaner
4. Case, right air cleaner
   (Candy blue green)
   (Candy ruby red)
   (Candy gold)
   (Non sanding)
5. Case, right air cleaner
   (Candy ruby red)
   (Candy Sapphire blue)
   (Candy topaz orange)
   (Non sanding)
6. Grommet B, air cleaner case
7. Grommet A, air cleaner
8. Washer, 19mm
9. Band, air cleaner connecting tube
10. Element, left air cleaner
11. Cover, left air cleaner
12. Case, left air cleaner
    (Candy blue green)
    (Candy gold)
    (Non sanding)
13. Case, left air cleaner
    (Candy ruby red)
    (Candy sapphire blue)
    (Candy topaz orange)
    (Non sanding)
14. Emblem, air cleaner case
15. Bolt, air cleaner
16. Bolt, right air cleaner
17. Bolt, air cleaner setting
18. Nut, push, 3mm
19. Washer, air cleaner setting
20. Bolt, hex., 6x10
21. Screw, pan, 5x16
22. Washer, plain, 6mm
23. Washer, spring, 6mm

cleaner connecting tube clamp and the air cleaner mounting bolt. Remove the tool box as shown in **Figure 51** by detaching the bolts on the rear engine mounting plate.

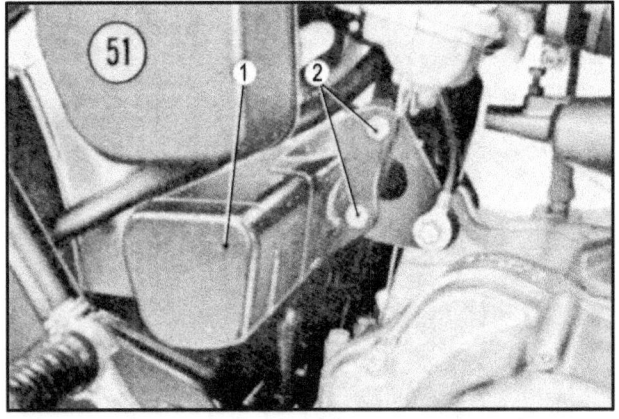

① Tool box ② 8mm hex bolt

3. Tap the air cleaner elements and blow them off with compressed air. Be sure they are not clogged with dust or foreign matter.

4. Replace the tool box and the air cleaners and check that the connecting tube between the cleaners is fastened properly so there are no air leaks.

Swinging Arm Disassembly

1. Removal of the swinging arm assembly is similar on all models, but minor differences do exist from the early CB to late model CB's and CL's. Pay attention to placement of washers and spacers during disassembly. Refer to **Figure 52** for details of the early models and to **Figure 53** for details of the later models.

2. Remove the rear wheel and rear shocks.

3. Take off the 14mm self-locking nut on the swinging arm pivot bolt and pull out the bolt.

4. Tap out the center collar and the pivot bushing.

Swinging Arm Inspection

1. Determine from **Figures 52 and 53** which type swinging arm the motorcycle is equipped with and use the following tables to check serviceable limits. (**Figure 54** is for the old style arm and **Figure 55** is for the new arm.)

2. Measure twist of the swinging arm as shown in **Figure 56** with the pivot bushing and center collar in place.

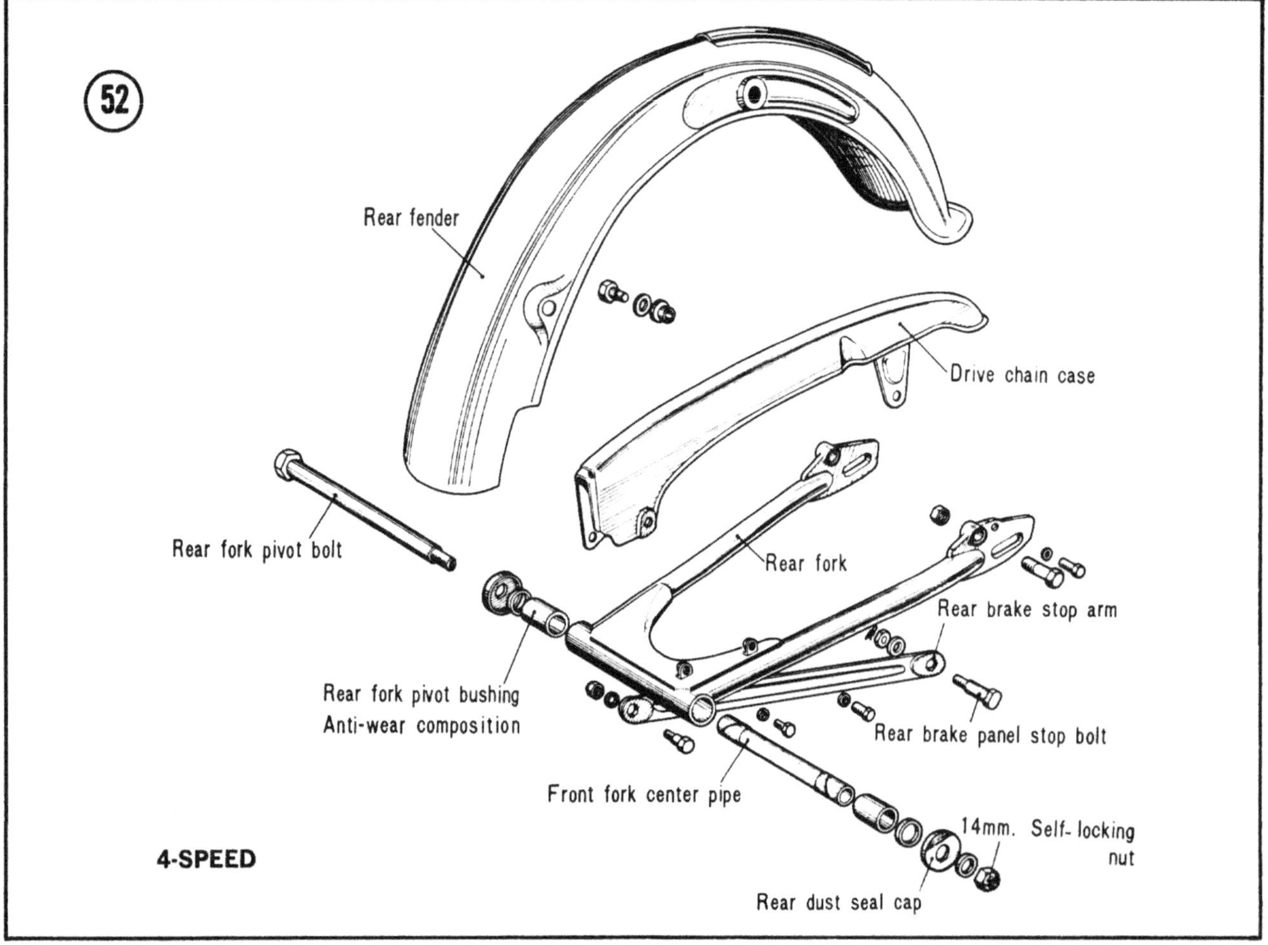

78

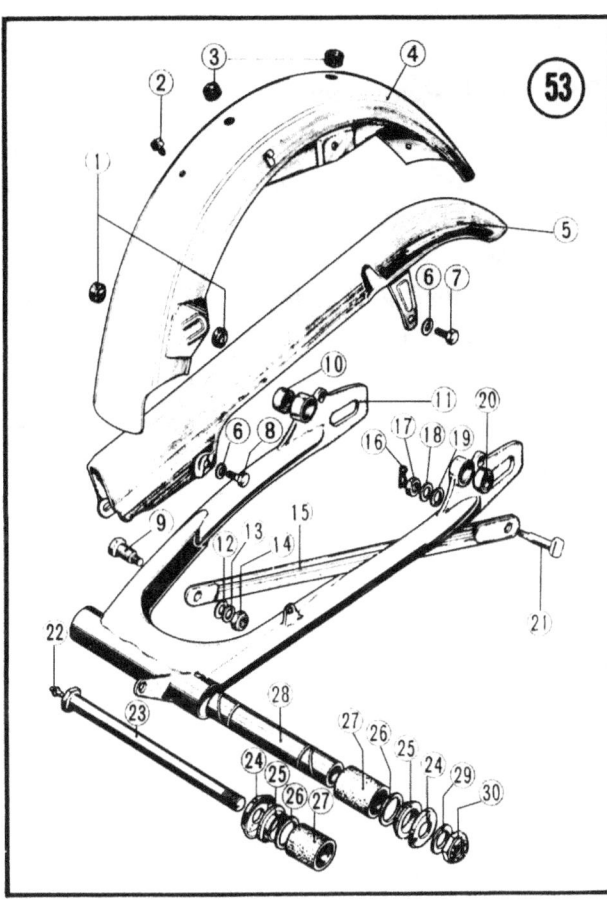

1. Measurement of rear fork center collar ⑤④

	Nominal value	Service limit
Full length	189.9 $^{+0}_{-0.3}$	Replace when less than 18.96
Inside diameter	14φ $^{+0.027}_{-0}$	Replace when more than 14.1
Outside diameter	21.5φ $^{-0.007}_{-0.028}$	Replace when less than 21.4

2. Inside diameter measurement of rear fork pivot bushing

	Nominal value	Service limit
Inside diameter	21.5φ $^{+0.033}_{-0}$ (After pressing in)	Replace when more than 21.6φ
Inside width	33 $^{-0.1}_{-0.2}$	

3. Measurement of rear fork pivot bolt.

	Nominal value	Service limit
Outside diameter	14φ $^{-0.032}_{-0.075}$	
Bending	0.01/ /100	0.02/ /100

① Front fuel tank cushion
② Wire cord grommet
③ Wire cord grommet
④ Rear fender
⑤ Drive chain case
⑥ 6mm flat washer
⑦ 6×16 hex bolt
⑧ 6×12 hex bolt
⑨ Rear brake stopper arm bolt
⑩ Rear cushion under rubber bushing
⑪ Rear fork
⑫ 10mm spring washer
⑬ Flat washer
⑭ 8mm self lock nut
⑮ Rear brake stopper arm
⑯ 8mm lock pin
⑰ 8mm hex nut
⑱ Rear fork thrust bushing
⑲ 10mm spring washer
⑳ Rear cushion under rubber bushing
㉑ Rear brake panel stopper bolt
㉒ Grease nipple
㉓ Rear fork pivot bolt
㉔ Rear fork dust-seal cap
㉕ Rear fork thrust bushing
㉖ Rear fork felt ring
㉗ Rear fork pivot bushing
㉘ Rear fork center collar
㉙ Rear fork pivot bolt washer
㉚ 14mm self lock nut

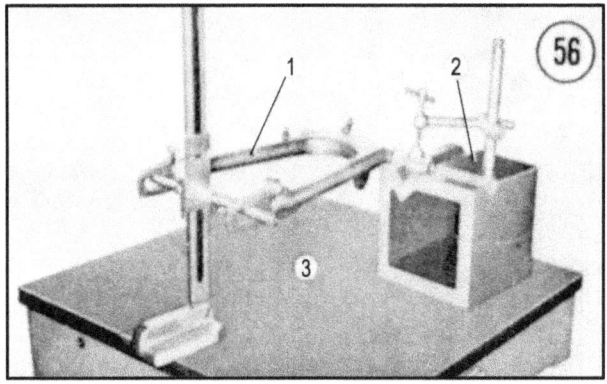

① Rear fork ② Square block ③ Surface plate

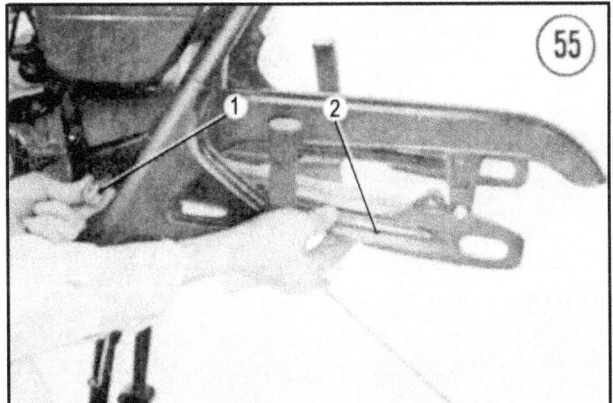

① Rear fork pivot bolt
② Rear fork

3. Inspect the rear brake stop arm for damage or bends and check the drive chain for wear.

Swinging Arm Reassembly

1. Refer to **Figures 52, 53** for details of swinging arm reassembly.

2. Drive in the pivot bushing and center collar. Soak the felt ring in oil and place the seal caps in position. Insert the pivot bolt in the side bracket and guide the swinging arm into

place. Secure with the 14mm self-locking nut.

3. Replace the wheel, shocks and adjust brake pedal play and chain tension.

Rear Shock Disassembly

1. Old and new type shocks are removed and disassembled in the same manner.

2. Remove the side hand hold shown in **Figure 57** and the upper and lower mounting bolts.

① 10mm cap nut
② 6mm bolt

3. Use a shock compressing tool as shown in **Figure 58** if possible. Compress the shock and remove the spring seat stop. The cover and spring may then be removed.

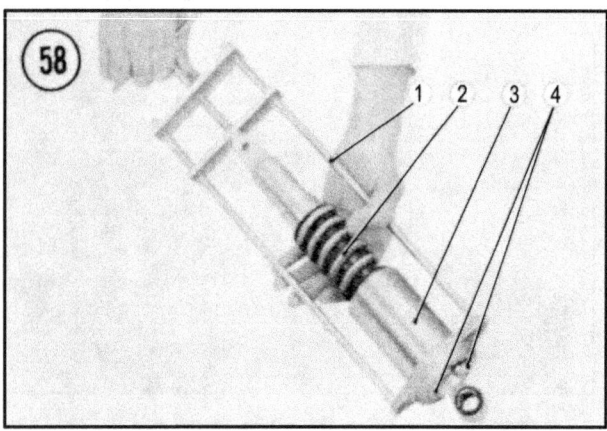

① Rear cushion disassembly tool
② Rear cushion spring
③ Rear cushion upper case
④ Rear cushion spring seat stopper

4. Measure spring length against a new spring to determine if replacement is necessary. Old type springs should have a free length of 199mm or more and new types should be 195mm or more.

5. Replace the dampening unit if leakage is found, as the units are not rebuildable. Check that the damper rod is not bent, and that the spring seat stop is in good condition.

Rear Shock Reassembly

1. Extend the shock to its full rebound position for reassembly and use the special tool to compress the shock so the stop may be inserted in place.

2. Check the shock for smooth action as shown in **Figure 59**.

3. Refer to **Figure 60** for mounting details.

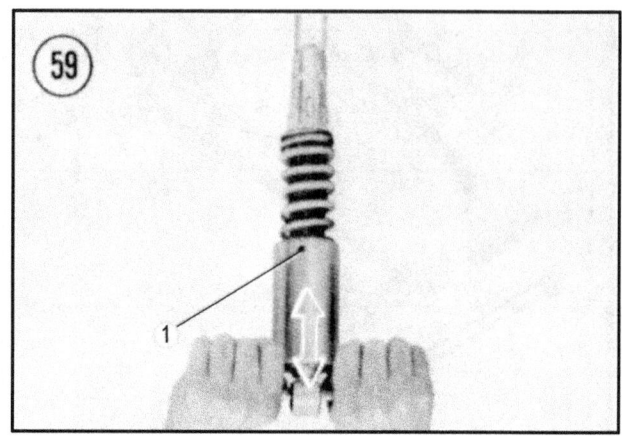

① Rear cushion assembly

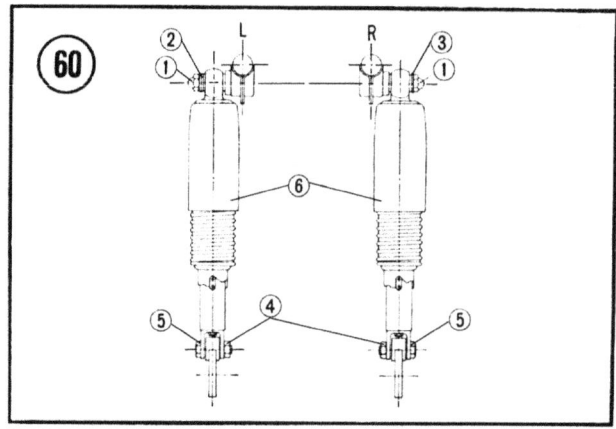

① 10mm cap nut   ④ 10mm thin nut
② Side grip   ⑤ 10×36 hex bolt
③ Special washer   ⑥ Rear cushion

Front Wheel Disassembly (Drum brake)

1. Support the motorcycle under the engine so that the front wheel is raised off the ground.

2. Refer to **Figures 61, 62, and 63** for details of front wheel construction.

3. Disconnect the brake cable and the brake torque link as shown in **Figure 64**. Disconnect the speedometer cable from the speedometer gear box.

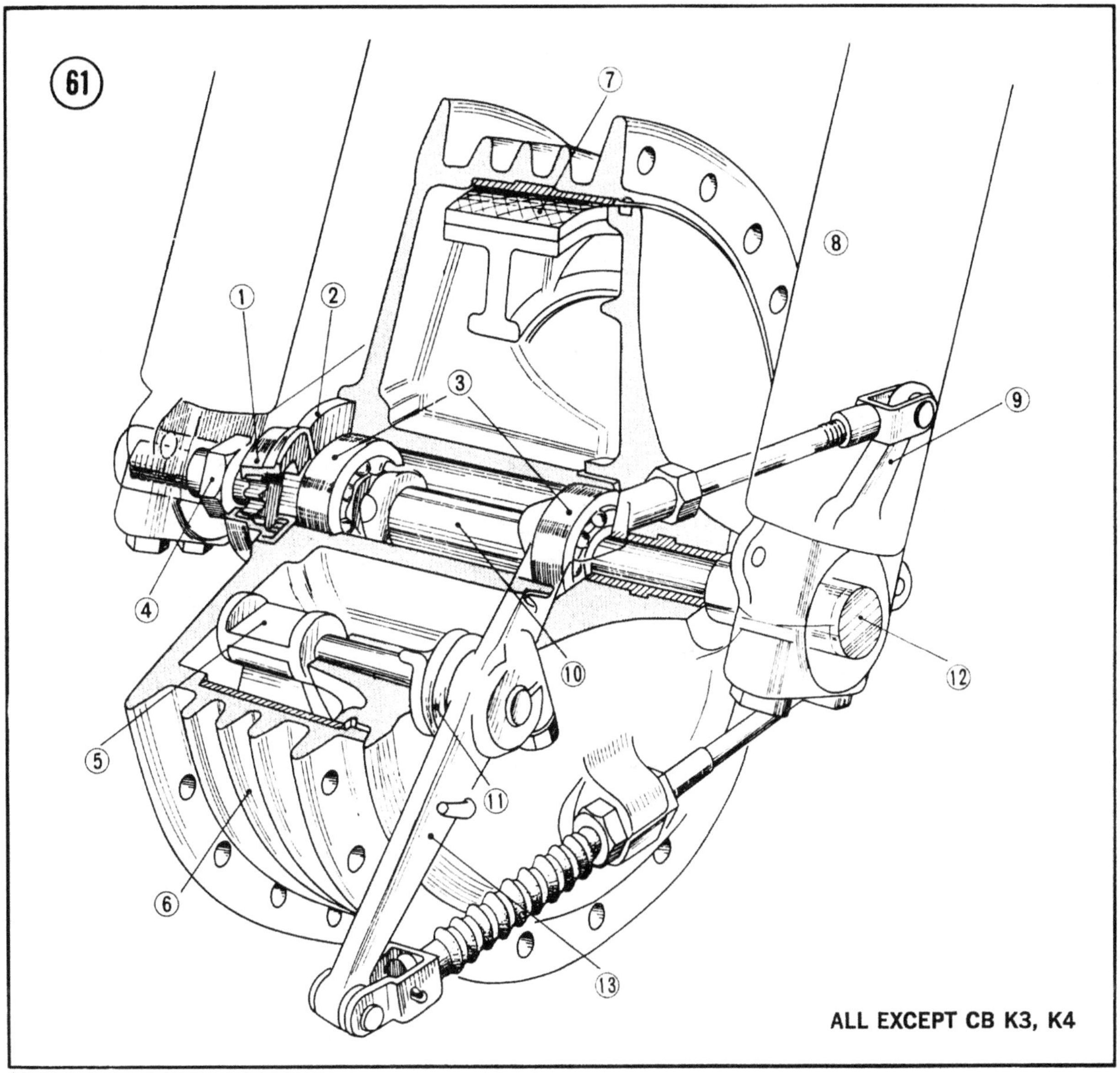

61

ALL EXCEPT CB K3, K4

① Speedometer gear box
② Front wheel bearing retainer
③ 6302 Z ball bearing
④ Front wheel axle nut
⑤ Front brake cam
⑥ Front wheel hub
⑦ Front brake shoe
⑧ Brake rod
⑨ Front brake arm B
⑩ Front axle spacing collar
⑪ Brake arm spring
⑫ Front wheel axle
⑬ Front brake arm

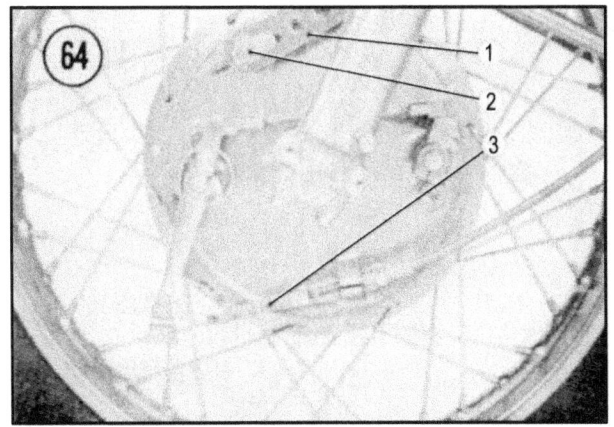

① Front brake torque link
② Front brake torque link bolt
③ Front brake cable

4. Take off the axle holder nuts on both sides to free the wheel.

5. Remove the axle nut and take out the axle. Pull the brake panel, complete with speedometer gear box, away from the hub.

6. Remove the bearing retainer as shown in **Figure 65.** The bearing and front axle spacer can then be removed. Remove the front brake arm and the actuating cam.

7. Remove the brake shoes as shown in **Figure 66.** Refer to **Figure 67** for details.

Front Wheel (Drum brake) Inspection

1. Use the accompanying tables to determine

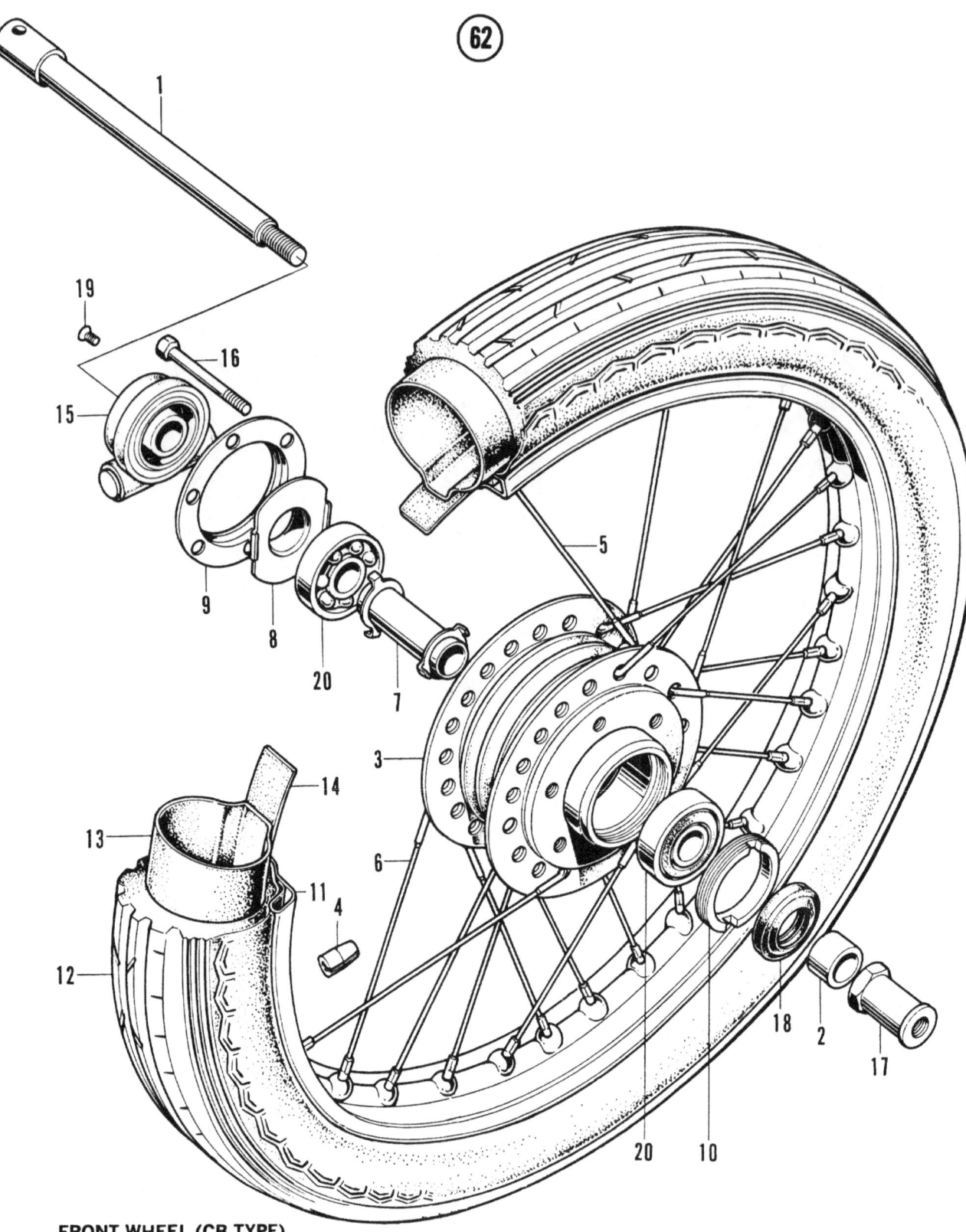

FRONT WHEEL (CB TYPE)

1. Axle, front wheel
2. Collar, front wheel
3. Hub Comp., front wheel
4. Balancer, wheel (20g)
   Balancer, wheel (15g)
   Balancer, wheel (10g)
   Balancer, wheel (5g)
5. Spoke A, front (DAIDO)
6. Spoke B, front (DAIDO)
7. Collar, front axle distance
8. Retainer, gear box
9. Cover, gear box retainer
10. Retainer, front wheel bearing
11. Rim, front wheel (DAIDO)
12. Tire, front wheel
    (Dunlop S 3.25-19" 4PR)
13. Tube, front wheel (3.25-19")
14. Flap, front tire (19")
15. Box Assy., speedometer gear
16. Bolt, 8x106
17. Nut, front wheel axle
18. Dust-Seal, 22368 (ARAI)
19. Screw, oval, 5x15
20. Bearing, ball, 6302Z

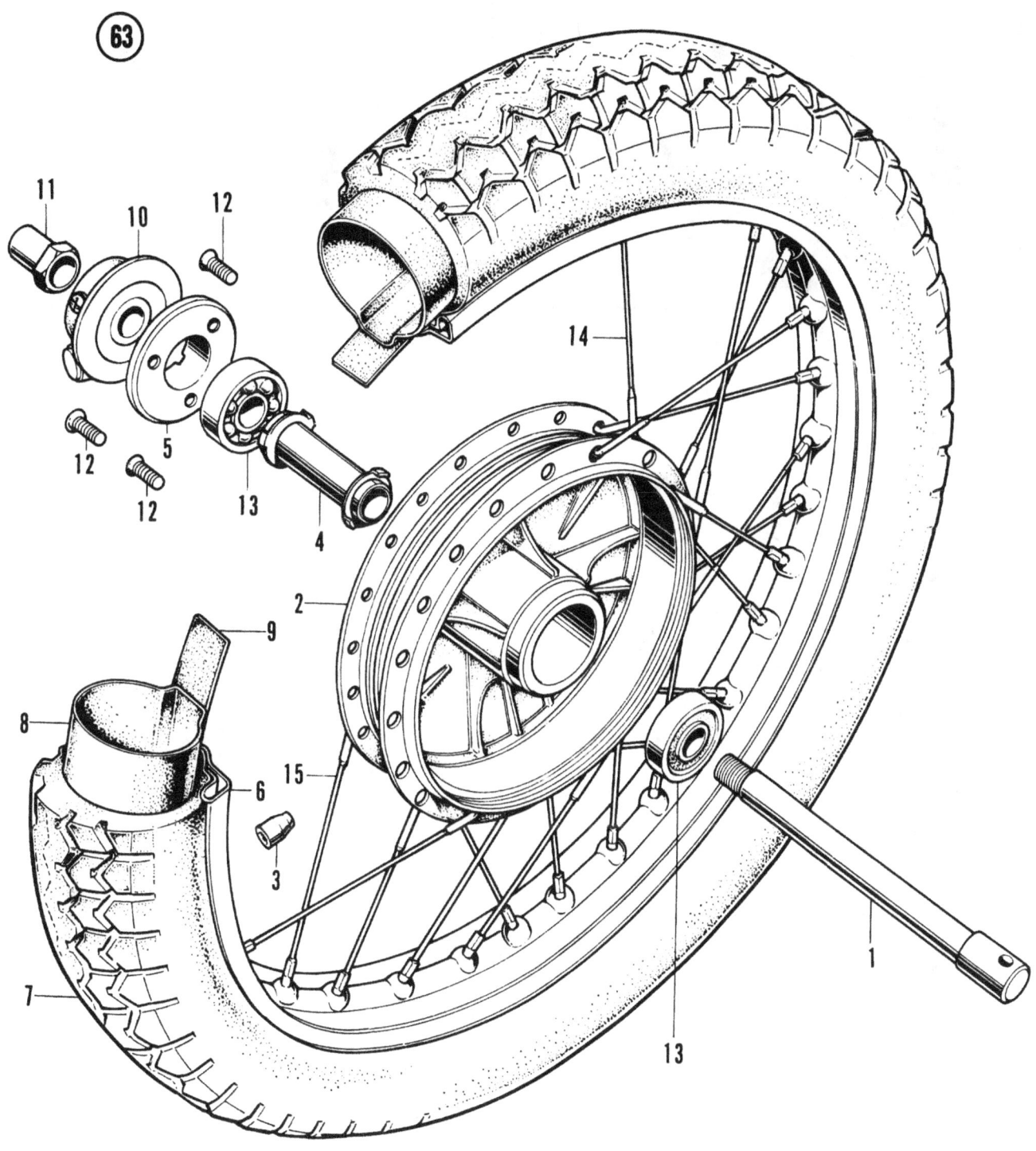

FRONT WHEEL (CL TYPE)

1. Axle, front wheel
2. Hub Comp., front wheel
3. Balancer, wheel (20g)
   Balancer, wheel (15g)
   Balancer, wheel (10g)
   Balancer, wheel (5g)
4. Collar, front axle distance
5. Retainer, front wheel bearing
6. Rim, front wheel (DAIDO)
7. Tire, front wheel
   (S. 3.25-19" 4PR. Dunlop)
8. Tube, wheel (3.25-19" Dunlop)
9. Flap, tire (19" Dunlop)
10. Box Assy., speedometer gear
11. Nut, front wheel axle
12. Screw, flat, 6x12
13. Bearing, ball, 6302Z
14. Spoke B, #9x155 (Inside)
15. Spoke B, #9x154.5 (Outside)

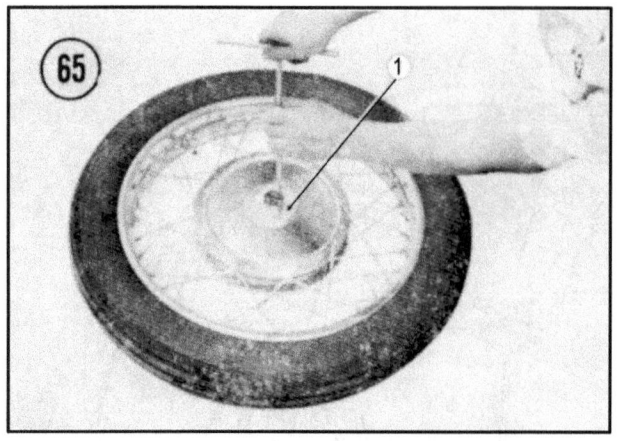

① Front wheel bearing retainer

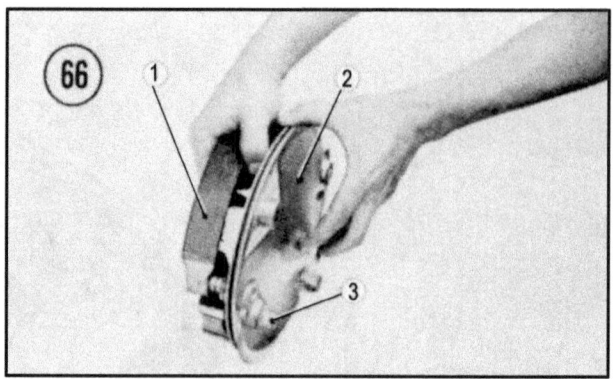

① Front brake shoe
② Front brake panel
③ Front brake cam

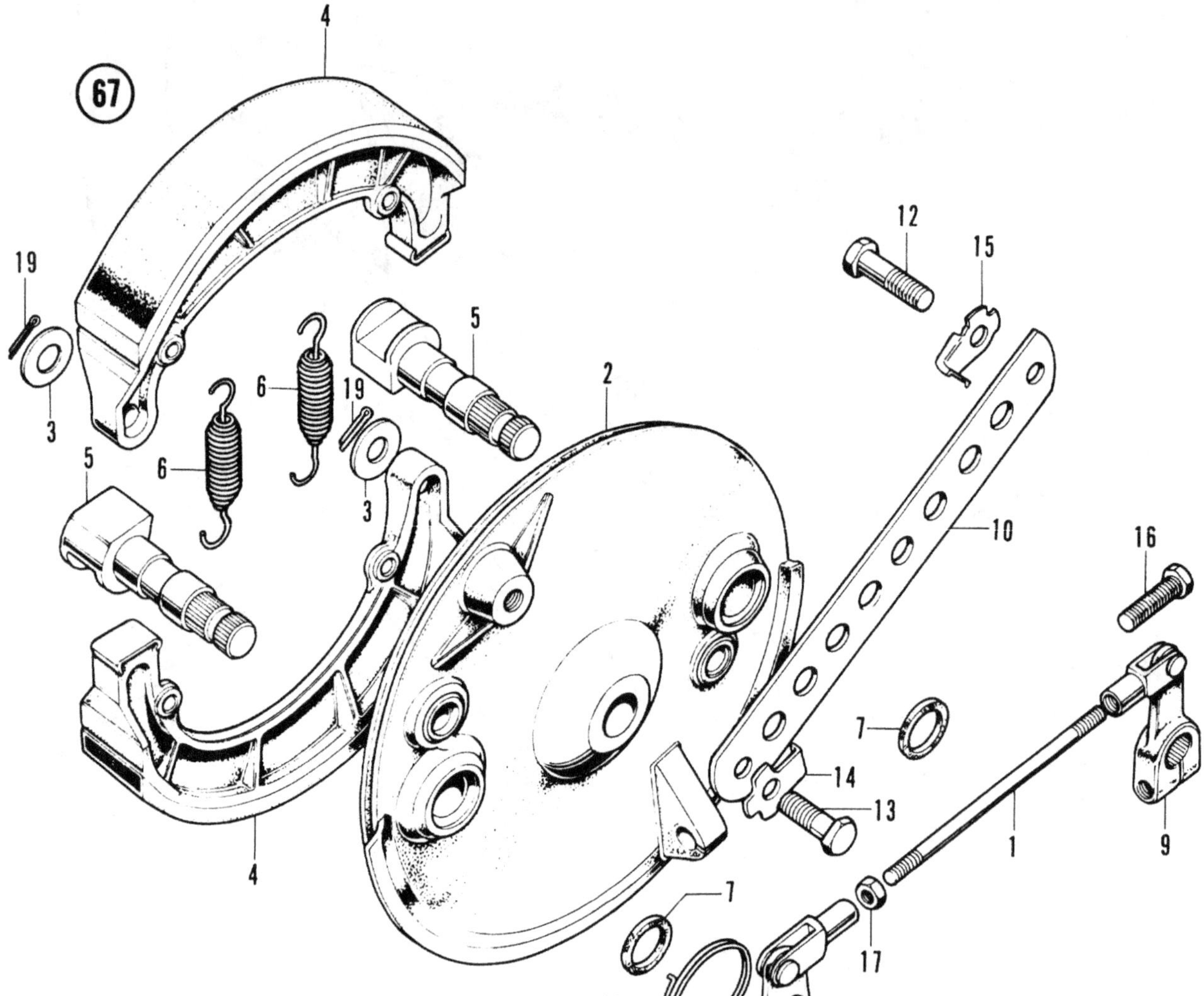

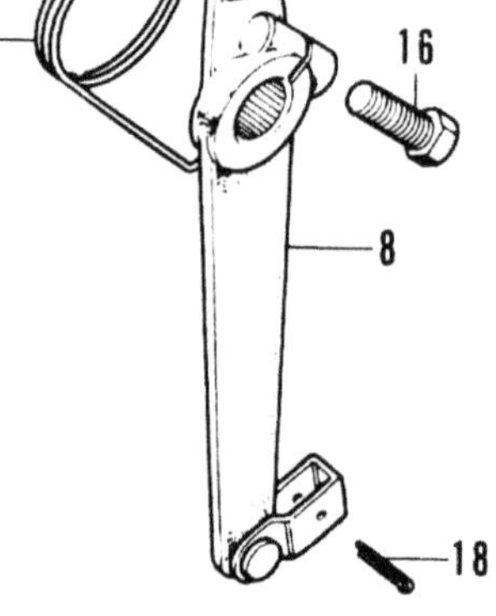

FRONT BRAKE SHOE — PANEL (CL TYPE)

1. Rod, rear brake
2. Panel Comp., front brake
3. Washer, anchor pin
4. Shoe Comp., front brake
5. Cam, front brake
6. Spring, brake shoe
7. Dust-Seal, brake cam
8. Arm A, front brake
9. Arm B, front brake
10. Arm, front brake stopper
11. Spring, brake arm
12. Bolt B, front brake stopper arm
13. Bolt, front stopper arm
14. Washer, tongued, 8.2mm
15. Washer B, tongued, 8.2mm
16. Bolt, hex., 6x20
17. Nut, hex., 6mm
18. Pin, cotter, 2.0x18
19. Pin, cotter, 2.5x20

serviceable limits for wheel and brake components. Refer to **Figures 68 and 69**.

2. Inspect the anchor pin for straightness and check the wheel for loose spokes at this time. Runout is checked as shown in **Figure 70**.

3. Balance the wheel by revolving it slowly and letting it stop of its own accord. Attach balancing weights (available in four sizes as shown in **Figure 71**) to the lightest point on the wheel, that is the point which ends up at the top. Repeat as necessary to obtain the best balance with the fewest number of weights.

Front Wheel (Drum brake) Reassembly

1. Grease the ball bearings and pack the wheel hub with grease. Refer to the drawing for details if necessary and insert the spacing collar. Use a bearing installer, making sure the seal side of the bearings faces outward.

2. Hook the brake shoe return spring and install the anchor pin and cam and assemble the front brake panel.

1. Rim runout ⑥⑧

Item	Standard value	Servicealbe limit
Side runout	Dial runout within 0.5 mm (0.020 in)	Replace or repair if over 2.0 mm (0.079 in)
Vertical runout	Dial runout within 0.5 mm (0.020 in)	Replace or repair if over 2.0 mm (0.079 in)

2. Axle bend and wear.

Item	Standard value	Serviceable limit
Inside diameter	14.996~14.984 mm (0.589~0.590 in)	
Bend	Within 0.05 mm (0.002 in)	Replace if more than 0.2 mm (0.0079 in)

3. 6302 Z ball bearings axial and radial clearance.

Item	Standard value	Serviceable limit
Axial clearance	Not more than 0.05 mm (0.002 in)	Replace if over 0.1 mm (0.004 in)
Radial clearance	0.007~0.002 mm (0.0003~0.0009 in)	Replace if over 0.05 mm (0.002 in)

4. Brake shoe spring.

Item	Standard value	Serviceable limit
Free length	67.4 mm (2.6535 in)	Replace if over 70 mm (2.765 in)
Tension	6 kg (75 mm) (13.32 lds) (2.953 in)	

5. Front brake shoe diameter and lining thickness.

Item	Standard value	Serviceable limit
Outside diameter	199.8~200 mm (7.866~7.844 in)	
Thickness	4.5 mm (0.1722 in)	Replace if under 2.0 mm (0.079 in)

6. Front brake cam thickness.

Item	Standard value	Serviceable limit
Thickness	10 mm (0.394 in)	If worn, deformed, or unusual, replace.

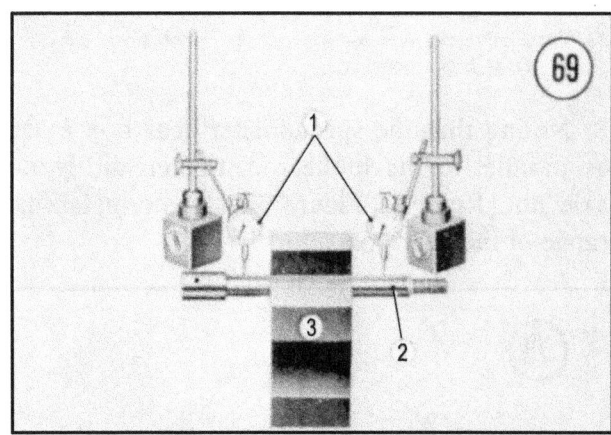

① Dial gauge
② Front wheel axle
③ V block

① Dial gauge
② Front wheel rim

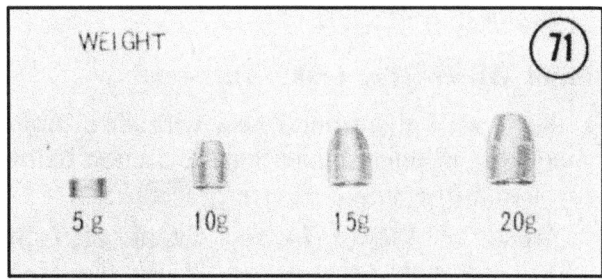

3. Note that punch marks on the brake arm and brake cam must be aligned. Refer to **Figure 72.**

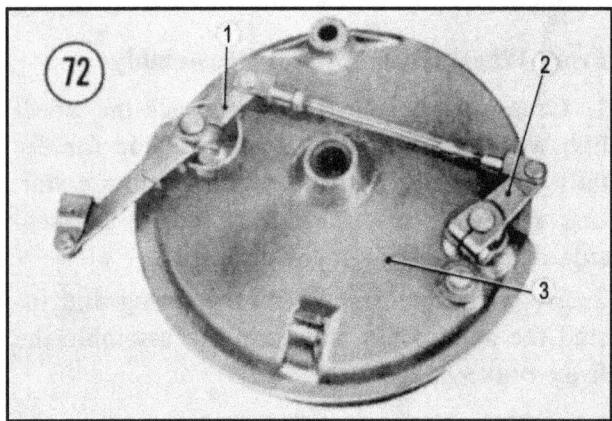

① Front brake arm A   ② Front brake arm B
③ Front brake panel

3. Noting that the speedometer gear box must be parallel to the brake rod, tighten the front axle nut. Refer to **Figure 73** for the installing range of the gear box.

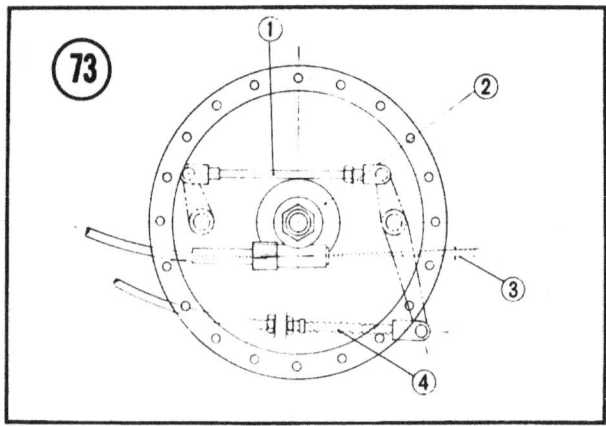

① Front brake arm rod   ② Speedmeter gear box
③ Installing range   ④ Front brake cable

4. Mount the front wheel in place, connect the stopper arm and tighten the front axle holder bolts.

5. Connect the speedometer cable.

6. Adjust brake free travel after connecting the brake cable. Free play should be from 15 to 30mm (0.6 to 1.2")

Front Wheel (Disc brake) Disassembly

1. Service of the front wheel with disc brake is covered in this section. See the section below for actual disc brake service procedures.

2. Refer to **Figure 74** for details of front wheel and hub construction. Raise the front wheel off the ground by blocking up the engine with a suitable support.

3. Detach the speedometer cable from the hub. Remove the axle holder nuts to free the front wheel assembly.

4. After the wheel has been removed, take care not to actuate the brake lever. The caliper piston may be forced out of its cylinder with subsequent loss of hydraulic fluid. If this occurs, the brake system will need servicing.

5. Remove the front axle nut and pull out the axle. Remove the speedometer gearbox.

6. Bend the tabs of the locking washers away from the disc holding nuts and remove the nuts. The disc will lift off.

7. Remove the gearbox retainer cover and the retainer.

8. Remove the wheel bearing retainer and dust seal. See **Figure 75.**

9. Remove the front wheel bearing.

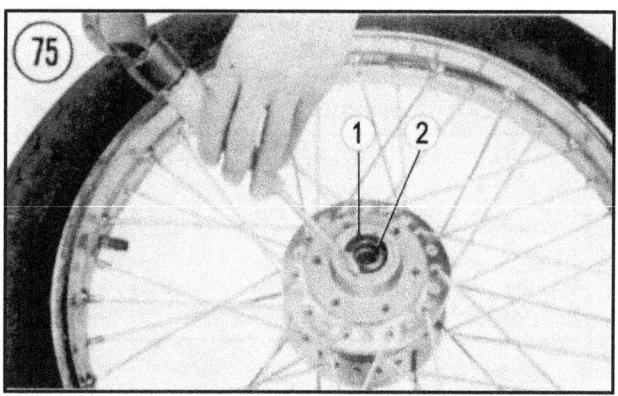

① Front wheel bearing retainer
② Dust seal

Front Wheel (Disc brake) Inspection

1. Place the brake disc on a flat plate and check it for flatness. Use a dial gauge as shown in **Figure 76**. A difference of more than 0.012" (0.3mm) indicates need for replacement. If disc thickness is less than 0.217" (5.5mm) replace the disc.

2. Rim runout should be checked as shown in **Figure 77.** More than 0.08" (2.0mm) indicates rim repair or replacement is necessary.

3. Measure the ball bearings as shown in **Figure 78** for axial and diametrical runout. If axial runout exceeds 0.004" (0.1mm) or if diametrical runout exceeds 0.002" (0.05mm) replace the bearings.

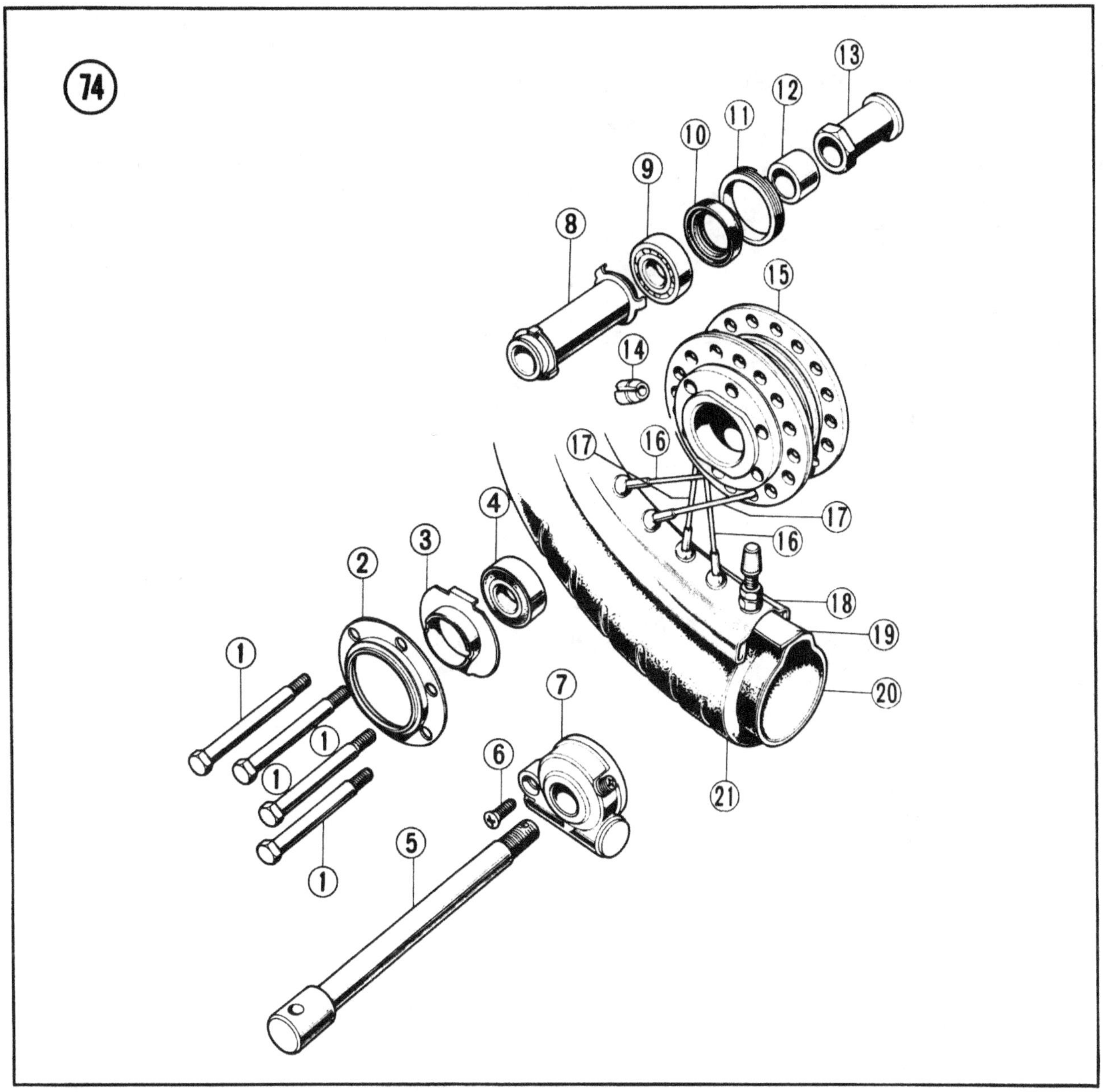

(74)

① 8 × 10 mm bolt
② Gear box retainer cover
③ Gear box retainer
④ 6302 Z ball bearing
⑤ Front wheel axle
⑥ 5 × 15 mm oval screw
⑦ Speedometer gear box
⑧ Front axle distance collar
⑨ 6302 Z ball bearing
⑩ 22368 dust seal
⑪ Front wheel bearing retainer
⑫ Front wheel collar
⑬ Front wheel axle nut
⑭ Wheel balancer
⑮ Front wheel hub
⑯ Front spoke A
⑰ Front spoke B
⑱ Front wheel rim
⑲ Front tire flap
⑳ Front wheel tube
㉑ Front wheel tire

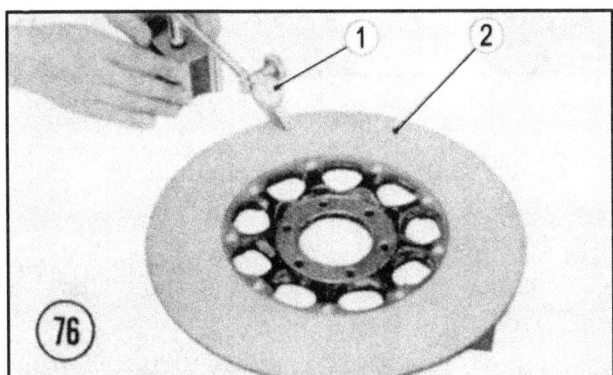

(76)

① Dial gauge ② Front brake disc

(77)

① Dial gauge

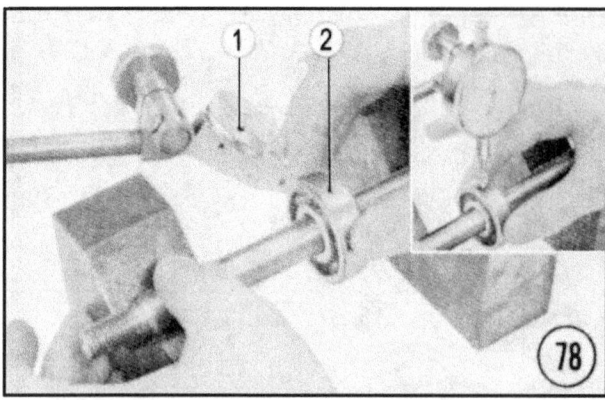

① Dial gauge   ② Ball bearing

Front Wheel (Disc brake) Reassembly

1. Replace the wheel bearings in the front hub with a drift of the proper size or bearing driver (Honda tool No. 07048-30001) as shown in **Figure 79**.

① Bearing driver

2. Install the dust seal in the bearing retainer and mount the retainer in place.

3. Install the gearbox retainer, lining up its tab with the flat on the hub, and fit the retainer cover, passing the disc mounting bolts through it.

4. Mount the disc in place using new lock washers and bending up their tabs as shown in **Figure 80**.

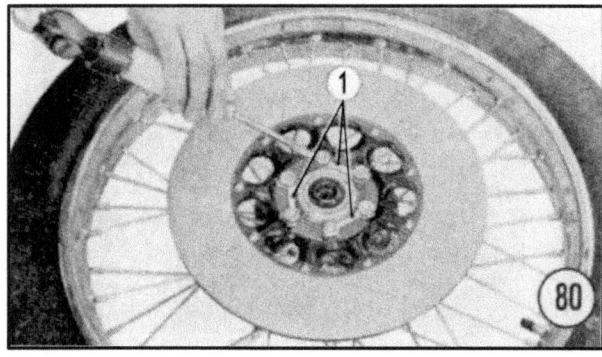

① Tongued washer

5. Pass the axle through the gearbox and then the hub, and tighten the axle nut.

6. Install the wheel in the forks and secure it with the axle holders and nuts.

7. Connect the speedometer cable, tightening the set screw shown in **Figure 81**.

8. Balance the wheel as outlined in the section on assembling the front wheel (drum type brake).

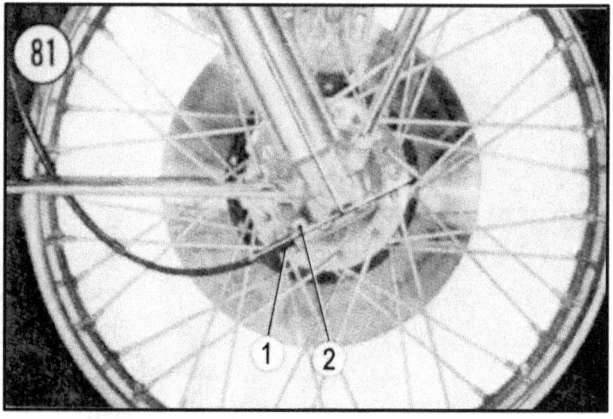

① Speedometer cable
② Setting screw

Front Brake (Disc type) Disassembly

1. Remove the front wheel as outlined above.

2. Disconnect the hydraulic line by removing the bolt shown in **Figure 82**. Refer to **Figures 83 and 84** for details.

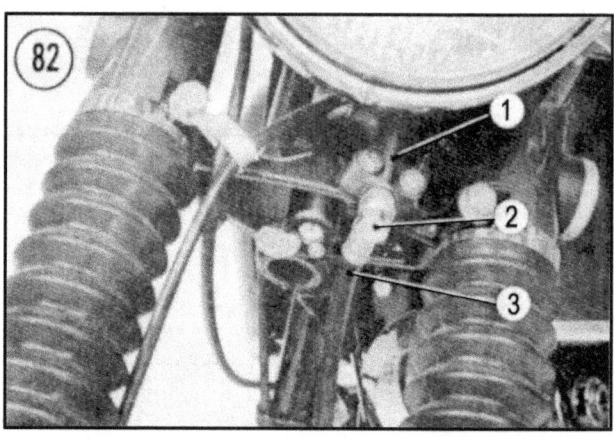

① Joint   ② Oil bolt   ③ Oil hose

3. Unscrew the three caliper mounting bolts and remove the caliper assembly from the bottom fork tube. See **Figure 85**.

4. Unscrew the two set screws and remove both calipers.

5. Remove pad A, pad seat and piston from caliper A.

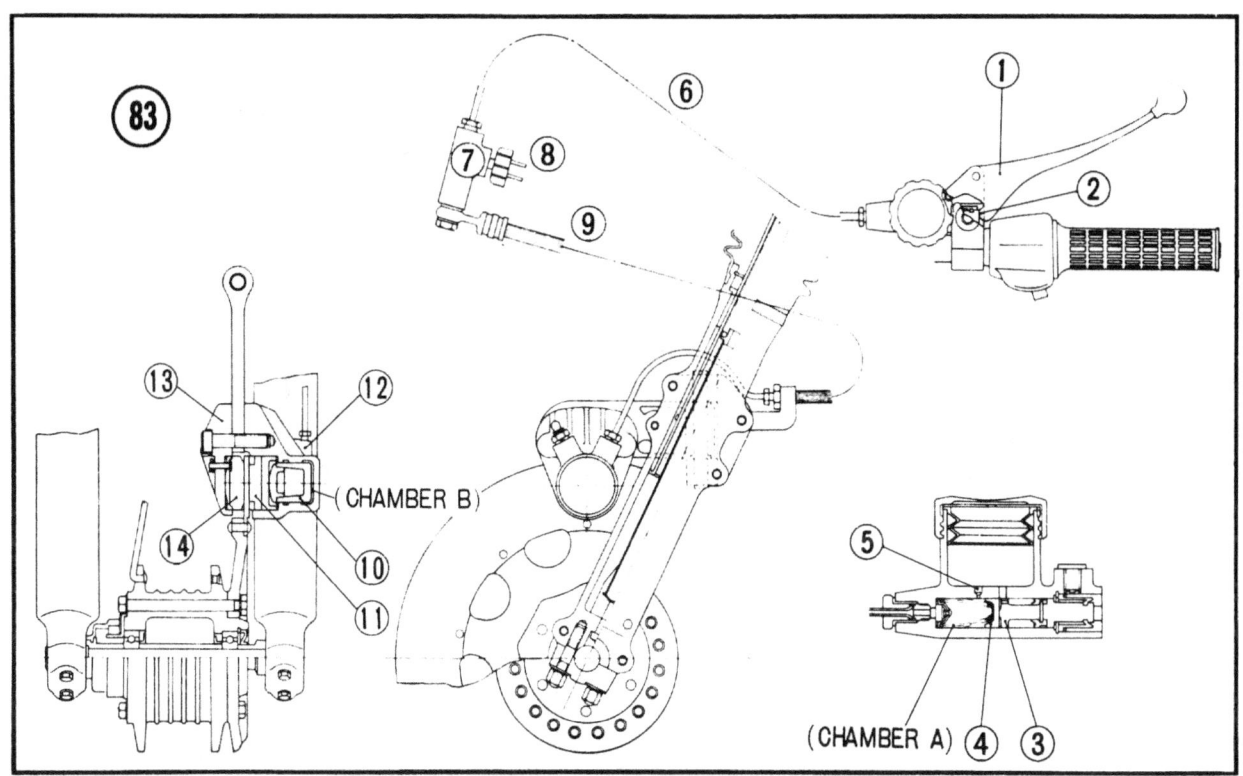

① Front brake lever
② Front brake lever cam
③ Master cylinder
④ Primary cup
⑤ Fluid passage
⑥ Front brake hose B
⑦ Three way joint
⑧ Stoplight switch
⑨ Front brake hose
⑩ Piston
⑪ Pad A
⑫ Caliper A
⑬ Caliper B
⑭ Pad B

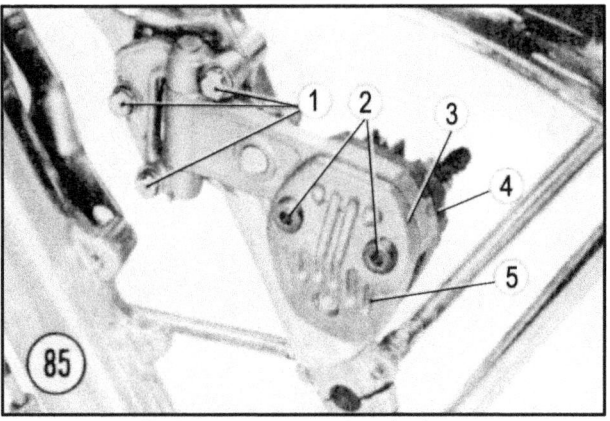

① Caliper mounting bolts
② Hollow head set bolts
③ Caliper   ⑤ Caliper B
④ Caliper A

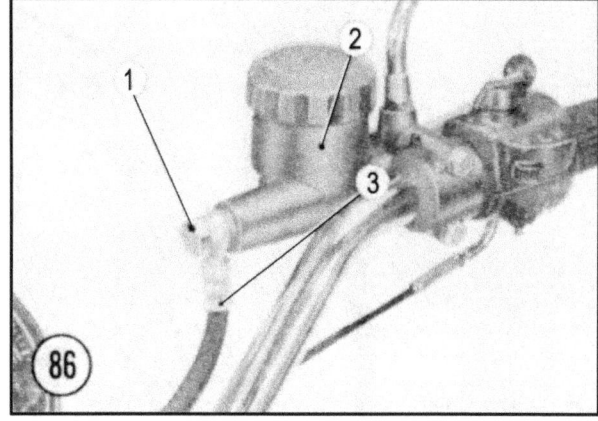

① Oil bolt   ③ Oil hose
② Master cylinder

6. Remove the cotter pin and pad B from caliper B.

7. To remove the master cylinder, unscrew the oil bolt shown in **Figure 86.** Unscrew the two master cylinder mounting bolts and remove the master cylinder from the handlebar.

8. Refer to **Figure 87** for details and remove the stopper washer and boot from the master cylinder.

9. Remove the circlip as shown in **Figure 88.**

10. Remove the washer, piston, secondary cup, primary cup, spring and check valve.

Front Brake (Disc type) Inspection

1. Check the clearance between the front of the caliper and the brake disc face. When it becomes 0.06 to 0.08" (1.5mm to 2mm) the friction pads should be replaced as a set.

2. If too large a stroke of the brake lever is necessary to actuate the front brake, check for low fluid level in the reservoir, air in the line,

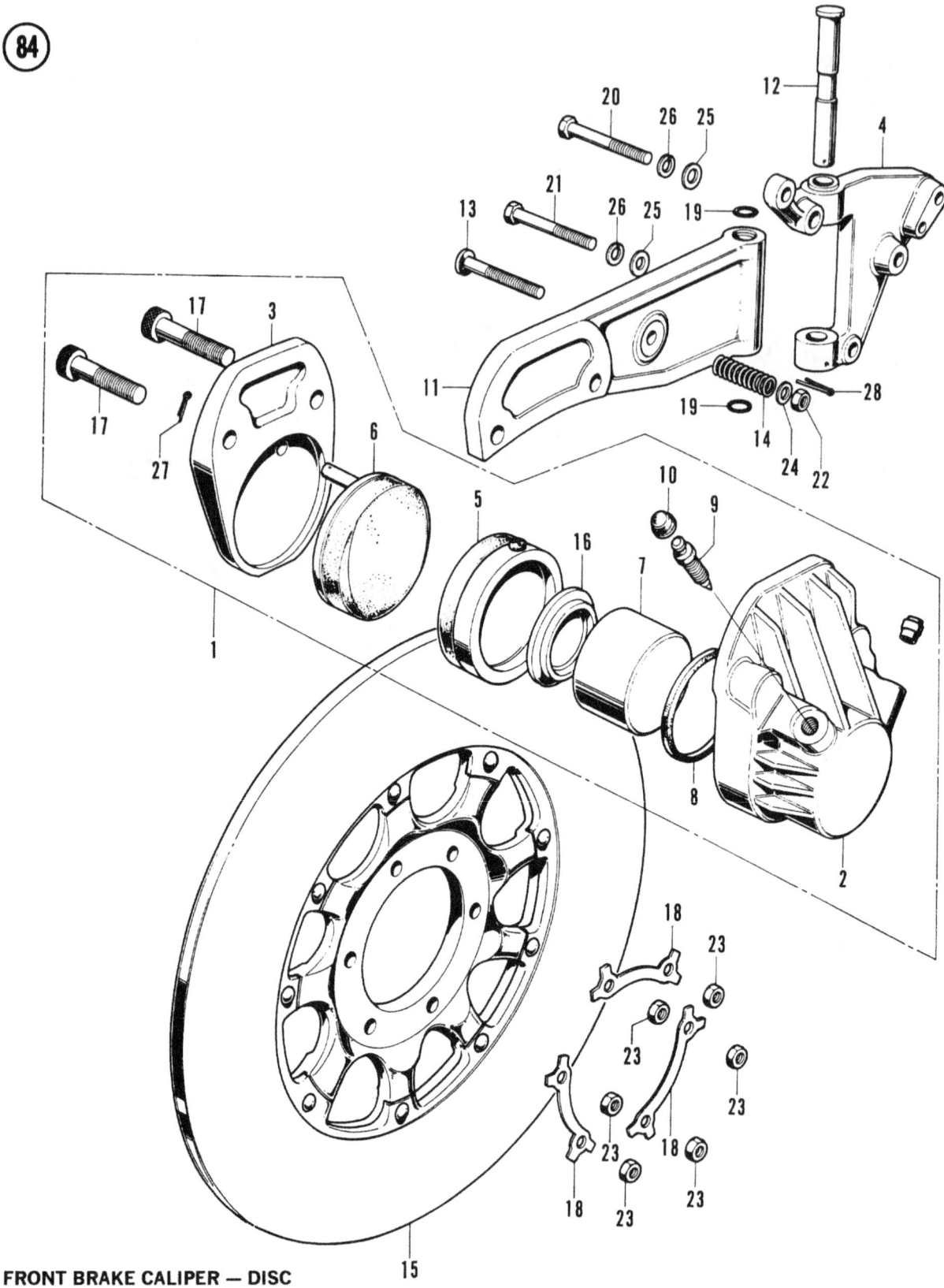

FRONT BRAKE CALIPER — DISC

1. Caliper Assy. (Tokiko)
2. Caliper A (Tokiko)
3. Caliper B (Tokiko)
4. Joint, caliper holder
5. Pad A Comp.
6. Pad B Comp.
7. Piston (Tokiko)
8. Seal, piston (Tokiko)
9. Bleeder (Tokiko)
10. Cap, bleeder screw (Tokiko)
11. Holder, caliper
12. Pin, caliper holder
13. Bolt, caliper adjusting
14. Spring, caliper adjusting
15. Disk Comp., front brake
16. Seat, pad
17. Bolt, caliper setting (Tokiko)
18. Washer, tongued, 8mm
19. O-Ring, 10x1.7
20. Bolt, hex., 8x40
21. Bolt, hex., 8x50
22. Nut, hex., 6mm
23. Nut, hex., 8mm
24. Washer, plain, 6mm
25. Washer, plain, 8mm
26. Washer, spring, 8mm
27. Pin, split, 1.6x12
28. Pin, split, 2.5x30

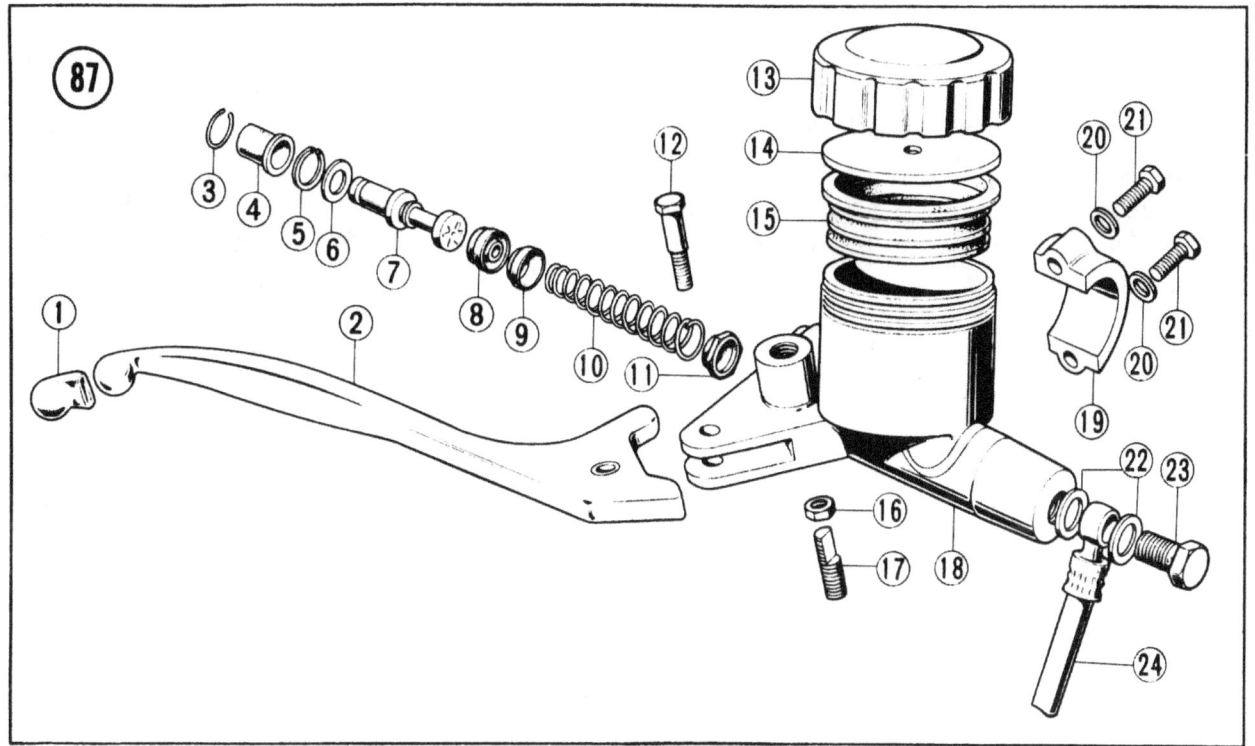

- ① Brake lever cap
- ② Brake lever
- ③ Stopper washer
- ④ Boot
- ⑤ 18 mm internal circlip
- ⑥ 10.5 mm washer
- ⑦ Piston
- ⑧ Secondary cap
- ⑨ Primary cap
- ⑩ Spring
- ⑪ Check valve
- ⑫ Handle lever pivot bolt
- ⑬ Oil cup cap
- ⑭ Master cylinder plate
- ⑮ Diaphragm
- ⑯ 8 mm hex nut
- ⑰ Lever adjusting bolt
- ⑱ Master cylinder body
- ⑲ Master cylinder holder
- ⑳ 6 mm spring washer
- ㉑ 6 mm hex bolt
- ㉒ Oil bolt washer
- ㉓ Oil bolt
- ㉔ Front brake hose

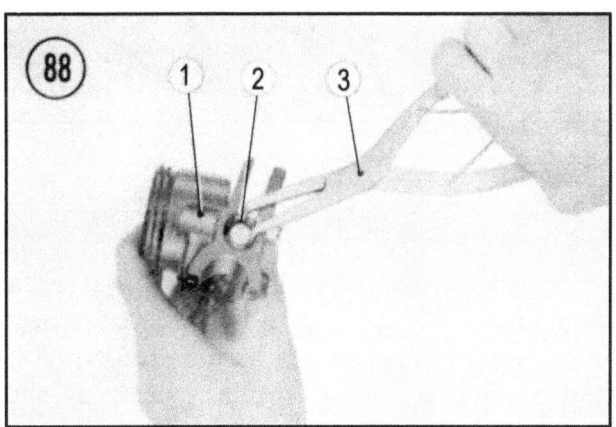

① Master cylinder body
② Circlip
③ Special pliers

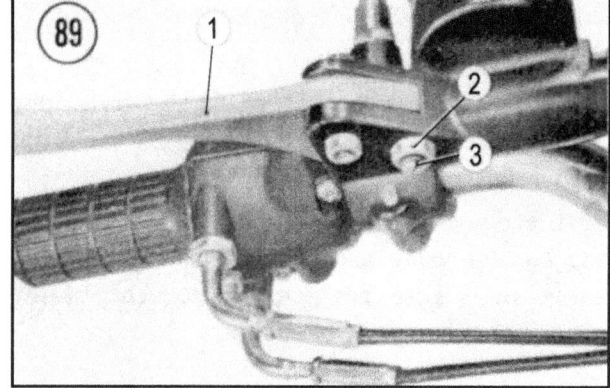

① Front brake lever
② Lock nut
③ Brake lever adjusting bolt

or misadjustment of lever free play. Add fluid or bleed the line as outlined in the reassembly section. Adjust free play by loosening the lock nut and turning the adjusting screw shown in **Figure 89**.

3. Measure the caliper cylinder and piston. When clearance between them exceeds 0.004" (0.11mm) the worn part or parts should be replaced. Replace the cylinder if it is worn past 1.504" (38.215mm) and the piston if it is smaller than 1.500" (38.105mm).

4. Measure the master cylinder and piston. When clearance between them exceeds 0.0045" (0.115mm) the worn part or parts should be replaced. Replace the cylinder if it is worn past 0.553" (14.055mm) and the piston if it is smaller than 0.549" (13.940mm).

5. Check the caliper piston seal and the oil

hose for wear or damage and replace if necessary.

Front Brake (Disc Type) Reassembly

1. Apply a small quantity (.3 to .5g) of silicon sealing grease to the calipers as shown in **Figure 90**. Keep grease off the braking surfaces of the pads.

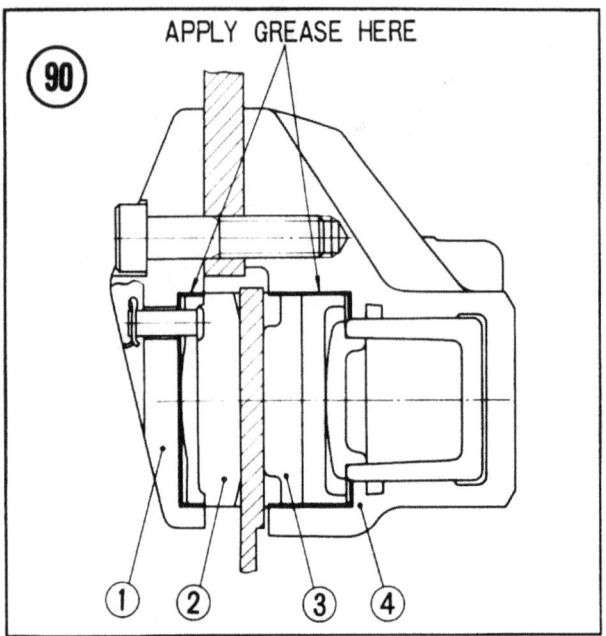

① Caliper B ③ Pad A
② Pad A ④ Caliper B

2. Reassemble the caliper and master cylinder assemblies and attach them to the fork tube and handlebar respectively. Replace the front wheel as outlined earlier.

3. Bleed the brakes. Take off the dust cap on the bleeder valve and attach a bleeder hose as shown in **Figure 91**. Set the free end of the hose in a clean glass container.

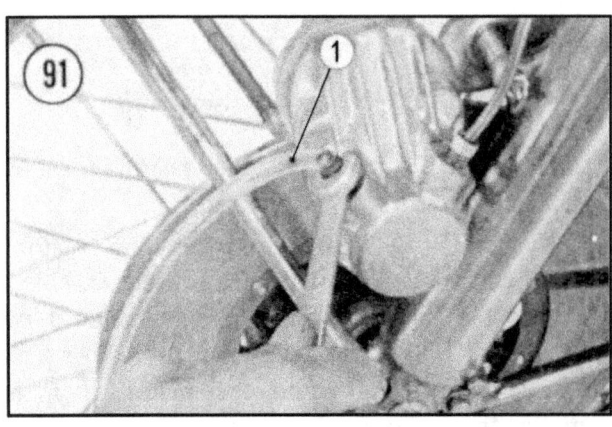

① Bleeder hose

4. Fill the hydraulic reservoir with SAE Type 70 R 3 brake fluid. Pump the brake lever until pressure can be felt and hold it tight. Open the bleeder valve and squeeze the lever all the way to the handlebar. Close the bleeder valve without releasing the lever. Repeat the process until no more bubbles appear in the fluid in the glass container. Replenish the fluid in the hydraulic reservoir as needed, using fresh fluid. Do not use the fluid pumped through the system.

When no more bubbles appear and the brake lever holds without any trace of sponginess the system has been properly bled. Tighten the bleeder valve, remove the bleeder hose and replace the dust cap. Check that the reservoir is full and replace the reservoir cap. See **Figure 92**.

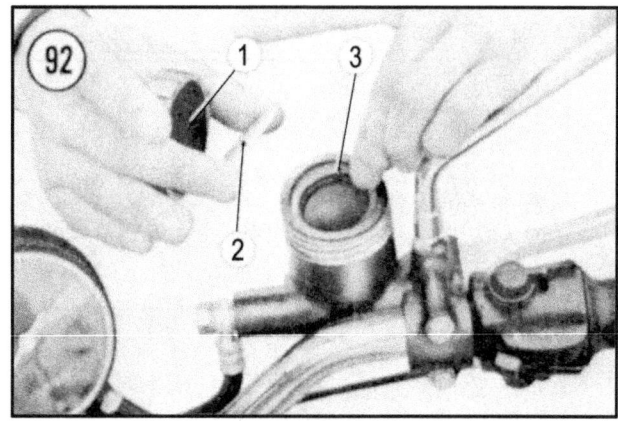

① Reservoir cap
② Washer
③ Diaphragm

To fill the system with fluid if it has been completely drained, open the bleeder valve, operate the brake lever, close the bleeder valve and release the lever keeping the hydraulic reservoir full all the time. When fluid comes out of the bleeder, the system is full but must still be bled as above.

5. Adjust the brake caliper clearance by raising the front wheel off the ground so it may be rotated. Loosen the caliper stopper bolt lock nut and turn the stopper bolt clockwise until the friction pad contacts the disc and some resistance is felt as the wheel is turned. Turn the bolt in the opposite direction (counterclockwise) just until no resistance is felt. Now turn the bolt 1/8 to 1/4 turn more and tighten the lock nut. See Insert in **Figure 93**.

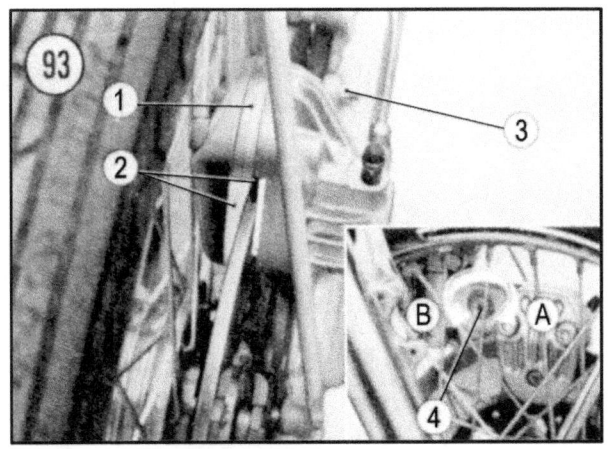

① Brake caliper
② Friction pads
③ Stopper bolt lock nut
④ Stopper bolt

Rear Wheel Disassembly (All models)

1. Refer to **Figures 94, 95, 96 and 97** for details of rear hub and brake construction.

① Drive chain   ② Drive chain clip

2. Remove the drive chain master link and the drive chain as shown in **Figure 98.**

3. Remove the adjusting nut from the rear brake rod and separate the rod from the brake arm. Remove the backing plate stop nut and free the stop arm from the backing plate.

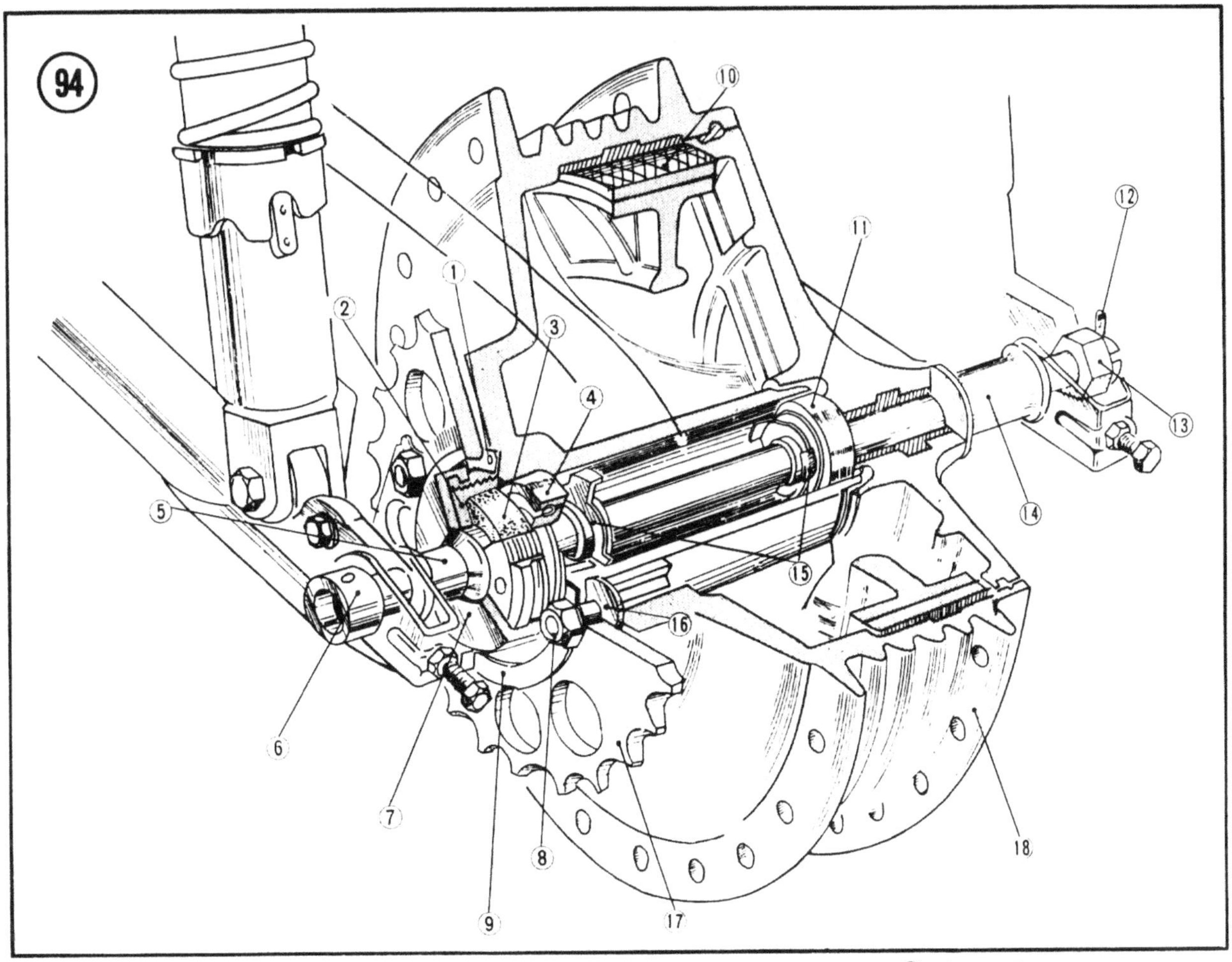

① 73.8 mm circlip
② Rear wheel bearing retainer
③ 34559 dust seal
④ 6305 Z ball bearing
⑤ Rear wheel side collar
⑥ Rear wheel axle
⑦ Bearing retainer
⑧ 10 mm nut
⑨ 10 mm tongue washer
⑩ Rear brake shoe
⑪ 6304 Z ball bearing
⑫ 4.0 × 10 mm center pin
⑬ Rear axle nut
⑭ Rear brake panel collar
⑮ Rear axle spacing collar
⑯ Driven sprocket bolt
⑰ Final driven sprocket
⑱ Rear wheel hub

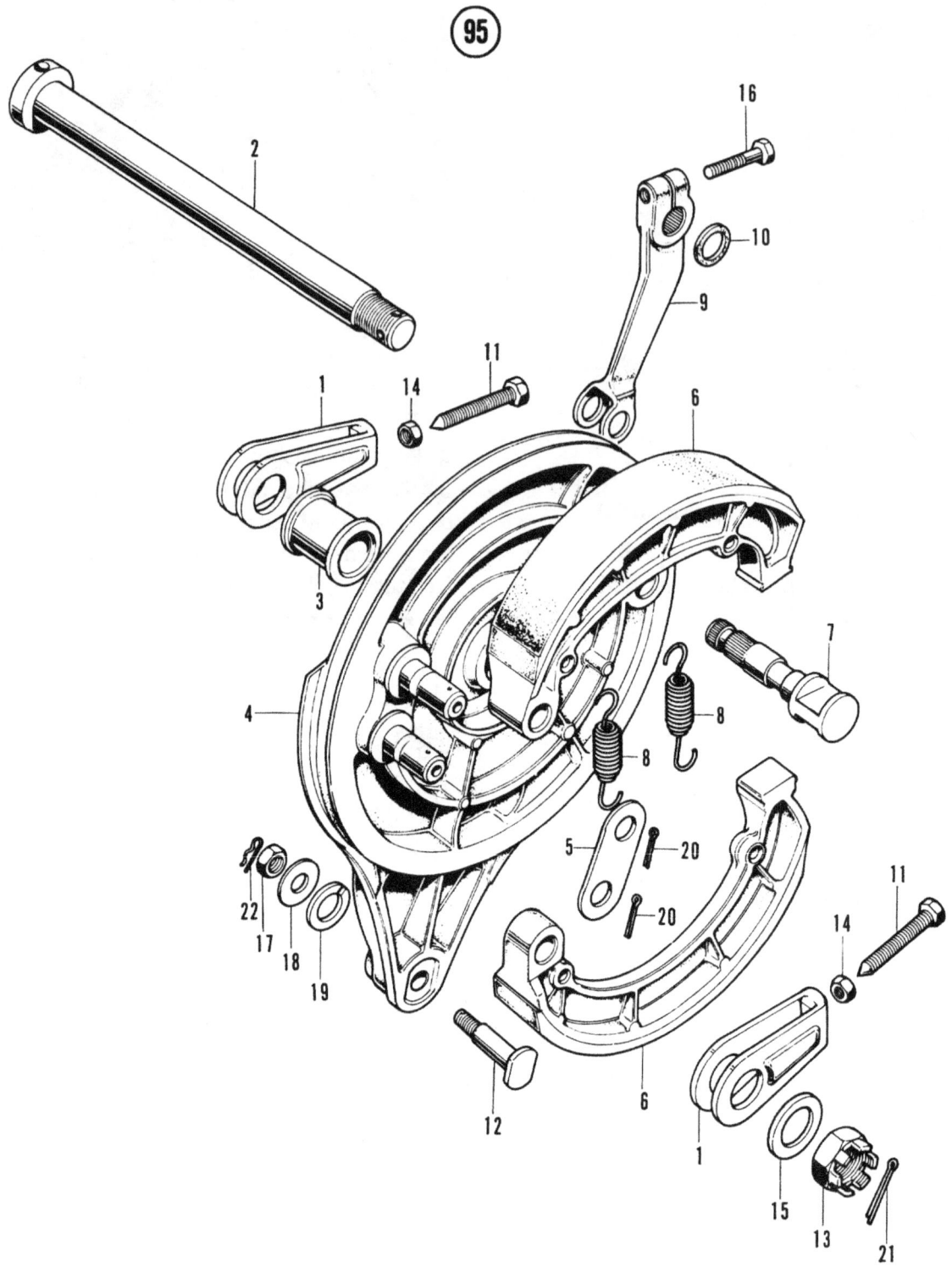

REAR BRAKE — PANEL

1. Adjuster, drive chain
2. Axle, rear wheel
3. Collar, rear brake panel side
4. Panel Comp., rear brake
5. Washer, anchor pin
6. Shoe Comp., rear brake
7. Cam, rear brake
8. Spring, brake shoe
9. Arm, rear brake
10. Dust-Seal, rear brake
11. Bolt, chain adjusting
12. Bolt, rear brake panel stopper
13. Nut, rear axle
14. Nut, chain adjusting
15. Washer, 18.5x34
16. Bolt, hex., 6x20
17. Nut, hex., 8mm
18. Washer, plain, 8mm
19. Washer, spring, 10mm
20. Pin, cotter, 2.5x20
21. Pin, cotter, 4.0x30
22. Pin, lock, 8mm

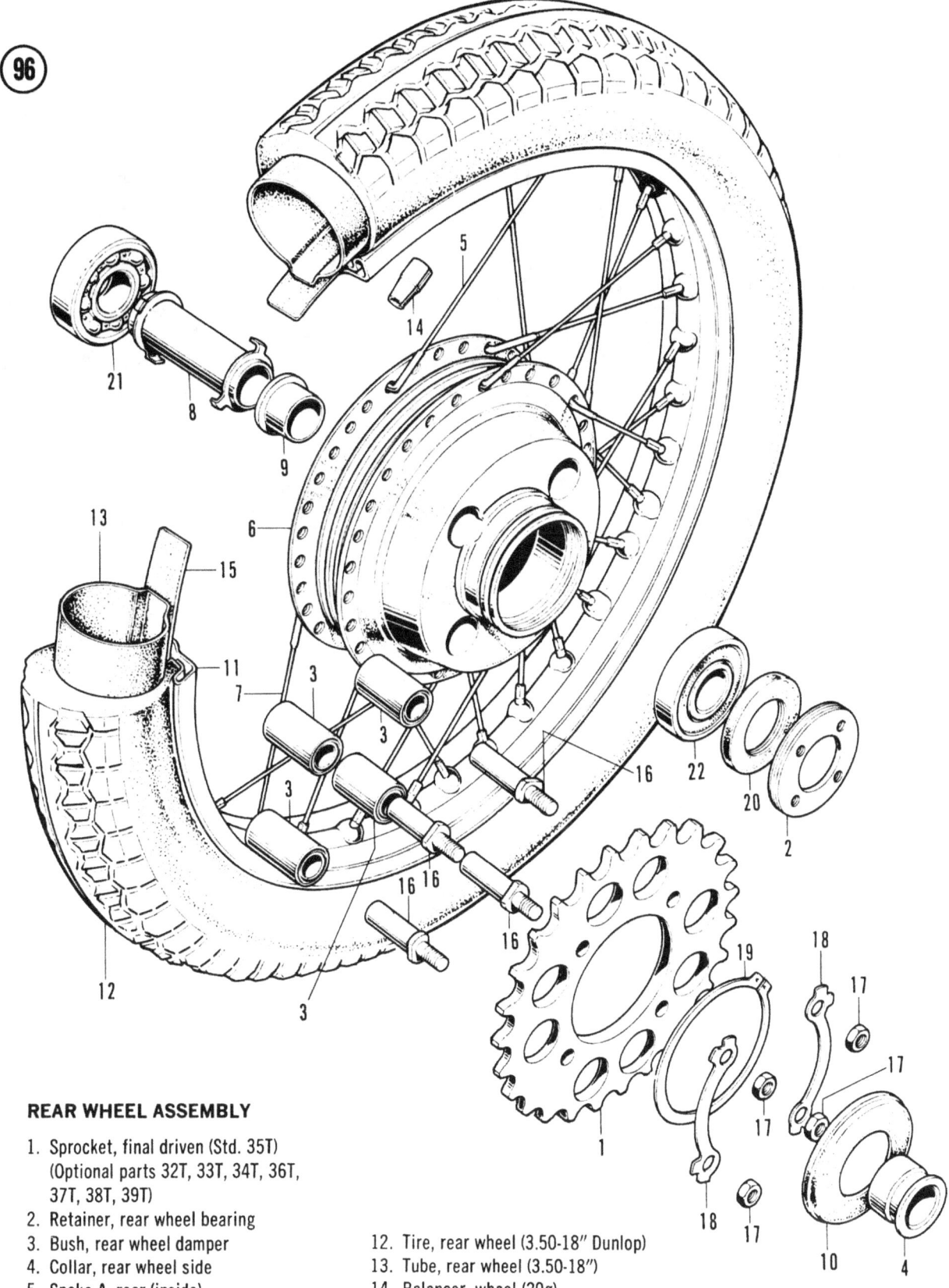

REAR WHEEL ASSEMBLY

1. Sprocket, final driven (Std. 35T) (Optional parts 32T, 33T, 34T, 36T, 37T, 38T, 39T)
2. Retainer, rear wheel bearing
3. Bush, rear wheel damper
4. Collar, rear wheel side
5. Spoke A, rear (inside)
6. Hub Comp., rear wheel
7. Spoke B, rear (outside)
8. Collar, rear axle distance
9. Collar B, rear axle distance
10. Cap, bearing retainer
11. Rim, rear wheel (DAIDO)
12. Tire, rear wheel (3.50-18" Dunlop)
13. Tube, rear wheel (3.50-18")
14. Balancer, wheel (20g)
    Balancer, wheel (15g)
    Balancer, wheel (10g)
    Balancer, wheel (5g)
15. Flap, tire (18")
16. Bolt, driven sprocket fixing
17. Nut, driven sprocket
18. Washer, tongued, 10mm
19. Circlip, 73.8mm
20. Oil-Seal, 34559
21. Bearing, ball, 6304Z
22. Bearing, ball, 6305Z

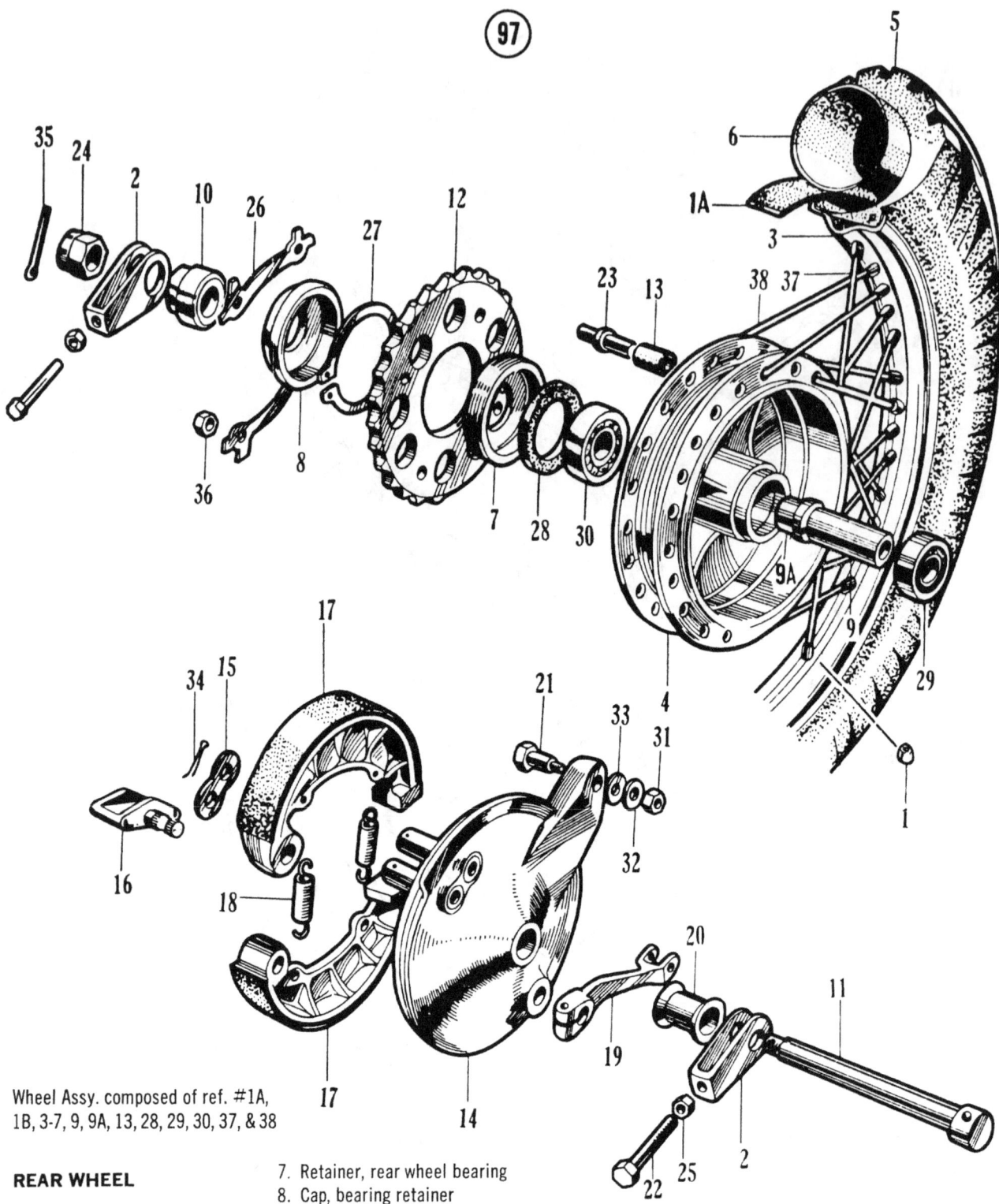

Wheel Assy. composed of ref. #1A, 1B, 3-7, 9, 9A, 13, 28, 29, 30, 37, & 38

REAR WHEEL

1. Balance, wheel 20G
   Balance, wheel 15G
   Balance, wheel 10G
   Balance, wheel 5G
1A. Flap, tire
2. Adjuster, drive chain
3. Rim, rear wheel
4. Hub, rear wheel
5. Tire, rear wheel 3.50x18
6. Tube, wheel 3.25/3.50x18
7. Retainer, rear wheel bearing
8. Cap, bearing retainer
9. Collar A, rear axle distance
9A. Collar B, rear axle distance
10. Collar, rear wheel side
11. Axle, rear wheel
12. Sprocket, final driven 35T
    (Optional—34T, 32T, 34T, 36T, 37T, 38T, 39T)
13. Bush, rear wheel damper
14. Panel, rear brake
15. Washer, rear brake anchor pin
16. Cam, rear brake
17. Shoe, rear brake
18. Spring, rear brake
19. Arm, rear brake
20. Collar, rear brake panel
21. Bolt, rear brake panel stopper
22. Bolt, chain adjusting
23. Bolt, driven sprocket fixing
24. Nut, rear axle
25. Nut, chain adjuster
26. Washer, tongue, 10mm
27. Circlip, 73.8mm
28. Oil-Seal, 34559
29. Bearing, ball, 6304Z
30. Bearing, ball, 6305Z
31. Nut, hex., 8mm
32. Washer, flat, 8mm
33. Washer, spring, 10mm
34. Pin, cotter, 2.5x20mm
35. Pin, cotter, 4.0x30mm
36. Nut, thin, 10mm
37. Spoke A, rear
38. Spoke B, rear

4. Pull the cotter pin out of the axle and remove the axle nut. Pull out the axle and remove the rear wheel as shown in **Figure 99.**

5. Take off the hub bearing retainer cap and remove the circlip.

① Rear wheel

6. Straighten the tabs on the drive sprocket retaining nuts and remove the nuts as shown in **Figure 100.** Lift off the sprocket.

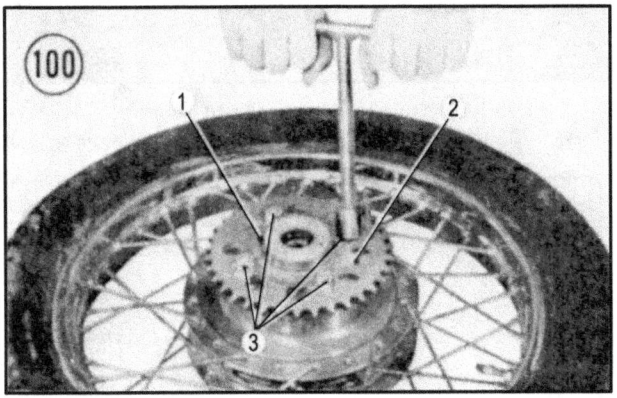

① 73.8 mm circlip   ② Final driven sprocket
③ 10 mm nut

7. Use a wheel bearing retainer wrench (special tool) to remove the bearing retainer as shown in **Figure 101.** Pull out the two wheel bearings and the rear axle spacer.

① Bearing retainer extractor   ② Bearing retainer

8. Remove the two cotter pins and anchor pin washer shown in **Figure 102.** Remove the brake arm so the brake shoes may be taken off.

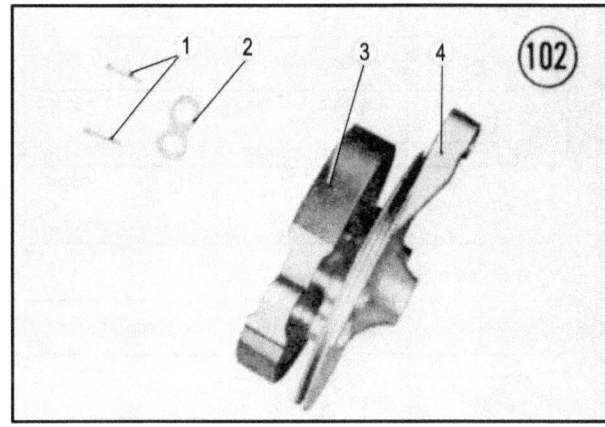

① 2.5 × 20 mm cotter pin
② Rear brake ancher pin washer
③ Rear brake shoe
④ Rear brake panel

Rear Wheel Inspection

1. Inspect the rear wheel, hub, brake and axle assemblies using the accompanying tables to determine serviceable limits. In addition, check the anchor pin for straightness, spokes for tightness, and balance the wheel if necessary as outlined in the section on front wheel (drum brake) service. **(Figure 103).**

Rear Wheel Reassembly

1. Grease the ball bearings thoroughly and pack the hub with grease. Insert the spacer and drive the bearings in place with a drift of the proper size or a bearing installer as shown in **Figure 104.** Be sure the seals are pointed outwards when the bearings are installed.

2. Replace the final drive sprocket and mount it using the special lock washer shown in **Figure 105.**

3. Install the brake shoes in place on the backing plate and hook up their springs. Install the brake cam and arm and secure with the anchor pin washer and cotter pins. Align punch marks on the brake cam and arm when fitting them together.

4. Fit the brake assembly or backing plate into the brake drum and remount the wheel. Reconnect the drive chain, making sure the closed end of the clip faces in the direction of chain travel. See **Figure 106.**

1. Rim runout.

Item	Standard value	Serviceable limit
Side runout	Within 0.5 mm (0.0197 in) (dial deflection)	Replace or repair if over 2.0 mm (0.0787 in)
Vertical runout	Within 0.5 mm (0.0197 in)	Replace or oepair if over 2.0 mm (0.0787 in)

2. Axle bend and wear.

Item	Standard value	Serviceadle limit
Outside diameter	19.947~19.98 mm (0.785~0.787 in)	
Bend	Within 0.05 mm (0.0020 in)	Replace if under 0.2 mm (0.0079 in)

3. Final driven sprocket root diameter.

Item	Standard value	Serviceable limit
Root diameter	167.23~167.37 mm (6.5757~6.5763 in)	Replace if over 166.3 mm (6.5472 in)

4. Ball bearing axial and radial clearance.

Item	Standard value	Serviceable limit
Axial clearance	Within 0.05 mm (0.0020 in)	Replace if over 0.01 mm (0.0004 in)
Radial clearance	0.01~0.02 mm (0.0004~0.0008 in)	More than 0.05 mm (0.0020 in)

5. Rear brake shope spring.

Item	Standard value	Serviceable limit
Free length	56.4 mm (0.2205 in)	Replace if over 59.5 mm (2.3425 in)

6. Rear brake shoe diameter.

Item	Standard value	Serviceable limit
Outside diameter	179.8~180.0 mm (7.078~7.087 in)	
Shoe thickness	5.0 mm (0.197 in)	Replace if under 2.0 mm (0.079 in)

7. Rear brake cam thickness.

Item	Standard value	Serviceable limit
Diameter	10 mm (0.39 in)	Replace if worn, deformed or unusual.

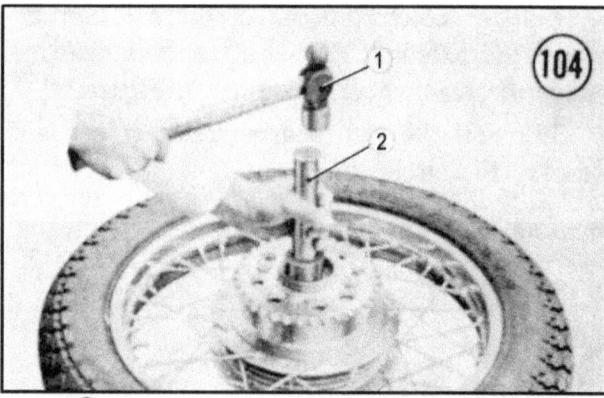

① Hammer   ② Bearing driver

① Final driven sproket   ③ Tongued washer
② 73.8 mm circlip   ④ 10 mm sprocket retaining bolt

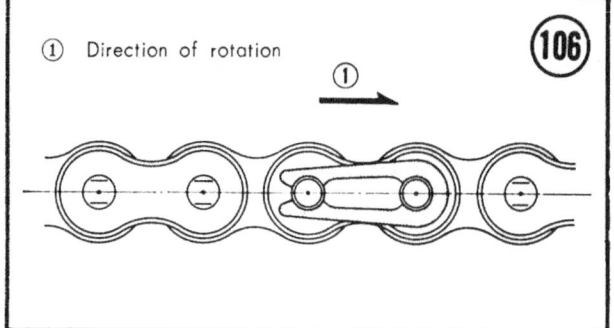

① Direction of rotation

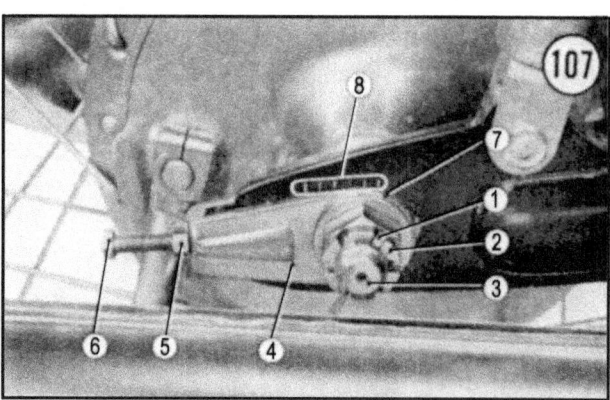

① Cotter pin   ⑤ Lock nut
② Axle nut   ⑥ Adjusting bolt
③ Rear wheel axle   ⑦ Index mark
④ Chain adjuster   ⑧ Reference mark

5. Adjust the chain before tightening the axle nut. Using the adjusting bolt on the chain adjuster, move the rear axle in its mounting until 0.4 to 0.8" (1 to 2cm) of slack are found in the longest run of the chain. Sight along the chain to check for straightness and use the reference marks on the swinging arm to ensure the rear wheel is lined up properly. See **Figure 107.**

6. Reconnect the brake stop arm and the rear brake rod. Adjust brake pedal play (see **Figure 108**) to 1". Tighten or loosen the brake rod adjusting nut as shown in **Figure 109.**

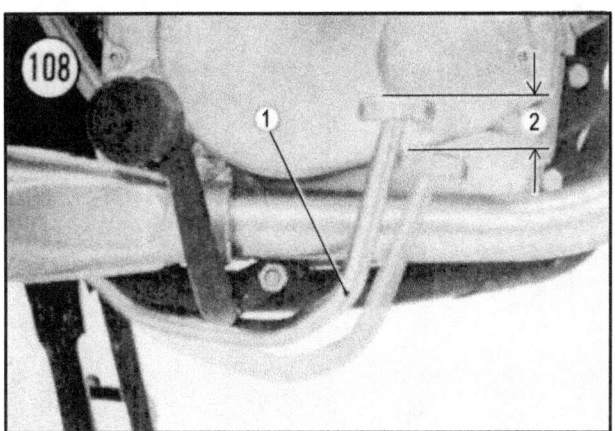

① Rear brake pedal   ② Free play

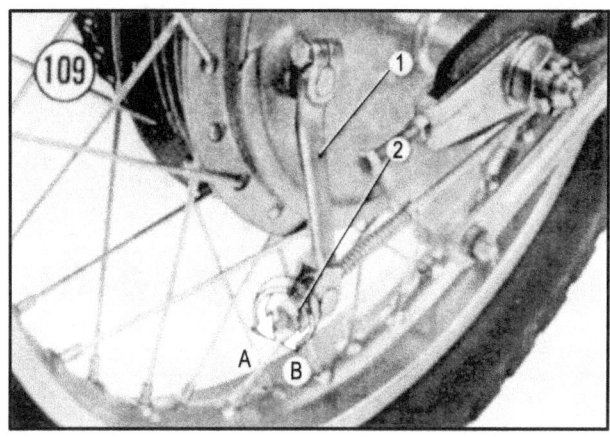

① Rear brake arm   ② Adjusting nut

SECTION FIVE

ELECTRICAL SERVICE

Electrical service procedures in this section have been kept as general as possible so they will apply to a maximum number of 450 Honda models. For specific servicing of wiring or wire looms, refer to the wiring diagrams at the end of this section, and determine which applies to your motorcycle. In most cases, differences will be obvious if they exist. For example on early CB 450's, two types of coil and breaker point assemblies were used. Type I used a pair of coils and a pair of breaker points while Type II used one coil and one set of points. Both types are illustrated; however, models using Type II were never imported into the U.S., although a few have been brought in privately. (See **Figures 1, 2, 3, 4, and 5**). Use common sense to choose the correct wiring diagram, for example, if your bike is fitted with turn signals, use the diagram that includes them.

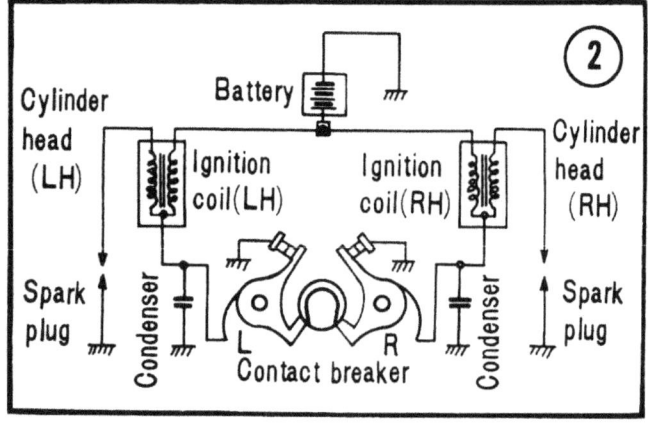

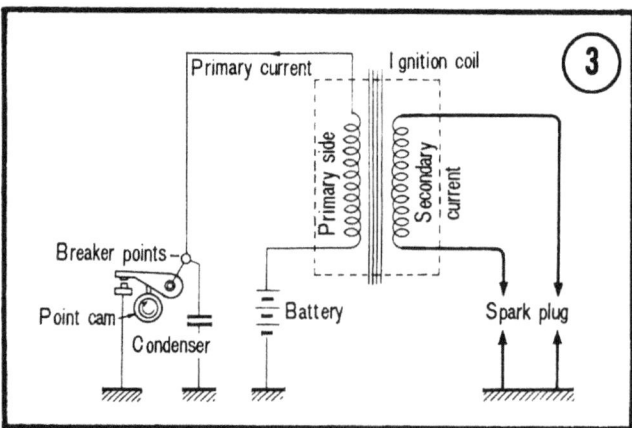

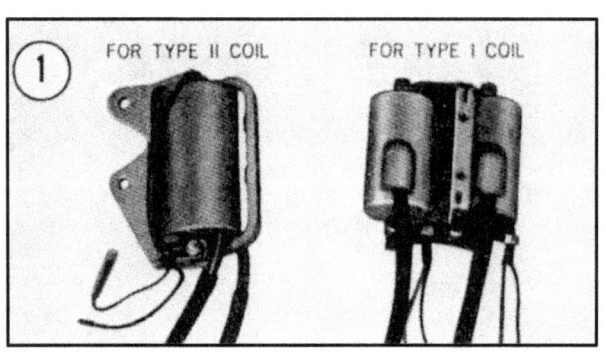

Ignition System

1. Proper operation of the ignition system depends on coil, condenser, points and plugs being in good condition.

2. Make a visual inspection of related wiring

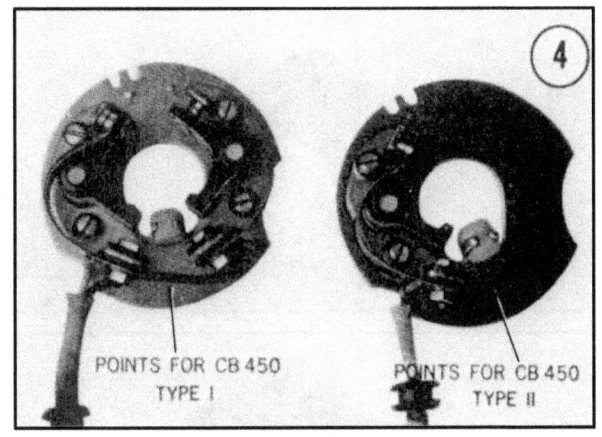
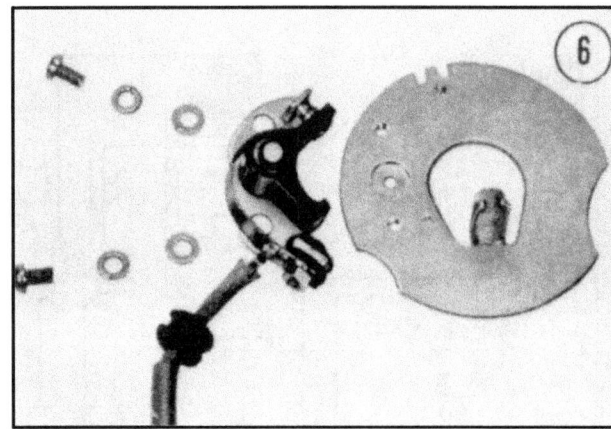
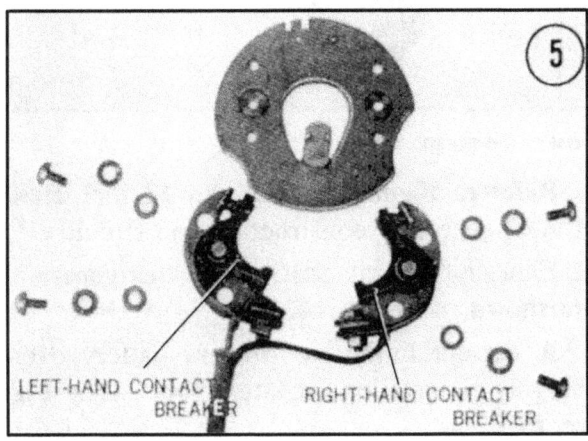
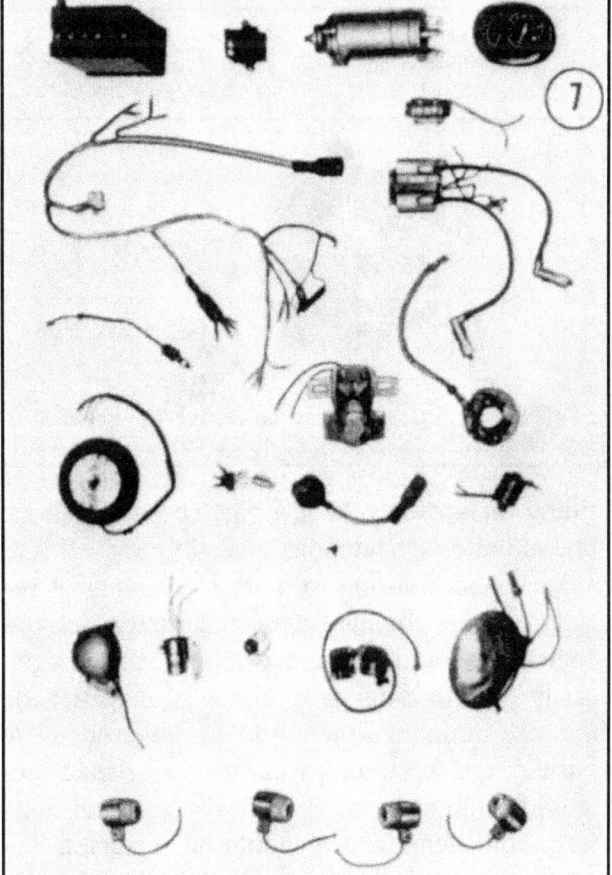

and the components, checking for evidences of burning or overheating. (**Figure 7**).

3. The best test for coil, condenser and spark plug operation is to replace the suspected misfunctioning items with known good ones one at a time.

4. Test the coil or coils for shorts (0 or extremely low resistance) between the primary and secondary terminals with an ohmeter. Clean all dirt and grease from around the terminals. Coils sometimes function on a tester yet fail when they get hot in service.

5. Test the condensers for leaks in their insulation and capacitance value which should be .24 microfarads.

6. Check the points for proper gap (See Section Two) and clean them if necessary. Grease the felt lubricating wick lightly.

7. Replace the breaker arm if the pivot hole is excessively worn.

8. Breaker terminal, insulators and wiring should be kept scrupulously clean at all times.

9. Use contact cleaner (the spray can type is best) to properly clean the points.

10. Refer to **Figures 4, 5, and 6** for details of the early ignition system.

11. **Figure 7A** shows the later ignition system.

12. A mechanical spark advance unit as shown in **Figure 8** is fitted and may be found under the contact breaker assembly. Check that the springs are not broken and the mechanism is free to operate. Advance should begin at 1,800-2,000 rpm with fully advanced condition reached at 3,400 rpm.

13. Spark plugs should be checked every 1,000 miles for condition. An accurate plug reading or check can best be accomplished by

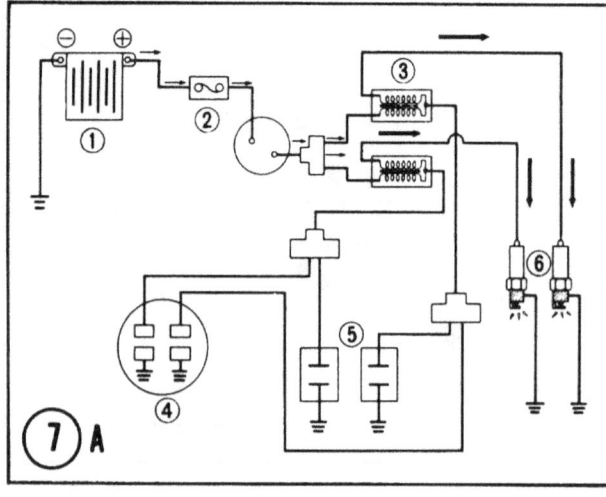

① Battery ② Fuse
③ Ignition coil ④ A.C generator
⑤ Condenser ⑥ Spark plug

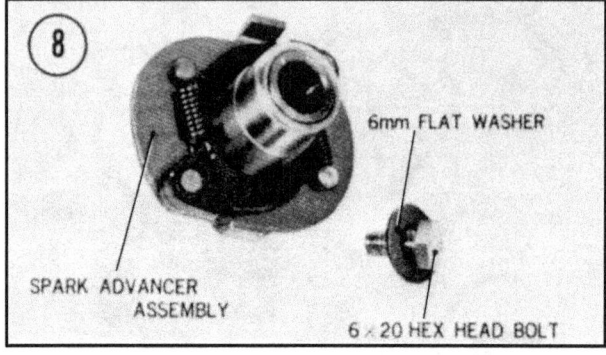

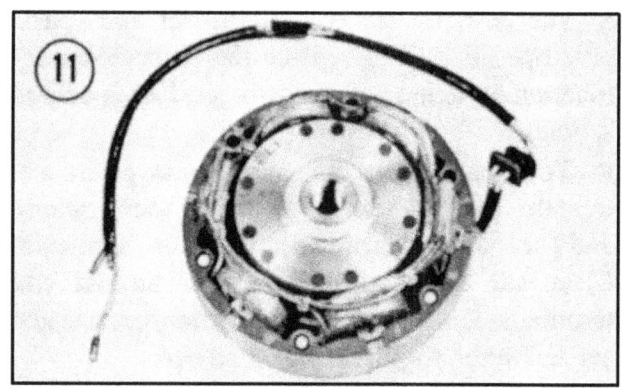

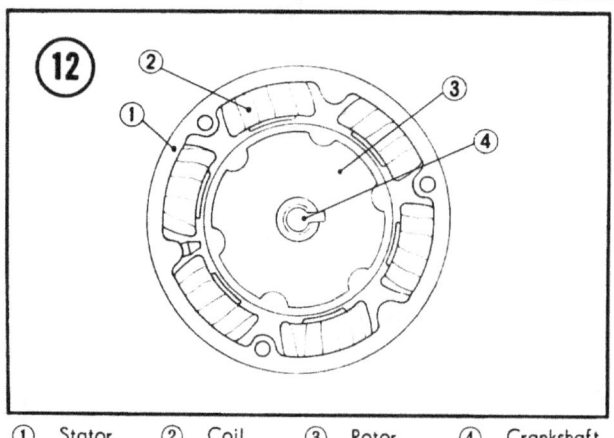

① Stator ② Coil ③ Rotor ④ Crankshaft

riding the motorcycle at a high speed for about one minute, declutching and shutting off the engine, and coasting to a stop. Meaningful results can be obtained with experience but the beginner should be able to spot danger signs easily. The normal plug has a light brown or tan appearance around the electrodes. A burned and worn appearance may indicate late ignition timing or an excessively lean fuel mixture, both items which should be corrected immediately to prevent engine damage. A wet, oily electrode surface could indicate ring, piston or valve defects or a plug of the incorrect heat range. In most cases the CB and CL 450's are fitted with NGK B8ES 14 mm plugs. A hotter plug may be fitted for severe stop and go driving and a colder one should be used for touring or racing.

14. Noise suppressor caps are fitted to the plug wires as shown in **Figures 9 and 10**. Caps shown apply to 4-speed models; 5-speed caps are similar but have a 45° bend. Replace them if they become excessively worn and use care to ensure the plug wires are properly seated.

Power System

1. Refer to **Figures 11, 12 and 13** for details of A.C. generator construction and circuitry.

2. Charging characteristics for the generator are shown in **Figure 14**.

3. A current limiter to prevent battery overcharging is installed on later models. See **Figure 15**.

4. **Figure 16** shown a hook-up diagram for installing the limiter on a motorcycle without one.

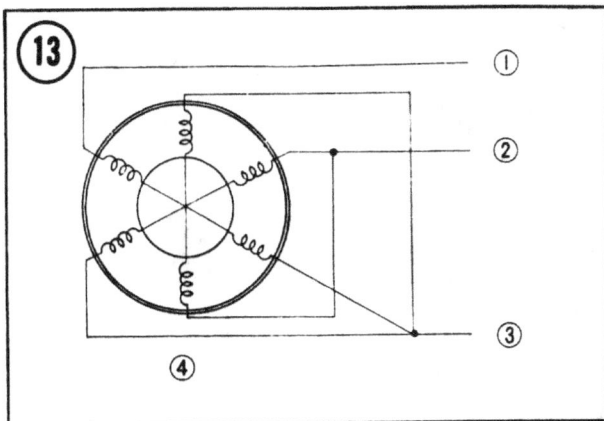

① Yellow (daytime)   ② Pink (night time)
③ Brown (common)   ④ Generator

Load	Charging initial rpm	Charging current (A)		
		3000 rpm	5000 rpm	10000 rpm
Day: Ignition coil	1000 rpm Max	3.5±0.5	4.5±0.5	5.7 Max
Night (I) Ignition coil +12V 35W (H·L) +8W (T·L) +3W (B·L) +3W×2 (M·L)	1800 rpm Max	1.1 +0.5 −0.1	1.9 +0.5 −0.3	3.2 Max
Night (II) Ignition coil +12V 25W (H·L) +8W (T·L) +3W×2 (M·L)	1500 rpm Max	2.1±0.5	2.9±0.5	4.0 Max

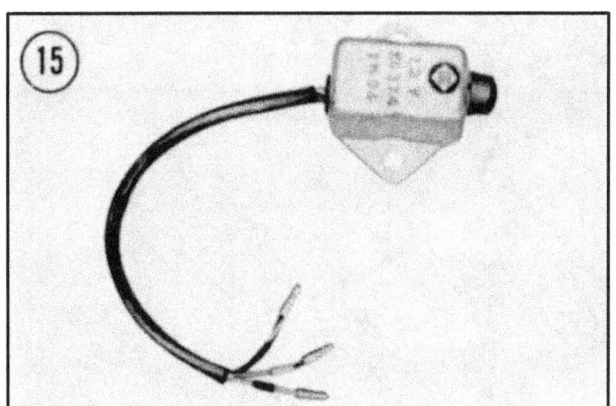

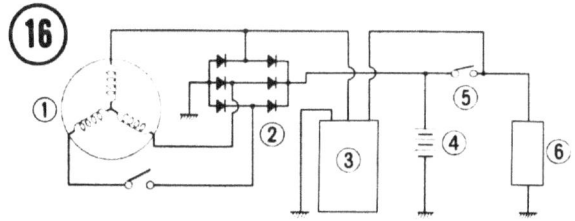

① AC generator   ② Selenium rectifier
③ Current limiter   ④ Battery
⑤ Ignition switch   ⑥ Load

5. When servicing the limiter, which is a silicon rectifier, do not remove the rubber cap and do not tamper with the nut found under the cap. The ignition switch should be in the "off" position during installation or removal.

6. Two types of rectifiers are shown in **Figures 17 and 18.** Rectifiers are damaged by wrong electrical connections, heat and humidity. In addition, the motorcycle should not be operated with the battery disconnected for any length of time as this will damage the rectifier.

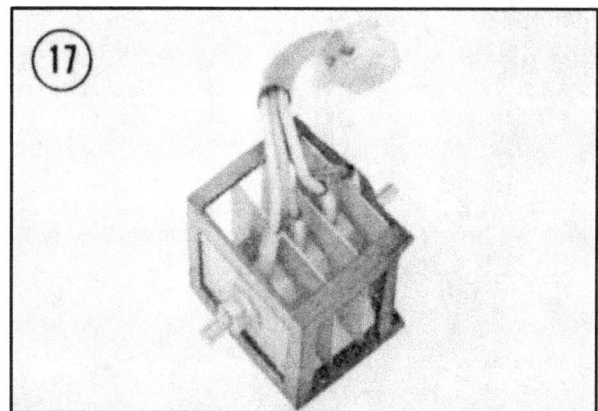

7. Rectifier circuitry is shown in **Figure 19.** Battery and rectifier mechanical details are shown in **Figure 20.**

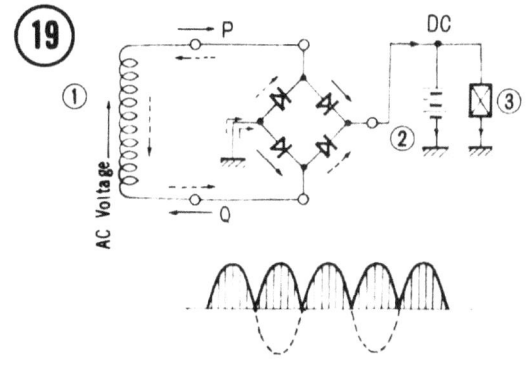

① Generating coil   ② Battery   ③ Load

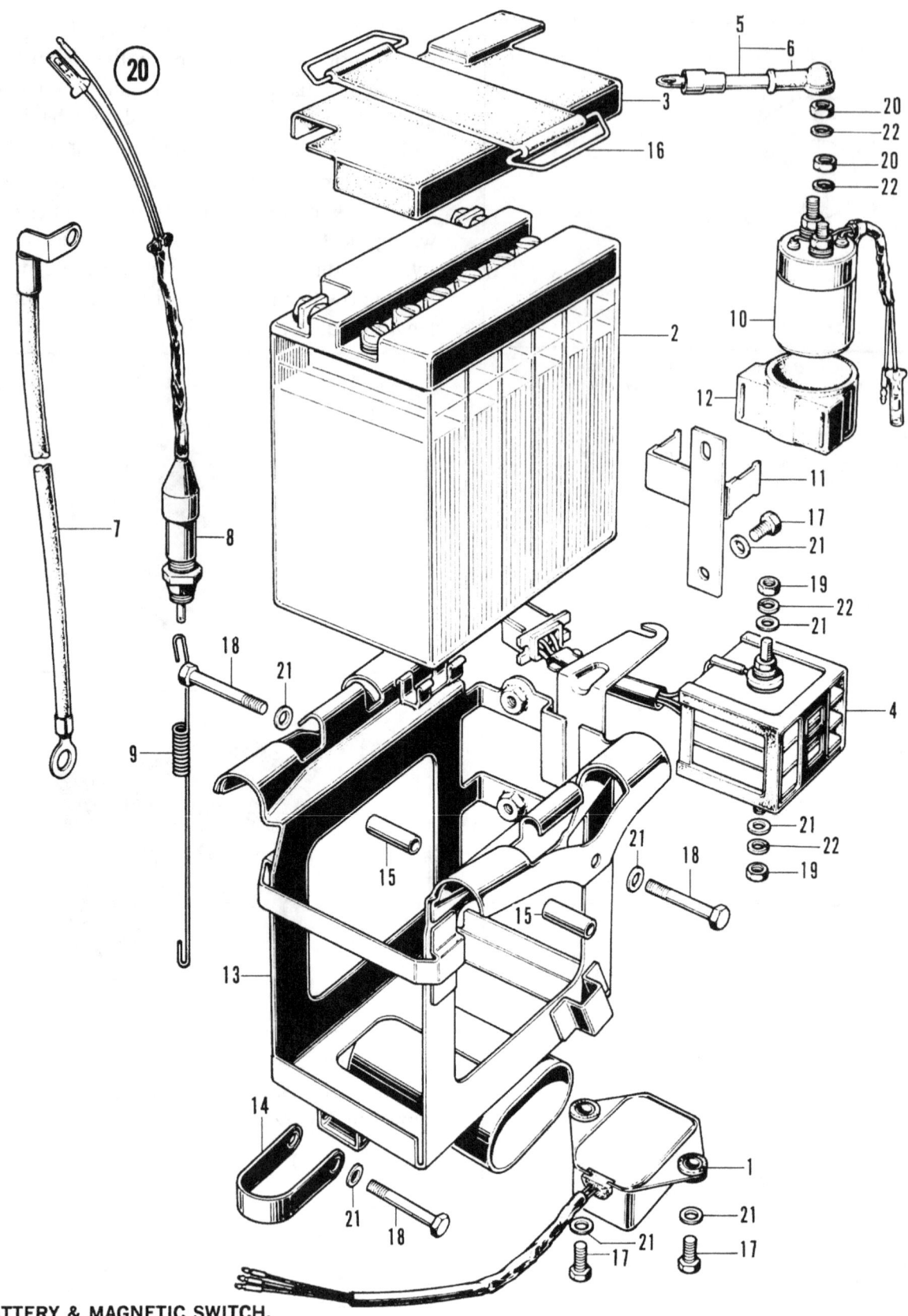

BATTERY & MAGNETIC SWITCH, 5-SPEED

1. Regulator, pointless
2. Battery Assy. (12V12AH)
3. Cover, battery
4. Rectifier Assy., selenium (Shindengen)
5. Cable, starter battery
6. Cover, starting motor terminal
7. Cable, battery earth
8. Switch Assy., stop (T.E.C.)
9. Spring, stop switch
10. Switch Assy., starter magnetic
11. Stay, magnetic rubber
12. Rubber, magnetic shock
13. Box, battery (black)
14. Stay, battery box lower (black)
15. Collar, battery box
16. Band, battery
17. Bolt, hex., 6x12
18. Bolt, hex., 6x40
19. Nut, hex., 6mm
20. Nut, hex., 6mm
21. Washer, plain, 6mm
22. Washer, spring, 6mm

Battery Service

1. Battery neglect is common among motorcyclists. Frequently inspect the battery for signs of damage and low electrolyte level.

2. Keep the battery filled to the level mark on the outside case as shown in **Figure 21.** Failure to do this will reduce service life. If the battery's plates are exposed to air for any length of time, sulfation occurs. In many cases damage is irreversible.

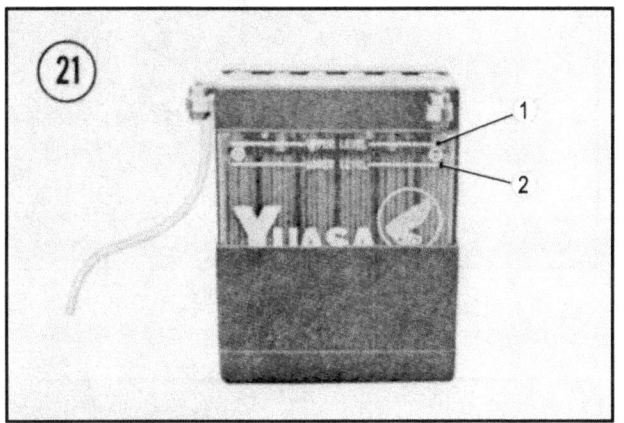

① Upper level mark   ② Lower level mark

3. Keep the battery charged at all times. If a lot of night time driving is done, the generator may not keep the battery charged. Remove the battery periodically and charge it with a service (trickle) charger.

4. Keep the battery terminals and outside surfaces clean to cut down on current leaks. Silicon spray may be applied after the terminals are connected to avoid corrosion.

Electric Starter Service

1. Refer to **Figures 22, 23, 24 and 25** for details of the starter motor and the planetary gear reduction mechanism.

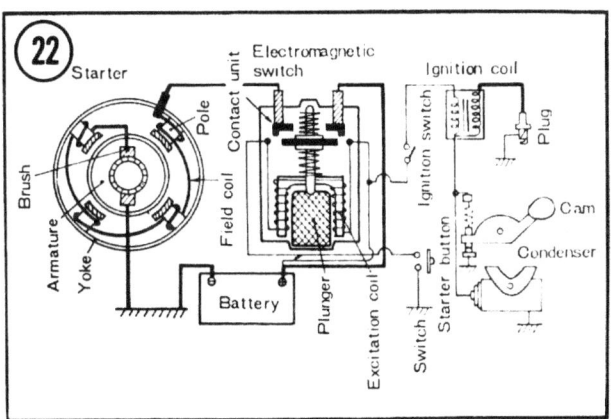

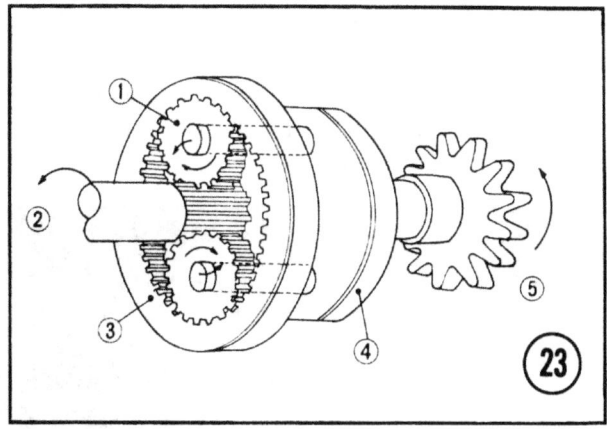

① Planetary gear   ② Motor shaft
③ Internal gear   ④ Sprocket shaft
⑤ Starting sprocket

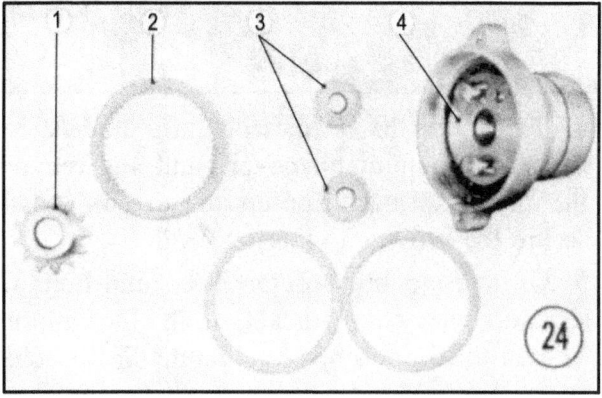

① Starting Sprocket   ② Internal gear
③ Planetary gears   ④ Sprocket shaft

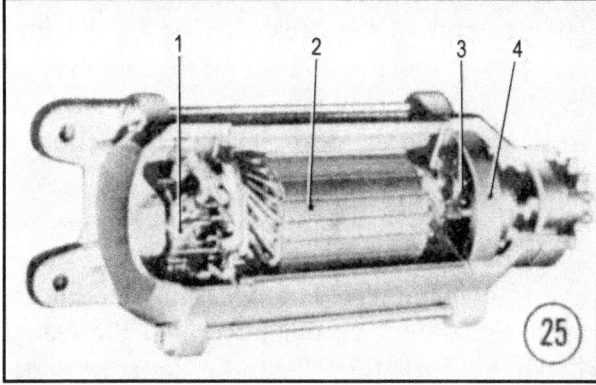

① Commutator   ② Armature
③ Planetary gear   ④ Internal gear

2. The starting motor receives very little use in most cases and generally requires infrequent service. Brush and commutator wear should be checked, carbon dust (from the brushes) should be blown out with compressed air, and the gear case should be greased periodically.

3. To remove the starter, take off the left crankcase cover and remove the starter cable from its terminal. Early CB 450's had a starter motor side cover (see **Figure 26**) held by two

phillips head screws. Remove the two 6mm bolts from the right side and pull the motor out, carefully disconnecting the chain from its sprocket. Do not force the motor out, or serious damage may result.

4. To service the brushes on early models, remove the commutator cover band and remove the brush springs. Loosen the screws which secure the brushes to the field coil.

5. On late models, unscrew two 5mm bolts to separate the end bracket from the motor. Loosen the 3mm screw holding the brush holder to the field coil and remove the bracket. Remove the brushes from their holder.

6. Reassemble in reverse order of disassembly, being careful so the brush lug on the positive side doesn't touch the inside of the end bracket on the later model starter. Check that the brush leads (wires) don't hamper the action of the brushes.

7. In **Figure 27,** diagram A shows the normal condition of a commutator. Diagram B shows a worn commutator. The mica must be undercut if the copper becomes worn to the extent shown. Undercutting should be done by someone with a thorough knowledge of the techniques involved.

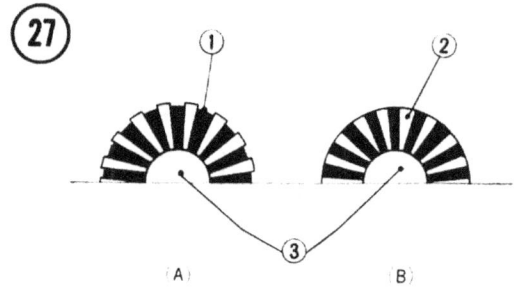

① Mica piece ② Commutator (copper) ③ Motor shaft

8. Reassemble the starter, using care to avoid damaging gaskets and O rings in order to keep the assembly waterproof.

Starting Clutch Service

1. Refer to **Figures 28, 29 and 30** for details of starting clutch construction and operation.

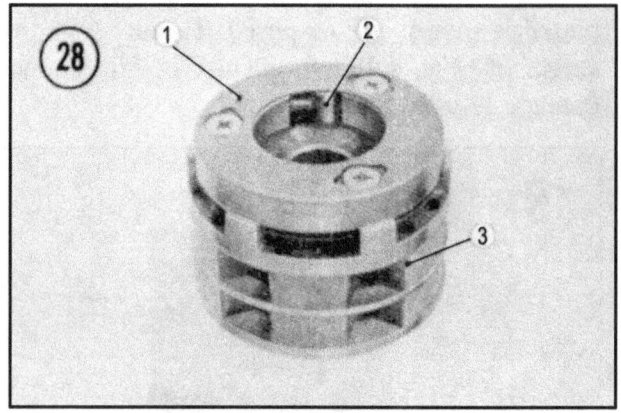

① Starting clutch outer
② 10.2×11.5 roller
③ AC generator rotor

① Starting clutch side plate
② Starting sprocket
③ Starting clutch outer
④ 8×18 knock pin
⑤ 10.2×11.5 roller
⑥ Starting clutch roller spring
⑦ Starting clutch roller spring cap

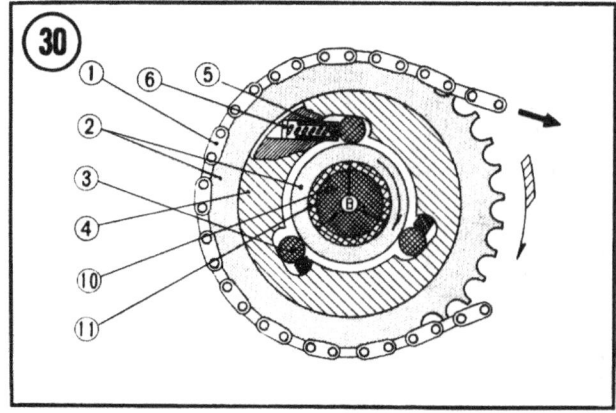

2. Handle the clutch rollers very carefully and grease them before reassembly. Use silicon grease.

3. Check that starting clutch parts have not become magnetized. Irregular operation could result. Replace if the parts show attraction for each other.

Solenoid Service

1. Refer to **Figures 31 and 32** for details of solenoid construction and service.

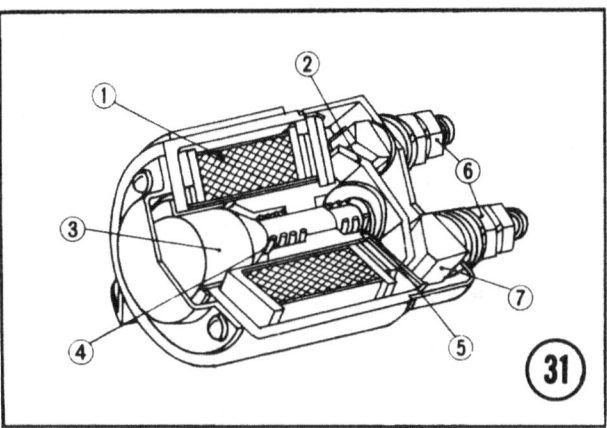

① Magnetic coil (primary coil)
② Contact (operating side)
③ Plunger
④ Return spring
⑤ Contact return spring
⑥ Terminals
⑦ Contact (fixed side)

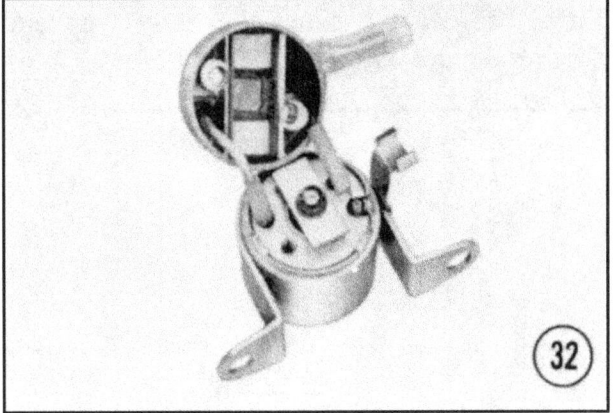

2. The cover may be removed as shown to clean the solenoid contact points. File them clean if burnt, and wipe them if oil is found. Check the O ring and replace if worn to keep oil out of the solenoid case.

3. If the trouble is not cleared up, the starter switch, solenoid coil, plunger or wiring may be defective.

Horn Service

1. If the horn is weak or inoperative, check that the battery is fully charged and all circuits are in working order.

2. Remove the horn cover and adjust tone and loudness with the adjusting screw. On late models, (as shown in **Figure 33**) do not turn the adjusting screw more than two turns in either direction.

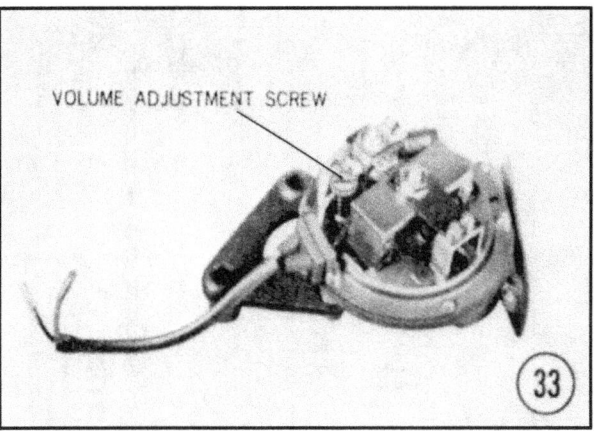

Tail and Stop Light Service

1. A 12 volt, 23/7 Watt combination bulb is used in the stoplight and tail light assembly.

Indicator Light Service

1. All indicator lights are 12 volt, 3 Watt.

Speedometer and Tachometer Service

1. Instruments should be serviced by a qualified technician.

Headlight Service

1. Very early CB 450's used a sealed beam headlight (see **Figure 34**). Later models use the type shown in **Figure 35**.

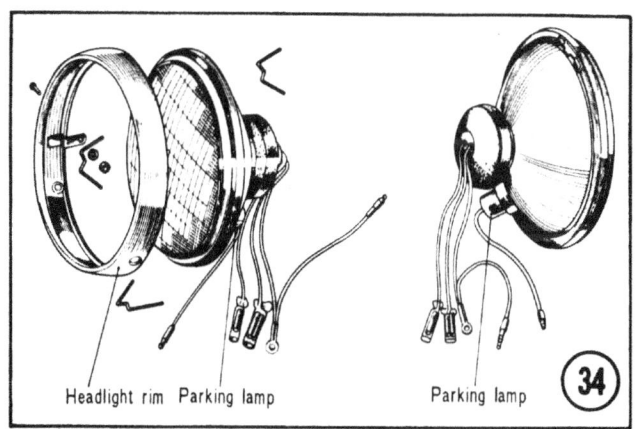

Headlight rim   Parking lamp   Parking lamp

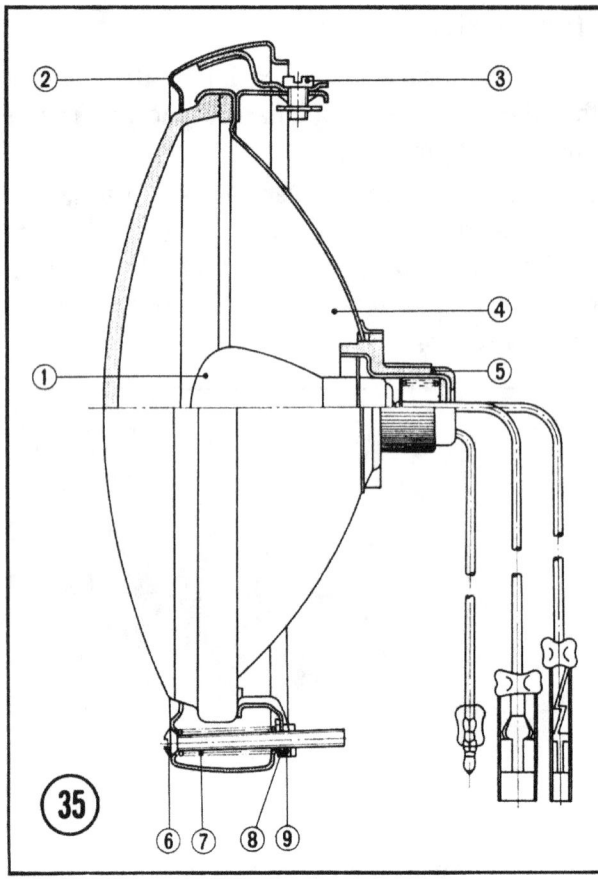

① Headlight fixing bolt ② Adjusting screw

① Headlight bulb   ② Headlight rim
③ Unit holder screw ④ Headlight unit
⑤ Headlight socket ⑥ Beam adjust screw
⑦ Beam adjust spring ⑧ Washer
⑨ Beam adjust nut

2. The headlight may be adjusted in a horizontal direction by turning the adjusting screw (No. 2, **Figure 36**) in or out. Vertical adjustment is accomplished by loosening the headlight mounting bolts and tilting the entire headlight assembly.

3. The headlight bulb is a 12 volt, 35/25 Watt unit.

Turn Signal Flasher Relay Service

1. The flasher relay is a negative grounded unit. Ensure that the case is mounted firmly with no paint or rust preventing a good ground connection.

2. Use bulbs of the correct type (12 volt, 25 Watt) and check them immediately if the turn signals fail to operate.

Wire Harness Service

1. Two types of wire harness arrangement are shown. **Figure 37** shows the early type and **Figures 38 and 39** depict the later type.

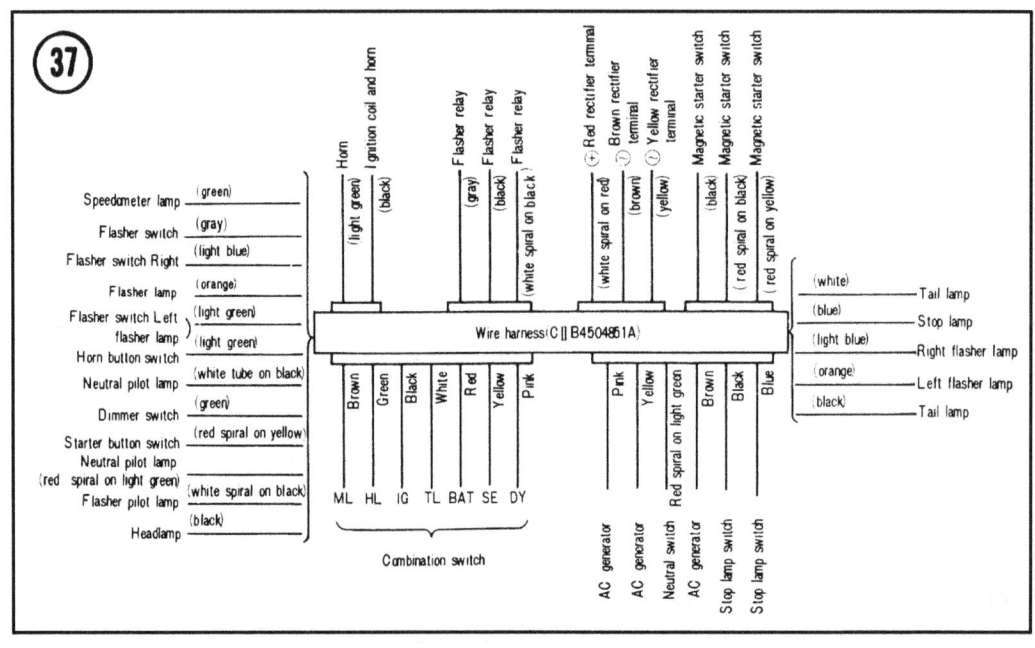

2. In servicing and testing, be extremely careful you are using the correct diagram.

3. If internal failure occurs in the wiring harness, an additional wire or cable must be attached to the harness to replace the damaged or defective one. Otherwise, an entire new harness must be installed.

Using a Service Tester

1. A service tester is a great aid in accurately checking electrical components. Most testers are similar in operation to the one shown here.

2. If the tester requires an outside power source, a 6 or 12 volt battery may be used except when testing a coil. For coil tests, use a battery of the same voltage as the coil being tested.

3. These instructions apply to a Jonan Service Tester, model ST-4B4. See **Figure 40**.

Continuity Testing

1. Use the continuity test to search out broken or disconnected wires or for checking suspected fuses.

2. Connect the power source (battery) as shown in **Figure 41**, using the red/white dual cable. Connect the red wire to the positive battery terminal and the white wire to the negative terminal.

3. Turn the selector switch to "Continuity" and check that the power source pilot light is lit.

4. Hook up the free lead to terminal "x" on the tester.

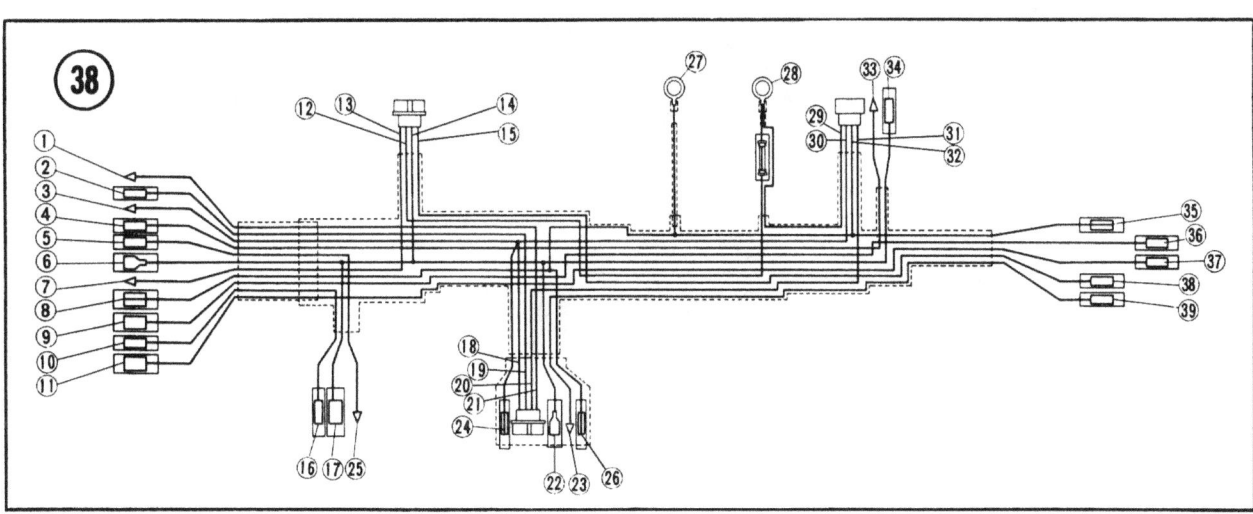

Ref. No.	Wire color	Connected to
①	Lt. green/red	Neutral pilot lamp.
②	White/yellow tube	Lighting dimmer switch
③	Yellow	Lighting dimmer switch
④	Yellow/red	Starter button switch
⑤	Gray	Turn signal switch
⑥	Black	Lighting-dimmer switch, neutral pilot lamp.
⑦	Brown/white	Speedometer lamp, Lighting dimme rswitch.
⑧	Green	High beam hedlight, R. L. turnr signal lamp.
⑨	Lt. blue	R. front turn signal lamp, turn signal switch.
⑩	Lt. green	Horn button switch
⑪	Orange	L. front turn signal lamp, turn signal switch.
⑫	Red	Main ignition switch
⑬	Brown/white	Main ignition switch
⑭	Black	Main ignition switch
⑮	Brown	Main ignition switch
⑯	Lt. green	Horn
⑰	Black	Horn, flasher relay ignition coil
⑱	Yellow	A. C. generator
⑲	White	A. C. generator
⑳	Pink	A. C. generator

Ref. No.	Wire color	Connected to
㉑	Lt. green/red	A. C. generator
㉒	Black	Regulator, stop switch
㉓	Green/Yellow	Regulator, stop switch
㉔	Yellow	Regulator
㉕	Gray	Flasher relay
㉖	Green	Regulator
㉗	Green	Battery (negative terminal)
㉘	Red	Battery (positive terminal)
㉙	Red/white	Selenium rectifier
㉚	Yellow	Selenium rectifier
㉛	Pink	Selenium rectifier
㉜	Green	Selenium rectifier
㉝	Yellow/red	Starter magnetic switch
㉞	Black	Starter magnetic switch
㉟	Green	R. L. rear turn signal lamp, tail light
㊱	Lt. bule	R. rear turn signal lamp
㊲	Orange	L. rear turn signal lamp
㊳	Brown	Tail light
㊴	Green/Yellow	Stop light

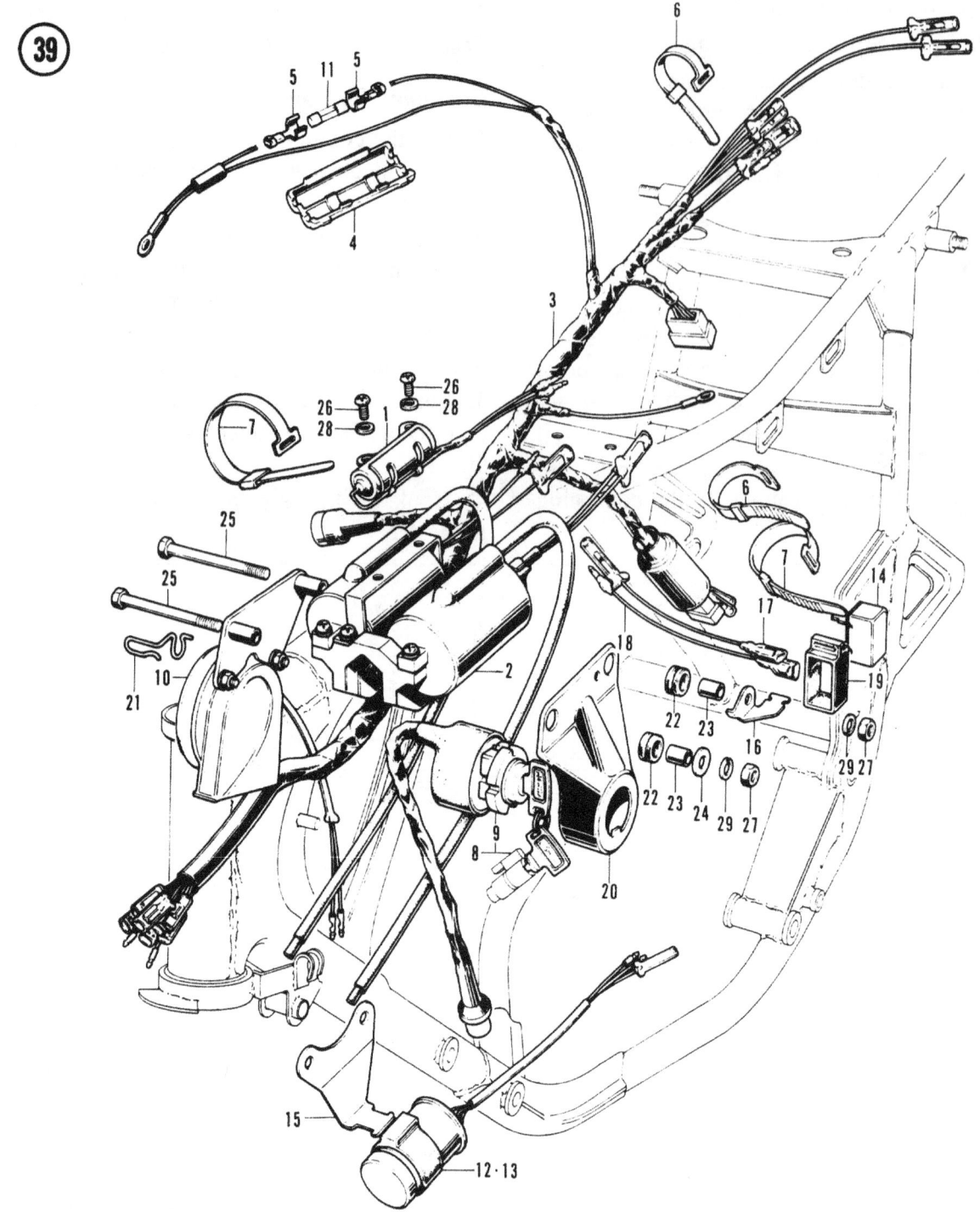

WIRE HARNESS, IGNITION COIL, & COMBINATION SWITCH, 5-SPEED

1. Condenser Comp. (Kokusan; T.E.C.)
2. Coil Assy., ignition (Kokusan; T.E.C.)
3. Harness, wire
4. Case, fuse connector
5. Connector, fuse
6. Band A, wire harness
7. Band B, wire harness
8. Switch-Kit, combination (T.E.C.)
9. Switch Assy., combination (T.E.C.)
10. Horn Assy., (Mitsuba)
11. Fuse (15A)
12. Relay Assy., winker
13. Relay Assy., winker (Used in Germany)
14. Relay Assy., winker (Used in U.S.A.)
15. Stay, winker relay (Not used in U.S.A.)
16. Stay, winker relay (Used in U.S.A.)
17. Sub-Cord A, winker relay (Used in U.S.A.)
18. Sub-Cord B, winker relay (Used in U.S.A.)
19. Suspension, winker relay (Used in U.S.A.)
20. Bracket, main switch (black)
21. Clip, tachometer cable
22. Rubber, number bracket cushion
23. Collar, number bracket setting
24. Washer, 18mm
25. Bolt, hex., 6x80
26. Screw, pan, 5x8
27. Nut, hex., 6mm
28. Washer, spring, 5mm
29. Washer, spring, 6mm

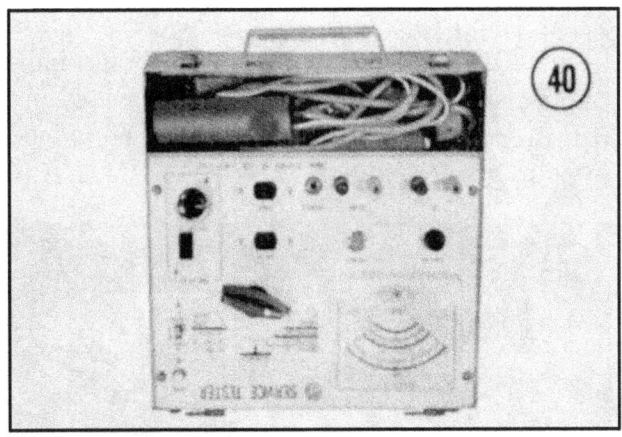

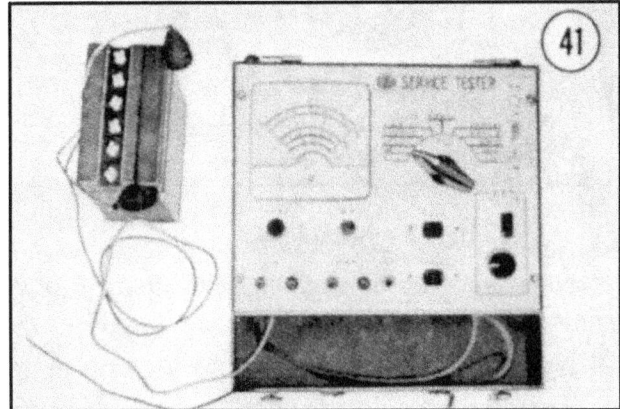

5. Touch the lead wires to the item being tested. If an unbroken current path exists, the continuity lamp will light up.

Measuring Resistance

1. Connect the power source as for the continuity check. Turn on the resistance switch.
2. Short circuit the test leads as shown in **Figure 42** and zero the meter by turning the scale adjusting knob.

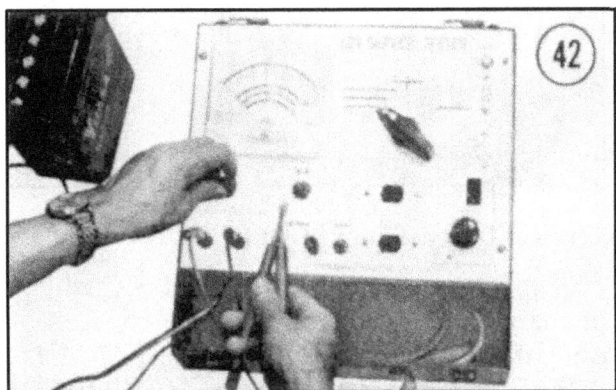

3. Connect the leads using the schematic diagram to determine positive and negative terminals on the rectifier. Measure resistance in both directions. More than 100 ohms indicates satisfactory negative resistance. Note that the rectifier must be removed from the motorcycle circuit for measurement.

Condenser Tests

1. Before making tests of condenser resistance insulate the points and disconnect the coil primary line connector. For the capacity measurement, disconnect the point wire lead in addition to taking the above steps.

2. Connect a power source to the tester and switch on the "insulation" switch. Short circuit the lead wires and zero the meter by turning the scale adjusting knob.

3. Connect the condenser into the circuit. The meter needle will swing in a positive direction and then return. Take a reading when the needle is almost stable. Five Megohms or more means the condenser insulation is good. One to 5 Megohms indicate satisfactory insulation while less than 1 Megohm means the condenser should be replaced.

4. Discharge the condenser when the test is complete by touching the condenser lead to the metal body as shown in **Figure 43** to avoid a shock.

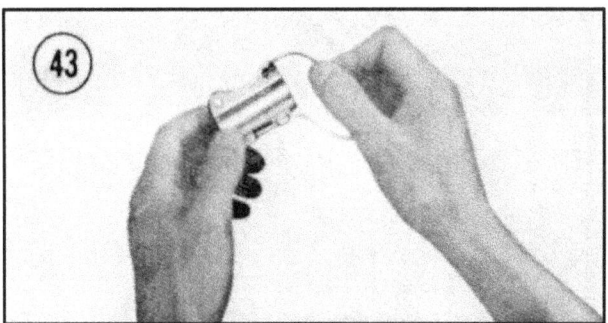

5. To measure condenser capacitance, remember to insulate the points, and disconnect the coil primary line connector and the point wire lead. Hook up a power source and turn the switch to "resistance."

6. Short circuit the leads and zero the meter as before.

7. Turn the selector switch to "Condenser." See **Figure 44.**

8. Place the condenser in the test circuit and take a reading from the meter. 0.21 microfarads to 0.26 microfarads indicates condenser capacitance is satisfactory. Anything under the low figure means the condenser needs replacing.

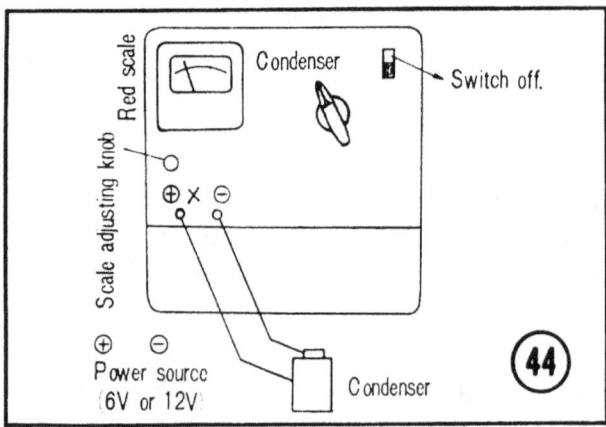

D.C. Voltage Measurement

1. No power source is required for this test. Set the selector switch to "D.C. Voltage." Connect the item being tested into the circuit, using the red test lead on the positive side and the black test lead on the negative side. This meter measures up to 30 volts.

D.C. Current Measurement

1. No power source is required for this test.

2. Connect the tester leads into the D.C. Current terminals as shown in **Figure 45**.

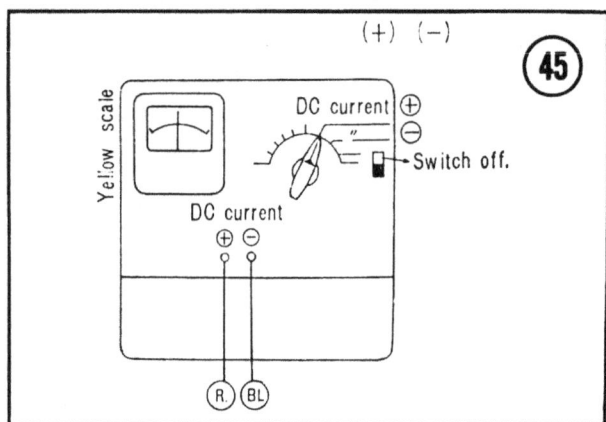

3. Disconnect the B terminal of the wire harness from the positive battery terminal. Connect the tester black lead to the battery and connect the wire harness B terminal to the red test lead. See **Figure 46**.

4. Turn the selector switch to "D.C. Current (+)". Start the motor and check that the needle swings to the positive side to indicate a charging condition. As the engine speeds up, if the needle moves in a negative direction, the selector switch may be moved to "D.C. Current (−)".

5. At 1,500 rpm the needle should read close to the "0" mark on the meter and should indicate a rising value as the engine is speeded up. If this occurs, the power circuit may be judged to be in good condition.

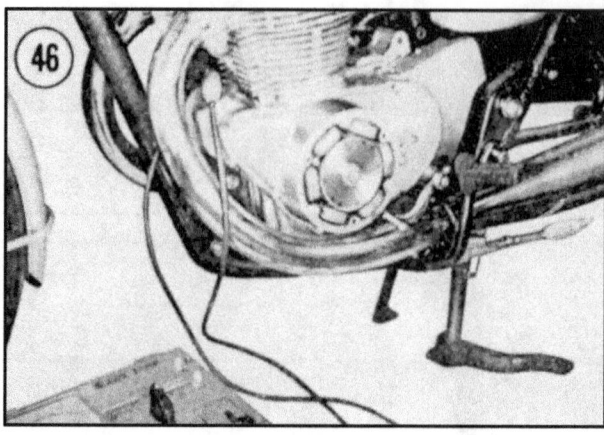

Service Tester Tachometer

1. Measurement of engine speed up to 6,000 rpm can be made with the service tester.

2. No power source is required.

3. Turn on the "Tachometer" switch and connect the tachometer plug into the jack marked "tachometer" on the tester. Read the green meter scale marked "6,000 rpm". Refer to **Figure 47**.

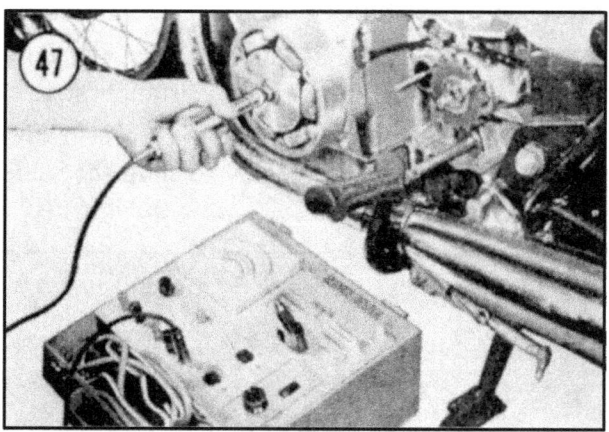

Service Tester Timing Light

1. Timing can be set exactly and the condition of the advance mechanism can be checked by using the timing function of the tester.

2. Remove the generator cover and point cover to give access to timing marks and points as outlined in Section Two.

3. Connect the power source to the tester and set the function switch to "Timing."

4. Connect the red/white twin lead cord to the "Timing" socket on the tester.

5. Using the hex bolt shown in **Figure 48,** connect the left cylinder spark plug into the circuit with the alligator clip. Replace the spark plug cap on the hex bolt.

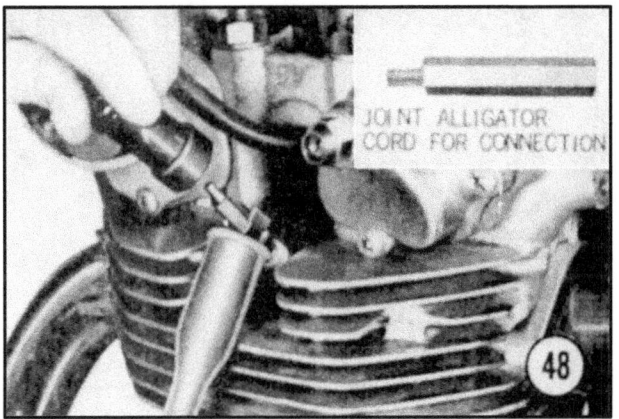

6. Start the engine and the timing light will begin flashing. By pointing the light at the marked portion of the generator rotor, timing can be checked. If the marks do not line up as outlined in Section Two, paragraph 6 of the Ignition Timing section, loosen the contact breaker installing screw and adjust until proper. Remember that right cylinder timing is adjusted by changing point gap after the left cylinder has been properly timed.

7. Check that the advance mechanism is working by revving the engine above idle and watching the mark on the generator rotor. It will move when the advance mechanism begins to operate.

Coil Tests

1. Coil efficiency should be tested if hard starting is experienced.

2. Connect the power source and ground the tester.

3. Connect the white lead with the connecting plug to the (—) terminal and the red lead to the (+) terminal.

4. Connect the red high voltage lead from the tester socket to the high voltage coil lead as shown in **Figure 49.**

5. Turn the selector switch to "Coil Test" and observe the spark in the window as the graduated knob is turned. A 6mm spark should be obtained.

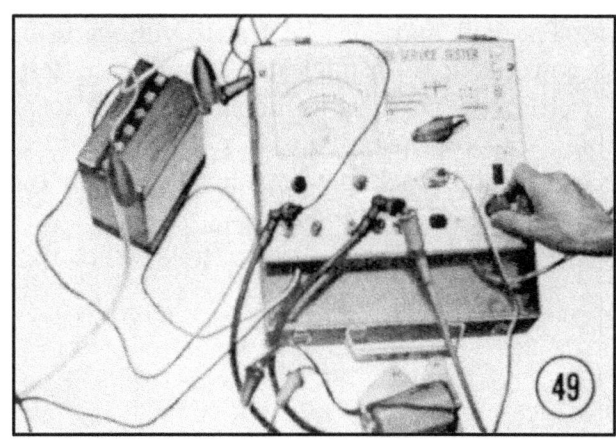

6. The spark should be pulled toward the third electrode as shown in **Figure 50.** If it is pulled away from the third electrode as shown in **Figure 51,** reverse the primary side positive and negative terminals. Normally the spark will be smaller when it is pulled toward the third (tertiary) electrode and the measurement should be applied.

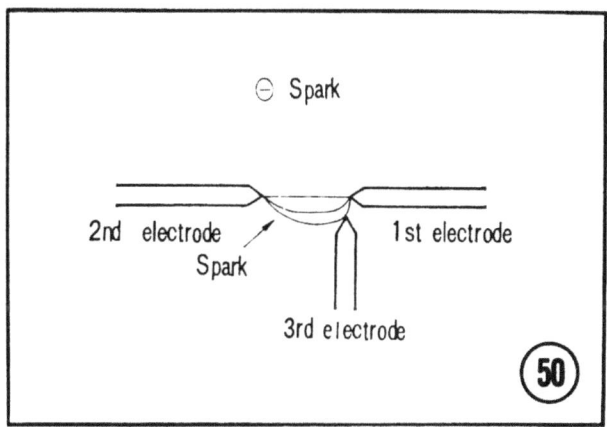

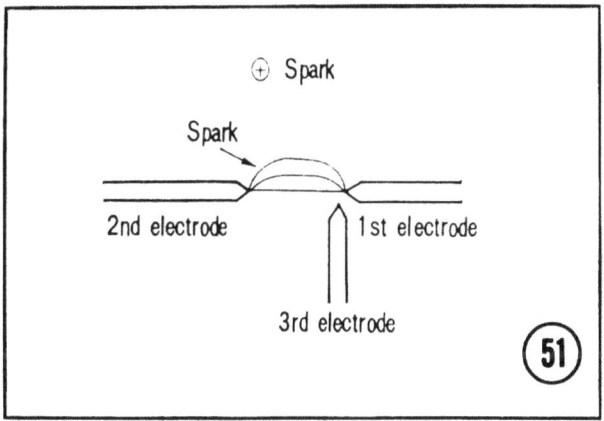

7. Caution: If the coil is being tested on the motorcycle, ground the black cable (which comes out with the power source cord) to the motorcycle body or engine. Omitting this may cause a heavy shock.

8. The coil may also be tested without using a power source for the tester. Connect the tester electrode gap cord to the inside of the spark plug cap by using the hex bolt provided. Ground the black power source cable to the motorcycle body or engine.

9. Set the selector switch to "Coil Test" and turn the ignition switch "on." Turn over the engine by kickstarter or electric starter and observe and measure the spark as in the preceding test.

SECTION SIX

WIRING DIAGRAMS

4 Speed ....,,,,,,,,,... Page 116

5 Speed USA (Without Front Brake Stoplight) .... Page 117

5 Speed USA (With Front Brake Stoplight ......,,,,,,,..... Page 118

5 Speed - General Export Model - Not USA .... Page 119

5 Speed - UK and Sweden Only .... Page 120

CL 450 K6 .... Page 121

CB 450 K7 .... Page 122

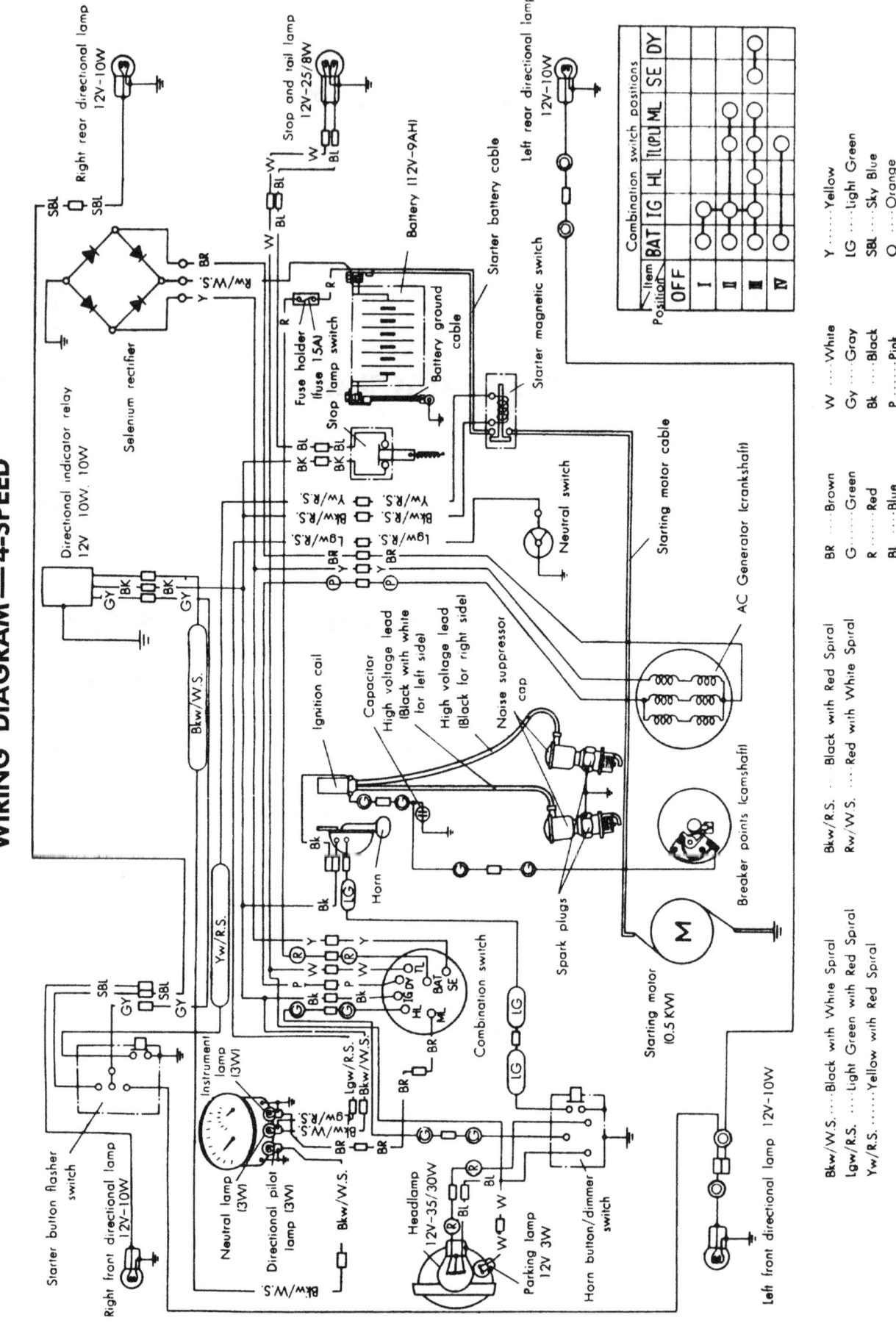

WIRING DIAGRAM—5-SPEED (U.S. without front brake stoplight)

WIRING DIAGRAM—5-SPEED (U.S. with front brake stoplight)

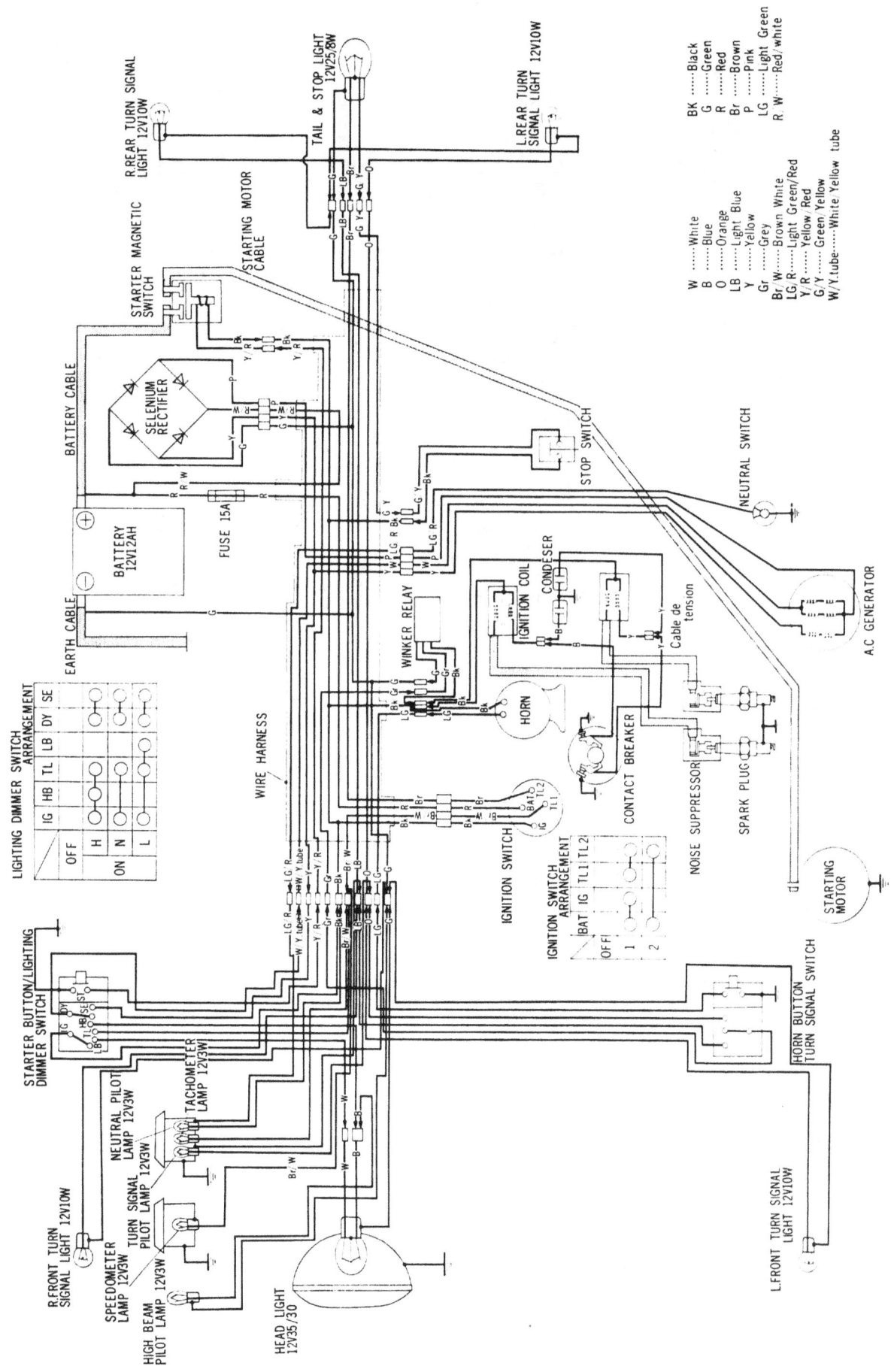

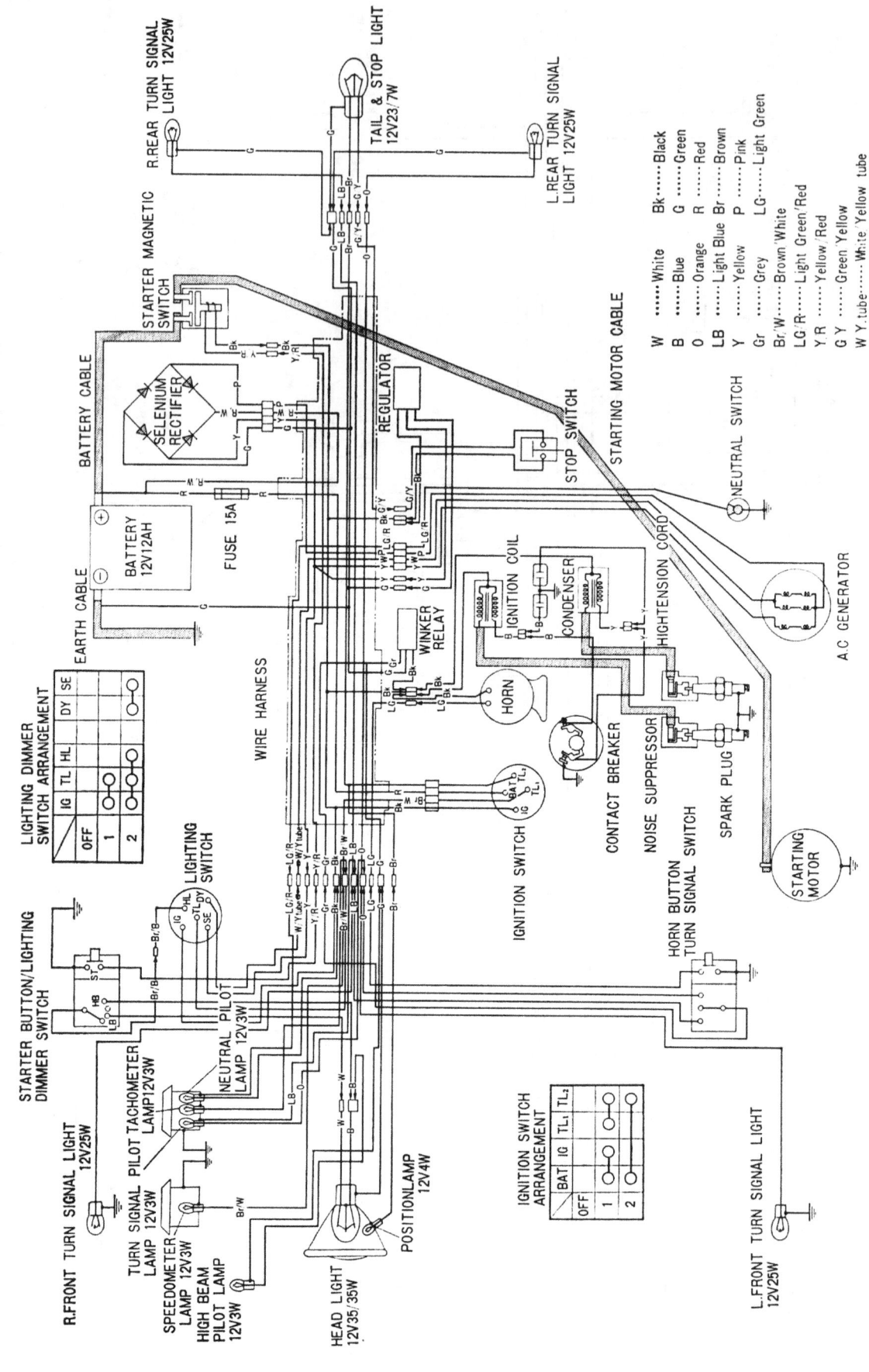

CL 450 K6 WIRING DIAGRAM

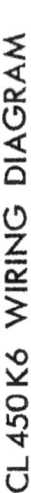

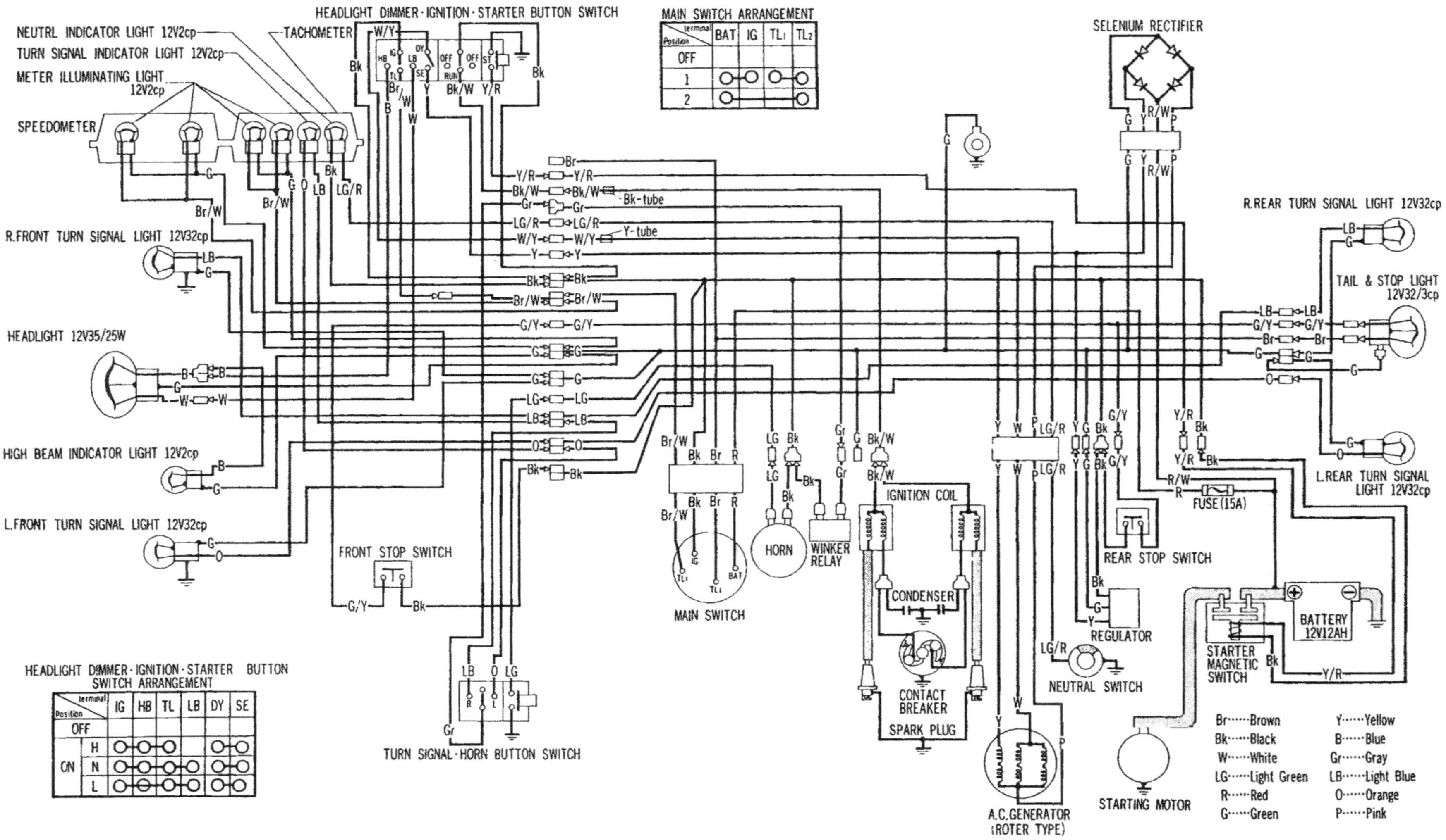

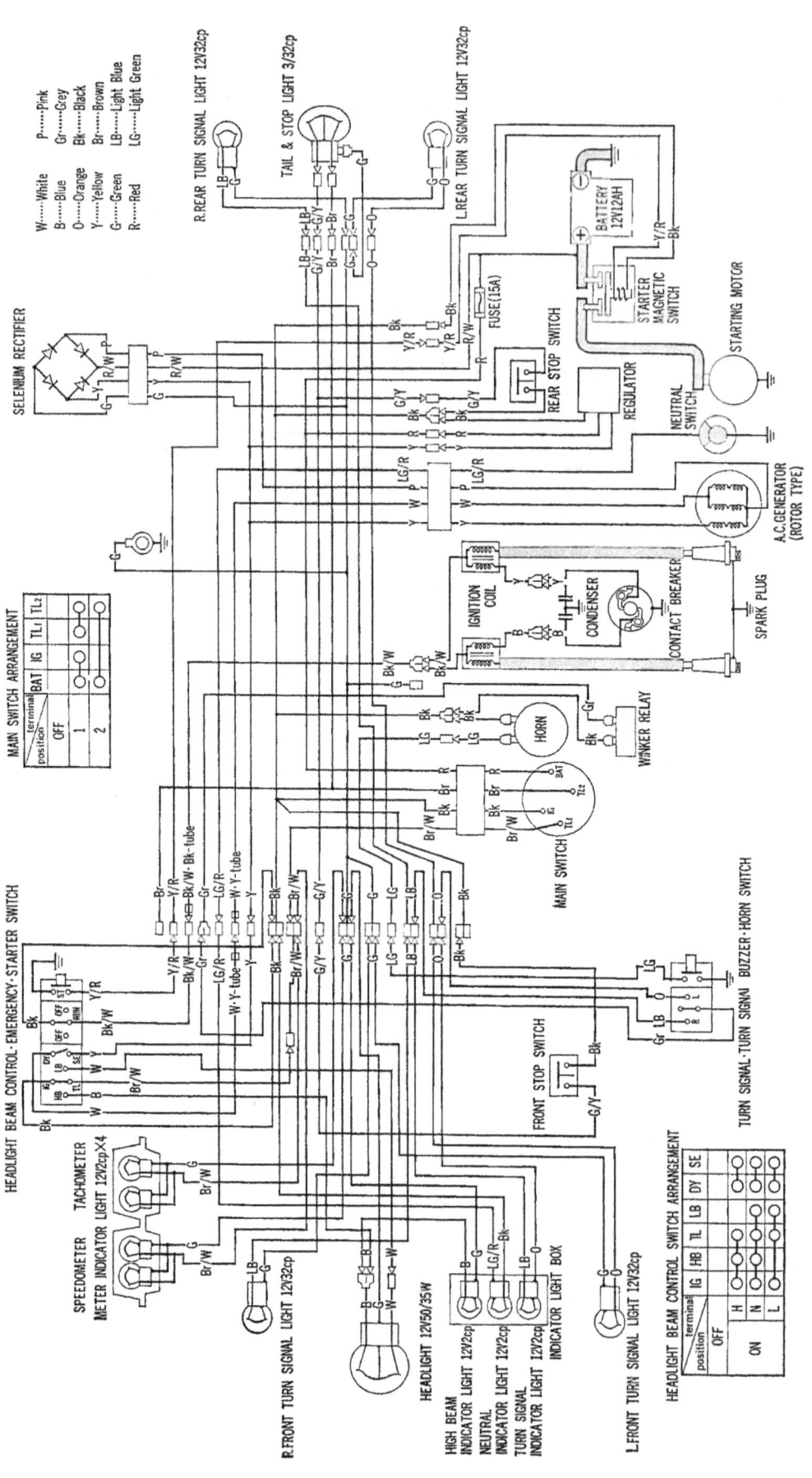

SECTION SEVEN

CB/CL 450 K1~K7 SUPPLEMENT

1. COMPARISON OF CB/CL 450 K1 TO CB/CL 450 K3

Part or item	CB/CL 450 K1	CB/CL 450 K3	Modified part
Tank cap	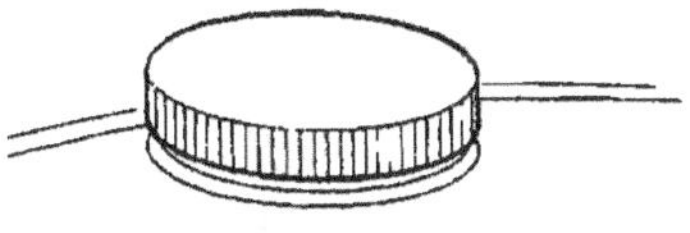 Fig. 7.1 • The tank cap is of a screw-on type	 Fig. 7.2 • The tank cap can be opened by pressing it down and by moving the operating lever	
Kill switch	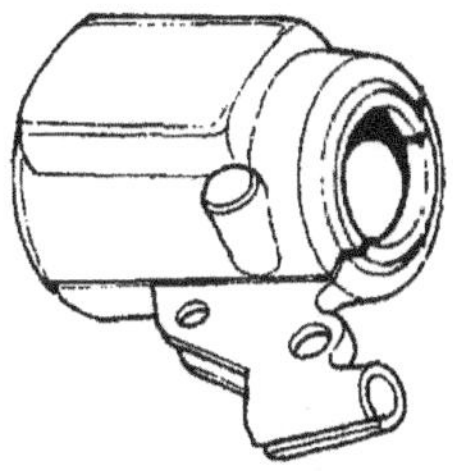 Fig. 7.3 • The kill switch is not used. The surface of the switch assembly finished by buffing.	 Fig. 7.4 • The kill switch is used. The surface of the switch assembly is finished by black, semi-lustered painting.	
Front brake	• Drum type	• Disc type	
Front forks	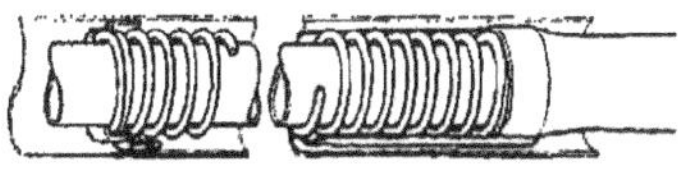 Fig. 7.5 • Springs: External installation • Oil: Condor No. 3 hydraulic oil • Pistons: Fixed type • Damping force: 52 kg/0.5 m/sec.	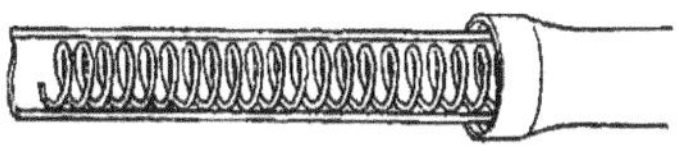 Fig. 7.6 • Springs: Internal installation • Oil: Ultra 10 W-30 • Pistons: Oscillating type • Damping force: 40 kg/0.5 m/sec.	
Steering dampers	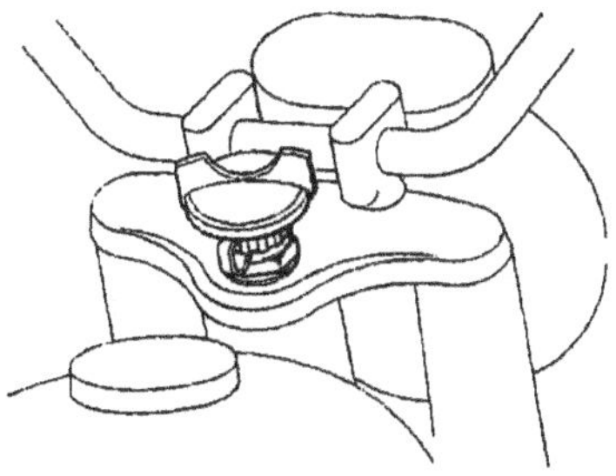 Fig. 7.7 • with friction damper	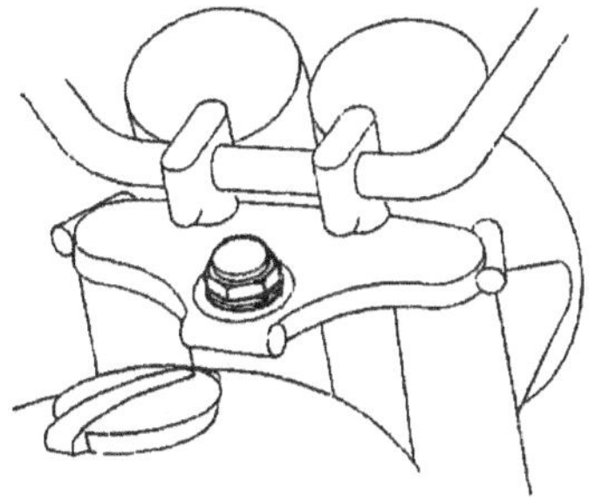 Fig. 7.8 • Without friction damper	

Part or item	CB/CL 450 K1	CB/CL 450 K3	Modified part
Transmission countershaft	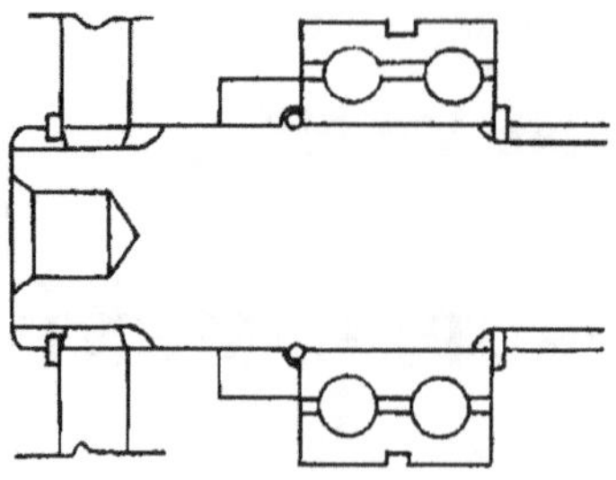 Fig. 7.9	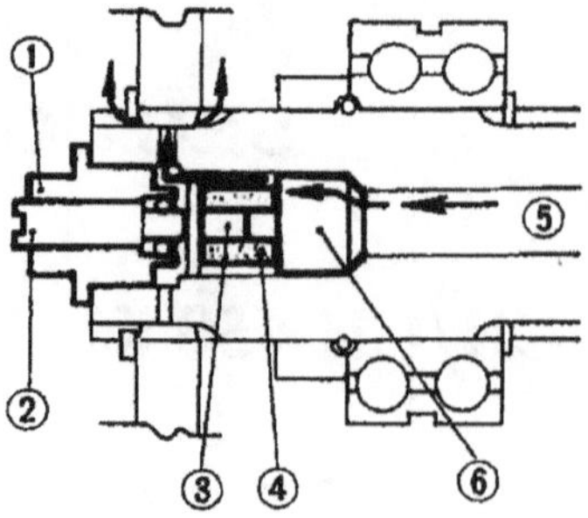 Fig. 7.10 ① Oil reserving plug ② Adjusting screw ③ Stopper ④ Rubber orifice ⑤ Oil ⑥ Oil reserving element	
Oil pump assembly	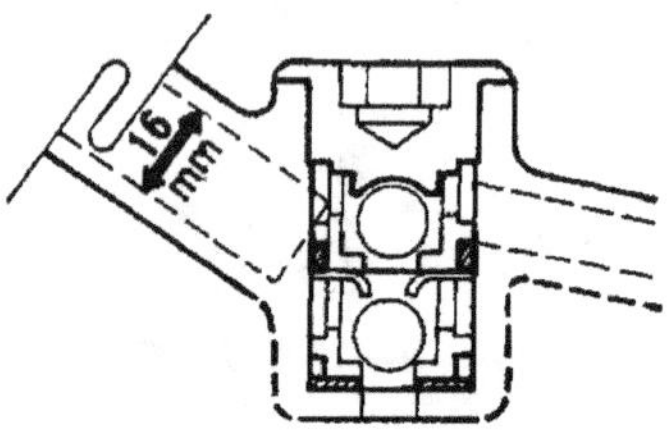 Fig. 7.11 • Plunger diameter: 16 mm (0.6299 in.)	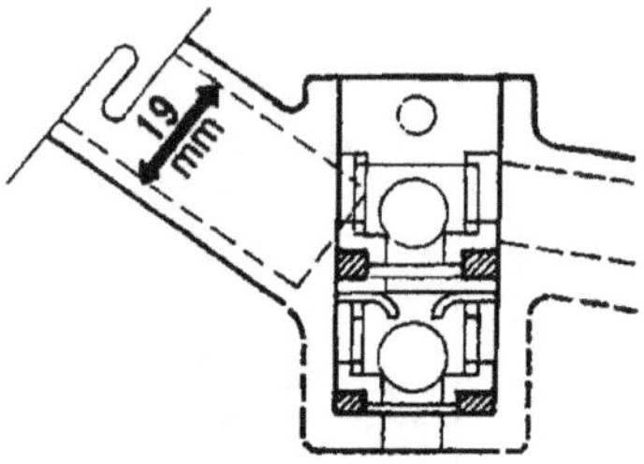 Fig. 7.12 • Plunger diameter: 19 mm (0.7480 in.)	

2. COMPARISON OF CB/CL 450 K3 TO CB/CL 450 K4

Part or item	CB/CL 450 K3	CB/CL 450 K4	Modified part
Fuel tank	(CB type) 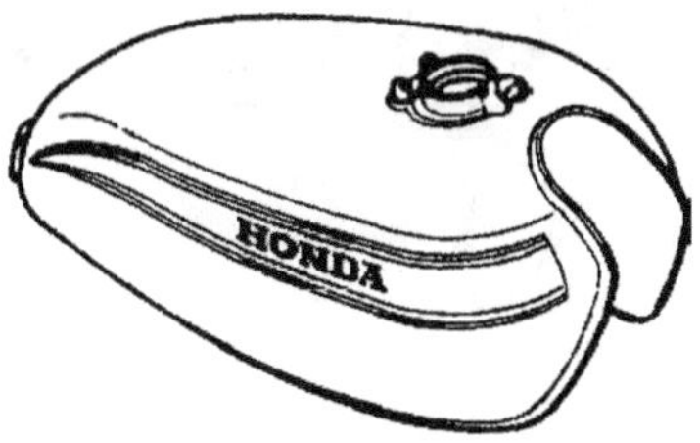 Fig. 7.13	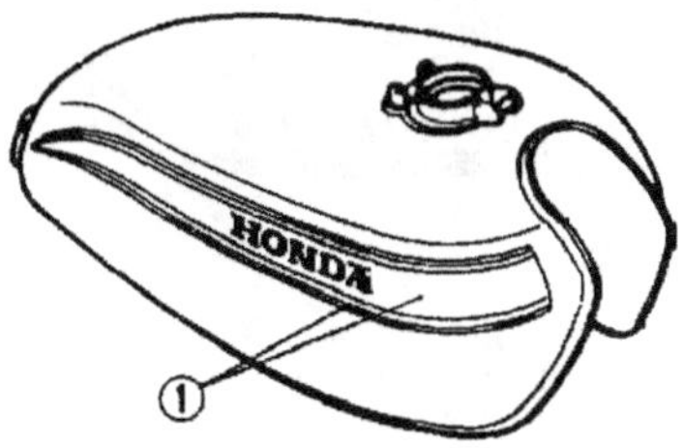 Fig. 7.14 ① Black Color of stripes are changed	
	(CL type) 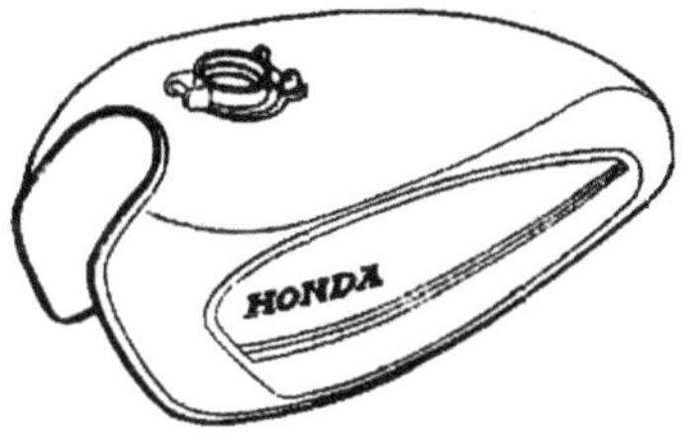 Fig. 7.15	Shape of stripes are changed 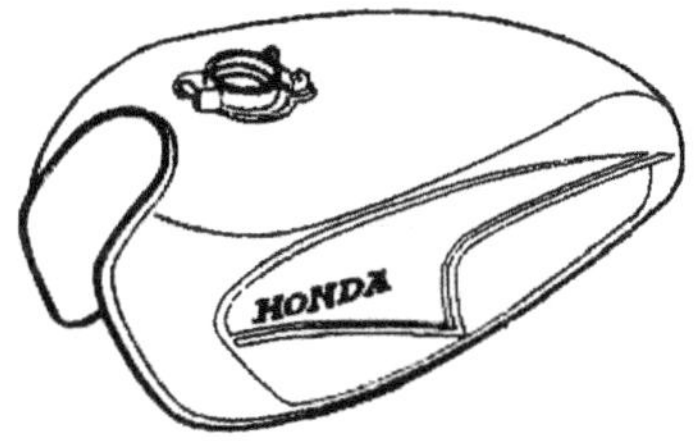 Fig. 7.16	
Double seat	(CB type) 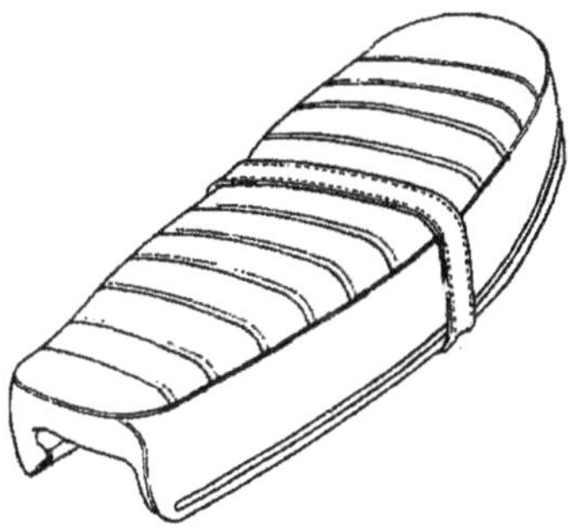 Fig. 7.17	Pattern is changed 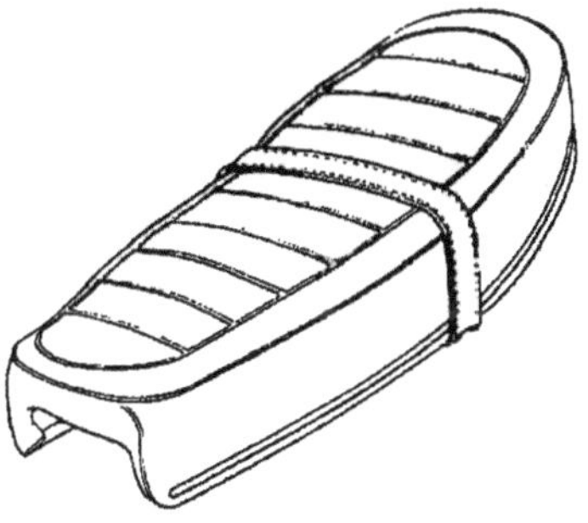 Fig. 7.18	
	(CL type) 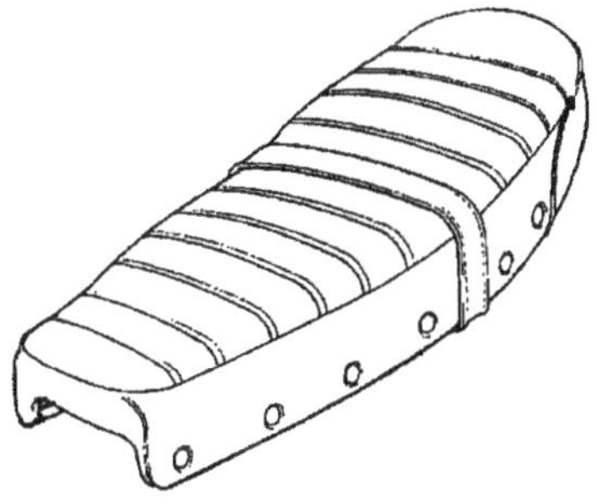 Fig. 7.19	Pattern is changed 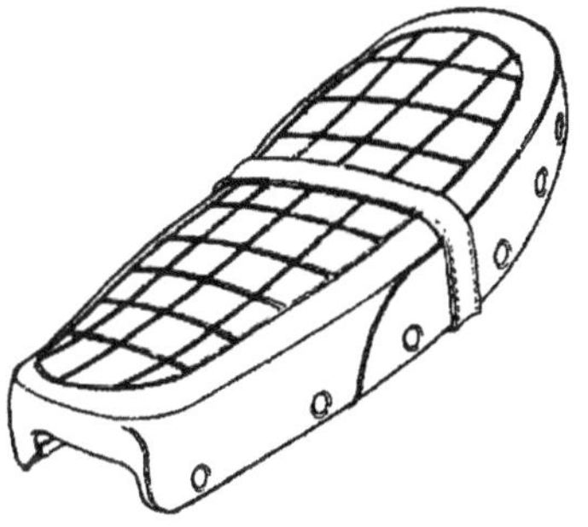 Fig. 7.20	

Part or item	CB/CL 450 K3	CB/CL 450 K4	Modified part
Air cleaner emblem	 Fig. 7.21	 Fig. 7.22 • DOHC is changed to double overhead cam • Emblem plate changed from one to two pieces • Double Over Head Cam emblem is applicable to K3 model by providing two holes on air cleaner cover	
R.L. exhaust muffler	(CL type) 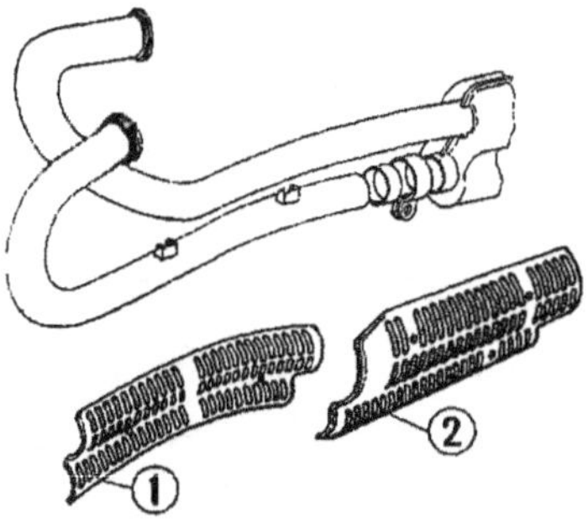 Fig. 7.23 ① Exhaust pipe protector ② Muffler protector	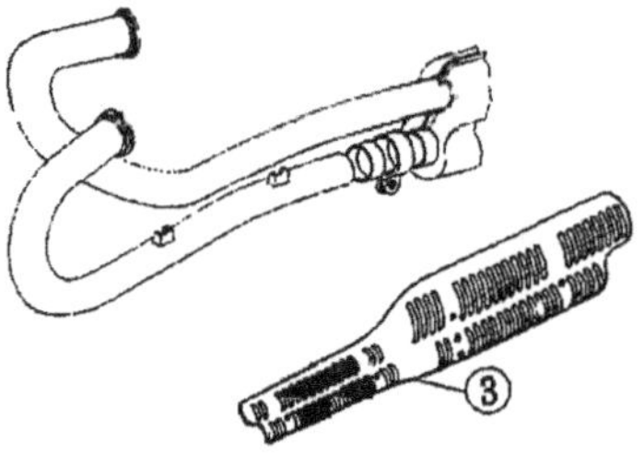 Fig. 7.24 ③ Exhaust pipe muffler protector • Protector is changed from two piece to one piece	
	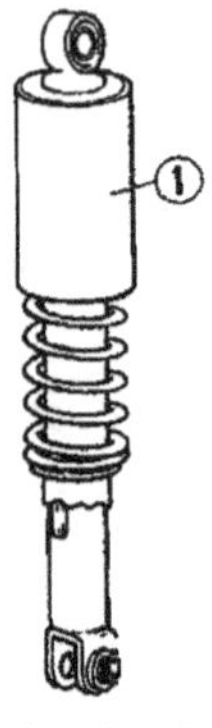 Fig. 7.25 ① Upper cover	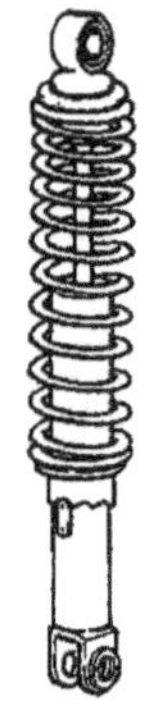 Fig. 7.26 Rubber mount is discontinued	

3. COMPARISON OF CL 450 K3, K4 TO CL 450 K5

Part or item	CB/CL 450 K3, K4	CB/CL 450 K5	Modified part
Fuel tank	(CL only) 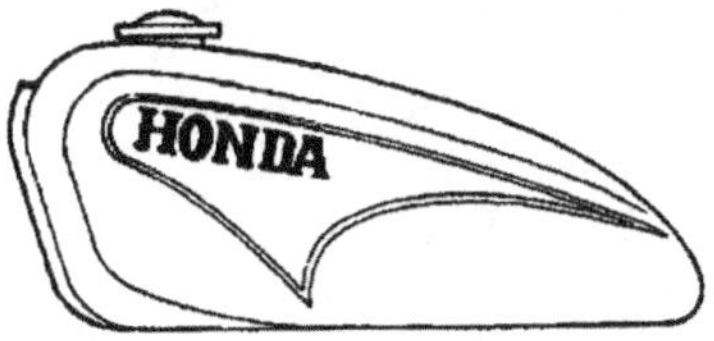 Fig. 7.27	(CL only)  Fig. 7.28 • The body and stripes were changed in type	• Stripes
Speedometer	 Fig. 7.29　① Speedometer	 ② Tachometer　Fig. 7.30 • The speedometer and tachometer were reversed in position. (The tachometer is interchangeable with the model CL 450 K3 tachometer.)	• Speedometer cable • Tachometer cable
Exhaust mufflers	(CL only) 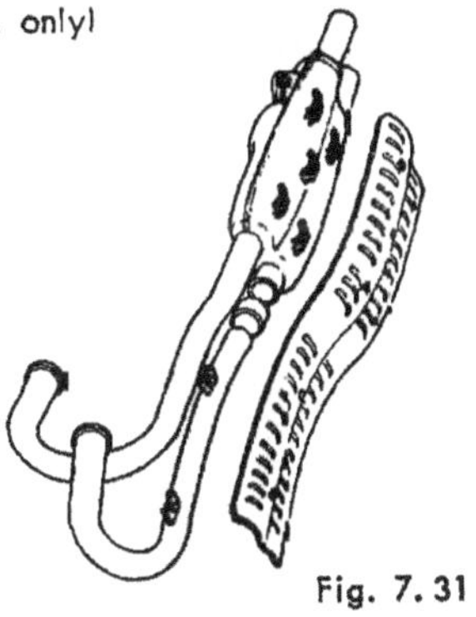 Fig. 7.31	(CL only) 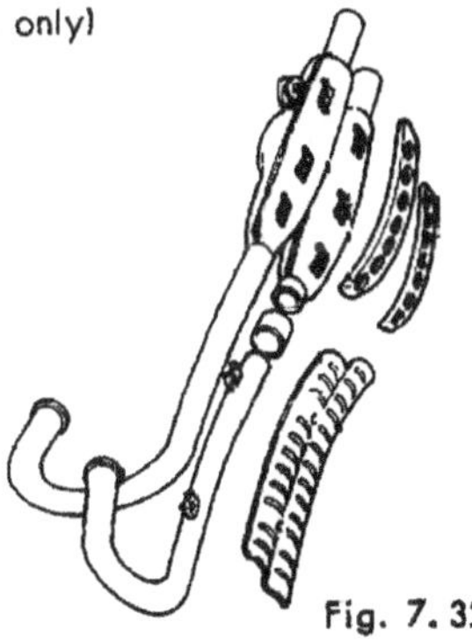 Fig. 7.32 • The right and left mufflers can be separated from the exhaust pipes and each protector separated into half. The components are not interchangeable as a single part, but they are interchangeable as an assembly.	• Muffler protectors • Exhaust pipe protectors • Muffler stays A and B • Muffler brackets
Brake pedal	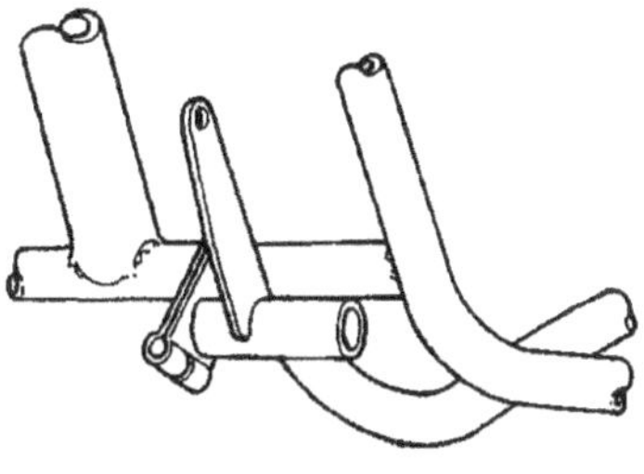 Fig. 7.33	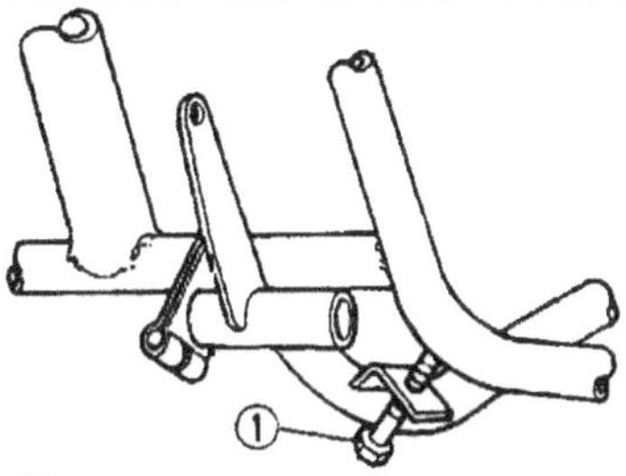 ① Adjust bolt　Fig. 7.34 • An adjuster was added to the brake pedal to adjust the pedal up and down.	

Part or item	CB/CL 450 K3, K4	CB/CL 450 K5	Modified part
Front forks	 **Fig. 7.35** • Type: Piston type • Oil: ATF • Internal construction: Same as the model CB 750 K1	 **Fig. 7.36** • Type: Rod type • Oil: ATF • Internal construction: Same as the model CB 500	• Frame body • Seat catch • Helmet holder • Seat hinges
	The front forks of both models are not interchangeable.		
Rear shock absorbers	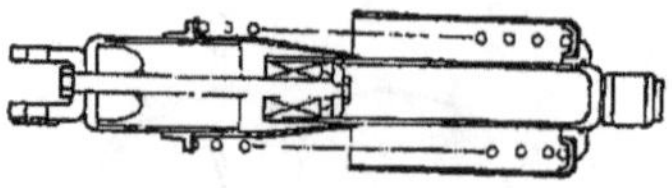 **Fig. 7.37** • Double tube type	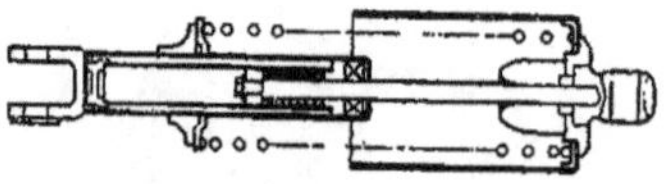 **Fig. 7.38** • Double tube, double acting type (The upper covers are removed from the model CB 500 rear shock absorbers.)	
	The rear shock absorbers of both models are not interchangeable in appearance, but they may be interchangeable on either side in pairs.		
Seat	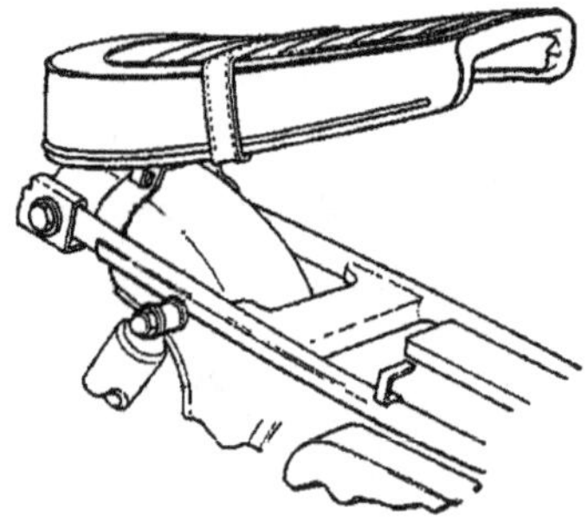 **Fig. 7.39**	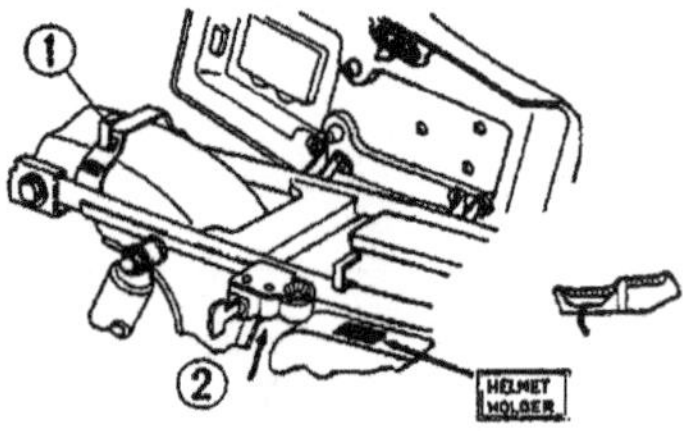 **Fig. 7.40** ① Helmet ② Seat catch • The seat is opened or closed sideways. • A helmet holder was added to hang a helmet. • The seat and frame body are not interchangeable with those of the model CL 450 K3.	
Fixing bolt	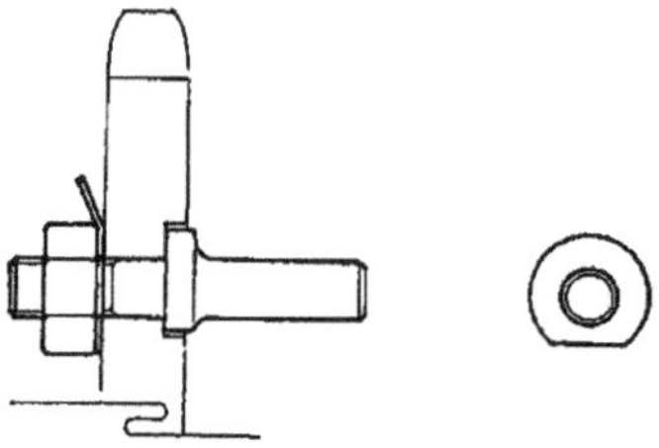 **Fig. 7.41**	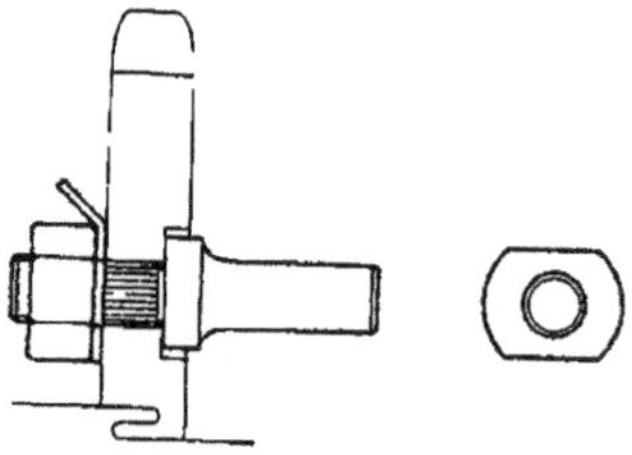 **Fig. 7.42** ① Knurled • The final driven sprocket fixing bolt is knurled.	
	The fixing bolt is not interchangeable as a unit, but it is interchangeable as an assembly including a sprocket, fixing bolt, tongued washer and nut.		

4. COMPARISON OF CB/CL 450 K5 TO CB/CL 450 K6

Part or item	CB/CL 450 K5	CB/CL 450 K6	Modified part
Fuel tank	(CB type) 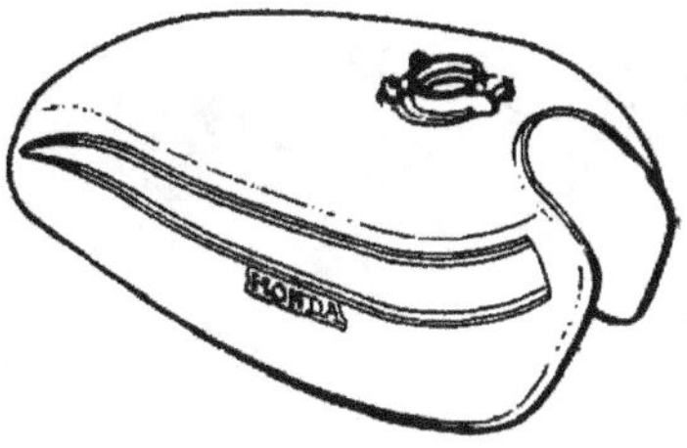 (CL type) 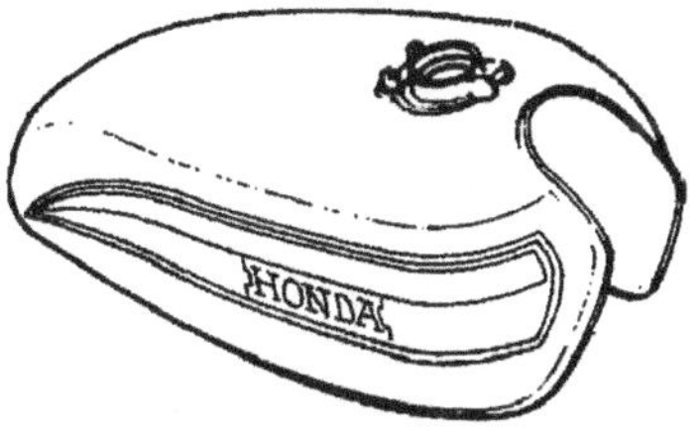 Fig. 7.43	(CB type) 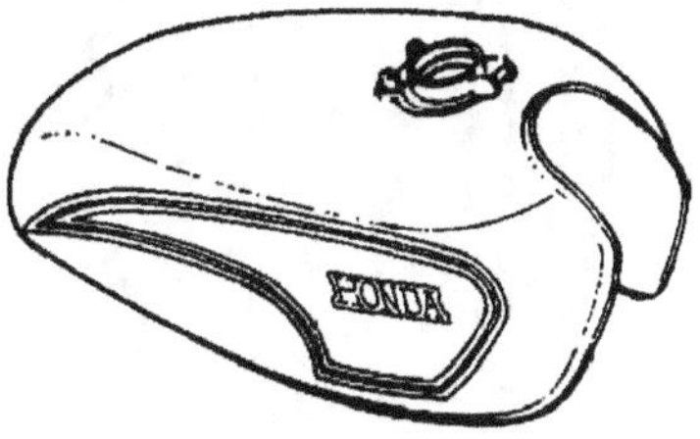 (CL type) 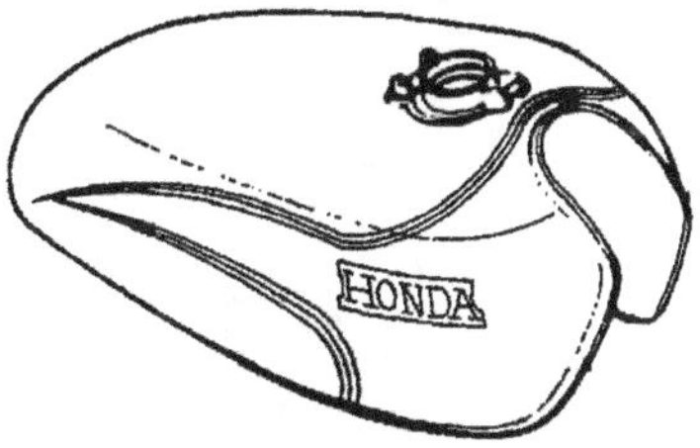 Fig. 7.44 • The stripes were changed in shape.	
Speedometer Tachometer	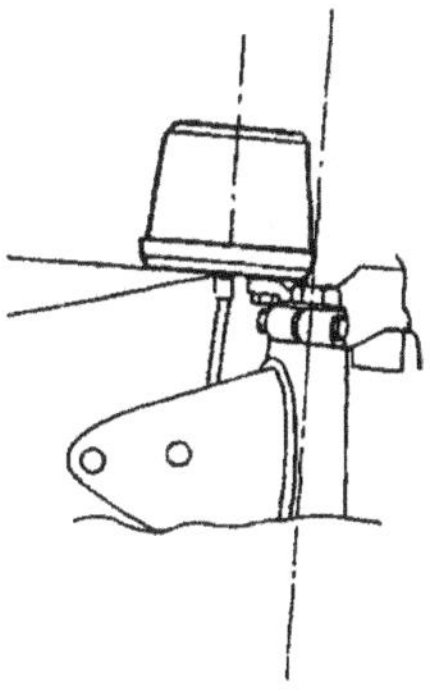 Fig. 7.45	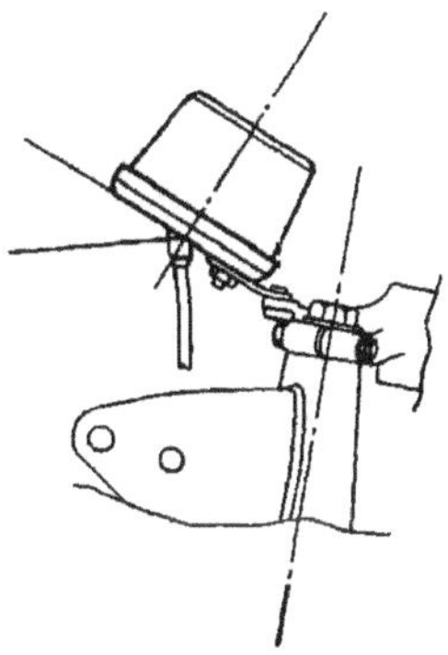 Fig. 7.46 • The speedometer and tachometer were changed in mounting angle and their dial plates were changed to the transparent illumination type for better visibility.	
Disc cover	 Fig. 7.47 • The disc cover and stays are not used.	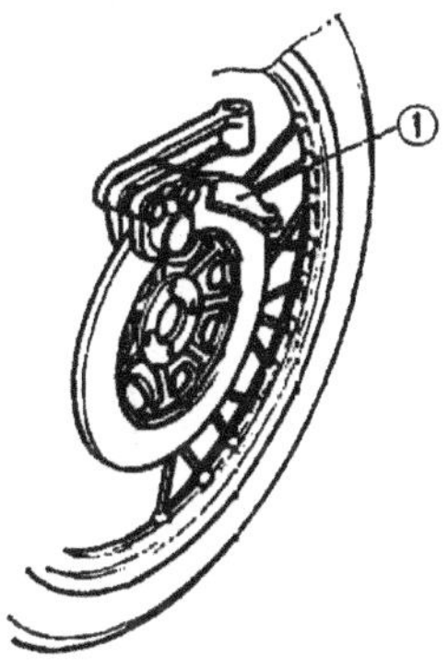 Fig. 7.48 ① Disk cover	

Part or item	CB/CL 450 K5	CB/CL 450 K6	Modified part
Sprocket side plate	 Fig. 7.49 • The side plate is not used.	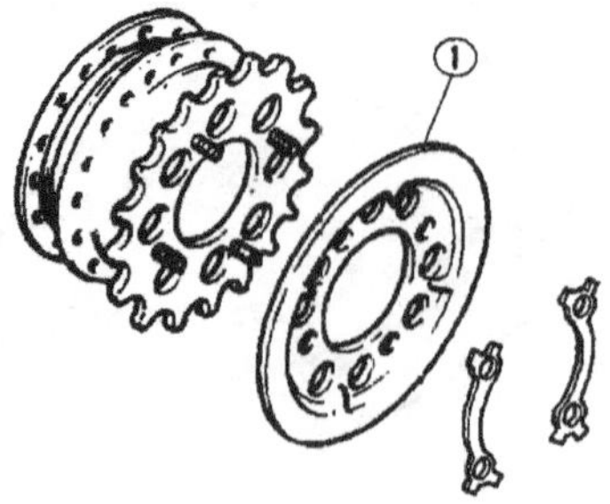 Fig. 7.50 ① Sprocket side plate	
Kill switch	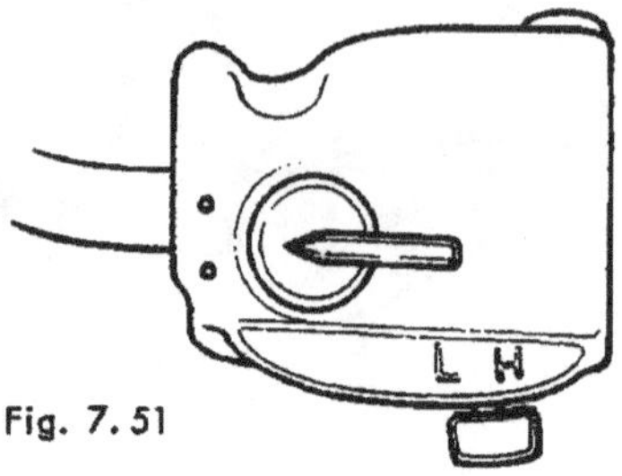 Fig. 7.51	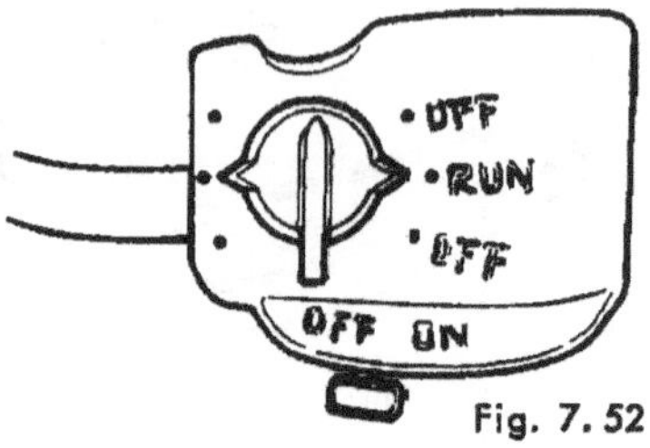 Fig. 7.52 • The kill switch knob was changed in shifting pattern from the up-down motion to the right-left motion.	
Pilot lamp box	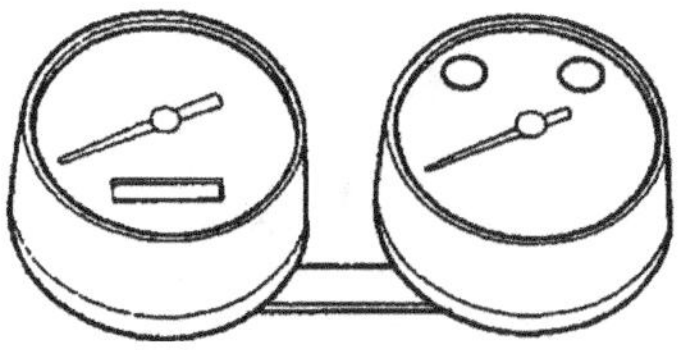 Fig. 7.53 • The pilot lamp box is not used.	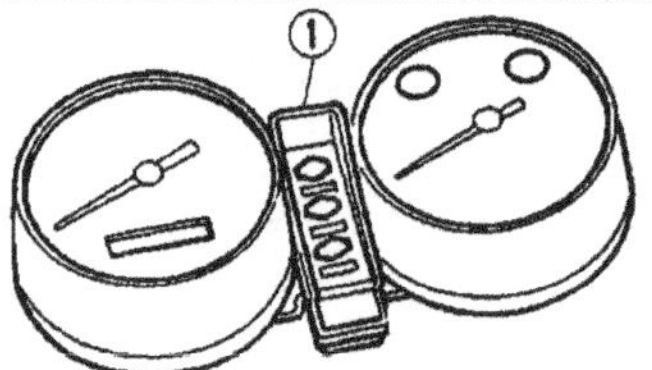 Fig. 7.54 ① Pilot lamp box • The pilot lamps are grouped for improved serviceability.	
Silicon rectifier	 Fig. 7.55	 Fig. 7.56 • The silicon rectifier was changed in shape. The new rectifier can also be used in the model CB 350 K5.	
Fuel tube cover	Fig. 7.57	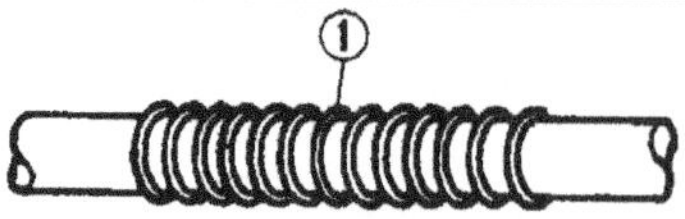 Fig. 7.58 ① Fuel tube cover • A tube cover was added.	

5. COMPARISON OF CB 450 K6 TO CB 450 K7

Part or item	CB 450 K6	CB 450 K7	Modified part
Rear fork pivot bushings	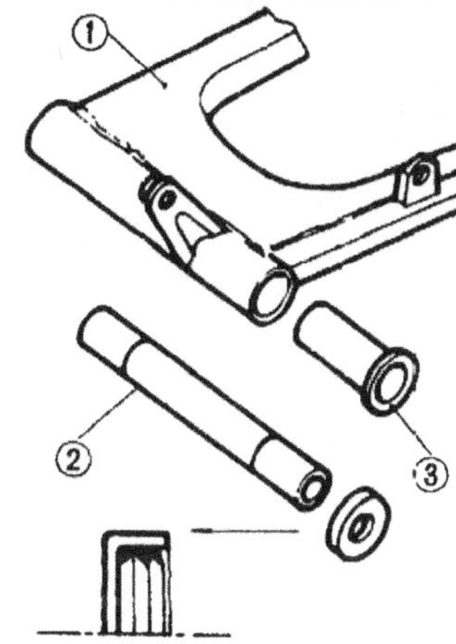 Fig. 7.59 ① Rear fork ② Rear fork pivot shaft ③ Rear fork pivot bush	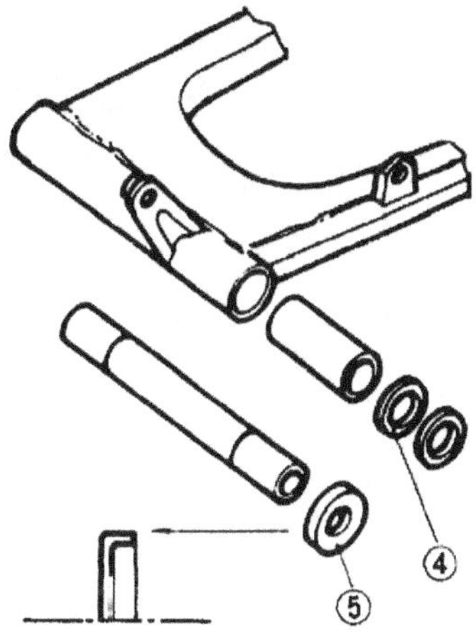 Fig. 7.60 ④ Felt ⑤ Dust seal cap	• Rear fork • Rear fork pivot shaft • Dust seal caps • Felt rings
Fuel tank	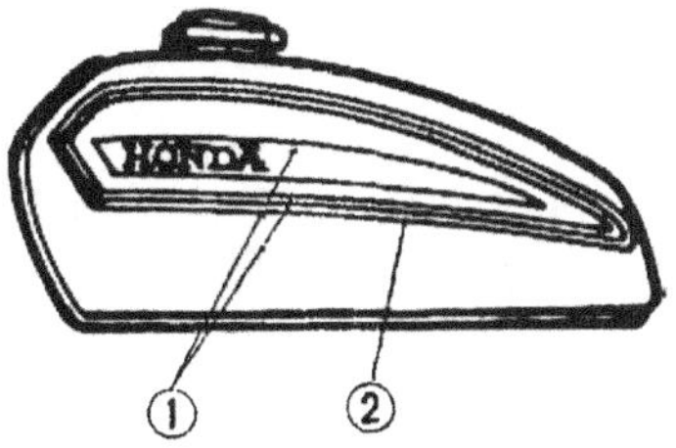 Fig. 7.61　① Gold	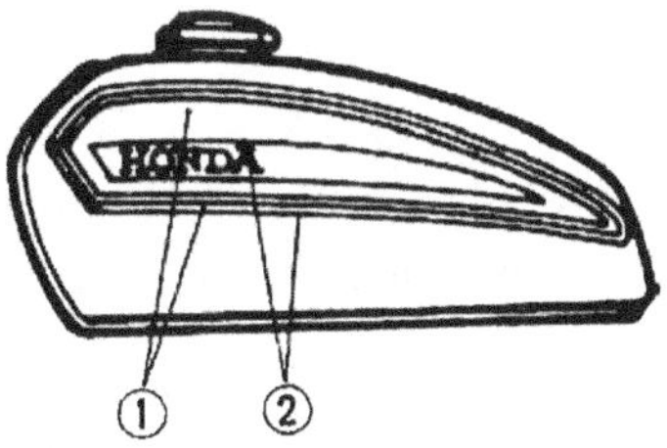 ② Black　Fig. 7.62 • The stripes were changed in color.	
Driven sprocket	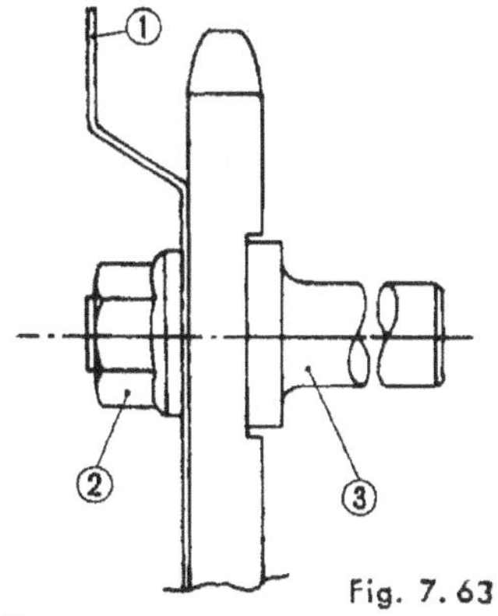 Fig. 7.63 ① Side plate ② U.B.S. nut ③ Fixing bolt	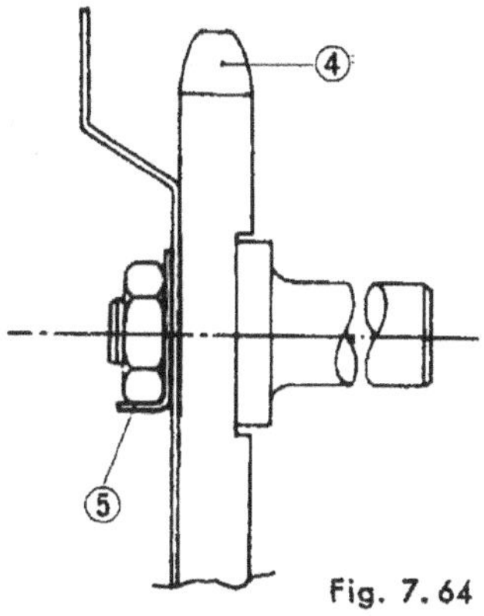 Fig. 7.64 ④ Sprocket　⑤ Tanged washer • The hitherto-used tongued washer was abolished and a U.B.S. nut was newly employed.	
Rear grip pipe	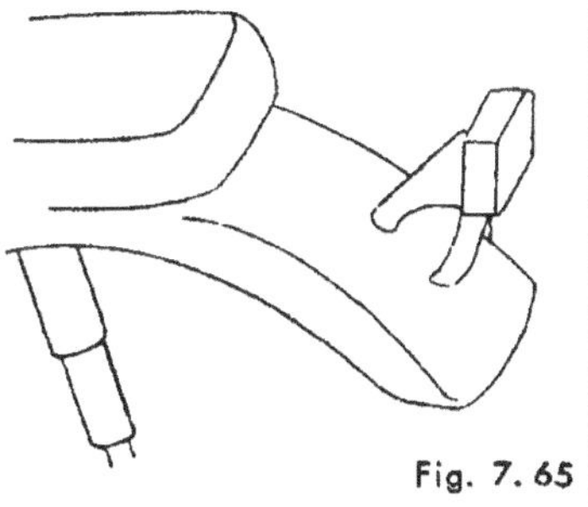 Fig. 7.65	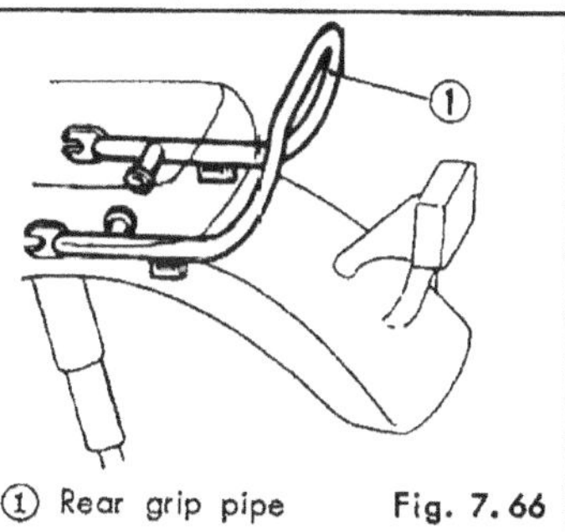 Fig. 7.66 ① Rear grip pipe • A rear grip pipe was added.	

SECTION EIGHT

GUIDE TO TROUBLESHOOTING

Diagnosing motorcycle ills is relatively simple if you use orderly procedures and keep a few basic principles in mind.

Never assume anything. Don't overlook the obvious. If you are riding along and the bike suddenly quits, check the easiest, most accessible problem spots first. Is there gasoline in the tank? Is the gas petcock in the "on" or "reserve" position? Has a spark plug wire fallen off? Check the ignition switch. Sometimes the weight of keys on a key ring may turn the ignition off suddenly.

If nothing obvious turns up in a cursory check, look a little further. Learning to recognize and describe symptoms will make repairs easier for you or a mechanic at the shop. Describe problems accurately and fully. Saying that "it won't run" isn't the same as saying "it quit on the highway at high speed and wouldn't start," or that "it sat in my garage for three months and then wouldn't start."

Gather as many symptoms together as possible to aid in diagnosis. Note whether the engine lost power gradually or all at once, what color smoke (if any) came from the exhausts and so on. Remember that the more complicated a machine is, the easier it is to troubleshoot because symptoms point to specific problems.

You don't need fancy equipment or complicated test gear to determine whether repairs can be attempted at home. A few simple checks could save a large repair bill and time lost while the bike sits in a dealer's service department. On the other hand, be realistic and don't attempt repairs beyond your abilities. Service departments tend to charge heavily for putting together a disassembled engine that may have been abused. Some won't even take on such a job — so use common sense and don't get in over your head.

OPERATING REQUIREMENTS

An engine needs three basics to run properly: correct gas-air mixture, compression, and a spark at the right time. If one or more are missing, the engine won't run. The electrical system is the weakest link of the three. More problems result from electrical breakdowns than from any other source. Keep that in mind before you begin tampering with carburetor adjustments and the like.

If a bike has been sitting for any length of time and refuses to start, check the battery for a charged condition first and then look to the gasoline delivery system. This includes the tank, fuel petcocks, lines and the carburetor. Rust may have formed in the tank, obstructing fuel flow. Gasoline deposits may have gummed up carburetor jets and air passages. Gasoline tends to lose its potency after standing for long periods. Condensation may contaminate it with water. Drain old gas and try starting with a fresh tankful.

Compression or the lack of it, usually enters the picture only in the case of older machines. Worn or broken pistons, rings and cylinder bores could prevent starting. Generally a gradual power loss and harder and harder starting will be readily apparent in this case.

WHAT TO DO IF THE ENGINE WON'T START

Check gas flow first. Remove the gas cap and look into the tank. If gas is present, pull off a fuel line at the carburetor and see if gas flows freely. If none comes out, the fuel tap may be shut off, blocked by rust or foreign matter or the fuel line may be stopped up or kinked. If the carburetor is getting usable fuel, turn to the electrical system next.

Check that the battery is charged by turning on the lights or by beeping the horn. Refer to your owner's manual for starting procedures with a dead battery. Have the battery recharged if necessary.

Pull off a spark plug cap, remove the spark plug and reconnect the cap. Lay the plug against the cylinder head so its base makes a good connection and turn the engine over with the kickstarter. A fat, blue spark should jump across the electrodes. If there is no spark, or a weak one, there is electrical system trouble. Check for a defective plug by replacing it with a known good one. Don't assume a plug is good just because it's new.

Once the plug has been cleared of guilt, but there's still no spark, start backtracking through the system. If the contact at the end of the spark plug wire can be exposed it can be held about 1/8 inch from the head while the engine is turned over to check for a spark. Remember to hold the wire only by its insulation to avoid a nasty shock. If the plug wires are dirty, greasy or wet, wrap a rag around them so you won't get shocked. If you do feel a shock or see sparks along the wire, clean or replace the wire and/or its connections.

If there's no spark at the plug wire, look for loose connections at the coil and battery. If all seems in order here, check next for oily or dirty contact points. Clean points with electrical contact cleaner or a strip of paper. With the ignition switch turned on, open and close the points manually with a screwdriver.

No spark at the points with this test indicates a failure in the ignition system. Refer to the Electrical Service Section in this manual for checkout procedures for the entire system and individual components. Refer to the Tune-Ups and Maintenance Section for checking and setting ignition timing.

Note that spark plugs of the incorrect heat range (too cold) may cause hard starting. Set gaps to specifications. If you have just ridden through a puddle or washed the bike and it won't start, dry off plugs and plug wires. Water may have entered the carburetor and fouled the fuel under these conditions, but wet plugs and wires are the more likely problem.

If a healthy spark occurs at the right time, and there is adequate gas flow to the carburetor, check the carburetor itself at this time. Make sure all jets and air passages are clean, check float level and adjust if necessary. Shake the float to check for gasoline inside it and replace or repair as indicated. Check that the carburetors are mounted snugly and no air is leaking past the manifolds. Check for a clogged air filter.

Compression may be checked in the field by turning the kick-starter by hand and noting that an adequate resistance is felt or by removing a spark plug and placing a finger over the plug hole and feeling for pressure. Use a compression gauge if possible. Compression should generally read 150 lbs. per square inch or more.

Valve adjustments should be checked next. Sticking, burned or broken valves may hamper starting. As a last resort, check valve timing as described in the Engine Service Section.

POOR IDLING

Poor idling may be caused by incorrect carburetor adjustment, incorrect timing, ignition system defects, an intake manifold leak or leakage between the carburetors at the balance tube. Check the gas cap vent for an obstruction.

MISFIRING

Misfiring can be caused by a weak spark or dirty plugs. Check for fuel contamination. Run the machine at night or in a darkened garage to check for spark leaks along the plug wires and under the spark plug cap. If misfiring occurs only at certain throttle settings, refer to the carburetor service section for the specific carburetor circuits involved. Misfiring under heavy load as when climbing hills or accelerating is usually caused by bad spark plugs.

FLAT SPOT

If the engine seems to die momentarily when the throttle is opened and then recovers, check for a dirty main jet in the carburetor, water in the fuel or an excessively lean mixture.

LACK OF POWER

Poor condition of rings, pistons or cylinders will cause a lack of power and speed. Check that valves are correctly adjusted. Ignition timing should be checked along with the automatic spark advance.

OVERHEATING

If the engine seems to run too hot all the time, be sure you are not idling it for long periods. Air cooled engines are not designed to operate at a standstill for any length of time. Heavy stop and go traffic is hard on a motorcycle engine. Spark plugs of the wrong heat range can burn pistons. An excessively lean gas mixture may cause overheating. Check ignition timing. Don't ride in too high a gear. Broken or worn rings and valves may permit compression gases to leak past them, heating heads and cylinders excessively. Check oil level and use the proper grade lubricants.

BACKFIRING

Check that the timing is not advanced too far. Check the automatic advance mechanism for broken or sticking parts. Check fuel for contamination.

ENGINE NOISES

Experience is needed to diagnose accurately in this area. Noises are hard to differentiate and harder yet to describe. Deep knocking noises usually mean main bearing failure. A slapping noise generally comes from loose pistons. A light knocking noise during acceleration may be a bad connecting rod bearing. Pinging, which sounds like marbles being shaken in a tin can, is caused by ignition advanced too far or gasoline with too low an octane rating. Pinging should be corrected immediately or damage to pistons will result. Compression leaks at the head-cylinder joint will sound like a rapid on and off squeal.

PISTON SEIZURE

Piston seizure is caused by incorrect piston clearances when fitted, fitting rings with improper end gap, too thin an oil being used, incorrect spark plug heat range or incorrect ignition timing. Overheating from any cause may result in seizure.

VIBRATION

Excessive vibration may be caused by loose motor mounts, worn engine or transmission bearings, loose wheels, worn swinging arm bushings, a generally poor running engine, broken or cracked frame or one that has been damaged in a collision. See also Poor Handling.

HIGH OIL CONSUMPTION

High oil consumption and loss of compression often go hand in hand. Check condition of rings, pistons, cylinders and valves. Worn valve stems or valve guides may be at fault. Use the correct grade of oil.

CLUTCH SLIP OR DRAG

Clutch slip may be due to worn plates, improper adjustment or glazed plates. A dragging clutch could result from damaged or bent plates, improper adjustment or even clutch spring pressure.

TRANSMISSION PROBLEMS

A grinding when shifting may be a result of worn synchronizers on the transmission gears or a sticking or non-disengaging clutch. Bent or broken teeth may cause hard shifting. A bent shifting rod or mainshaft or layshaft could cause hard shifting. Popping out of gear could be due to worn dogs on the gears or misadjustment in the shifting mechanism.

POOR HANDLING

Poor handling may be caused by improper tire pressures, a damaged frame or swinging arm, worn shocks or front forks, weak fork springs, a bent or broken steering stem, misaligned wheels, loose or missing spokes, worn tires, bent handlebars, worn wheel bearings or dragging brakes.

BRAKE SYSTEM

Sticking brakes may be caused by broken or weak return springs, improper cable or rod adjustment or dry pivot and cam bushings. Grabbing brakes may be caused by greasy linings which must be replaced. Brake grab may also be due to out of round drums or linings which have broken loose from the shoes. Glazed linings or brake pads will cause loss of stopping power.

LIGHTING SYSTEM

Bulbs which continuously burn out may be caused by excessive vibration, loose connections that permit sudden current surges, poor battery connections or installation of the wrong type bulb.

A dead battery or one which discharges quickly may be caused by a faulty generator or rectifier. Check for loose or corroded terminals. Shorted battery cells or broken terminals will keep a battery from charging. Low water level will decrease a battery's capacity. A battery left uncharged after installation will sulphate, rendering it useless.

A majority of light and horn or other electrical accessory problems are caused by loose or corroded ground connections. Check those first and then substitute known good units for easier troubleshooting.

INDEX

A

Air cleaner 75, 77
Air cleaner, servicing 8

B

Backfiring 134
Battery 10
Battery construction 104
Bearings, transmission 44
Brake, front disc 86
Brake, front drum 81
Brake problems 135
Brake, rear 95
Brakes, adjustment 10
Brakes, front 81
Breaker plate 6

C

Cam chain, adjustment 9
Cam chain, tensioner 15, 22
Cam follower 16
Camshaft assembly 20
Carburetors 48-53
Carburetors, cleaning & adjusting 7
Clutch, adjustment, ... 9
Clutch assembly 4
Clutch, disassembly 27
Clutch, inspection 29
Clutch slip or drag 134
Coil testing 113
Condenser checks 111
Crankshaft, inspection 36
Cylinder, disassembly & inspection ... 23
Cylinder head, disassembly 14
Cylinder head, inspection & cleaning .. 14

D

D.C. voltage 112
Drive chain 10
Drive chain installation 98
Drive chain, master link 13

E

Electrical service 100
Engine, design 1-3
Engine removal 12
Engine, replacement 13
Engine service 12
Exhaust pipes 75

F

Flat spots 134
Fork crown 60
Frame disassembly 72
Frame service 54
Front forks 61
Fuel system, maintenance 8
Fuel tank inspection 71
Fuel tank removal 71

G

Gear operation 5
Gears, backlash 40

H

Hand controls 54
Handlebars 54
Hard starting 133
Headlights 107
High oil consumption 134
Horn service 107
Hydraulic brake control 91

I

Idle, adjusting 7
Idling 133
Ignition system 100
Ignition timing 6
Indicator lights 107

K

Kick stand service 72
Kick starter 48

L

Left crankcase cover disassembly 29
Lighting problems 135
Lights 107
Lubrication system 4

M

Maintenance, periodic 8
Misfiring 134
Muffler 75

N

Noises, engine 134

O

Oil change, intervals	9
Oil filter, disassembly	26
Oil filter, maintenance	8
Oil pump assembly	30, 31
Overheating	134

P

Piston, disassembly	24
Piston seizure	134
Point gapping	6
Poor handling	135
Poor idling	133
Power, lack of	134
Power system	102

R

Rectifiers	103
Resistance checks	111
Right crankcase cover, disassembly	26
Rings, piston, inspection	24

S

Shocks, rear	80
Solenoid	107
Spark plugs	7
Speedometer service	107
Starter, electric	105
Starting	133
Starting clutch	106
Steering stem	70
Swinging arms	78

T

Tachometer assembly	18
Tachometer service	107
Tachometer, testing	112
Tail lights	107
Tappet clearance	16
Throttle valves, synchronizing	7
Torque specifications	11
Torsion bar	19
Tower crankcase assembly	34
Transmission, 4-speed	37
Transmission, 5-speed	45
Transmission problems	135
Troubleshooting	132
Tuning	6
Turn signals	108

U

Upper crankcase assembly	33

V

Valves, adjusting	7
Valves, inspection, & service	19
Valve timing	15
Vibration	134

W

Wheel, front	80
Wheel, rear	93
Wiring diagrams	115
Wiring harness	108

VELOCEPRESS MANUALS - MOTORCYCLE

1930'S BRITISH MOTORCYCLE CARBS & ELEC COMPONENTS (BOOK OF)
1930'S BRITISH MOTORCYCLE ENGINES (OVERHAUL & MAINTENANCE)
1930'S BRITISH MOTORCYCLE GEARBOXES & CLUTCHES (BOOK OF)
AJS 1932-1948 SINGLES & TWINS 250cc THRU 1000cc (BOOK OF)
AJS 1945-1960 SINGLES 350cc & 500cc MODELS 16 & 18 (BOOK OF)
AJS 1955-1965 SINGLES 350cc & 500cc (BOOK OF)
ARIEL UP TO 1932 (BOOK OF)
ARIEL 1932-1939 PREWAR MODELS (BOOK OF)
ARIEL 1933-1951 (WORKSHOP MANUAL)
ARIEL 1939-1960 4 STROKE SINGLES (BOOK OF)
ARIEL 1958-1964 LEADER & ARROW (BOOK OF)
BMW R26 R27 (1956-1967) FACTORY WORKSHOP MANUAL
BMW R50 R50S R60 R69S (1955-1969) FACTORY WORKSHOP MANUAL
BRIDGESTONE 90 SERIES FACTORY WSM & PARTS CATALOGUE
BRIDGESTONE 175 SERIES FACTORY WSM & PARTS CATALOGUE
BSA BANTAM ALL MODELS FROM 1948 ONWARDS (BOOK OF)
BSA SINGLES & V-TWINS UP TO 1927 (BOOK OF)
BSA SINGLES & V-TWINS UP TO 1930 (BOOK OF)
BSA SINGLES & V-TWINS UP TO 1935 (BOOK OF)
BSA SINGLES & V-TWINS 1936-1939 (BOOK OF)
BSA OHV & SV SINGLES 250-600cc 1945-1959 (BOOK OF)
BSA OHV & SV SINGLES 250cc (ONLY) 1954-1970 (BOOK OF)
BSA OHV SINGLES 350 & 500cc 1955-1967 (BOOK OF)
BSA TWINS 1948-1962 (BOOK OF)
BSA TWINS 1962-1969 (SECOND BOOK OF)
CYCLEMOTOR (BOOK OF)
DOUGLAS 1929-1939 PREWAR ALL MODELS (BOOK OF)
DOUGLAS 1948-1957 POSTWAR ALL MODELS FACTORY SHOP MANUAL
DUCATI 160cc, 250cc & 350cc OHC MODELS FACTORY SHOP MANUAL
HONDA 50 ALL MODELS UP TO 1970 INC MONKEY & TRAIL (BOOK OF)
HONDA 90 ALL MODELS UP TO 1966 (BOOK OF)
HONDA 125-150cc TWINS C/CS/CB/CA FACTORY WORKSHOP MANUAL
HONDA 250-305 TWINS C/CS/CB FACTORY WORKSHOP MANUAL
HONDA 450 CB/CL 1965-1974 K0 TO K7 WORKSHOP MANUAL
HONDA C100 SUPER CUB FACTORY WORKSHOP MANUAL
HONDA C110 SPORT CUB 1962-1969 FACTORY WORKSHOP MANUAL
HONDA TWINS & SINGLES 50cc THRU 305cc 1960-1966 (BOOK OF)
HONDA TWINS ALL MODELS 125cc THRU 450cc UP TO 1968 (BOOK OF)
J.A.P. ENGINES 1927-1952 & MOTORCYCLES 1934-1952 (BOOK OF)
LAMBRETTA 1947-1957 ALL 125 & 150cc MODELS (BOOK OF)
LAMBRETTA 1957-1970 LI & TV MODELS (SECOND BOOK OF)
MATCHLESS 1931-1939 ALL MODELS 250cc THRU 990cc (BOOK OF)
MATCHLESS 1945-1956 350 & 500cc SINGLES (BOOK OF)
MATCHLESS 1955-1966 350 & 500cc SINGLES (BOOK OF)
NEW IMPERIAL ALL SV & OHV FROM 1935 ONWARDS (BOOK OF)
NORTON 1932-1939 PREWAR MODELS (BOOK OF)
NORTON 1932-1947 (BOOK OF)
NORTON 1938-1956 (BOOK OF)
NORTON 1955-1963 MODELS 19, 50 & ES2 (BOOK OF)
NORTON 1955-1965 DOMINATOR TWINS (BOOK OF)
NORTON 1957-1970 TWINS FACTORY WORKSHOP MANUAL
NSU PRIMA 1956-1964 ALL MODELS (BOOK OF)
NSU QUICKLY 1953-1963 ALL MODELS (BOOK OF)
PANTHER 1932-1958 LIGHTWEIGHT MODELS 250 & 350cc (BOOK OF)
PANTHER 1938-1966 HEAVYWEIGHT MODELS 600 & 650cc (BOOK OF)
RALEIGH MOPEDS 1960-1969 (BOOK OF)
RALEIGH MOTORCYCLES 1919-1933 (BOOK OF)
ROYAL ENFIELD 1934-1946 SINGLES & V TWINS (BOOK OF)
ROYAL ENFIELD 1937-1953 SINGLES & V TWINS (BOOK OF)
ROYAL ENFIELD 1946-1962 SINGLES (BOOK OF)
ROYAL ENFIELD 1958-1966 250cc & 350cc SINGLES (SECOND BOOK OF)
ROYAL ENFIELD 736cc INTERCEPTOR FACTORY WORKSHOP MANUAL
RUDGE 1933-1939 (BOOK OF)
SUNBEAM 1928-1939 (BOOK OF)
SUNBEAM 1946-1957 S7 & S8 (BOOK OF)
SUZUKI 50cc & 80cc UP TO 1966 (BOOK OF)
SUZUKI T10 1963-1967 FACTORY WORKSHOP MANUAL
SUZUKI T20 & T200 1965-1969 FACTORY WORKSHOP MANUAL
SUZUKI TWINS 1962 ONWARDS 125-500cc WORKSHOP MANUAL
TRIUMPH 1935-1939 PREWAR MODELS (BOOK OF)
TRIUMPH 1935-1949 (BOOK OF)
TRIUMPH 1937-1951 (WORKSHOP MANUAL)
TRIUMPH 1945-1955 FACTORY WORKSHOP MANUAL
TRIUMPH 1945-1958 TWINS (BOOK OF)
TRIUMPH 1956-1969 TWINS (BOOK OF)
VELOCETTE 1925-1970 ALL SINGLES & TWINS (BOOK OF)
VESPA 1951-1961 (BOOK OF)
VESPA 1955-1963 125 & 150cc & GS MODELS (SECOND BOOK OF)
VESPA 1955-1968 GS & SS (BOOK OF)
VESPA 1963-1972 90, 125 & 150cc (THIRD BOOK OF)
VILLIERS ENGINE UP TO 1959 INC. 3 WHEELERS (BOOK OF)
VILLIERS ENGINE UP TO 1969 (BOOK OF)
VINCENT 1935-1955 (WORKSHOP MANUAL)

VELOCEPRESS TECHNICAL BOOKS – MOTORCYCLE

CATALOG OF BRITISH MOTORCYCLES (1951 MODELS)
INDIAN PONYBIKE, BOY RACER & PAPOOSE ILL PARTS LIST & SALES LIT
MOTORCYCLE ENGINEERING (P.E. Irving)
SPEED AND HOW TO OBTAIN IT (Motor Cycle Magazine UK)
TUNING FOR SPEED (P.E. Irving)

VELOCEPRESS MANUALS - THREE WHEELER'S

BSA THREE WHEELER (BOOK OF)
VINTAGE MORGAN THREE WHEELER (BOOK OF)

VELOCEPRESS MANUALS - AUTOMOBILE

ALFA ROMEO GIULIA WORKSHOP MANUAL 1300 TO 2000cc 1962-1975
ALFA ROMEO GIULIA TECH MANUAL CARBURETED CARS FROM 1962
ALFA ROMEO GIULIA TECH MANUAL FUEL INJECTED CARS FROM 1969
AUSTIN-HEALEY 6-CYLINDER WORKSHOP MANUAL
AUSTIN-HEALEY SPRITE & MG MIDGET WORKSHOP MANUAL 1958-1971
BMW 600 LIMOUSINE FACTORY WORKSHOP MANUAL
BMW 600 LIMOUSINE OWNERS HAND BOOK & SERVICE MANUAL
BMW 2000 & 2002 1966-1976 WORKSHOP MANUAL
BMW ISETTA FACTORY WORKSHOP MANUAL
CORVAIR 1960-1969 WORKSHOP MANUAL
CORVETTE V8 1955-1962 WORKSHOP MANUAL
FIAT 500 FACTORY WORKSHOP MANUAL 1957-1973
FIAT 600, 600D & MULTIPLA FACTORY WORKSHOP MANUAL 1955-1969
JAGUAR E-TYPE 3.8 & 4.2 SERIES 1 & 2 WORKSHOP MANUAL
JAGUAR MK 7, 8, 9 & XK120, 140, 150 WORKSHOP MANUAL 1948-1961
METROPOLITAN FACTORY WORKSHOP MANUAL
MGA & MGB OWNERS HANDBOOK & WORKSHOP MANUAL
MG MIDGET TC, TD, TF & TF1500 WORKSHOP MANUAL
PORSCHE 356 1948-1965 WORKSHOP MANUAL
PORSCHE 911 2.0, 2.2, 2.4 LITRE 1964-1973
PORSCHE 912 WORKSHOP MANUAL
TRIUMPH TR2, TR3, TR4 1953-1965 WORKSHOP MANUAL
VOLKSWAGEN TRANSPORTER, TRUCKS & WAGONS 1950-1979 WSM
VOLVO 1944-1968 ALL MODELS WORKSHOP MANUAL

VELOCEPRESS TECHNICAL BOOKS - AUTOMOBILE

FERRARI 250/GT SERVICE AND MAINTENANCE
FERRARI GUIDE TO PERFORMANCE
FERRARI OWNER'S HANDBOOK
FERRARI TUNING TIPS & MAINTENANCE TECHNIQUES
HOW TO BUILD A FIBERGLASS CAR
HOW TO BUILD A RACING CAR
HOW TO RESTORE THE MODEL 'A' FORD
MASERATI OWNER'S HANDBOOK
OBERT'S FIAT GUIDE
PERFORMANCE TUNING THE SUNBEAM TIGER
SOUPING THE VOLKSWAGEN
SOLEX CARBURETORS (EMPHASIS ON UK & EU AUTOMOBILES)
SU CARBURETORS (EMPHASIS ON UK AUTOMOBILES)
WEBER CARBURETORS (EMPHASIS ON ALFA & FIAT)

VELOCEPRESS BOOKS & GUIDES - AUTOMOBILE

ABARTH BUYERS GUIDE
COMPLETE CATALOG OF JAPANESE MOTOR VEHICLES
FERRARI 308 SERIES BUYER'S AND OWNER'S GUIDE
FERRARI BERLINETTA LUSSO
FERRARI BROCHURES AND SALES LITERATURE 1946-1967
FERRARI BROCHURES AND SALES LITERATURE 1968-1989
FERRARI OPP, MAINTENANCE & SERVICE H/BOOKS 1948-1963
FERRARI SERIAL NUMBERS PART I - ODD NUMBERS TO 21399
FERRARI SERIAL NUMBERS PART II - EVEN NUMBERS TO 1050
FERRARI SPYDER CALIFORNIA
HENRY'S FABULOUS MODEL "A" FORD
MASERATI BROCHURES AND SALES LITERATURE

VELOCEPRESS BOOKS – RACING

CARRERA PANAMERICANA - MEXICAN ROAD RACE (BOOK OF)
DIALED IN - THE JAN OPPERMAN STORY
IF HEMINGWAY HAD WRITTEN A RACING NOVEL
VEDA ORR'S NEW REVISED HOT ROD PICTORIAL

AUTOBOOKS WORKSHOP MANUALS & BROOKLANDS ROAD TEST PORTFOLIOS

FOR A COMPLETE LISTING OF THE AUTOBOOKS & BROOKLANDS TITLES THAT WE CURRENTLY HAVE AVAILABLE, PLEASE VISIT OUR WEBSITE.

For a detailed description of any of the above titles please visit
www.VelocePress.com